RENEGADES
SHOWMEN
& Angels

RENEGADES
SHOWMEN
& Angels

A THEATRICAL HISTORY
OF FORT WORTH
FROM 1873–2001

JAN L. JONES

Library of Congress Cataloging-in-Publication Data

Jones, Jan, 1947-
   Renegades, showmen, and angels : a theatrical history of Fort Worth from 1873-2001 /
by Jan L. Jones.
      p. cm.
   Includes bibliographical references and index.
   ISBN-13: 978-0-87565-318-1
   ISBN-10: 0-87565-318-9 (cloth : alk. paper)
   1. Theater—Texas—Fort Worth—History—20th century. 2. Theater—Texas—Fort
Worth—History—19th century. 3. Performing arts—Texas—Fort Worth—History—
20th century. 4. Performing arts—Texas—Fort Worth—History—19th century. I. Title.
   PN2277.F67J66 2006
   792.09764'5315—dc22
                              2005029652

Cover and text design by Bill Maize; Duo Design Group
Printed in Canada

For Haley, Taylor, Colby, and Garrett

CONTENTS

CHAPTER ONE

COWBOYS AND CULTURE:
1870-1880

"We saw one man carried away—not so much by
the performance as by a policeman."
~*Fort Worth Daily Standard*, 1876

Fort Worth's recorded theatrical history began like a tragicomic episode lifted straight from the pages of one of the lurid melodramas so popular with nineteenth-century audiences, complete with a rogue's gallery of characters worthy of a Dickens novel—gamblers, thugs, prostitutes, and dipsomaniacs. Take the strange case of William Webster.

On a subfreezing night in January 1877, Webster, the piano player of Theatre Comique was missing—nothing too unusual perhaps. Theatre Comique and its neighbor, the Centennial Theater, were just two more of the clapboard, nondescript structures that had sprung up along Main Street in the six months since the arrival of the railroad. More saloons than bastions of culture, their roughneck clientele were as likely to shoot the keys off the piano as watch the stage show. In Fort Worth's boomtown atmosphere, where dance halls, variety theaters, and saloons had steadily proliferated over the past half year, a man who did not want to be found could easily get lost in the shuffle of homesteaders, capitalists, gamblers, and last-chance drifters being deposited by the trainload almost daily at the newly constructed T&P depot along Front Street.

Webster, the absentee musician, may well have fallen into the last-chance category—acquaintances had taken note of his hard drinking and bouts of delirium tremens. There were no witnesses to his middle-of-the-night disappearance from the tent city hastily thrown up around the courthouse square as temporary housing for the crush of new settlers, but this too was not surprising in a town struggling to cope with the strain placed on city services by hundreds of new arrivals monthly. Since July of 1876, the stress of formerly uncommon distractions—pistol shots and bouts of fisticuffs between drunken rowdies in the rapidly expanding entertainment district—made law enforcement unlikely to search for one bibulous piano player.

The lantern light discovery of a corpse at the base of the Trinity River bluffs some hours later and its subsequent identification as Webster only generated more questions than answers. A hastily called inquest failed to discover whether the piano player's headlong descent off the cliff had been a case of simple misadventure, or the result of some chronic disaffection that led him to take his own life. In a final ironic coda to the tragedy, with no minister to conduct the service and only a straggle of official mourners, including the mayor, the band of the Centennial Theater escorted Webster to his last resting place, "[paying] this last respect to one of their own profession" with "a solemn air suited to the occasion."[1]

The case of the ill-fated Webster was, in many respects, merely a symptom of the civic turmoil that had recently engulfed the city, a problem often accompanying the growth of railway lines into previously isolated frontier towns during the last half of the nineteenth century. Once a railroad was in place, the population increased steadily as respectable homesteaders and merchants arrived in quest of land and the chance to carve out a fresh niche in untapped regions. This, in turn, opened the door for improved cultural offerings such as touring theatrical troupes, variety (later called vaudeville) entertainers, and opera companies.

Unfortunately, railroads also deposited society's ne'er-do-wells right along with the respectable churchgoers. Yet in nineteenth-century expansionist thinking, town fathers sometimes tolerated questionable enterprises such as gambling and prostitution as evils necessary to attract the skilled if not always law-abiding artisans and laborers needed to assure a community's long-term survival. New development engendered by the railroad's arrival undoubtedly both alarmed and encouraged longtime residents, some of whom had arrived following the Civil War more than a decade earlier and stuck it out through the period when Fort Worth was little more than a nondescript pioneer outpost. Only four years earlier, the editor of the *Lexington* (Virginia) *Gazette,* touring through North Texas, sent home accounts of his travels, characterizing the town as "a shabby village on a small river not over ankle deep, the only tavern built of mud and rocks and the fare execrable."[2]

The loyalists remained through 1872, long enough to witness an encouraging spurt of growth as the Texas & Pacific line pushed as close as Marshall, 175 miles to the east. Between the end of 1872 and September 1873, Fort Worth grew from a population of a few hundred to between three and four thousand. Speculators made handsome profits selling lots at inflated prices, but then a national financial panic struck. Railroad executives announced the indefinite suspension of the approaching rail line at Eagle Ford, twenty-six miles short of the city. To save the town, local officials suspended all city business except for the spring cattle drive, agreeing to work without salaries until matters improved. Not until the summer of 1876 did the panic sufficiently ease to complete the rail line into Fort Worth.[3]

Dallas, to the east, had already experienced the double-edged sword of railroad expansion. In a seven-month period between July of 1872 and February of 1873, two railroads had established their terminus in the city. Three years later, on July 15, 1876, with the Texas and Pacific only four days away from Fort Worth, the *Dallas Herald* felt compelled to warn its western neighbor that the "accumulation of adventurers and disreputable characters" brought by the railroad "will be to Fort Worth what the Red River raft is to that river. They will block up there and make the place a social pandemonium until the road goes on. Good Lord deliver us from a terminal town." [4]

Nobody seemed too concerned about this prospect at first. Entertainment for the city's residents before the advent of the rails had been a make-do proposition at best. Most opportunities through the 1860s and 1870s came in the form of dances and amateur theatricals held in the city's second courthouse or in Goodwin's Hall, occupying the second floor above a livery stable located at First and Houston. There was also the occasional passing circus. The courthouse, in fact, served as the town's cultural hub, with A. B. Fraser placed in charge of theatrical business by county officials and authorized to charge $7.50 a night rental. Although few records of the city's earliest histrionic ventures exist, the first probably occurred sometime around 1870. Still, the reality remained that few professional troupes cared to brave travel in the state, much of which still had to be traversed by stagecoach.[5]

Residents, meanwhile, entertained themselves as best they could. Professor Daniel Gordon organized a dancing school in the courtroom, "where every other night," according to the *Democrat* "[pupils] might have been seen performing uncertain and indescribable gyrations." In February 1873, after attending a fancy dress ball and "burlesque art exhibit" in the courthouse, *Democrat* editor, Buckley Paddock, himself recently arrived from Mississippi, observed wryly, "The leading citizens seem to be poking fun at their own plight while enjoying the 'culture' they can devise." That same month he noted the organization of the Thespian Club, the city's first recorded amateur troupe. After the company's inaugural performance did not go as planned, Paddock remained supportive: "The attendance was not very large, nor was the performance as good as we have seen, but," he added, "the club was hurried into . . . the exhibition before they were fully prepared, and . . . blunders were made that were wholly unavoidable."[6]

What early dramatic societies might have lacked in histrionic skill, they made up in devotion to civic causes. June 1877 performances of *The Streets of New York* raised money to purchase equipment for the Tarrant Rifles, a volunteer militia. The company shortly established the Home Dramatic Club and toured Fort Griffin, Fort Belknap, and other communities to the west. In 1881, the Amateur Dramatic Club of Fort Worth presented *The Lady of Lyons* with proceeds going to a library fund.[7]

Paddock's 1873 correspondence with his wife, who had yet to join him in Texas, also reveals the editor's sardonic commentary on the quality and types of amusements reaching the city from the outside. After attending a concert by the Davis Family, he complained, "[The performance] is a poor thing—four scrawny women, without voice enough to call chickens, trying to sing. The instruments are as bad as their voices." More to his taste was the Wild Men of Borneo Combination, a company that appeared in the local Masonic Hall several nights later. The wild men, he reported, "are perfect curiosities . . . about three feet high. They pick out the two largest [men] in the audience and bring them on the stage—[one] little fellow . . . lifts them both at once."[8]

Paddock used the *Democrat* both to rally support for any sort of public improvements and to criticize residents who neglected their civic responsibilities. After the initial setback in the railroad's efforts to reach Fort Worth in 1873 and the subsequent collapse of the city's economic boom, he crusaded for renewed negotiations with T&P, pointing out the benefits Dallas had achieved as a result: "Dallas . . . boasts nine churches, four or five schools, theater, graded streets and other improvements, all done in a little more than twelve months." At the same time Paddock criticized a similar lack of citizen initiative in Fort Worth: "Now let's look at our own city and see what has been done by her people to beautify and improve her. Here it is—$0000.00." He urged residents to make the building of a town hall or theater a priority, saying, "There is not a week passes but that it would be wanted for two or more nights. Public entertainments would be much more frequent if there was a suitable place provided for them."[9]

Yet even after the T&P finally reached the city on July 19, 1876, town officials discovered they still faced an uphill battle persuading professional stock theater companies and minstrel troupes, two of the more popular forms of legitimate entertainment during the era, to make the long jump between Dallas and Fort Worth because available bookings could not offset the dual problems of poor, often makeshift facilities and high rail fares. Getting performers even to consider an appearance in a backwater settlement required a combination of artful persuasion and monetary guarantees. Late in 1876 the *Austin Statesman* tracked the unusual measures employed by Buckley Paddock to lure an itinerant touring company to the city:

> Dallas people made the agent of Callender's Minstrels believe that Fort Worth was no bigger than one's fist, and the Minstrels concluded not to go thither; but Paddock heard of the outrage, had the census taken and houses counted, . . . and the minstrels were roped in. Paddock is perfectly blest, and Dallas is in sack cloth and ashes.[10]

B. B. Paddock, newspaper editor, and later mayor of Fort Worth and president of the city's Board of Trade. His journalistic campaigning in the *Daily Democrat* contributed to stricter regulation of Hell's Half Acre's variety halls, while his zeal for municipal improvements spurred completion of the Texas and Pacific rail line into town in 1876 and the construction of the Fort Worth Opera House in 1883.

Courtesy, Fort Worth Public Library, Local History and Genealogy

By October, the *Democrat* could report, "Emigrants are arriving daily from all portions of the old states. Every train that arrives is crowded to the utmost." With the coming of the railroad and renewed prosperity, some entertainments finally moved out of the courthouse as four different theaters made their appearance through the summer and fall of 1876. The Adelphi opened in July at Second and Main but lasted only a few weeks before being replaced in the same location by Theatre Comique. Nearby, the Centennial Theater made its debut in October, followed in November by Evans Hall above Dahlman Brothers' store on the courthouse square.[11]

Four days before the arrival of the railroad, the *Democrat* announced, "The Adelphi Theater has in preparation a new drama by the renowned artiste, Will C. Burton, entitled *Struck By Lightning* with a powerful caste[sic] which will be presented in a few days and of which notice will be given." With the opening of the Adelphi, the city's first recorded variety theater, it appeared that finally a local entrepreneur had found a way around Fort Worth's lingering stigma of provincialism. Buckley Paddock quickly, if somewhat immoderately, endorsed the addition in the pages of the *Democrat,* remarking, "This cosy [sic] place of amusement, the first regularly established theater in our city, is nightly growing in popularity and deservedly so. They present . . . an entertainment equal to that given in the . . . finest theaters of the older states; a first class company giving a programme so kaleidoscopic in its variety as to leave the audience in a state of doubt as to whether they are on this earth or in fairy land."[12]

The "kaleidoscopic variety" proved to be little more than melodramas with titles like *Sing Bad the Tailor* and *Red Dick* that gave fair warning of their literary merit. All were from the pen of Will Burton. Burton served as playwright and leading man for a company of actors whose named performers included Baby Murray, Harry Devere, Mr. Monroe, and the Misses Clark and Burton. Harry Devere doubled in the role of theater manager. Each evening, the Adelphi's "leetle deutscher band" toured surrounding streets, gathering in an audience while "pealing forth . . . glorious strains of harmonious discords."[13]

Barely three weeks later the *Democrat* announced the abrupt departure of the new theater's troupe of thespians with the headline, "Skedaddled, Defunct, non-est and gone out is the Adelphi Company." Sometime in the early morning hours of August 8 the troupe "jumped town," hauling off $300 worth of liquor and whatever else of the building's portable assets could be stowed in two wagons hired with the previous night's receipts. The absconders stripped the building almost to the bare walls, leaving only chairs, benches, some glassware, and the stage curtain. The *Democrat* commented dryly that if the group's profits had been less than the rent on the wagons, "they would undoubtedly, have been yet among us." The theater's out-of-luck musicians and several local merchants were left holding unpaid bills of between $600 and $800 with no goods left to confiscate.[14]

Just over a week later, the Adelphi announced plans for a return engagement under a new moniker—Theatre Comique. The owners engaged Harry Devere and Will Burton, evidently not among the mutinous players, to manage the new enterprise and announced not only plans to reopen but to expand the operation, adding four new scenes to the stage and constructing two private boxes at balcony level, connected to each other by a promenade containing additional seating above an expanded auditorium. The principal improvement was the construction of a generous portico wrapping around the building's second story where patrons might escape the heat inside. This second attempt at opening a variety hall proved more successful, although perhaps not without some differences of opinion that led to the eventual dismissal of Devere as manager.[15]

In mid-September the *Democrat* reported, "Mr. Will C. Burton will hereafter take the entire charge and management . . . in the place of Harry Devere." Little is known about Burton's origins, but he had earlier worked variety houses in San Antonio and may have been just one of many opportunists following the establishment of rail lines and mother lode discoveries to burgeoning towns. This supposition is supported by one reporter's observation, "Burton's reputation as a manager of variety theaters is too well-known to require comments." References in both the *Democrat* and *Daily Standard* testify to the manager's versatility as actor and playwright as well. While voicing doubts about the talents of the Comique's resident acting company, the *Standard* still praised Burton, saying of one dubiously titled playlet, *Red Dick,* "Its composition evinces considerable talent in the author and if well-rendered would make an interesting drama."[16]

Burton may have given his best performance after leaving Fort Worth. Drifting through several western communities, he stuck for a time in Weatherford, where he opened a variety hall and disorderly house and feuded with another theater inmate, Jack Rush. Late one night, in May 1880, Burton, his brother, and another man ambushed Rush, gunning him down in a hallway of Rowdy Kate Lowe's sporting house. At his trial Burton was quickly judged guilty and sentenced to hang, but when legal appeals failed to win a reversal of his punishment, he began acting "like a crazy man." The scene gained the actor a reprieve. In January 1881, a second jury judged him insane, and he was remanded instead to prison.[17]

By October, business at the reconstituted Comique was booming. Torches flared in front of the building each evening as a silhouetted tightrope walker balanced precariously on a rope stretched between the theater and a neighboring building, over the heads of the gathered crowd. Inside, the entertainment fell into one of several categories that defined a fairly standard variety format: the presentation of the female form, short melodramas, and irreverent ethnic humor, liberally laced with sexual double entendre. All were well suited to the tastes of an all-male, largely unsophisticated clientele, many of them traveling men, farmers, or cowboys. There were also skits burlesquing well-known plays, the government, or politicians. One of the more popular female attractions in October 1876 was Alice Bateman, described as, "the finest clog dancer [and] good looking too." Bateman sometimes appeared with William Noonan in an "Irish" skit, treating the audience to a liberal dose of suggestive dialogue, which caused a reporter to assert "the two . . . would make not only Billy Burton blush for joy, but a 'pertater' or a 'shelalah' would have no chance in that crowd," a reference both to the skits' ethnic dialogue as well as objects sometimes wielded by the crowd against inept performers. Noonan and blackface comedian Gus Canfield were described as just two of "many 'phunny' fellows" appearing.[18]

At the conclusion of the variety acts, an all-night dance often commenced, with female performers serving double duty as dance partners for customers, steering them frequently toward the bar for liquid refreshments. The boisterous atmosphere promoted at the Comique sometimes worked to blur the line between actors and patrons, make-believe and reality. A local constable pushed through the crowd toward the stage one night as a fight broke out. He quickly subdued the belligerents, only to discover he had just disrupted the evening's last show by arresting two performers engaged in mock pugilistic display. The *Standard* recorded the incident's conclusion at the expense of the embarrassed policeman: "Instead of [the actors] being 'sent up,' [the constable] had to 'set 'em up.'"[19]

At about the same time, a second variety hall, the Centennial, prepared to receive customers just a few doors away on Main Street. The new hall, like the Comique, housed a combination saloon, dance hall, gambling house, and variety theater. Its layout, compared with the Comique and other variety halls, seemed fairly standard. The building, according to published descriptions, was eighty feet deep. On street level a dance floor occupied most of one side, while a bar on the opposite side took up the remaining space. At the rear sat the stage, 22 1/2 by 18 feet, a comparatively minor fixture. The Centennial's real draw, less publicly obvious on the building's second floor gallery, were the gambling rooms and small apartments from which the variety actresses met privately with admirers. In the gallery, patrons could treat the ladies to high-priced liquid refreshments, or for a dollar, rent the key to one of the rooms, where a couple might engage in a more private liaison. Once inside the apartment, additional refreshments required an additional fee, but the patron could enjoy his visit undisturbed.[20]

The Centennial's atmosphere was no less boisterous than its rival the Comique. One hundred or more cowboys might jostle for space at its bar on any given evening. As the night wore on and customers began to loosen up through several hours of steady drinking and often prurient burlesque acts, one or more drovers might decide to demonstrate their ability with a six-shooter, more often than not limiting the potshots to lights or glassware. Occasionally though, patrons would indicate their displeasure with an onstage act by firing over the heads of performers, which would result in a scurrying to safety of both actors and audience members, much to the amusement of the cowboys.[21]

The duplicitous role of the city's variety theaters and performers is well documented in local newspapers. The more public face of a variety hall, revolving around the simple notion of providing cheap, unrefined, if often crude entertainment to its clientele, in reality acted as a means to an end—separating customers from their money in the more profitable areas of the business—liquor, prostitution, and gambling. J. B. Roberts, a reporter who covered the city for several early Fort Worth newspapers, summed up the practice: "It was generally understood that whoever went to a honk-a-tonk and lost his roll had no kick coming to him. . . . The times were free and easy and everything went, as the boys said." The variety show and the activities of the theater's cadre of so-called actresses were all carefully orchestrated by management to generate the most revenue in the least amount of time before a customer had the chance to take his money somewhere else.[22]

In 1906, a correspondent sent undercover by the *Fort Worth Record* recorded the scene in what was then the city's largest variety theater, the Standard:

> I made my way into the auditorium where a vaudeville show
> was in progress. Men and boys [listened] to the suggestive songs of
> a peroxide blonde . . . dressed decollette and [singing] in a voice
> about as musical as a stick rattling along a picket fence. . . . When
> not busy entertaining . . . she was fattening her temporary bank
> account by wheedling men into buying drinks . . . in small stalls
> where they are separated from their money and other detachable

valuables with the utmost neatness. Men without money are
passed up with a suddenness that must make their teeth chatter.
[Actresses] had work to do and the sooner the gentleman . . . was
separated from his cash, the sooner they [were] ready for the next
victim.[23]

Outwardly, the proprietors of both Theatre Comique and the Centennial each promoted the image of a high-class establishment. The Centennial engaged Thomas N. Wilson, described as "the great tragic actor," whose repertoire, in reality, ran almost exclusively to self-penned melodramas with such mawkish titles as *Married On the Scaffold, A Life For a Life, The Spy of 1776,* and *Justice, or the Lost Heiress.* Both theaters also sponsored benefits, most directed toward raising money for the Fort Worth Hook and Ladder Company, which in March and September 1876 had battled two disastrous fires with a hand-drawn wagon, the city's only piece of fire equipment.

The fires, which exacted a heavy toll in civic pride, destroyed the courthouse and several businesses. Under pressure from the *Daily Standard,* the city council finally purchased a $6,000 horse-drawn pumper, but the acquisition severely drained city cash reserves. At one point, the competition to stage benefits became so fierce that the Comique and Centennial scheduled rival fund-raisers on the same night. Owners finally called a truce, with the Centennial agreeing to reschedule. Ironically, the theaters' philanthropic zeal worked against the firemen, limiting the amount raised to just a few hundred dollars.[24]

In February 1873, shortly after his arrival in Fort Worth, Buckley Paddock noted in the *Democrat,* "Fort Worth is a moral and orderly town. Been here two months and haven't seen a drunk . . . a policeman or a police court." By 1876, that had all changed. The altruistic efforts of the variety theaters did little to mask growing evidence of the halls' more sordid activities and the clientele these pursuits habitually attracted. By November 1876, only three months since the first train pulled into town, the *Standard* noted, "The theaters are crowded every night, and among the audiences [are] many rustics who are seemingly carried away by the performance. We saw one man carried away—not so much by the performance as by a policeman." [25]

Both newspapers recorded fights inside the theaters and in their vicinity with regularity, the sparring not limited just to customers. In late October the *Standard* reported, "There was a little fist cuff [sic] at the Comique Saturday night after the show between some of the performers, but no damage was done." In December, a *Democrat* reporter witnessed another incident involving two female "entertainers" employed as dance girls, who "pitched into one another, pulled, scratched and tore each other's clothes until each was apparently satisfied. They were then marched off to the mayor's office and received their merited punishment."[26]

As the year turned, matters only got worse. In January a "bloody fight" broke out in front of the Centennial between two miscreants named California Bill and Fred Swain. Three gamblers playing cards just south of the theater exchanged several shots in a disagreement turned violent. One player was hit three times. There were also accusations of property damage. After the death of a valuable horse that tore itself loose from its hitching post and became impaled on a broken wagon trace, the *Democrat* complained, . . the brass bands [of the Centennial and Comique] never seem to think it incumbent of them to cease their tooting when a team becomes restive or frightened . . . and though lives or property may be lost or endangered, the tooting always goes on." In March, just two months after the death of William Webster, the Comique's hapless piano player, the *Standard* added to the growing tally of violence the demise of Alice Willard, an actress in the Centennial, during the evening's usual round of carousing and entertainment. The newspaper's enigmatic observation, "Her death was rather sudden," suggested there was more to the story than what was reported.[27]

Part and parcel with the rough clientele their establishments attracted were the proprietors of the city's earliest variety theaters. Before 1876 John T. Leer operated one of the town's most notoriously sordid saloon dance halls, the Red Light, but sometime in 1876 or 1877, he began partnering with Joe Lowe, a man recently arrived in Fort Worth, in the operation of the new Centennial Theater. Leer's history is confusing. The first Fort Worth city directory, issued in 1877, describes him as proprietor of the Comique Saloon, located at Eighth and Houston; his name also appears on old trade tokens of the same period for Theatre Comique. Whether Leer first operated Theatre Comique at Second and Main and then moved its location to Eighth and Houston, or whether he might have bought out the original Comique is unclear.[28]

What does emerge clearly from documented incidents involving Leer is a contradictory image—a man both capricious and volatile by turns, with a talent for making enemies. In October 1876 Leer sponsored one of the Centennial's benefits for the city's new fire company, but in January 1877 he was arrested after riding his horse into a dance hall operated by John Stewart and Henry McCristle near what was described by the *Democrat* as "the old theater Comique" on Houston Street.[29]

Brandishing a cocked six-shooter, Leer demanded a drink. Employees persuaded him to leave, but as the horse stepped off the building's front porch, it stumbled and fell, throwing an obviously inebriated Leer. Constables took him into custody on the spot, but he quickly posted bail and returned to the dance house, where he fired several shots through the front windows. Two bullets found their marks, striking McCristle "square" in the back and Stewart in the leg. Authorities hauled Leer back to jail once again, but neither victim was seriously hurt. After a relatively short stay in the county jail, Leer evidently was released, because in 1878 he himself was wounded after being shot from ambush in his livery stable by a disgruntled former partner.[30]

Joe Lowe, proprietor of the Centennial Theater, is notorious among western historians. He had already earned his nickname "Rowdy Joe" by the time of his arrival in Fort Worth sometime in 1876. An affinity for brawling and an irascible disposition had led to at least one previous murder charge during 1873 in Wichita, Kansas, after he feuded with and killed Ed "Red" Beard, a rival saloon operator. Beard and Lowe had engaged in at least two earlier shootouts that injured several bystanders, so when Joe was acquitted of Beard's murder, he was rearrested for attempted murder. [31]

Lowe and his wife, a notorious madam in her own right nicknamed "Rowdy Kate," decided to run for it. By 1876, the pair had drifted to Fort Worth, no doubt planning to cash in on the town's boom. On October 1, the *Democrat* announced, "The Centennial Hotel is undergoing a thorough change and will be opened next week by Mr. Joe Lowe as a theater." The article added that Harry Devere, late of the Comique, "has gone to St. Louis to engage a first class company." By the end of October, crowds had increased to the point that Lowe and Devere added another act, two female Negro delineators, "which will certainly attract."[32]

Rowdy Joe lived up to his nickname almost immediately. By mid-November, he had rankled county commissioners, refusing to pay taxes on properties that included the Centennial and the Red Light, a dance hall notorious for catering to the more prurient needs of trail hands accompanying the cattle herds that pushed regularly through Fort Worth. To curb Lowe's belligerence, city aldermen passed an ordinance prohibiting "the sale of intoxicating liquors in houses where shows of any kind are carried on." The action, however, seemed to be aimed directly at Lowe. Immediately after passage of the law, the council tabled any action until the city secretary could "notify [Lowe] that unless he pays his taxes regular, the same will be approved." Lowe got the message and shortly after, the council rescinded the ordinance.[33]

Lowe's partnership in the Red Light, in addition to his interest in the Centennial, helps demonstrate his true proclivities as vice lord. In November 1878 the *Democrat* devoted much of one page to an exposé of the Red Light, calling it and other dance halls in the city a repository of crime, where vice, recklessness, dissipation and wickedness abound in all its manifold phases. The prolific thief . . . and ordinary murderer . . . find refuge in these assemblies. . . . The ordinary young men of the town and not unfrequently those who attain to some standing in society seek these holes of infamy. One-third of all the arrests are made within their boundaries.[34]

Gambler Joseph "Rowdy Joe" Lowe. From 1876 to 1879 he operated the city's largest and most prosperous variety theater/bordello, the Centennial Theater.

Courtesy, N. H. Rose Collection, Western History Collections, University of Oklahoma

Despite the raucous nature of the variety theaters' clientele and proprietors, the town's rapidly expanding gambling district continued its explosive growth. City officials found themselves holding a handful of contradictory cards—the need to regulate the human cesspool of brothels, saloons, and variety halls while still profiting from the revenues they could bring in. Evidence of this conflicted stance had surfaced shortly after the city's incorporation in 1873, when officials first adopted, and then abandoned in quick succession, ordinances regulating houses of prostitution and making illegal the carrying of deadly weapons.

Timothy I. Courtright, also known as "Longhair" Jim Courtright, who served as city marshal from 1876–1879, was discouraged by some city officials from interfering with gun-toting cowboys unless the cowboys used the guns. But by 1878 the situation was clearly out of hand. Lacking an ordinance with the teeth to shut down the variety halls altogether, town deputies fell back on a statute banning disorderly houses (bordellos) in an attempt to control vice purveyors, including Lowe. County court records indicate that he was arrested at least six times during 1878 and 1879 for the offense but was always quickly back in business after payment of a simple fine.[35]

Joe Lowe continued as a burr under the saddle of city officials through 1879. In August 1878, Lowe's manager, Billy Cregier was shot and killed inside the Centennial after arguing with a customer over a bar tab. Then in November 1878, the county attorney ordered Lowe's arrest after several of Lowe's female performers, living on the top floor of a boardinghouse rented by Lowe from D. C. Dunn, were seen attending theatrical performances in the Centennial. The charge more than likely stemmed from an ordinance passed just one month earlier, banning known prostitutes from public places after nine P.M. and was simply the latest strategy in the ongoing battles between city authorities and local vice operators. Lowe, claiming the ladies were nothing more than actresses, demanded a trial.[36]

In court, the county attorney focused on the purpose of the boardinghouse, arguing, "the employees of the house, though they lived in the house, must be freed from the taint of bad reputation as to virtue." For his defense, Lowe contended "if [the actresses] behaved themselves as decent people and committed no lewd acts, they were entitled to witness theatrical performances as other people." The county attorney, however, insisted, "though they acted in every way decent, yet having a lewd reputation, they were under the denunciation of the statute." The jury sided with the county—Lowe was ordered to pay $100.[37]

A December 30th fire capped a year already filled with personal and legal annoyances for Lowe. About one A.M., a fire broke out in Townsend's Keno Room above the

Eureka Restaurant and spread quickly to other businesses nearby. A brisk south-westerly wind swirled sparks between the buildings and across the street toward the Occidental and Lowe's Centennial, where the roof and clapboard walls first smoldered and then ignited. Before the theater could become fully involved, the fire department arrived and doused it with a steady stream of water; however, the flames consumed two entire blocks and at least eighteen businesses on either side of Main Street between First and Second streets. At two-thirty, passengers still ten miles out on the westbound train from Dallas reported seeing the cupola atop the courthouse clearly etched in the glare of the inferno.[38]

While the Centennial suffered only minor damage and was quickly back in business, the infamous boardinghouse, home to both Lowe and his coterie of female entertainers, burned to the ground. The next day the *Democrat* tallied the property losses at $25,000, much of it uninsured. Lowe and his variety actresses lost personal possessions totaling $2,500; Ella Davis "lost nearly all her handsome wardrobe, and a five years collection of music."[39]

Just two weeks after the fire, the *Democrat* reported, "Joe Lowe is going to Colorado next month on a prospecting tour. He thinks of closing his theater next March unless business improves." Whether or not the Centennial actually went into a decline, what does seem clear is that the same irascible temperament that earned Joe his "rowdy" reputation, chafed under the new restrictions laid by Fort Worth authorities on its vice industry. After traveling to Leadville in February, he returned in March but only for a short time. An item in the *Democrat* noted, "The Centennial Variety Theater has closed for good. . . . [Lowe] may open up again during the spring cattle drive, but it is not probable that he will, as his mind is set on going to Leadville." [40]

By the end of the month he had already set up shop in Colorado. In the mid-1880s he moved on again, this time to Denver, where he continued to rankle law enforcement over a fifteen-year period while operating a series of variety theaters and sporting houses. In 1899 his contentious nature finally caught up with him when a former policeman, evidently nursing a longstanding grudge, gunned him down in the back room of a saloon. Ironically, as he aged, Lowe had taken to leaving his gun at home. He died unarmed.[41]

While Lowe's migration disposed of one problem for town fathers, it by no means signaled the end of the variety theater dilemma. The Centennial continued to operate, as did at least one new establishment, the Apollo Garden, located on Houston between Fifth and Sixth. Listed in an earlier city directory as a saloon, the *Democrat* noted its expansion to a variety theater in August and September 1879: "This theater has been opened with the best theatrical and musical talent that influence and money could command. The stage has been refitted and the interior of the house is well adapted for accommodating the crowds that assemble."[42]

The emergence of the Garden and other theaters following Lowe's departure suggests that recently passed ordinances were having little effect on the variety business. Adding to the problem, city aldermen seemed as divided on an outright ban of the theaters as they had been just after the arrival of the railroad in 1876. Such an observation is supported by a dispute that developed in 1885 over the licensing of John Leer, a full six years after Lowe's departure.

Leer, who had disappeared from city directories for several years following his legal problems of the 1870s, reemerged as one of several proprietors of Theatre Comique. When he sought to expand his variety operation with a dance hall, the *Daily Gazette* was quick to record the ambivalent stances of several aldermen, seemingly in spite of Leer's known reputation as a troublemaker: "Alderman Darter moved to table the request, but Alderman Alexander said that [Leer] had been granted the privilege of running a variety theater and it would not be any additional shock to his own modesty and morals . . . if a dance house was run in connection with it." The potential monetary loss of several hundred dollars in additional revenues for the city clearly became the overriding factor in the vote that followed. Over Darter's protests, the council issued the license, the reporter noting with particular irony the circular logic of alderman W. R. Haymaker: "He didn't think a dance house in addition to the variety would do any more harm than had already been done."[43]

In Fort Worth's ongoing love-hate relationship with its vice district, the next influential purveyor of variety entertainment in the city, unlike Rowdy Joe Lowe, had solid ties to the community. When George Bird Holland died in 1921 at age eighty-six, no less a personage than J. Frank Norris, outspoken, often flamboyant leader of Fort Worth's First Baptist Church and Hell's Half Acre's most vitriolic critic, preached him into the next world. Holland's obituary, flattering and respectful by any standard, spanned five columns in the *Star-Telegram,* characterizing his life and accomplishments as, "exceptional . . . for even the Texas pioneer." What the article failed to reveal were the ironies of Holland's long, often picaresque career and his relationship with Norris.[44]

CHAPTER TWO

VARIETY THEATER:
1873-1913

"The glory one finds
Is of various kinds
In this great and glorious land;
But the highest as yet
Is to play a cornet
In a vulgarity theater band."
~*Fort Worth Daily Gazette*

George Bird Holland and J. Frank Norris encountered each other for the first time in 1911 as tensions ran high between pro- and anti-liquor forces in the months preceding a referendum election called by the legislature to settle the issue of statewide prohibition. Norris, an outspoken advocate of the ban, stoked the anti-liquor bonfire nightly for several weeks from a tent set up at Fifth and Throckmorton, just blocks from Hell's Half Acre. Following a counter rally in the city auditorium led by pro-liquor supporters that included the mayor, Norris sympathizers left the meeting to warn him that a mob intended to cap the evening by hanging him from a telephone pole. Hoping to protect his family from witnessing his own lynching, Norris decided to confront the crowd before they could reach his house. He went to the site of the rally, where, he recalled later, "I saw a man standing up on a slab with a rope in his hand, and I walked up to him, since he was calling my name. 'Are you looking for me?'" Norris asked. Startled, the man dropped the rope, and the crowd, caught off guard perhaps by Norris' audacity, scattered.[1]

The man with the rope was George Bird Holland. Norris did not learn this, though, until some time later, when during a service at First Baptist Church, he looked out from the pulpit and observed the same man—"an old bear . . . with a mustache long enough to tie behind his ears," sitting on the back row. Although he returned to the church several times, Holland repeatedly dodged any direct contact with the evangelist by slipping out quickly at the end of each service. Norris finally spotted his man walking along Main Street one day. Holland, in his late seventies by then, was still an imposing figure. Norris recalled years later: "He had a white sombrero hat, Confederate gray uniform coat . . . down below his knees, two rows of brass buttons . . . a heavy walking cane over his arm . . . boots with spurs . . . and bells on the spurs." Norris introduced himself, never mentioning the rope incident, and after learning Holland's identity, invited him to return to services. Meanwhile he made inquiries. Friends warned Norris about Holland's reputation for courting trouble, one telling him, "[Holland] had so many notches on his gun he . . . lost count."[2]

Owner of a string of variety theaters tied for over thirty years to illegal liquor sales and prostitution and personal friend with the likes of train and bank robber Frank James, George Holland, no doubt, deserved his reputation for pandering to the basest instincts of his customers. City councilman J. H. Henderson once described Holland's various theaters and honky-tonks as "a disgrace to nineteenth century civilization." But Holland also had solid ties to Tarrant County going back over fifty years and a past that contained heroic elements by frontier standards.[3] Before the Civil War, Holland, whose parents homesteaded in White Settlement, near the border of Tarrant and Parker Counties, took part in skirmishes between Indians and settlers. In 1861 he

George Bird Holland, *left*, owner of several of the city's most notorious variety halls, including My Theatre and Theatre Comique. In later years, Holland formed an unlikely friendship with First Baptist Church preacher, J. Frank Norris, *right*, whose crusades against the excesses of Hell's Half Acre brought him death threats. Holland-*Fort Worth Record*, 10 February 1921

Norris-Courtesy Fort Worth Public Library, Local History and Genealogy

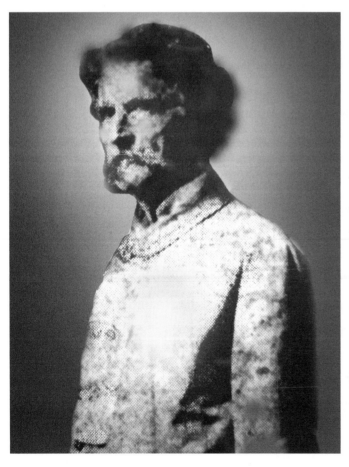

enlisted in Company K, Seventh Texas Calvary, serving through several southern and western campaigns. Following the war, he continued service for a time in a Texas Ranger or local militia unit.

Whatever reservations Norris may have had, he persisted in his efforts to befriend Holland. Holland continued to attend services, and one Sunday night showed up accompanied by an entourage of thirty-five fellow gamblers and saloon keepers, explaining to Norris, "I . . . told my gang how you perforated my hide . . . and I want-ed them to come out and get the same thing." Norris had them all escorted to seats of honor at the front. Following the incident, Norris offered Holland a Bible, a gift he accepted only after querying the evangelist skeptically: "I hadn't been inside a church in forty years when I started to go to your church. Do you know who I am?" Norris countered, "They tell me you are one of the meanest white men in town." Holland's unvarnished response made no effort to dispute the truth of the epithet: "You've got my number correct." Despite this outward show of bravado, Norris' unorthodox tactics clearly blindsided Holland and marked the beginning of an improbable friendship that endured until Holland's death. So powerful was the change that in 1915 Holland and Norris stood together in front of a packed First Baptist assembly, as Holland handed over a half-drunk bottle of liquor and publicly renounced his past life.[4]

One early Fort Worth city guide suggests that George Holland, not John Leer or Rowdy Joe Lowe, was responsible for opening the city's first variety theater sometime around 1875, bankrolled by a group of local businessmen hoping to capitalize on the lucrative stockman and cowboy trade. Holland's obituary also makes mention of a previous theater, although this may have been one of his known establishments, My Theater, which, in 1879, was located at the corner of Houston and Weatherford streets. If Holland did operate an earlier theater, a more likely date for the enterprise would seem to be 1876, when the *Daily Democrat* named the Adelphi "the first regularly established theatre in our city." While not mentioning its precise location, the news-paper urged citizens to "turn out and support this new evidence of our city's prosperity and enterprise." Nowhere in press accounts are owners or proprietors named, but when the Adelphi failed, Theatre Comique opened almost immediately in the same location, suggesting determined underwriting if nothing else. By 1877, the year of the city's earliest surviving directory, and again in the 1878-1879 directory, there is no more listing of Theatre Comique, perhaps indicating that competition from the Centennial had forced it from business by then.[5]

Even though the absence of records clouds the disappearance of this first Theatre Comique sometime between 1876 and 1879, Holland clearly maintained an active role

in Fort Worth's vice industry. Late in 1879, several months after Joe Lowe's anticlimactic exit from the city, two separate notices appearing in the *Democrat* announced
a performance of *The Daughter of the Regiment* by John F. Andrews' Star Minstrels and
the extended engagement of "acrobatic song and dance men" Thompson and Beason,
appearing in the play *Buffalo Bill,* both at My Theater. These advertisements, coupled
with the absence of any theater listing other than the Centennial for the 1878-1879 city
directory, suggest that Holland's variety hall opened following Lowe's exit in a direct
attempt to fill the void left by the closing of the Centennial.[6]

Holland, in fact, ran numerous ads for My Theatre in the *Democrat* beginning in
1879. In July 1880, he achieved notoriety of a different sort after two of his actresses
turned verbal sparring over choice parts in a melodrama into a scrap that briefly
landed them both in jail. By 1882, the city directory still named Holland as proprietor
of My Theatre but noted his relocation to Second and Main, the same corner where
the Centennial had operated from at least 1876 through 1879. While the name Theatre
Comique also appears in the 1882 directory, it is no longer used as the name of a
theater but as a business heading for variety theaters. Based on ads, news items, and
city directory listings, Holland operated My Theatre continuously from 1879 through
at least 1884, although he abandoned his Houston Street location sometime in 1881
or 1882.[7]

By September 10, 1881, when an ad soliciting talent for the theater appeared in a
New York newspaper, Holland declared his operation "the largest and finest hall in
the South." Ads placed locally were equally self-congratulatory, proclaiming it "The
Palace Theatre of the South." The number of acts alone suggests a sizeable venture.
Already signed to appear were Wentworth and Lorain, the Dolan Brothers, the
LeClairs, the Darley Sisters, Ida Hart, Lizzie Haywood, Annie Petrie, Sadie Hasson,
and Kittie Whitland. Still needed to complete the bill were several variety acts typical of the period: a "first-class male song and dance team, one female impersonator,
one dramatic star and six specialty ladies." A footnote added, "First class artists apply
at once."[8]

As the largest variety hall in town, My Theatre attracted a broad cross section of
clientele ranging from cowboys and drifters to prominent citizens. Clothier Nat
Washer, who, with his brother Jake established Washer Brothers in the early 1880s,
later recalled the strategic arrangement of the building's floor plan. Customers passed
through saloon and gaming areas in front to reach the stage show at the rear, where
"for a modest admission fee one could witness an immodest display of unattractive
but still alluring 'serio-comic' singers, as they were then termed." Washer's conclusion

was not surprising: "The environments were more conducive to exciting than to entertaining sensations." Sometime in 1885 or 1886, Holland either opened a new theater or, more likely, changed the name of his existing operation to Theatre Comique. If he had been the original proprietor of a previous Theatre Comique, such a name change would have made sense. However, all of these facts and suppositions still do not tell the complete story.[9]

An interview with early resident E. H. Keller, conducted by the Federal Writer's Project in the 1930s, offers other intriguing possibilities. Keller, who immigrated to Fort Worth in 1873, remembered Holland as proprietor of My Theater but maintained that Joe Lowe had earlier operated the same theater. While Keller's somewhat ambiguous responses stop short of naming My Theater and the Centennial as the same establishment, newspaper accounts at Holland's death make further reference to Holland's ownership of both Lowe's Centennial as well as My Theater, opening the possibility that it was Holland who purchased Lowe's Fort Worth business interests at Lowe's exit and who may even have partnered with him at various times between 1876 and 1879. These same anecdotal accounts, however, still manage to confuse matters by naming My Theatre, rather than the Adelphi or Theatre Comique, as "the first ever established [in Fort Worth]." Whether or not My Theatre was actually the establishment's original name, the possibility exists that the Centennial, My Theatre, and the second Theatre Comique were all operated by Holland at one time or another and may have existed at various times in the same facility.[10]

Whatever the case, by the 1880s, Holland's theatrical enterprise dominated the local variety business, expanded considerably beyond mere "serio-comic" singing—twenty-four individuals in the 1882 city directory listed their occupations and employer specifically as variety performer, actor, or musician of My Theatre. Nearly all of Holland's employees boarded at Lawson and Hurley's Merchant's Restaurant, less than a block from the theater, indicating a sizeable and well-organized operation. Additionally, no entertainer listed in the directory specified any other theater in the city as a place of permanent employment, although two or three individuals gave their occupations simply as variety performer or musician without specifying a full-time employer. If other saloons were running variety shows in competition with Holland, these were small and ineffective by comparison. As further evidence of Holland's domination of the variety business, the city director reported to city council in 1884 that only one variety theater, evidently My Theater, remained in operation in the city.[11]

Between 1879 and 1881, Holland's variety business had grown to the point that he began construction of an all-new theater at the corner of Second and Throckmorton, backed by a group of local capitalists. The brick building, constructed at a cost of $12,000, faced south onto Second Street. Dominating the new theater's interior was a second-floor circular gallery. Except for minor finishing details, workmen had completed the structure by early October, and Holland intended to occupy it within days. The only setback during construction had been heavy rains that drenched the theater's wooden framework and brick walls and delayed completion of the building's tin roof. At five A.M. on October 1st, the roof and three walls of the building suddenly collapsed inward, likely dragged down by the added weight of rain-swollen flooring in the gallery and upper rooms. The building, unoccupied at the time except for a sleeping vagrant who somehow escaped with only minor injuries, was declared a total loss. After surveying the ruins, local architects placed blame for the collapse on "green" brick and the added weight of swelled roof timbers. More ominously, inspectors concluded, if the theater had opened on schedule, inadequate trussing of the gallery, combined with the weight of the expected opening night crowd, would have produced the same collapse, even without rain.[12]

Three days after the incident, seemingly untroubled by his run of bad luck, Holland opened the show intended for the new theater to sympathetic sell-out crowds at his old location. While at first he optimistically maintained his intention to rebuild on Throckmorton, he later voided the contract, announcing plans instead to erect an even more expansive theater at Main and Fourth. These plans evidently fell through also, much like his ill-fated gallery. Late in 1881 or early 1882, he moved his entire operation to the corner of Second and Main, where he remained through 1886, occupying what had been one of early Fort Worth's busiest hotels, the Pacific House. Constructed by W. J. Boaz and J.P. Alexander in the early 1870s, the frame structure had originally stood at a corner of the courthouse square until expansion of the city's business district southward led to its relocation sometime after 1874.[13]

Evidently the move worked to Holland's advantage: By 1885, his staff had expanded to at least thirty-six. Besides the ubiquitous "actresses," personnel included ten actors, a property man, stage manager, stage carpenter, scenic artist, ticket agent, and orchestra leader. His regular bill combined melodramas and burlesques such as *Texas Jack, The Lady of Lions* [Lyons], *Norah Creina,* and *Sam Bass, the Road Agent* with what his ads called "startling novelties . . . and all the latest sensations of the day."

Beginning in the fall of 1885, local newspapers, city council minutes, and city directories chronicled significant changes in George Holland's theater operations, culminating in Holland's disappearance from city records for the next five years. What may have led him to abandon his local interests is open to speculation, but city records suggest increased competition from other variety hall proprietors as a factor. Holland had gone virtually unchallenged for several years, but around 1885 or 1886 W. E. Graves obtained a variety license and opened Fashion Theater at 1616 Main.[14]

Holland made several changes in his own operation in a relatively short period of time, perhaps in response to this new challenger, although other issues seemed to play equal roles. The most obvious change was a new name for the theater. Sometime in 1885 or 1886 My Theatre became Theatre Comique, a name dating back ten years to the arrival of the railroad.[15]

While the "new" theater's address in the 1885-1886 city directory remained the same as My Theater and Holland's individual listing as proprietor stayed unchanged as well, Theatre Comique's business listing revealed a second adjustment—Alexander Wilson was added as additional proprietor—perhaps indicating Holland's need for help in managing his growing business interests. Complicating the picture even further, John Leer reemerged in June 1885 as a third proprietor of Theatre Comique, although this could simply have been an indication that Wilson's management was unsatisfactory. Why Holland would offer part interest in his operation to several new partners is not entirely clear, but a *Gazette* article in 1886 suggests that he intended to open a new variety theater "near the foot of Houston street" and had already applied for the necessary permits.[16]

Leer moved to increase the theater's visibility almost immediately. When a disastrous fire destroyed much of Galveston in the fall of 1885, he sponsored several benefit performances raising money for the victims, motivated perhaps more by the need for publicity than any true spirit of benevolence. He followed this in December with a turkey dinner targeting the many homeless children who lived around the city in packing crates and abandoned buildings, many of them eking out an existence as bootblacks and newsboys. In December, despite his previous altercations with law enforcement, Leer also managed to obtain a license from city aldermen to operate a dance hall in connection with the variety theater.[17]

Besides increased pressure from competitors in the Fort Worth vice trade, another possible factor in George Holland's vanishing act was the growth of his variety demi-empire beyond Fort Worth. As early as 1883 the *Gazette* took note of this expanding theatrical "circuit," observing that Holland already owned five theaters in the state and was in the process of renovating an "opera house" in Terrell, although this last move did not go unopposed. A second story one month later noted that a lawsuit filed against Holland in Terrell's city court sought to shut down the same theater, though a jury eventually ruled in his favor. Neither report provided additional details of

Holland's variety halls, but his 1921 obituary listed theaters in Fort Worth, Terrell, Dallas, Waco, Laredo, El Paso, and Cripple Creek, Colorado.[18]

Perhaps overriding all other factors in Holland's vanishing act were his frequent tangles with city officials. Between 1879 and 1886, he was repeatedly hauled into court and fined on a variety of charges, most stemming from unlicensed liquor sales, operating a theater without a permit, or keeping a disorderly house. At least once, however, he was hauled in on the more serious charge of aggravated assault, although after waiving a plea, he was judged not guilty.[19]

Events in the first half of 1886 conspired unexpectedly to further sour Holland's already contentious relationship with city officials. In the weeks leading up to the spring city elections, slated for April 6, "repair" work closed Theatre Comique for over a month, at a time when the licenses of Holland, Leer, and Graves were, coincidentally, slated for quarterly renewal. As matters turned out, whatever the true reasons behind Holland's eventual decision to close his theater or sell out his share of the business, his timing could not have been worse.[20]

Pressure on Holland and other business owners in the city's vice district after 1879 paralleled often inconsistent attempts by city officials to tighten operating restrictions for variety theaters and other vice-related establishments. From the mid-1870s through the 1890s, public outcry against the variety theaters steadily mounted, fueled by such violent incidents as the gunning down of Billy Cregier and John Leer's dance hall rampage.

The press campaigned against the theaters, providing documentation of often lurid incidents such as the 1890 arrest of William de Orme, a "song and dance man," who assaulted a variety actress, kicking her so hard in the stomach "that blood spurted from her mouth." In 1899, a customer severely injured Frank Jenkins, stage manager of Hurley's Theater, slashing him repeatedly with a broken whiskey bottle after Jenkins interrupted the customer's tête-à-tête with an actress. City aldermen struggled to maintain order, hampered by an understaffed police force and their own reluctance to sacrifice the revenues generated by the vice industry for city coffers, and in some cases, for their own pockets.[21]

Pro- and anti-liquor forces on the city council remained at odds for much of the 1880s, the battle often clouded by the quid pro quo politics of town economics. This ambivalence of city officials is aptly illustrated by contradictory ordinances passed within a fortnight of each other during 1880. The first prohibited the sale, giving away, or consumption of liquor in connection with variety performances. The second, passed a few days later, amended the first to allow such sales once proprietors negotiated a registration process that included applying to the council in writing, paying a quarterly licensing fee of $62.50, posting an additional $250 bond, gathering written consents from neighboring dwellings and businesses, and hiring special policemen at owners' expense. In 1884 the council added an ordinance targeting "loud talking, laughing, hissing, whistling, cat-calling, snorting, throwing paper or other missiles . . . or any other act or conduct tending to harass, annoy or disturb any of the spectators or actors or performers in any theatre or opera house while any performance is going on."[22]

Conservative forces may have believed the new ordinances would close the variety theaters, but the regulations had the opposite effect. Even with additional tightening of the licensing ordinance in 1885, Graves, Leer, and Holland were all repeatedly granted operating licenses.[23]

On April 6 citizens elected several new aldermen and voted in H. S. Broiles as mayor to replace the retiring John Peter Smith. One day later, the newly elected council met to consider several matters, including the routine quarterly renewal of variety licenses. In a surprise action, aldermen voted five to two to suspend the permits of all variety halls, including Holland's proposed second theater. While it is possible that the actions of the council may have been a response to some sort of organized rebellion by theater owners against the complex licensing procedures, there is no indication of this in the press or in city council minutes. It seems more likely that conservatives on the council found themselves unexpectedly in the majority at an opportune moment and decided to capitalize on the situation to close the theaters permanently.[24]

Conservative crowing was short-lived. On April 19, the day of the council's formal installation, variety proprietors approached Broiles armed with several petitions. Five aldermen signed the documents in support of the theaters in addition to most neighboring businesses. Even C. B. Daggett Jr., an alderman who, two weeks earlier, had voted to shut the houses down, signed. Broiles caved in to the pressure, claiming majority rule. Over the next several weeks, he remitted the fines of operators who had remained open in defiance of the closure and issued temporary operating permits to all existing theaters. These actions drew criticism from city attorney William Capps, who claimed Broiles had no legal authority to grant such permits without the council's vote. By May 5, the special permits expired, a technicality ignored for the most part by the halls' operators and regulars. Two weeks later, the *Gazette* reported, "The show part of the variety theaters was not going last night but the dizzy females . . . champagne and beer still flourished."[25]

Aldermen continued to skirt the issue until June 1, when John Leer and W. E. Graves forced the issue, appearing before the council with new petitions. A reporter observed, "A broad smile rested on the face of nearly all present, as it was believed that the council was evenly divided on this question and fun was expected." After efforts to table the issue failed, the council finally voted with predictable results. The mayor, who sided with those in favor of granting the licenses, broke the four-to-four tie. Broiles explained it was "better to receive for the city a certain amount of revenue than have nothing."[26]

Unexpectedly, a pair of victories emerged from the council's abortive efforts to rid Fort Worth of its variety theaters once and for all. Missing from the hearings to reopen the show houses was George Holland. The simplest and most logical explanation, given Holland's acerbic disposition, is that he balked at continuing efforts to regulate his operation, refused to pay his bond and other fines, and cleared out. Circumstantial evidence supports this. Holland had remained open in defiance of the order and on May 21, 1886, was arrested for operating a variety theater without a license. While John Leer and W. E. Graves continued to appear meekly before the council at regular licensing intervals, Holland did not reapply to run a theater in the city until 1892. Theatre Comique may have stayed in business through the early part of 1887, but a small news item in December 1886 noted that a half interest in the theater and an adjoining structure had been sold "under execution" for $270.[27]

Although the variety hall at the corner of Second and Main did not close down for good until 1890, the name Theatre Comique disappeared from city directories by 1888. Following Holland's departure, Leer renamed the operation Leer's Vaudeville, but the name change, and perhaps Leer's ownership seems to have been short-lived. Newspaper accounts suggest several enterprises attempted to force new life into the show house, but none, including Leer's, survived long enough to make it into city directories. Although W. E. Graves operated from the site for a short time during 1887, it is not clear if he continued the operation under the name Theatre Comique.[28]

With the disappearance of Theatre Comique from Second and Main and increased pressure applied by various civic and religious organizations, the city's vice industry continued a slide to the south end of town, where it gradually congealed by the 1890s in the area below Ninth Street between Houston and Jones. Known collectively as Hell's Half Acre for close to a decade, the "district," in reality, defied any half-acre boundaries and was actually a magpie collection of saloons, brothels, variety halls, and gambling dens scattered widely throughout the blocks south of the courthouse.

Far from signaling the decline of the variety theaters, the demise of Theatre Comique offered fresh opportunities to several new operators. Over the next ten years

J. D. Andrews, C. W. Hurley, Gus Wood, and John M. Moore, all moved to fill the gap left by the closing of the last uptown variety hall. Lee Riley, a Dallas hack driver with more glorified theatrical delusions than common sense, was less adept at securing his piece of the lucrative Fort Worth vice market. Riley persuaded local man Buck Cooper to partner with him in opening a variety theater in the Acre, and as down payment, gave Cooper 125 newly minted silver dollars. Cooper took the money to the Farmers and Mechanics' Bank to deposit, where bank clerks detained him and contacted police after they recognized the coins as part of a missing silver shipment that had disappeared from the same bank's vault only hours after its arrival a month earlier. Cooper was eventually exonerated after Riley and a bank guard confessed to pulling off the inside job.[29]

Through the 1890s and into the first years of the twentieth century, several new variety theaters opened, all in or near Hell's Half Acre. In 1890, J. D. "Dan" Andrews opened Andrews' Pavilion Theater, conducting business from the northwest corner of Jones and Twelfth until 1895 or 1896. The Gem Theater, recorded only in brief news items, was also operating in 1890, although its exact location and proprietor are unknown. C. W. Hurley and Mrs. B. Hurley conducted business from Hurley's Summer Garden and Theater, opened around 1896 at 1214 Jones. Later they changed the name of the theater to People's. Sometime around 1895, Gus Wood went into business at 114 West Front, across from the T&P depot, calling his enterprise the Front Street Theater, and in 1905 E. N. Dinwiddie and Mannie Kramer were operating the Star Theatre at 1400 Rusk. Most significantly perhaps, between 1891 and 1892, George Holland returned to Main Street, opening Holland's Varieties.[30]

Since Holland's last attempt to cut himself a slice of the variety trade in 1886, ongoing efforts at reform were led by several no-nonsense mayors including H. S. Broiles, John Peter Smith, and Buckley Paddock. Elected on a reform platform, Broiles' get-tough policies, backed by County Attorney R. L. Carlock and District Judge R. E. Beckham, made significant inroads in police corruption and succeeded in shutting down forty-five gambling operations, several of which operated behind closed doors in previously untouchable "uptown" establishments. During this period Holland and John Leer chose to abandon for good the high ground of uptown.[31]

Reform measures targeting the variety theaters continued throughout the 1890s, sometimes hampered by the very officials elected to maintain order. In July 1890, the city council ordered the closing of both the city's existing variety theaters when it was discovered that neither had paid the required licensing fees or obtained the necessary permits to operate. Final approval of the action was blocked, however, when Mayor

Pro-tem J. P. Nicks, acting in the absence of Mayor W. S. Pendleton, refused to sign the order. Pendleton, who served less than four months of his term before deserting his wife to run off with a telephone operator, resigned three days later, forcing a special election.[32]

On August 4, voters reelected John Peter Smith, a city founder and one of the most popular mayors of the 1880s. Within days of taking office, Smith had vetoed permits already granted by the council, including one that would have allowed J. D. Andrews to reopen a variety hall at the corner of Second and Main. Churches meanwhile rallied behind the new mayor, gathering hundreds of signatures in support of his actions. The *Gazette* used the municipal sparring to poke fun at the exaggerated importance claimed for the theaters by some on the council:

> The glory one finds
> Is of various kinds
> In this great and glorious land;
> But the highest as yet
> Is to play a cornet
> In a vulgarity theater band.[33]

As support for Smith's actions grew, some council members retreated, at least temporarily, from their original positions. It was long enough for Smith to push through an ordinance prohibiting the sale or giving away of liquor in any place where dramatic presentations took place. However, a second, more restrictive ordinance, which would have prevented saloons from operating within 100 feet of any theater, failed to pass by a slim margin. And though the new ordinance represented an important step forward, the failure of the council to sever the connection between the saloons and the variety theaters ensured that the halls would remain open for another twenty years.[34]

The return of George Holland coincided generally with the election of Buckley Paddock as mayor in 1892, significant since Paddock, Broiles, and Smith all supported active prosecution of repeat offenders in the Acre over the longstanding policy of allowing guilty parties simply to pay a fine and return to business. Holland became a victim of this shift in policy soon after reopening his variety hall at 1115 Main. After he was brought to trial in the city court and found guilty of keeping a disorderly house in August 1893, his lawyer appealed the verdict to the state court of criminal appeals. When that court rejected the appeal, Holland was ordered to jail despite his last minute offer to turn over property to the court to settle the judgment against him.[35]

Holland never operated a variety theater on Main Street again. Instead, by 1897, he reopened as Holland's Varieties at Twelfth and Jones, a corner that served as a revolving mill for theaters over several years: Hurley's, People's, and still later, Andrews' Pavilion were all located at the intersection. A reporter covering the hearing granting Holland an operating license noted aldermen "swallowed without making more than a wry face, but it . . . turned the civic stomach." Sure of himself and

In the 1890s, city founder and popular two-time mayor John Peter Smith pushed through new ordinances aimed at shutting down the Acre's variety theaters. Despite his efforts, the halls prospered well into the 20th century.

Courtesy, Fort Worth Public Library, Local History and Genealogy

defiant as ever, Holland had conducted business for a month before even bothering to appear before the council.[36]

Into old age Holland seemed to relish his reputation for pushing the legal limits of decency. One resident recalled, "If there was anything ever invented by man to attract the base instinct of the human which was not put on at Holland's, it was an oversight on the part of the management." By 1899 Holland had moved once again to 1405 Rusk, one block south of the Standard Theater, but by 1901 he was back at Twelfth and Jones, still just steps away from his chief rival. Around 1905 Holland moved the theater one last time—to 115 E. Thirteenth, and by 1907, now past sixty, he had closed down for the last time.[37]

By the 1890s, a steady influx of homesteaders was gradually displacing the gamblers and ruffians of the boomtown days. Fort Worth, with a population now above thirty thousand, increasingly occupied itself with more typical municipal issues: building churches and schools, improving water, sanitation, and fire services, and paving streets. The founding in 1890 of both the Fort Worth Dressed Meat and Packing Company and the Fort Worth Brewing Company helped industrialize the city and brought much needed revenues, diminishing the importance of Hell's Half Acre's saloons and variety theaters to the local economy but failing to eliminate them altogether. Far from cowering under the double-barreled threat of moral and municipal progress, Hell's Half Acre roared on, more or less contained in the area below Ninth Street but far from eradicated. Emblematic of this ability to regenerate itself, between 1893 and 1894 the Standard Theater debuted at the corner of Twelfth and Rusk. Unlike the clapboard Centennial and Theatre Comique, the Standard was all brick, the Acre's largest and grandest variety theater since the wide open days of Rowdy Joe Lowe and George Holland.[38]

By the time the Standard appeared, however, the traditional western honky-tonk and variety show, catering openly and unapologetically to the most prurient inclinations of its clientele, faced not only increased legal censure but was rapidly losing ground to changes occurring in the eastern show business establishment. Replacing variety was vaudeville, a style of entertainment that had first emerged well before the Civil War but by the 1890s was rapidly gaining public acceptance for its staging of "polite" variety bills, sanitized to attract audiences that included women and children. The term "variety," with its ribald associations, fell into disuse, giving way to the more acceptable "vaudeville," the term increasingly favored by image-conscious proprietors hoping to add a gloss of respectability to their bills.

The Standard Theater, located in the heart of Hell's Half Acre, was the first to try to broaden its audience base by disassociating itself from the old term, referring to its bill in newspaper ads as "burlesque and polite vaudeville," an ambiguous designation at best. The Phoenix Theater, opened around 1901 by J. P. Balderson at 1213 Calhoun, began its life as a variety theater but followed the lead of the Standard and shortly became a vaudeville house under the ownership of Phil Epstein. Epstein, who had served as the Standard's orchestra leader for several years, purchased the Phoenix between 1901 and 1902, changed its name to the Crown, and operated it until 1905, when he sold out to J. N. Brooker and moved up permanently into the "polite" family market as music director of the new Majestic Theater. Only the older variety halls like Holland's and People's held on to the term variety—by 1904, all remaining theaters, with the exception of Greenwall's, the city's legitimate opera house, designated themselves by the new term—vaudeville.[39]

John M. Moore, a prominent businessman in Hell's Half Acre, built the Standard. Previously, with his wife Ella, he had operated Rankin and Moore, a saloon in North Fort Worth. Around 1895 the couple opened the Palace Hotel and Saloon at 1201 Main and the Atlanta House Hotel at 1114, less than a block north. In 1898 when millionaire capitalist and stockman Winfield Scott constructed the luxury Metropolitan Hotel at Main and Eighth Street, he persuaded Ella Moore to operate it for him. [40]

Superficially at least, the Standard operated on a higher plane than its predecessors in the variety trade. By the 1930s when variety had long become synonymous with burlesque and strip tease, one veteran merchant in the Acre maintained that while only men attended the Standard, and it had something of an unsavory reputation, "it was conducted on a higher moral tone than many of the best [burlesque] theaters. . . . Never did a woman appear there without stockings or tights. The displays . . . would not have been permitted at the Standard. I never heard even the word 'damn' spoken there." Referring to the striptease artist who had gained national attention at the 1933 Chicago Century of Progress Exposition, he continued, "Do not get the idea that the Sally Rands of today would have been permitted to do their fan dances at the old Standard."[41]

The Standard, however, is best remembered for the two colorful characters who took it over in 1897. Frank DeBeque had a convenient relationship with his wife Maggie—she tended the Standard's boardinghouse where performers and employees lived just behind the theater and protected the family's financial interests. Frank ran the theater, and he and Maggie both performed occasionally in the shows—he as an acrobat and gymnast, she as an Indian club juggler and slack wirewalker. DeBeque, whose real name was Frank Riggins, indulged in the sporting life and was an inveterate gambler with an eye for horseflesh, occasionally even running his own string of ponies on the side. Maggie worried that Frank's propensity for taking risks could endanger their considerable investments in Fort Worth—they bought the Standard in 1897 and later purchased 775 acres of ranchland in Arlington Heights just west of town, where Frank bred his horses and built Maggie a seven-room house.[42]

When the DeBeques took over the Standard Theater in 1897, the two already had Dallas arrest records stretching back at least a decade. Frank's encounters with law enforcement extended mainly to charges of public intoxication, although the *Dallas Herald* documented other more serious accusations against him, including embezzlement. Maggie, whose real name may have been Maggie Mawhorn, operated under several aliases including Elnora Mitchell, Maggie Lawler, and Maggie DeBeque, working as a variety actress in Dallas' Mascot Variety Theater and Camp Street Opera House, both notorious sporting houses. In 1892 deputies arrested Maggie after a man charged that she had stolen $250 from him. She was arrested again, along with another variety actress, a few months later on the curious charge of dressing in men's prize-fighting costumes and then slugging it out in a manner the arresting officer described as "cross-countering and upper cutting . . . to make the pugilistically inclined turn green with envy." Each combatant was charged $5 for her fun.[43]

Performances at the Standard ran from eight-thirty until midnight—ten to fifteen acts on the bill each night, most considered too coarse or rough for mixed audiences. Clearly a "low-class" vaudeville house, the Standard, nevertheless, stayed open longer than any other Fort Worth variety theater, operating from 1896 until sometime around 1913. By 1901, advertisements proclaimed it "the Koster and Bials of Texas," a comparison with what had briefly been one of New York City's most prominent vaudeville houses. Koster and Bials' Music Hall sported crystal chandeliers, vaulted ceilings, and classical statuary. Fort Worth in the 1890s was hardly New York, though Standard management worked hard to accommodate a clientele ranging from prominent stockmen and local bluebloods to the more usual cowboys and drummers that frequented the Acre. Tickets for ground floor seating ranged in price from fifteen to twenty-five cents, while stage boxes for private parties ran as high as $3. Single seats in a booth cost fifty cents.[44]

The Standard emulated its New York counterpart in other ways, sometimes granting patrons free admission. Since theaters' main income came from liquor sales, free shows actually boosted profits. Another practice adopted by the Standard was the Koster and Bials entertainment formula: a motley bill that ranged even to the occasional operetta afterpiece or burlesques of classical fare but always with the clear objective remaining—the immodest display of the feminine form. On the hall's ground level, far less elegant than Koster and Bials, sawdust covered the floor, and customers sat on wooden benches. Private booths and boxes on the floor above lined the balcony rail and offered more luxurious table seating from which to view the show.[45]

Despite its eclectic nature, a hallmark of most vaudeville theaters, the level of talent playing the Standard remained inferior to acts booked into the so-called high-class theaters. Only a handful ever broke into these polite vaudeville circuits or later made the transition to motion pictures. Among the few making the jump were Buster Keaton, Bert and Johnny Swor, and Ben Turpin. Turpin, billing himself as the Happy Hooligan, parlayed crossed eyes into a career that spanned circus, burlesque, and film. When he switched to Mack Sennett's Keystone features in 1917, he became a major comedy star.[46]

Though now virtually forgotten, Bert and Johnny Swor, a pair of brothers raised in Farmer's Branch near Dallas, became leading blackface comedians, appearing as end men with both the Lew Dockstader and Al G. Fields minstrel organizations. The siblings made the jump to high-class vaudeville billing themselves for a time as Two Black Crows; later, Bert performed as a monologist and as part of the comedy team Moran and Mack. Both later performed in the family-oriented Majestic. One of Bert's signature bits, imitated by other comedians of the period, involved the teary reading of a sappy letter from home, concluding with the line, "God bless and keep you—from your loving Ma and Pa."[47]

Probably the most recognizable name to play the Standard was Buster Keaton, who, at the time of his appearances sometime before 1908, was a precocious child performer, part of his parents' "knockabout" vaudeville act. He earned individual fame much later, after crossing over into silent movies.[48]

In January 1906, chief of police James H. Maddox complained to a reporter, "I have more trouble with variety theaters than with any other class of people. A great many thieves lay [sic] about such places and I consider it necessary to the peace and protection of the people that I be allowed to close them up." Three months earlier, in October 1905, Maddox had launched a fresh assault on the theaters, ordering proprietors to stop all liquor sales and shutter their operations by December 1. The crackdown came in the wake of earlier changes in ordinances controlling variety theaters, seeking to plug loopholes that previously allowed customers and proprietors to avoid prosecution when selling or purchasing liquor in rooms or buildings adjoining a theater instead of the theater itself. Deputies arrested proprietors of several theaters and dance halls, including the Star, Crown, and Standard. In comments to reporters,

Maddox ignored the decency issues so often raised by critics of the variety perform-ances, citing instead the flouting of liquor laws coupled with the often predatory tac-tics employed by female entertainers, who could boost their salaries as much as thirty per cent by convincing customers to "treat" them:

> These entertainers get a percentage of all they can persuade a
> man to buy. I have known men to go to such a place with a large
> amount of money and . . . be picked up on the outside the next
> morning without a cent. When they get all he has, out he goes.
> There is no one to prosecute because he has spent his money
> while drunk.[49]

Maggie DeBeque, who had assumed full ownership of the Standard in 1905, was one of those arrested in the first sweep but avoided further prosecution by closing down immediately, claiming she had no interest in reopening. Spurred perhaps by Maddox's aggressiveness in taking action, the city council, whose members since the 1870s had routinely abetted variety theaters through sweetheart enforcement of toothless ordinances, reacted uncharacteristically. On December 18, 1905, they sup-plied the police with new ammunition for the campaign, voting to further amend existing liquor regulations for theaters. Unlike previous failed attempts, the measure passed unanimously, banning not only the sale of liquor in places where theatrical performances of any kind were given but its consumption as well.[50]

Some variety managers, including Frank DeBeque and Dave Houghton, fought back against the closures, their lawyers declaring the new ordinance unconstitutional and claiming false imprisonment. On the strength of these claims, People's, the Star, and the Crown shortly reopened, dispensing not beer but Teetotal, a drink claimed by its manufacturer to contain less than 1 percent alcohol while still mimicking the fla-vor of beer. The strategy resulted in a new round of arrests and an improbable court-room scene one reporter called "nothing short of ludicrous." One variety hall actress testified to consuming fifteen bottles of Teetotal without "getting dizzy about the head." Despite the questionable testimony, the judge found the Star Theater not guilty of selling intoxicating liquors.[51]

By January 1906, the DeBeques, heartened by the 1 percent strategy of other theaters, reopened the Standard. The council and police may well have felt new pres-sure to adopt a strict enforcement stance because more arrests followed shortly, including Frank DeBeque and the previously acquitted proprietors of the Star. By the end of January, police reported that only two variety theaters remained open. New violations of the ordinance had ended. No further mention was made of People's, and newspaper accounts suggest it made a voluntary decision to close, possibly to get charges dropped against its proprietors after assistant city attorney Virgil R. Parker announced his intention to continue prosecutions of all violators of the new ordinance. Dave Houghton, who had repeatedly voiced claims of unfair arrest, proclaiming the ordinance unconstitutional, was tried and convicted twice by juries during January and February. Each time he filed appeals, but shortly after his conviction on February 7, newspaper ads for the Star disappeared, suggesting that Houghton, too, had either given up the fight or gone bankrupt. By mid-year 1906, no variety theaters remained except the Standard and Crown, and by 1907, the Crown too, had disappeared. The Standard somehow avoided permanent closure, if not further controversy.[52]

Around midnight on December 22, 1906, John Nichols, a special policeman assigned to the Standard Theater, confronted a patron in the variety hall's lobby. Though obviously drunk, the man, a farmer named Barney Wise, argued with Nichols and drew a .38 revolver as the officer tried to arrest him. Shots were exchanged and a struggle ensued. Nichols fell to the floor dying. Frank DeBeque and two other men who witnessed the altercation subdued Wise until police arrived. Meanwhile, theater patrons carried the still-conscious Nichols to a cot in the rear of the theater, where he died minutes later.[53]

Public outrage followed. Editorial implications of police ineffectiveness and payoffs led to calls for the resignation of Chief Maddox and triggered sweeping raids of the Acre's most notorious dance halls and brothels. The resulting arrests jammed court dockets, leading to a petition circulated among local judges and other law enforcement officials demanding relief and the creation of a new criminal court. One week after the murder, the *Record* devoted much of one issue to a scathing exposé of the Acre and four of its most sordid establishments, including the Standard and the Crown. In an ironic twist, a jury acquitted Nichols' assailant after witnesses could not establish conclusively who had fired the first shot.[54]

The murder of John Nichols marked another turning point in Fort Worth's relationship with its variety theaters. By 1910, the Texas frontier had long since vanished, along with the young town style of law enforcement that tolerated the excesses of the sporting houses, dance halls, and variety theaters. While the Standard continued to operate until 1913, other theaters, including People's, the Star, and the Crown, had long since vanished, victims as much of changing public tastes as municipal crackdowns.

The growth of both vaudeville and motion pictures, bankrolled by investors who lavished profits on increasingly opulent show palaces, eventually helped trivialize the Acre's tawdry variety halls far more effectively than police raids and public outrage. When offered the choice of knocking back cheap liquor in a second rate theater or sitting in comfort to watch top-billed vaudeville acts, former variety clients increasingly chose the latter.

Frank and Maggie DeBeque, the last major variety holdouts, finally sold the Standard in 1909 to A. Phinney and Alvin Hill, who after their own tangles with law enforcement, closed the hall's saloon and beer garden permanently and announced that hereafter the theater would be operated as just that—a theater. The decision, as matters turned out, proved anticlimactic. By that time, several new theaters, including the Lyric, Phillips, Lyceum, and the Majestic, the city's "big-time" house, flanked Hell's Half Acre, offering "high-class" family-style vaudeville at prices far less than a stage-side booth and a bottle of rot-gut at the Standard. Done in by the competition and a quarter century past its glory days as the Koster and Bials of Texas, the old theater finally succumbed to the wrecking ball in 1934, joining George Holland's long-vanished Theatre Comique, which had burned to the ground in a fire of suspicious origins in 1907. Local newspapers helped give both theaters more decent burials than perhaps either deserved, eulogizing them as colorful remnants of Fort Worth's wide-open era. In truth, by the time the Standard met its fate, variety had ceased to play any role in the city's life, a second-rate performer long since given the hook by management.[55]

CHAPTER THREE

FROM MAKESHIFT HALLS
TO OPERA HOUSE:
1873-1884

"There's only one thing the matter with the play
and that is the double murder. It should have
been a triple one and should be performed
in the first act . . ."
Fort Worth Daily Gazette, 1883

By the 1870s, expansive accounts of Texas cattle ranches and limitless business opportunities were attracting British investors, and in 1877 Englishman Charles Leveson Gore and his young wife, May Robison, decided to try their luck in the American West. Within months of Rowdy Joe Lowe's arrival, the young couple stepped off the train in Fort Worth and registered at the El Paso Hotel. Gore eventually acquired a 380-acre tract of land three miles west of town in what would later become Arlington Heights. For a time, the pair camped out in a small house on the bluffs above the west fork of the Trinity River.[1]

Wealthier than most settlers, they acquired cattle and within months began constructing a much larger two-story house on a site west of Hulen and just south of Crestline Road and River Crest Country Club, near where, in the 1940s, All Saints Episcopal Church was constructed. Ignoring local Solomons who predicted the structure would collapse in the first good windstorm, the Gores completed the house and furnished it with bone china, silver, furniture, and rugs brought from England. The elaborate homestead quickly became a focal point for dances and other neighborhood events.[2]

The Gores survived two years in their prairie manor house before homesickness, rural isolation, and repeated bouts of fever convinced them to sell and try their fortunes in the more settled East. Sending May ahead to New York, Gore accepted an offer from P. H. Clark of Williamson County for an even trade—the land and house for seven hundred head of horses. The venture seemed foolproof—Gore would drive the herd north to market, turn a solid profit, and rejoin his wife, but en route, various misfortunes claimed much of the herd, and Gore sold what remained of the couple's western hopes at a loss. Disillusioned by the setbacks, Gore rejoined his wife in New York, intent on returning the family to England. When May stubbornly refused to leave America, they divorced; in a final tragic denouement to their Texas adventure, Gore died shortly after returning to London.[3]

Robison was invited to join a stock company, where she learned the acting craft over twenty years. A misprint in a theater program shortened her real name, Mary Jeanette Robison, to May Robson, providing her with her permanent acting persona.[4]

She aligned herself with Charles Frohman, one of New York's most powerful manager-producers and a founding member of the monopolistic American Theatrical Syndicate, which, by 1900, exerted draconian control over most theatrical bookings in the United States. Actors loyal to the system were assured the best available parts and a full season, while those who insisted on maintaining their independence were often relegated to obscurity. She built a solid reputation as a versatile comedienne, making character roles the focus of her career. [5]

In 1911, thirty years after leaving Fort Worth, Robson returned, this time to the Byers Opera House, as the star of her own company. During her stay, she visited old acquaintances and toured the home she and her husband had built in the late 1870s. Somewhat ironically, *The Rejuvenation of Aunt Mary,* the play in which she toured for over four years, revolved around the humorous misadventures of a rural spinster who abandons the country after encountering life in New York City. The local reviewer proclaimed her, "a soul-satisfying comedienne in an all-that-is-desirable comedy. She and the play are one rippling composition of melodious mirth."[6]

Robson's transformation was so complete that one reporter observed, "Many . . . older residents will remember Mrs. Gore, but few will associate her with May Robson, so completely did the actress swallow the sprightly girl from the antipodes . . . through sheer force of necessity."[7]

The course of Robson's career, rising through the stock company ranks and touring the country with traveling productions helps illustrate the late-nineteenth century theatrical practices that brought legitimate theater to Fort Worth. At the same time the raucous ambience and clientele of the variety theaters were galvanizing the attention of citizens and the local press, a small yet significant notice appeared in the *Democrat* in November 1876 announcing, "A plain stage has just been built in the large hall over Dahlman Brothers, and Mitchell is painting the drop curtains and scenes. Hundreds of chairs were moved in today for the accommodation of those who will visit the Minstrels on Friday and Saturday nights."[8]

Constructed by local businessman B. C. Evans at the northwest corner of Houston and First streets, Evans Hall became the first stage in Fort Worth built expressly for the presentation of theatrical productions and entertainments catering to the mainstream family or mixed audience. Despite the excitement clearly generated

British actress May Robson in 1884. Robson and her husband Charles Leveson Gore, homesteaded just west of Fort Worth in 1877, buying land near present-day River Crest Country Club, and furnishing it with silver, furniture, and rugs brought from England.

Courtesy Albert Davis Collection, Harry Ransom Center, University of Texas-Austin by the announcement, Evans Hall was still far removed from the ideal space envisioned by longtime citizens. Patrons entered the hall by an outside stairway on First Street, at the rear of the ground floor. The level floor of the hall made it difficult for persons seated in the rear to see. Even as it prepared to open, the *Standard* complained, "The hall . . . in dimentions [sic] is adequate for all present purposes, but it has not been arranged for public convenience. . . . Fort Worth should have a hall, an opera house especially adapted for amusements. . . . Will not our people build one?"[9]

If Evans Hall was still far removed from the opera houses proliferating in more established regions of the country, its construction, nevertheless, marked a significant step forward. Performance halls of any type stood on equal footing with courthouses,

Fort Worth merchant B. C. Evans in 1876 constructed a stage in a second-floor hall at the northwest corner of Houston and First to create Evans Hall, the city's first theater catering to mixed audiences.

Courtesy, Fort Worth Public Library, Local History and Genealogy

churches, libraries, and industry as symbols of community aspiration and pride, attracting new commerce and a better class of settler. The expansion of the railroad system westward was also producing changes in the long-established internal systems of American theatrical production. Before the Civil War, stock companies featuring a rotating repertoire of plays each season seldom strayed from well-established theaters, located chiefly in major urban centers such as Philadelphia, Boston, and New York. By the 1870s, however, this system had given way to a new trend—the "combination" company, a road variation of the older stock company system.[10]

In the last half of the century, legitimate plays of all sorts dominated performance bills, but minstrel shows, popular since the 1840s, still drew large crowds. Evans Hall opened November 17, 1876, with the Georgia Minstrels, a group bearing as its name an epithet commonly used to designate all-black minstrel companies. The *Democrat* noted, "These minstrels have made a national reputation and as they are the only genuine negroes in the minstrel business, they may be considered a curiosity in themselves, aside from their superiority as showmen."[11] A reviewer for the *Daily Standard* called the hall's second attraction, the Fay Templeton Star Alliance, a "first-class theatrical troupe" and its feature player, ten-year-old Fay Templeton a "charming little beauty."[12]

No more attractions were booked into the hall until January 1877, when the Selden-Irwin Combination played for a week, its performances once again built around a repertoire of such popular plays as *Our American Cousin* and Edward Bulwer Lytton's *The Lady of Lyons* and *The Two Orphans*. Problems with several of the players "wavering in their lines" brought criticism from local reviewers, although the *Standard* noted that leading man Harry Rainforth "adapts himself well" as Lord Dundreary in *Our American Cousin*.[13]

Also appearing was Katie Putnam, an actress who toured the United States extensively in the last three decades of the nineteenth century. Between 1877 and 1894, she returned to Fort Worth at least ten times. Putnam's reputation resided as much on personal charisma as any great acting or singing ability. She had built a considerable following emulating both the style and repertoire of Lotta Crabtree and Maggie Mitchell, two of the more popular actresses of the period. A local reviewer called her "the most inimitable piece of feminine cuteness now on the American stage." She performed twice during the hall's first season, appearing in *Fanchon the Cricket* and *Lena the Madcap*.[14]

March 1877 brought Madame Rentz's Female Minstrels high-kicking their way into Evans Hall with the city's first view of the cancan. Rentz and her entourage played to a predominately male audience with somewhat predictable results. Anticipation of the spectacle of barelegged chorines in short petticoats and exposed bloomers generated a traffic jam of buggies and wagons on Main Street. The troupe's appearance two years earlier at the Tremont Opera House in Galveston had precipitated a firestorm in the press that decried the "lewd and disgraceful exhibition" of the "Can-Can orgie."[15]

Fort Worth's male population shamelessly welcomed the troupe. Just before show time, near pandemonium erupted as several hundred men tried to shove their way into the hall. One journalist observed, "The entertainment was very interesting in many of its parts and would have been much better had [the entertainers] been favored with . . . better order." Later, seeking eyewitness commentary, the reporter claimed to have interviewed 187 men exiting the hall, all disavowing any knowledge of the event.[16]

The second season opened October 5, 1877, with Haverly's Minstrels, but the quality of bookings remained uneven. Seven combination companies braved the trip, including those of James Wallack, Selden Irwin, Henrietta Chanfrau, Fay Templeton's Star Alliance, and Katie Putnam's Dramatic Company. The Stoddart Comedy Company appeared twice, first in December 1877 and again a month later in January 1878. The Alleghanians offered a mix of Swiss bell ringing, vocal renditions of numbers from popular operettas, and a tuba band. The Peak family teamed with comedians Fred and Annie McAvoy and the Blaisdell Brothers in a performance benefiting the local fire department.[17]

In January 1879, tragedienne Jane Coombs brought the "classics," to Fort Worth for the first time with productions of Dumas' *Camille* and Shakespeare's *Romeo and Juliet*. The *Democrat*'s man-on-the-scene took exception to *Camille* calling it "simply too emotional to be enjoyable" with "too many overwrought, pathetic, sentimental parts to make it attractive as a popular play." By contrast, he declared Coomb's portrayal of Juliet, "faultless" with "a fine conception of the character." He was less forgiving of a certain Mr. Hall as Romeo, whose bungling of the fabled balcony scene drew titters of laughter from the audience and led to the observation, "[he] did not look like a Romeo or act like one."[18]

Evans Hall continued as Fort Worth's only legitimate hall for three more seasons, weathering intermittent dry spells while occasionally booking personages of some repute. William F. Cody, better known to admirers as Buffalo Bill, had parlayed youthful experiences as pony express rider, army scout, and buffalo hunter into a long and successful show business career, first launched in 1872. Cody appeared in

Fort Worth in December 1879 in a horse opera written to capitalize on the public's fascination with his larger-than-life adventures, first popularized in dime novels and newspapers. His dramatic vehicles merely presaged the pageantry and melodrama of Cody's later Wild West Show, launched in 1882, and his Fort Worth appearance was no exception. A street parade led by war-bonneted Indian chiefs and Cody's own brass band costumed in colorful military regalia preceded the night's presentation, *May Cody, or Lost and Won.* The melodrama, commissioned by Cody himself, featured his sharpshooting and prowess with a bullwhacker's whip.[19]

William F. "Buffalo Bill" Cody. Capitalizing on his fame as an army scout and pony express rider, the plainsman turned to acting in the 1870s. Following an 1879 appearance at Evans Hall, Cody peevishly complained that the hall had "no dressing rooms, no lights...in fact, no nothing."

Courtesy, William E. Hill Collection, Dallas Public Library

Professional performances in Evans Hall stopped in 1882, but local photographer C. L. Swartz documented this amateur performance c. 1900. Participating were such prominent citizens as Dr. Frank Boyd, seated second from left; and grocer E. H. Carter(seated, wearing a hat). Standing are Judge Joe Terrell, third from left, middle row; and B. B. Paddock, fifth from left. To the right of Paddock, l. to r., are Judge B. D. Tarleton and Mr. and Mrs. W. C. Stripling.

Courtesy, Fort Worth Public Library, Local History and Genealogy

Ultimately, Evans Hall, with its physical limitations and absence of even basic stage equipment, could not attract the talent available to cities with performance halls and opera houses constructed expressly for theatrical presentations. Buffalo Bill complained during his 1879 appearance that he had never encountered a hall with such poor accommodations—"no dressing rooms, no lights . . . in fact, no nothing," a reporter quoted him as saying.[20]

These shortcomings, coupled with the unwillingness of many star-led companies to troupe in virgin territory, undoubtedly hastened the demise of the hall. Whatever the cause, the hall suddenly closed in March 1881, cutting short the current theatrical season. A notice in the *Democrat* announced, "Messrs. Booth and Dryden, lessees . . . have been requested by the owners to cancel all engagements they may have with troupes or artists wishing to play here, as the hall will no longer be used for theatrical purposes." The abrupt closure seems to suggest that a rift of some sort had developed.[21]

"What shall we do?" moaned the *Democrat*. An editorial appearing the day after the announcement complained that the town's only remaining stage of any sort was located in the variety hall operated by George Holland and called for immediate construction of a full-fledged opera house:

> Think of it—Fort Worth, a city of enterprise and capital, with a population of ten thousand . . . and now without a hall for public entertainments. If there ever was an absolute necessity for an opera house, it is right now. . . . Work cannot be commenced too early, while a delay may subject us to inconveniences and losses. . . . The opera house should be finished before fall; otherwise no troupes will visit us. . . . Fort Worth needs an opera house, and Fort Worth should have an opera house at once.[22]

While planners courted investors and developed the working details of a proposed performance hall, theatergoers once again endured the pre-railroad indignities of a town bypassed by most entertainments, excluding traveling circuses and the risqué variety offerings of Holland's My Theater. During the 1881–1882 season, not one legitimate troupe or minstrel company scheduled an appearance in the city.[23]

Change came from an unexpected source. Around 1881, Fort Worth's considerable German population had founded the Deutsch Verein (German Society) to organize dances and other entertainments for German settlers, many of whom spoke very little English. The new civic organization held its inaugural ball January 14, 1882, in College Hall (more than likely the campus of Texas Wesleyan University at the corner of Jennings and Eleventh). Within months, the society built or leased its own hall on the south side of Seventh Street between Throckmorton and Houston.[24]

A revitalized theatrical season took shape in Deutscher Verein Hall during late 1882 or early 1883 with at least seven troupes booked to perform. In January 1883 Barlow and Wilson's Mammoth Minstrels appeared, followed by Andrews and Stockwell's Ideal Pantomime Company. Fay Templeton returned in February, still touring with what had become, at least in billing, her own "opera" company. The sixteen-year-old actress sang featured roles in *La Mascotte* and *Olivette*. Richardson's Dramatic Combination, the Boston Operatic Minstrels, and the ubiquitous Katie Putnam followed her. J. H. Haverly's English Opera Company rounded out the season on March 10 with *The Merry War*.[25]

In early 1883, the Fort Worth city director included as part of his annual report to the city council, a short notation: "A splendid new opera house will be erected in the coming season. It is already contracted and some of the material is on the ground." Completion of the hall, to be located at the northwest corner of Third and Rusk, was still ten months away, but the *Democrat* felt sufficiently heartened by the news to predict future theatrical success for the city, alluding to current tours of other Texas cities by the country's leading comic actor, Joseph Jefferson, and American prima donna Clara Louise Kellogg: "Galveston and Austin are already enjoying such dramatic and operatic entertainments. Fort Worth will attract the stars as soon as her grand new opera house is completed."[26]

Fueling the optimism was news in the summer of 1882 that a recently formed syndicate headed by two of Fort Worth's most prominent business leaders, Walter A. Huffman, and Captain Martin B. Loyd, was moving forward with final plans for the city's much-delayed first opera house. Chosen to design the new hall was the architectural firm of John Bailey McElfatrick and Son, in business since 1855, a prolific St. Louis company specializing in theatrical design. In the heyday of live theater during the late nineteenth century, the firm designed over sixty theaters in

Walter A. Huffman and Martin B. Loyd, two of the capitalists influential in construction of the Fort Worth Opera House in 1883. Huffman eventually became majority stock holder. Following his premature death in 1890, Huffman's widow sold the hall to Henry Greenwall.

Courtesy, Fort Worth Public Library, Local History and Genealogy

Captain M. B. Loyd

New York alone and an estimated two hundred nationwide, each structure's plan unique and reflecting the latest innovations in theatrical equipment.[27]

By July 1883, McElfatrick had new opera houses under construction in both Fort Worth and Dallas. Work on the Fort Worth hall, built at a total cost of $55,000, was followed closely in the local press through the spring and summer of 1883. Moving forward despite delays caused by the discovery of substandard bricks and design flaws that initially placed too much load on some exterior walls, construction proceeded under the direction of James W. Keplinger and son, George Keplinger, another St. Louis firm specializing in the unique configurations demanded by theatrical enterprises. On July 21, the *Gazette* reported:

> The opera house will be a bijou in its way. It is so compactly
> built, notwithstanding its great seating capacity, as to bring the
> actors and the audience into close communion. Even the bald heads
> will have no use for field glasses when giddy burlesquers face the
> footlights, and the shallowness of the stage gives no reason for flirt-
> ing behind the scenes.

Total seating capacity for the 70 by 110 foot hall was 1,214.[28]

Though negotiations to book an acting company for the premiere remained incomplete, by September 9, the *Gazette* reported,

> The new opera house is finished. The final touches and outside
> ornamentation will be put on this week, but the interior is ready for
> the grand opening with the exception of the chairs, and the build-
> ing will be locked and the keys given to the manager in a few days.

Surrounding the dress circle was a horseshoe balcony, supported by twelve iron pillars. This gallery rose in two additional levels: the family circle, or first balcony, and the theater's least expensive seats, the upper gallery, where patrons had to content themselves with sitting on wooden pews.[29] Two private boxes flanked the stage on either side, adjoining the dress circle and family circle.[30]

The stage, appointed with the latest innovations in machinery both for raising and storing scenery and creating special effects, measured approximately thirty-two by sixty-eight feet. A permanent frame and bridge permitted scenic artists to be raised and lowered for painting drops and gave stagehands access to stage machinery. Other "bridges," adjustable grooves, or gaps, in the stage floor, allowed for raising and lowering set pieces and the creation of certain illusory effects from a seven-foot space beneath the stage floor.[31]

Noxon, Albert and Toomey, a third St. Louis firm of scenic artists, received the contract for outfitting the stage area of the new theater. Equipment included thirteen drop and wing settings and all the accompanying set pieces, flats, and furniture commonly found in theaters of the era: palace chamber, modern chamber, bastillion prison, rustic kitchen, perspective street, dark wood, landscape, garden, rock pass, oak chamber, Gothic chamber, and horizon. In addition there were such pieces as a pavilion, cottage, garden statues, flower vases and balustrades, rocks, bridges, and water.[32]

With drapery and wing legs installed, the remaining performance space measured thirty feet deep from grand drape to backdrop and thirty feet wide from wing drape to wing drape. The vertical distance from the stage floor to the rigging gallery measured fifty-two feet. Illumination for scenes came from five rows of adjustable gas-powered border lights and reflectors, thirty-two burners in each overhead row, which could be raised and lowered for various effects. A reporter noted the lights "make the stage as bright as day."[33]

The Fort Worth Opera House, c. 1883. Following its purchase in 1890, the hall was renamed Greenwall's Opera House.

Courtesy, Jack White Photograph Collection, Special Collections, University of Texas-Arlington Library

Merchant Max Elser, who served as ticket agent for Evans Hall from 1876-1882. In 1883, he became the first manager of the newly constructed Fort Opera House.

Courtesy, Fort Worth Public Library, Local History and Genealogy

Charles H. Benton, manager of the new Dallas opera house, scheduled to open just days after the Fort Worth premiere, worked closely with Max Elser, manager of the Fort Worth Opera House, to acquire talent for both houses. Elser, a Fort Worth merchant who had served as ticket agent for Evans Hall, had been instrumental in bringing the first telegraph line to the city. Evidently, he remained in town to oversee final arrangements for the theater's opening while Benton made the long journey to New York for meetings with agents.[34]

Though Benton managed to secure a number of bookings, the *Gazette* reported, "he had to do some tall talking with some of the managers to induce them to make Texas dates." Alluding to the problem of remoteness that continued to plague many Texas theaters, the article explained, "The long 'jumps' and high railroad fares in the state are too vividly remembered in companies with the sorry experience of many combinations in the past." [35]

Bookings for the hall's inaugural season covered several genres: The ever-popular minstrel troupes included Callender's Minstrels with Billy Kersands, Ida Siddons' Mastadons, and M. B. Leavitt's Gigantean Minstrel Festival; popular melodrama, including *The French Spy, Fogg's Ferry,* and *East Lynne;* Shakespearean specialists Thomas Keene and Frederick Warde; and Joseph Jefferson, the most beloved American comedian of the era, in his signature role, *Rip Van Winkle.* Comedy came in the form of *Tourists in a Pullman Palace Car,* Roland Reed in *Cheek,* and Charles Hoyt's *A Bunch of Keys;* actress Rose Eytinge with her own company, presented *Felicia* and *Oliver Twist.* Opera was also represented in presentations by Maurice Grau's Opera Company, Hess Opera Company, and perhaps the premiere event of the season, the appearance in concert of American-born opera prima donna, Minnie Hauk.[36]

Large ads in the *Gazette* had earlier proclaimed the premiere "a memorable fashion event" in the "Palace Amusement Temple of Northern Texas" with "the Most Brilliant Gems of the Operatic Diadem." Ticket prices for each performance during the four-day event ranged from $1.50 for parquet seating to the top price of $8.00-$10.00 for a private box. Seating in the upper gallery, the least expensive, went for fifty cents. The Chicago Ideals Opera Company, an offshoot of the famed Boston Ideals, opened the new hall on Wednesday, October 10, 1883, with a performance of *Iolanthe,* Gilbert and Sullivan's latest offering, and followed it with three more of the team's most popular operettas—*Patience, The Sorcerer,* and *H.M.S. Pinafore.* [37]

With the completion of its new opera house, Fort Worth made a sizeable jump in cultural status, joining a loosely organized but growing theatrical circuit connecting major towns throughout the state. The first season of operation for the opera house was not without problems, however. Barely three weeks after the opening, a play entitled *The Black Dwarf,* featuring the improbable scenario of trapeze artists firing pistols, resulted in a fire that ignited an onstage drop curtain during the performance. The *Dallas Weekly Herald* reported, "The curtain was ordered down, when actors and actresses rushed on the stage and a panic among the audience was only prevented by a number of citizens who ordered all to keep their seats. The curtains were dropped to the stage and the fire extinguished, when the performance continued."[38]

Though quick thinking had averted a tragedy in this case, the event led to another, more startling, discovery—there were no fire extinguishers of any sort in the building. The *Gazette* crusaded for immediate modifications, pointing out "every well-appointed theater in the county has [extinguishers] in addition to . . . facilities for flooding the stage with water in case of necessity." There were also continuing problems with ticket sales, a clear sign that the new theater needed to work harder at coordinating city events, building audiences, and improving publicity. This became obvious in mid-November, when the opera house attracted an audience of fewer than fifteen, while a crowd estimated at two thousand gathered to witness the races at Fort Worth's newly opened Driving Park. Copy space in the newspaper ran mostly to coverage of the horse races and to cockfights at Byne's Council Room pit, with only negative mention of the opera house.[39]

The negative press notices resulted from a contract dispute between manager Max Elser and the acting company of *A Friend,* the latter claiming that Elser had failed to publicize the play or provide a house orchestra for two successive performances. On the first night of the run, the play, a potboiler revolving around a double murder, went on without incident, despite the absence of musicians to provide the proper ambience. Still minus an orchestra on the second night, the dispute flared again backstage, with Elser and the actors' spokesman, Marlande Clarke, bickering hotly over profit margins and salary adjustments. After the audience of only eleven people waited for over an hour, the first act commenced, but at the beginning of the second act, Clarke abruptly halted the performance.

Stepping to the apron, he announced, "As Mr. Max Elser has not acted fair and square by me, and the house is so small, I have no other recource [*sic*] but to ring down the curtain and take what legal steps I may." The slender house, expecting entertainment, instead found themselves minor characters in the pocket melodrama. A reporter in attendance noted, "The audience were somewhat surprised, but showed their appreciation of the situation by the loudest applause possible from eleven persons." Next day, with the troupe finally departed, manager Elser characterized the dramatic offering as "unfit for ladies to see," adding sardonically, "There's only one thing the matter with the play and that is the double murder. It should have been a triple one and should be performed in the first act."[40]

Despite such incidents, the clear winners in the new opera house's first season were local theatergoers. Patrons suddenly could select from among at least forty-five offerings that ranged from minstrelsy, acrobatics, and magic to a dramatic platter that included Shakespeare, melodrama, operetta, and farce. Between November 1883 and April 1884 several stars of national reputation, including Frederick Warde, Joseph Jefferson, Roland Reed, Louis James, and Rose Eytinge braved the trip across Texas to Fort Worth. In addition, prizefighters John L. Sullivan, Steve Taylor, and Mike Gillespie gave boxing demonstrations, and internationally known opera diva Minnie Hauk sang in concert.

Completion of the hall also helped spark renewed ambition among local amateurs. In what may have been the city's first locally produced operetta, prominent local musicians and singers banded together to stage *The Chimes of Normandy* in February 1884. Among cast and orchestra members were Mrs. A. S. Pettus, Fannie Murphy, W. T. Maginnis, Nat Washer, and Leopold August. Following the resignation of Max Elser around 1884 or 1885, Mr. and Mrs. Charles Benton assumed management of the opera house. Mrs. Benton organized a children's acting troupe, and in 1886 the Fort Worth Dramatic Society staged a number of plays, including *East Lynne* and *Wives of the Period*.[41]

Over the next seven seasons the performance hall continued to benefit from a steady increase in national railroad touring by major companies and stars, as well as significant efforts during the 1880s to consolidate Texas opera houses into an organized circuit. Behind many of the state improvements were the efforts of a pair of Galveston businessmen, brothers Henry and Morris Greenwall. The city's theatrical fortunes and those of the Greenwall family were destined to remain bound together for the next thirty-four years, well into the second decade of the twentieth century.

CHAPTER FOUR

SHAKESPEARE, MELODRAMA, AND THE GREENWALLS: 1884-1900

*"The present play is a species of melo-musical-comic drama,
with a slight tinge of the tragedy,
if such can be comprehended."*
~*Fort Worth Daily Gazette,* December 1890

As late as 1887, five years after the opening of the Fort Worth Opera House, a local reviewer still grumbled, "Away down in the south where everybody expects to meet with cowboys and coyotes, few first class companies have the courage to venture." Famed English actress Lillie Langtry, whose tour of the state brought her to Fort Worth for two nights in April 1888, seemed fearful of venturing anywhere in the state much beyond Galveston. She confessed embarrassment to a Galveston reporter after exaggerated newspaper accounts of western violence led her to believe gangs of roving bandits would accost her in Texas. Rather than risk being "held up by cowboys," she left most of her jewelry behind in New Orleans. She girded herself admirably for the perilous undertaking, traveling in the Lalee, her seventy-five-foot, air-conditioned private railroad car, a rolling palace that boasted not only Langtry's private boudoir upholstered in blue satin but sleeping compartments for staff, an office, kitchen, library and parlor fitted out in Nile-green silk brocade, embossed leather, and parquet wooden flooring.[1]

Rising American actress Minnie Maddern (later Fiske), who herself had bypassed Fort Worth on two tours before 1887, by 1888 also seemed disdainful of accounts of unbridled frontier mayhem. During her Fort Worth appearance, she made light of such reports saying, "People away from here have a very exaggerated idea of the rough-ness of the people. It is all so different from the impression people have in the north and east. The audiences . . . are cultivated, refined, and appreciative, and do not measure the success of the play by the number of men in it who die with their boots on."[2]

Despite such encouraging signs, the Fort Worth Opera House struggled in its first five seasons, undergoing several changes in management as its directors sought

Fearful of being "held up by cowboys," British actress Lillie Langtry left her jewelry behind in New Orleans during her 1888 Texas tour. Her Fort Worth stop came April 25-26.

Courtesy, William E. Hill Collection, Dallas Public Library

to attract profitable bookings. Max Elser had numerous ongoing business interests, including a stationery, books, and musical merchandise store, as well as contracts with several railroads to run fifteen hundred miles of telegraph line through Louisiana and Texas. Either he had agreed to serve as opera house manager only on an interim basis, or these interests eventually pulled him away from the theater.

Elser resigned sometime in 1884 or 1885, replaced by Charles Benton, who had previously managed the Dallas Opera House. Benton's wife, Agnes, served as opera house business manager and later seems to have taken on many of her husband's managerial duties as Benton became involved in the administration of additional theaters. In July 1886, Benton resigned, and George Dashwood, a local druggist, purchased the lease to become the opera house's third manager in just four seasons. Dashwood continued to manage the theater through at least the 1890–1891 season. Meanwhile, an expansion of theatrical touring, both in Texas and across the country in general, contributed to a steady improvement in the quality of Fort Worth's theatrical bookings. [3]

Several actors who had built highly profitable road careers around signature characterizations also appeared at the new opera house. In 1886 James O'Neill, father of twentieth-century dramatist Eugene O'Neill, enthralled local audiences for the first time as *The Count of Monte Cristo,* while Annie Pixley charmed them with her portrayal of plucky mining camp waif, *M'Liss, Child of the Sierras,* who battles ruffians and more sophisticated feminine rivals to keep the man she loves. Kate Claxton included the opera house on her tour first in 1887, playing blind Louise, the role she had originated in *The Two Orphans,* one of the most popular melodramas of the nineteenth century. She returned several more times through 1903. Cigar-smoking Lotta Crabtree, who began her career at age seven singing and dancing for gold nuggets in the California mining camps, played Fort Worth in *Pawn Ticket 210,* a vehicle created for her by David Belasco and Clay Greene. The show sold out with sales of $1,050, the largest receipts for a single performance since the opening of the opera house. [4] Even with the prestige of national stars, the opera house continued to be plagued by its share of third-rate offerings. *The Gazette* pronounced an 1888 performance of *Davy Crockett* so bad that "none [of the actors] can be said to rise above the mediocre, but some . . . veraciously can be said to fall below it." [5]

In 1885 James Wallick, whose appearances in so-called border dramas helped codify what would eventually become the western, starred in *The Bandit King,* James McCloskey's horse opera canonizing the exploits of bank robber Jesse James, or as he was called in the play, Joe Howard, an alias supposedly used by James. In McCloskey's version, James' escapades served as cover for his true purpose—breaking up an unscrupulous gang of desperadoes. [6]

Wallick cut a dashing figure as Howard, supported by a cast that included his two trained horses, Roan Charger and Bay Raider. The horses, which endeared themselves to audience members by tearing down wanted posters, descending a staircase, and

Many of the nineteenth century's best known actors made appearances at the Fort Worth Opera House between 1883 and 1900. Among them were, left to right, James O'Neill, father of playwright Eugene O'Neill, Annie Pixley, Lotta Crabtree, and Joseph Jefferson, known for his portrayal of Rip Van Winkle.

Courtesy, William E. Hill Collection, Dallas Public Library

rescuing a damsel from a burning building, sometimes received better notices from critics than their human co–stars. Such "hair-lifting" episodes as "a leap for liberty through the window on horseback," "the fearful plunge down the rapids," and "a duel to the death—a bowie knife fight on horseback," allowed Wallick to tour the play successfully for over ten seasons. Wallick and his equine sidekicks returned in 1886 with a similarly styled epic, *The Cattle King.* As range baron Bob Taylor, the actor once again played to a standing-room-only crowd.[7]

In January 1889 William A. Brady, another purveyor of the sensational, presented *After Dark,* one of several so-called tank dramas that employed realistic water effects. At one point, a murderer hurled his intended victim into London's Thames River—no painted drop but a canvas tank full of real water, six feet deep, that extended the width of the stage. Those in the gallery pressed against the balcony rails as Old Tom dove headfirst from the bow of a boat to rescue her. Moments later victim and rescuer emerged dripping from the "river" in full view of the audience. Just twelve days later, *Lost In New York,* another Brady production, featured "a vast river of real water 60 feet

long, 30 feet wide, 4 feet deep, containing 60,000 gallons," on which the audience saw "an actual steamboat running at full speed."[8]

Throughout much of Texas during the early 1880s, any formalized theatrical circuit remained, at best, loosely organized beyond coastal areas where acting troupes could easily jump by ship from New Orleans to Galveston and from there, the short distance to Houston. Troupes and stars, because of this lack of a consolidated system, made touring arrangements as best they could, booking in the late spring and summer with individual theater managers, who often made pilgrimages to New York, where, increasingly, the majority of play companies and actors were based. Once there, managers might have to deal individually with as many as forty different producers to broker a complete season. This haphazard arrangement began to change by the mid-1880s when Henry Greenwall, who had managed theaters in both Galveston and Houston, emerged as a consolidating force. Following the Civil War, Greenwall's older brother, Morris, persuaded him to move from New Orleans to the port city of Galveston, where the two established a brokerage firm. In 1867, one of their customers, actress Augusta Dargon, became stranded in the city after a disastrous tour that left her unable to pay off debts she owed to the Greenwalls. Instead of selling off her effects, the two brothers devised a mutually beneficial solution that allowed them not only to recoup their losses but gave Dargon a second chance at a profitable season— they leased a frame building, fitted it up as a makeshift theater, and formed a stock company featuring Dargon. When that building burned, they leased Turner Hall and continued to sponsor the actress.[9]

From that beginning, the brothers steadily expanded their theatrical enterprises. By 1871, they had persuaded Willard Richardson, founder of the *Galveston News,* to build the Tremont Theatre for their use. They next moved into Houston as well, leasing Perkins Hall, later called Pillot's Opera House. By 1872 they had already attempted to establish a theatrical circuit in the state, sending the Tremont stock company on tour through several towns beyond Houston and Galveston. The enterprise showed enough promise that the next year the Greenwall-sponsored troupe ventured as far north as Corsicana and Dallas, although there is no record that the company made it to Fort Worth, still at that point without a railroad.

Henry Greenwall clearly exerted enough influence in regional theatrical matters, to handle, informally at least, the Texas bookings for many touring companies. A comparison of bookings for the Tremont, Pillot's, and the Fort Worth Opera House between 1885 and 1890, the year Greenwall finally assumed full control of the Fort Worth theater, reveals a high level of coordination among these theaters, with attractions often appearing in Fort Worth and Dallas one week to ten days after concluding engagements in the southern part of the state.[10]

As Henry Greenwall worked to establish a Texas theatrical circuit, he also began consolidating his regional control in other ways, becoming manager of the Dallas Opera House between 1883 and 1885, taking over San Antonio's Turner Opera House in 1886, leasing the New Orleans Grand Opera House in 1888, and securing the Fort Worth Opera House in 1890.[11]

The growing scope of the manager's influence was evident by 1886. A disastrous 1885 theatrical season in New Orleans, the gateway through which many troupes and important performing artists often entered Texas, caused a number of prominent players to consider abandoning tours through the state altogether, fearing they could not generate sufficient revenue to cover expenses without the profitable New Orleans launch. Greenwall, who by then had spent nearly twenty years as a theatrical manager in the state, had, for the most part, built a solid reputation as a man of his word, generous to actors down on their luck.[12]

He evidently capitalized on this reputation in 1886, persuading a number of companies to tour the state by a new route, entering Texas through Arkansas instead of New Orleans. To accommodate the actors, Greenwall formed the Texas, Arkansas, and Louisiana Theatrical Circuit, guaranteeing touring companies sufficient dates to make reasonably short jumps throughout the state. Greenwall described the new route to a *Dallas Morning News* reporter in September 1886: "We commence at Pine Bluff, Arkansas. Then come Little Rock, Hot Springs, Texarkana, Palestine, Tyler, Denison, McKinney, Dallas, Fort Worth, Waco, Austin, Bryan, San Antonio, Galveston, Brenham, Beaumont, and Lake Charles, Louisiana." Greenwall booked attractions and assigned dates for theaters on the circuit under written certificates signed by individual managers, giving him authority to act on their behalf. As companies signed, he forwarded contracts to individual theaters and obtained receipts. The system sometimes broke down if paperwork was delayed or when managers, likely trying to maneuver around Greenwall's cut of the profits, repudiated the agreements.[13]

Perhaps in response to such controversies, a group of managers from Texas and Arkansas gathered in the spring of 1886 at the Fort Worth Opera House to discuss booking and routing issues. Editorial comments appearing in the *Gazette* before the meeting noted, "The amusement interests in Texas have long suffered because of the lack of cooperation on the part of managers. Companies tour the state in a haphazard . . . manner productive of general complaint." The meeting led to the formation of the Texas Theatrical Association. In June the group reconvened at the opera house to establish policies for its membership, voting that all managers should handle their own bookings and that no contract would be recognized without an individual manager's signature. A common routing ledger open to examination by all managers was to be set up through an established New York theatrical agency to help eliminate the sometimes duplicitous booking practices of previous seasons.[14]

In 1887 Edwin Booth, perhaps the greatest actor produced by America in the nineteenth century and certainly the most highly regarded tragedian of his time, toured Texas under Greenwall's aegis. He and his dramatic counterpoint, Lawrence Barrett, both friends of Greenwall, played Galveston, Houston, Dallas, Austin, and San Antonio but bypassed Fort Worth.[15]

Responding perhaps to the clamorous demand for tickets during 1887, Booth and Barrett mounted a second, more ambitious tour through the state in 1888, this time including a one-night stand in Fort Worth. Playing a program that included both *Julius Caesar* and *Othello* in Galveston and Houston, the pair modified the bill for their February 18 performance in Fort Worth, presenting *Hamlet* in place of *Othello* and performing a double-bill in one long evening. *Julius Caesar* earned only modest praise for the players, and it was clear from *Gazette* commentary that what the crowd had really come to see was *Hamlet*. Noting the difficulties imposed by any effort to compare Booth and Barrett, the reviewer nevertheless observed, "Barrett is not the material from which such actors as Booth are made. Yet there is about the acting of Barrett a certain native reality which commends itself."

Booth, at age fifty-four still playing Hamlet, was noted for his well-studied, unmannered interpretation of the character, traits the Fort Worth critic found worked both for and against him.

> The symmetry of Mr. Booth's Hamlet is an example of finished art; his acting, looked at technically, is not equaled on the English-speaking stage. It is carved like a statue, faultless in proportion; but today it is a statue into which a soul may or may not be breathed. To the casual observer it may stand for ... formal perfection; but to the practiced eye, the mechanism is in many places bare of the warm nerve covering of [emotion].

Despite Booth's failings, the reviewer concluded,

> We believe Mr. Booth has the power to brush away the heaviness and ... give us a Hamlet as superb in its spontaneity of passion, if not as tender in melancholy beauty, as any ... down the long gallery of three centuries.[16]

In the summer of 1890 the Fort Worth Opera House entered a new phase. On June 29, Walter A. Huffman, one of the capitalists most instrumental in organizing a syndicate to build the hall, died in Chicago, where he had gone for medical treatment. Huffman had eventually bought out other syndicate interests and leased the hall first to Charles Benton and then to George Dashwood. In the twenty years before his death, Huffman had invested heavily in Fort Worth real estate and civic projects, amassing a considerable fortune, but after gold speculation on Wall Street drove up interest rates in 1889, he had trouble raising money to pay off notes. Huffman's untimely death left his estate heavily in debt and opened the door for Henry Greenwall to expand his theatrical circuit. Preparing to embark from New York for Europe, Greenwall learned from his brother, Phillip Greenwall, that a consortium of eastern theater managers

Edwin Booth, one of the nine-teenth century's greatest actors, in his signature role, Hamlet. He made two tours through Texas during 1887-1888, playing the Fort Worth Opera House, February 18, 1888.

Courtesy, William E. Hill Collection, Dallas Public Library

planned to challenge his control in the south by making a cash offer to Huffman's heirs for the Fort Worth Opera House.[17]

Intending to make its move only after Greenwall was safely out of the country, the opposition posted a representative to make sure that the manager embarked. In the best cloak-and-dagger tradition of melodrama, Greenwall evaded the spy and secretly boarded a train for Fort Worth. A New York representative, meanwhile, guilesly displayed a telegram confirming that Greenwall had set sail. By the time Greenwall reached Fort Worth, the eastern consortium had already laid out an offer that included a cash down payment of $10,000 and expected to close the deal that same day. Greenwall's unexpected appearance and his counterbid—doubling the other investors' cash deposit, put an end to the upstart challenge to Greenwall's southern control and insured that the theater would remain a permanent fixture of his Texas circuit.[18]

Following seven seasons of uneven bookings and several changes in management, Henry Greenwall, the agent long most politic in shaping the state's theatrical fortunes, publicly announced on July 17 an agreement with the Huffman estate to purchase the performance hall for $40,000, although by the time the property actually changed hands on September 2, an additional thousand dollars had been knocked off the purchase price. Published estimates of the value of the seven-year-old structure, including land, indicate Greenwall picked up the property at bargain prices. The comparatively low price can be partially explained by the need of the Huffman heirs to settle indebtedness quickly but also by the costs of maintaining and upgrading the opera house's out-of-date lighting system and its aging stock of stage equipment and scenery. Greenwall announced that the house would be repainted and replastered for the upcoming season but that a more extensive renovation, including new scenery, would be undertaken in 1891.[19]

Purchase of the Fort Worth Opera House, which by its October 1st opening had been renamed the Greenwall Opera House, helped Henry Greenwall put a further lock on his control of major theatrical houses throughout the state. He continued his expansion two months later, announcing in November plans to construct a new $100,000 opera house in Waco. In Fort Worth, meanwhile, he instituted several changes in personnel—George Dashwood stayed on to oversee day-to-day operations of the opera house, but Greenwall's brother, Phillip Greenwall, relocated to Fort Worth from Galveston to supervise overall running of the circuit and coordination of the Dallas and Fort Worth theaters. Sol Braunig, who had previously served the Greenwall organization as treasurer of Sweeney and Coombs Opera House in Houston, was

HENRY GREENWALL.

PHIL W. GREENWALL.

In answer to actors' complaints about the hardships of Texas touring, Galveston theatrical manager, Henry Greenwall, left, established the Texas, Arkansas, and Louisiana Theatrical Circuit in 1886. After purchasing the Fort Worth Opera House in 1890, he installed his brother, Phillip Greenwall, right, as manager.

Courtesy, Fort Worth Public Library, Local History and Genealogy

moved to Fort Worth in 1891 to fill the same position, while A. B. Wolfe was appointed box office manager. George Conner, who had previously served as orchestra leader for George Holland, became music director. Henry Greenwall himself remained in New Orleans, where he had moved in 1888 to assume management of the Grand Opera House. From that city he continued to operate his southern circuit until his death at age 81 in 1913.[20]

Phillip Greenwall arrived in Fort Worth in September 1890 to begin preparations for the coming theatrical season. For the next twenty-seven years, he supervised the Texas circuit, first from the Greenwall Opera House, until it was torn down in 1908, and then from the Byers Opera House, constructed that same year. Following the death of Henry Greenwall in 1913, he assumed full control of all remaining Greenwall theatrical holdings, a position he held until his own death in 1917.[21]

Within the first year of direct management by the Greenwalls, several improvements became evident. Advertising increased substantially under a press strategy intended to raise public awareness of theatrical events. Large-type, two-column, front-page ads soon became a regular feature of the Sunday *Gazette,* spotlighting the coming week's lineup of attractions, as well as upcoming appearances by major stars. Inside the paper, two new Sunday columns made their entrances—one provided background on upcoming attractions and news of the theatrical season across the country, while the second, a syndicated feature, offered gossipy commentary on theatrical celebrities and events.

George Conner, music director of Greenwall's Opera House from 1890 to 1913. A composer, and arranger, he had previously served as musician and orchestra leader for George Bird Holland. George Conner obituary,

Courtesy, Tarrant County Historical Commission, Tarrant County Courthouse

Many theaters by 1890 had begun electrifying both as a safety measure and to improve on the dimness of gas lighting. As part of their upgrading of the opera house's equipment, within a year the Greenwalls began replacing the stage's outmoded gaslights with a combination of gas and electric "so constructed as to be absolutely safe from fire." (Fifteen years earlier, New York's Brooklyn Theater had caught fire during a play performance, killing 198 theatergoers.) The Greenwalls also instituted several new policies, including an eight-thirty curtain and a ban on latecomer seating before the end of the first act to "end the clatter of seats and the necessity of getting up to let someone to an inside seat in the middle of an act." Complaints about rowdy inmates of the gallery led to the posting of a special policeman and restricting "women of bad repute" to an isolated area so that there "need be no fear of undesirable neighbors in the house.[22]

The "new" Greenwall Opera House opened October 1, 1890, with a reprise of William A. Brady's gallery-pleasing spine tingler from the 1888–1889 season, *After Dark.* As far as quality of offerings, however, little changed at first, beyond the name Greenwall now tagged onto local advertising—the revolving door of sensational dramas, alternating with the ubiquitous minstrel shows and the occasional farcical comedy, continued much as before. The bewildering sameness of the entries led one local critic to conclude, as he searched in frustration for words to characterize the latest arrival,

> [the play] is one of the numerous melodramas and musical
> comedies which pervade this portion of the country, except that
> the present play is a species of melo-musical-comic drama, with
> a slight tinge of the tragedy, if such can be comprehended.[23]

The melodramatic trend continued through the next several seasons. *Paul Kauvar,* a drama set during the French Revolution, arrived in 1891, offering gruesome mob scenes and a simulated beheading on an operating guillotine, complete with wax head dropping into a waiting basket. *The Pulse of New York,* playing first in 1892 and again in 1893, featured "the great fire scene," "the great leap for life," and a "real elevated railroad train." In *The Bottom of the Sea,* a hit both in New York and on the road, ships collided spectacularly as the two rivals for the heroine's affections dived into the depths of one sinking vessel to battle for possession of her jewel box during a final watery duel. *The Fast Mail* offered thrills to suit the most lurid proclivities in theatrical mayhem—a stabbing, a train hurtling full-speed through a station, a steamboat explosion, a drowning in Niagara Falls, and an axing.[24]

Despite the sameness of much of the theatrical fare, the advent of the 1890s and the change in ownership for the opera house worked together to bring new stars to the city. Many of these rising stars showcased their talents in more recent works rather than such shopworn vehicles as Shakespeare or the endlessly recycled catalog of adventure-romance sensational dramas. Replacing stars like Booth and Crabtree were such versatile performers as Richard Mansfield, Tim Murphy, Robert Mantell, Minnie Maddern, Nat Goodwin, Lillian Russell, Otis Skinner, Eva Tanguay, and Eddie Foy.

Foy, who did regular turns in vaudeville as well, later appeared with his seven children in an act billed The Seven Little Foys. He took to the boards of the opera house at least twice during the 1890s in musicals—*Off the Earth* in 1897 and *Hotel Topsy Turvy* in 1900. Tim Murphy, appearing as Texas cattleman turned congressman Maverick Brander, brought Charles Hoyt's comically satirical take on Washington politics, *A Texas Steer,* to the opera house in 1895. Another popular star, Scottish leading man Robert Mantell adopted a "thundering" style—not always popular with critics but endearing him for many seasons to road audiences. He appeared at the opera house several times through the 1890s in the romantic drama, *Monbars.* The *Gazette* applauded the intensity and "virile force" of his stage presence.[25]

Lillian Russell, the capricious yet beautiful star of at least two dozen American musicals during the 1880s and 1890s, had developed a reputation among peers as self-serving and unpredictable because of her tendency to renege on contracts and to desert both husbands and shows. Despite her reputation, she made herself popular during Fort Worth appearances by furnishing coffee and sandwiches for backstage crews who labored through whatever weather conditions might occur, unloading and setting up heavy sets and equipment. She avoided displays of temperament and, following a run, routinely tipped each crewmember $10.[26]

Less obliging was Nat Goodwin, a man admired for his comedic genius but equally notorious for his erratic behavior and excesses. The feckless Goodwin arrived for back-to-back one-night stands of *The Nominee* in Dallas and Fort Worth during January 1895, already "in his cups" after a several-days' drinking and gambling binge that began in Cincinnati and progressed across country to Dallas' Oriental poolrooms. Despite his inebriated condition, Goodwin completed the Dallas performance but only after keeping the audience waiting for an hour. Next morning, following a confrontation with leading lady Ethel Winthrop, he fired her, throwing the company into disarray and leaving them uncertain whether the tour could continue. Remaining cast members departed for Fort Worth without him, while Goodwin resumed his private reconnaissance of the Dallas tenderloin. Only a chance

encounter with actor Robert Mantell, just concluding his own Fort Worth engagement, finally ended the spree.[27]

Mantell first persuaded Goodwin to rejoin his company, then personally escorted him to the Dallas depot; by an unfortunate coincidence, the train left later than usual, delaying the Fort Worth production until well past nine o'clock. Waiting at the opera house was Goodwin's already stressed ensemble and an increasingly disgruntled crowd described as "the best class of theater-goers." Goodwin sobered up sufficiently to flounder through a shortened performance, covering his unsteady condition with such finesse that the reviewer, his remarks colored, perhaps, by more than a little double entendre, commented, "it is not difficult to see how [Goodwin] has earned such metropolitan fame as a comedian." Afterwards, the actor beat a hasty retreat on the late train to Houston, hoping perhaps to avoid a lynch party.[28]

British actor Richard Mansfield was remembered as much for outspoken arrogance as for any histrionic skill he possessed. A bantam-sized man with a receding hairline and Napoleonic tendencies, his fits of self-importance became nearly legendary. Arriving in Fort Worth late on a stormy evening for a scheduled performance of

Popular with Fort Worth audiences during the 1890s were, l to r, actors Minnie Maddern, Lillian Russell, and Nat Goodwin.

Maddern, Goodwin, courtesy William E. Hill Collection, Dallas Public Library
Russell, Author's collection

RICHARD MANSFIELD 5266

Richard Mansfield's temperamental outbursts sometimes angered theater managers, but roles such as Cyrano de Bergerac and Dr. Jekyll and Mr. Hyde endeared him to audiences.

Author's collection

Cyrano de Bergerac, Mansfield at first refused even to disembark from his private rail-road car, despite an opera house already packed from dress circle to upper gallery. Anticipating trouble, Phil Greenwall ordered waiting stage crews to throw open the freight cars and haul the company's scenery and properties to the theater, expecting Mansfield to back down quickly. When the actor, instead, exploded into threats of lawsuits, Greenwall, a barrel-chested man standing well over six feet tall, stood his ground, promising countersuits for breach of contract.[29]

Confronted with this open show of force, Mansfield stalked off the train, getting as far as the opera house before balking again, raving backstage that he would never appear. Years later, the incident remained vivid for stage electrician Barry Burke, who recalled what happened next for *Fort Worth Press* columnist Jack Gordon:

Finally Phil Greenwall lost his temper: "You go on now or I'll knock the hell out of you!" Mansfield went. After the performance, Greenwall told Mansfield, "You can never play in a house of mine again." Mansfield perceived that Greenwall's physique was not to be reckoned with.[30]

With the purchase of the opera house by the Greenwalls assuring Fort Worth interests a continued place in the steadily expanding network of southern, southwestern, and western theatrical circuits, stars who formerly had avoided Texas were increasingly compelled to include Greenwall Circuit theaters on any important tour. Stuart Robson's 1892 appearance in *The Bachelors* and *She Stoops to Conquer* was billed as the society event of the season. He returned in 1894 to a standing-room-only reception in one of his most popular vehicles, *The Comedy of Errors.* Famed Polish actress, Helena Modjeska, who made her United States debut in 1877, played to a sold-out Greenwall's in 1893, starring as Portia to Otis Skinner's Shylock in *The Merchant of Venice.* Excelling in both comic and dramatic roles, Skinner had risen to stardom in his own right by 1894, playing the title role in *His Grace de Grammont* at the opera house in November and returning again in 1896 and 1897 in *Villon the Vagabond, The Lady of Lyons,* and *Soldier of Fortune.* Minnie Maddern, after a short retirement from the stage following her marriage to editor Harrison Grey Fiske in 1890, toured Texas and Fort Worth in 1896, playing Nora in Ibsen's somber drama of married life, *A Doll's House.*[31]

A somewhat ironic coup de théâtre for the Greenwall circuit came in February 1892 with the booking of legendary French actress Sarah Bernhardt. Texas stops on the Grand World Tour, as it was billed, included Fort Worth, Dallas, Houston, and Galveston. For Bernhardt's Fort Worth stop, railroad lines offered special excursion rates to accommodate the predicted standing-room-only crowd, and Phil Greenwall limited the number of tickets sold to any one person in an effort to curtail scalping similar to what had occurred during Booth's Texas tours. The *Gazette* went so far as to predict, "the event will doubtless be the most memorable, in an artistic and financial sense, ever known in the annals of the theatrical history of Fort Worth." One week before the engagement the paper reported "the inquiry for seats and the anxiety manifested by people . . . to secure tickets shows the greatest of living tragediennes will be greeted with a crowded house, filled from pit to dome."[32]

The expected throngs failed to materialize. Despite the glowing publicity notices, by February 1st, the day of Bernhardt's Fort Worth appearance, only about six hundred tickets had sold. Significantly, at more than double the usual top price of $1.50, and a full dollar more than Booth's top price, nearly all the remaining unsold seats were those going for $4.00, an indication perhaps that the city's cultural tastes still leaned decidedly more to ten-cent beer and *The Bandit King* than imported wine and French tragedy. At the evening's performance of *La Tosca,* Sardou's tale of betrayal and revenge, locals listened, mystified, as Bernhardt spoke her lines in French in an otherwise all-English production.

She made other changes that may have affected the play's emotional impact. Instead of leaping to her death from a parapet, her customary coup de grâce, inexplicably, Bernhardt chose a less dramatic exit—baring her breast to the soldiers' bullets as the curtain fell, an ending adopted by her chief American rival, Fanny Davenport. While lauding Bernhardt's dramatic skills, the local reviewer complained,

> Fort Worth does not appreciate high art, and even Bernhardt,
> who has been coached and praised by the press until her name is a
> household word, could not present a sufficiently strong presenta-
> tion of the art divine to draw the four shining dollars from the
> average man's pocket.[33]

In 1888, when Henry Greenwall gained control of the New Orleans Grand Opera House, a bitter war of retribution had commenced between ousted longtime manager David Bidwell and Greenwall. The battle that ensued for control of New Orleans' theaters eventually affected bookings for Fort Worth's opera house as well as Greenwall's two-hundred-theater southern and Texas circuits and became part of a chain of events that profoundly changed the entire country's theatrical booking system.

Seeking to reassert his dominance of New Orleans theater, Bidwell purchased H. S. Taylor's New York theatrical booking agency, placing it in the control of Abraham L. Erlanger, Charles B. Jefferson, and Marc Klaw. Ironically for Henry Greenwall, the alliance formed among Bidwell, Erlanger and Klaw by 1895 had germinated the seed of a much larger trust, although Bidwell, who died in 1893, did not live to participate in it. Just as railroad expansion contributed to the demise of traditional east coast resident repertory companies, the forming of a powerful alliance that came to be known as the Theatrical Syndicate signaled the beginning of the end of booking control by regional empresarios such as Greenwall. [34]

After investing nearly thirty years building his southern and Texas circuits, Henry Greenwall refused to give in to Klaw and Erlanger's demands to book only syndicate-sanctioned shows and actors. By the turn of the century, the monopoly controlled enough key theaters on important touring routes that many of the country's most influential actors, producers, and playwrights had capitulated to the trust to save their livelihoods. Greenwall continued to book independently through his own American Theatrical Exchange, but with little new coming to Texas by way of New York, and the empresario's Galveston interests in ruins following the 1900 hurricane, the long-term outlook for the Greenwall circuit and the Fort Worth Opera House remained in doubt

French actress Sarah Bernhardt in *La Tosca*, c. 1887. Despite her "legendary" status, Bernhardt's 1892 Fort Worth appearance failed to sell out.

Courtesy, Sarah Bernhardt Collection, Harry Ransom Humanities Research Center, University of Texas-Austin

at the turn of the century. The Greenwall theatrical fortunes lay increasingly in the hands of anonymous road companies performing endless revivals of timeworn melo-dramas and comedies and occasional appearances by the few major stars who remained Greenwall loyalists.[35]

THE PRIDE AND GLORY OF TEXAS AND PYRO-THEATER: THE SPRING PALACE AND *THE LAST DAYS OF POMPEII*

Let's give three cheers for the Texan's bride
Who casts all thought of rank aside—
Who gives up house and fortune, too,
For the honest love of a Texan true.

Edward J. Smith

With that eccentric judgment often applied by human nature to significant catastrophes, the Texas Spring Palace in later years became less a symbol of Texas greatness, as its builders intended, and more a cautionary drama, far more harrowing in its final denouement than any of the artless cliffhangers presented on the opera-house stages of the late nineteenth century. Years later, recalling the palace's fiery destruction and his own close encounter with death, one survivor observed simply, "We burned the candle of life at both ends."[1]

The palace, a Turkish confection of fanciful turrets, towers and onion domes—"Aladdin's wonderful palace," as official advertising characterized it—was laid out on the model of a Saint Andrews cross in four transecting wings that stretched by its second season 375 feet east and west and 225 feet north and south. The building and its contents were fashioned entirely from natural and native Texas products. Sixteen carloads of wheat, seven cars of millet, ten acres of corn stalks, eight acres of Johnson grass and alfalfa, two cars of cane, four cars of cactus, four cars each of mosses and coal, a car of seashells, and a car of pelts and hides all went into its construction. Holding all of it together required nearly two tons of tacks and nails and over half a ton of wire.[2]

Modeled after a trend in fairs and expositions that remained in vogue through much of the 1880s and 1890s, the Spring Palace emulated other temples of nature—ice palaces had been constructed in Toronto, while St. Paul and Sioux City, Iowa, boasted Corn Palaces. Later, Denver constructed a mineral palace. Originally conceived as a permanent exhibit building constructed of stone and iron, the palace was the brainchild of General R. A. Cameron, immigration commissioner for Texas of the Denver, Texas, & Fort Worth Railway. Cameron had made several trips to Iowa's Corn Palace and visualized the Texas shrine as a magnet with which to draw in capitalists and immigrants both for Texas and Fort Worth. Fort Worth, as an increasingly important railroad hub at the strategic northern gateway to the state, seemed the ideal location for such an exposition.[3]

Constructed between March and May of 1889 on the Texas & Pacific Railway reservation south of Front Street (present-day West Lancaster Avenue) between Main Street and Jennings Avenue, the two-story, 60,000-square-foot palace, its perimeter defined and ornamented by twelve three-storied towers of Moorish and Malay design, faced northward toward the county courthouse. Crowning the atrium within its central apex was a great dome and lantern—at 130 feet high and 60 feet in diameter, second only in size to the one atop the nation's capitol in Washington, D.C. Original plans had called for a building relatively spartan in dimensions—a mere 250 by 150 feet— although newspaper editor and Spring Palace president Buckley Paddock later admitted that management during the 1889 inaugural season ran to the "extravagant."[4]

Following completion of the building's superstructure in mid-April, hundreds of volunteer workers, spearheaded by local women's organizations, blanketed the

The Texas Spring Palace, shown in 1889, and promoted as a "grand musical entertainment in a castle of earth's wonders" featured performances of operettas and concerts by the Elgin National Watch Factory Military Band.

Courtesy, Fort Worth Public Library, Local History and Genealogy

framework inside and out with the carloads of assembled organic matter, working it into intricate tracery, geometric patterns, and carefully constructed "karporamata"—murals depicting Texas life and landscapes—all fashioned, like complex mosaics, out of the tons of grains, seeds, grasses, horns, shells, mosses, and hides. Paddock recalled in his memoirs, "There was not an inch of timber, except the floors, but that was covered with some product of Texas, wrought in the most artistic manner into pictures." Dominating the exterior at the palace's main north entrance, beneath the dome and a crescent halo of United States and Texas flags, was the head of a Longhorn steer sprouting like bovine royalty from a Texas Lone Star, all fashioned out of vari-colored corn, cedars, and cane.[5]

Unrelenting downpours hampered completion of the grounds and exterior decorations and threatened to drown out opening festivities. The Spring Palace finally opened with great pomp on May 29, 1889. In a break between showers around eleven o'clock a two-mile-long procession of tradesmen, local, and out-of-state dignitaries, ladies' clubs, veterans' organizations, bands, floats, and 750 schoolboys, all dressed in identical white jackets, tramped stolidly along muddy Houston and Main streets, past the ceremonial reviewing stand, to the gates of the palace. Inside, under the grand rotunda, what remained of the crowd heard laudatory speeches delivered by Buckley Paddock, Texas governor Sul Ross, and John M. Thayer, governor of Nebraska.[6]

Planners balked at labeling the exposition a state fair, instead tagging it a "grand musical entertainment in a castle of earth's wonders." Throughout its two seasons, a total of only seven weeks, the Spring Palace became a cultural mecca for the city and the entire region—site of operettas, recitals, and recitations performed by local talent, three daily band concerts, nightly dances, and occasional dress cotillions. At least one bride and groom tied the knot amidst its splendors. To provide an almost continuous musical backdrop, the Spring Palace orchestra was formed from a select group of Texas musicians under the direction of Professor Ault Reed. Other bands from different regions of the country were also engaged, including the most prominent, the famed Elgin National Watch Factory Military Band of Elgin, Illinois. The Mexican National Band, on tour through the south, also performed.[7]

The Elgin Band achieved national fame between 1887 and 1892 under the direction of Joseph Hecker, an Austrian conductor and composer hired by factory officials to reshape a local military-style band into an organization that could be used in watch factory promotions. Band members, brought in by Hecker from all parts of the country, supplied their own instruments and worked ten-hour days in the watch factory, playing concerts at night. On tour, band members continued to receive their full factory wages with the Elgin Company furnishing dress uniforms and music. The band's repertoire, running from popular airs to classical and sacred pieces, was so extensive that Hecker, from the beginning of his Elgin tenure, employed a full-time copyist. Expanding the group's range with his own compositions, he boasted the organization could play through much of a season before repeating a selection.[8]

The unlikely pairing of English comic opera moguls William S. Gilbert and Arthur Sullivan during the 1870s and 1880s resulted in an unprecedented string of popular hits, introduced America to a new style of satirical musical, and inspired countless stagings by professional and amateur companies. Not surprisingly, as committees planned entertainment venues for the initial season of the Texas Spring Palace in the winter of 1889, a Gilbert and Sullivan adaptation became another of the featured entertainments.[9]

Fort Worth's earliest recorded presentation of a Gilbert and Sullivan operetta was a performance in 1881 of *H. M. S. Pinafore* by the Fay Templeton Star Alliance. In October 1883, the new Fort Worth Opera House celebrated its grand opening with a four-night roster of Gilbert and Sullivan musicals, including *Patience, The Sorcerer, Iolanthe* and *H. M. S. Pinafore*, all performed by the Chicago Ideals Opera Company. *H. M. S. Pinafore, The Pirates of Penzance*, and a later bit of Gilbert and Sullivan fluff, *The Mikado*, appeared several times between 1881 and 1889, both at Evans Hall and the Opera House. While few actual records survive, an organization of local singers more than likely took on the task of preparing the Gilbert and Sullivan production for the Spring Palace. Active in the leadership of the group was William Fife Sommerville, a transplanted Scotsman who was appointed director-general of the Texas Spring Palace in 1889 and again in 1890.[10]

In the spring of 1886, local Gilbert and Sullivan enthusiasts under the direction of Sommerville, had staged an ambitious amateur production of *Patience*, with the lead roles going to Edward J. Smith and Fannie Bridges. Although the group limited musical accompaniment to a single pianist, they rented costumes from Chicago and hired two New York theatrical firms to provide incidental scenery and effects. The success of *Patience* evidently sparked the formation of the Fort Worth Musical Union, an organization of local singers and G & S enthusiasts, which in 1888 mounted an even more ambitious production of *The Pirates of Penzance*, directed by Sommerville. Dallas music teacher and conductor Hans Kreissig, who would found the Dallas Symphony Orchestra in 1900, drilled chorus members.[11]

Sommerville had come to Texas as assistant manager of the Matador Land and Cattle Company, a Texas investment syndicate formed in 1878 and later purchased by a consortium of Scottish venture capitalists in 1882. By 1885, handling company operations from an office in Fort Worth, he had been promoted to manager. In 1890, he was named a director of the newly formed Wichita Valley Railway Company, which supported the Matador interests. For *The Pirates of Penzance,* Sommerville assumed dual roles—serving both as director and leading man. Fresh lyrics poking fun at Fort Worth-Dallas rivalries and local civic leaders were interpolated into some of the tunes. Edward J. Smith, a young local businessman who starred in the 1886 production of *Patience,* may have contributed the lyrics. In 1889 Smith apparently agreed to create a full-length adaptation of a Gilbert and Sullivan musical for the Spring Palace.[12]

The Gilbert and Sullivan formula—topical, satirical tunes woven through absurd scenarios peopled with broadly drawn English character types, shamelessly skewered Victorian class and social mores and eventually became the inspiration for two Texas-themed musicals, both written by Smith for the Spring Palace exposition. The two-act operettas followed the G & S formula and story lines closely, retaining the familiar music, but replacing lyrics and British motifs with Texas characters, situations, and settings. Beyond extant librettos, and a smattering of eyewitness accounts, almost no records of the actual performances remain, although it seems likely that several of the performers from the previous year's production of *The Pirates of Penzance* took part. Little is known about Smith either, beyond what can be learned from city directories of the time. He had managed both the Western Union, and Gulf, Colorado, & Santa Fe telegraph offices over several years and served as editor and publisher of at least two publications, *Texas Rail and Wire* and a weekly newspaper focusing on society events, the *Sunday Mirror.* Old-timers recalled that Smith moved to Washington, D.C. during the 1890s to work as a *Gazette* correspondent.[13]

For the 1889 exposition, Smith wrote an ambitious parody of *The Mikado* that poked fun at stuffy eastern attitudes while glorifying free-thinking Texans. Titled *The Capitalist* and set in Fort Worth, the musical revolved around the efforts of Yankee-Doo, a cowboy, to persuade By-Gum, unhappily betrothed to her guardian the Lord High Excursionist, to marry him instead. By-Gum resists until Yankee-Doo reveals that he is actually the son of the famous Capitalist, exiled after his father tried to force him into an arranged marriage with Kitty Shea, an elderly spinster who expects Yankee-Doo to forsake the unspoiled beauties of Texas and return with her to the more settled east. Matters are resolved when the Lord High Excursionist, disgraced after attempting to banish Yankee-Doo to Dallas, learns that Kitty Shea is wealthy and is persuaded to marry her instead. The Capitalist, newly reconciled with his son, presents Yankee-Doo and By-Gum with a fine corner lot in boomtown Fort Worth, and all, including Kitty Shea, live happily ever after in Texas.[14]

As much unabashed propaganda as entertainment, the musical's story line blended state and local efforts to attract settlers, with hints that in Fort Worth class distinctions mattered little compared to initiative and hard work, allowing a man to achieve any goal—romantic or otherwise. When Yankee-Doo returns from selling his cattle herd, intent on courting By-Gum and settling down, he tells a gathering of businessmen:

> My cattle all are sold;
> And now no longer ranging
> For town lots I'd be changing
> These saddle-bags of gold.

They sing in reply,

> We now proclaim we've lots of room,
> And ask the whole world here to come.
> Of acres, we've two million score
> For those who knock at our front door,
> And fifteen million people more
> Won't make us overcrowded.[15]

In Smith's version, even the three sisters, By-Gum, Peek-a-Boo and Pretty-Thing, harmonizing on the celebrated G & S chorus, "three little maids from school," confess they "had made their pile/ by putting their money in Texas sile" but guilelessly offer to share their good fortune with new settlers:

> Three little maids of wealth and station,
> Come for to get some legislation;
> All for the cause of immigration,
> Three little maids from school.[16]

During its first season the Spring Palace lost $23,000, although enthusiasm for the project continued to run so high that Buckley Paddock later claimed it took directors less than one hour to raise the money needed to pay off creditors. Paid admissions for the four weeks of the exhibition totaled over 100,000, with several hundred making the trek from as far away as New England. The *New York Times* reported every state in the Union and most of the territories well represented. Still flush with the success of his creation, the palace's chief decorator, E. D. Allen, succumbed to a fit of hyperbole, proclaiming it "the most magnificent structure the eye of man has ever beheld." Many evidently agreed with him—directors laid plans almost immediately for a second season and by January 1890 declared themselves debt-free and fully subscribed. During the winter, construction crews began extending the east-west wings of the palace an additional 125 feet and the north-south corridor, seventy-five feet.[17]

For the palace's second season, directors once again engaged the Elgin Band, while Edward Smith produced a second Gilbert and Sullivan parody, drawing his new Texas tale, *Fort Worth,* from *H. M. S. Pinafore,* the seafaring fable of Captain Corcoran, in love with Little Buttercup, and his headstrong daughter, Josephine, who spurns the affections of an admiral for the love of Ralph Rackstraw, a common sailor. In land-locked Fort Worth, Captain Bigbug, foremost citizen of the town, admires the tamale vendor, Little Chilitop, "the rosiest, roundest, and reddest beauty in the huckster business," but can never marry her because of the social barriers blocking their path to connubial bliss. Despite his own romantic yearnings, Bigbug illogically expects his daughter, Josephine, to marry Colonel Longhorn, King of the Cowboys, with matters complicated by Josephine's secret love for Alf Ryestraw, an ordinary Fort Worth policeman. Outwardly, Josephine expresses little but contempt for Alf's declarations of affection and lowly rank, telling him, "This unwarrantable presumption on the part of a common policeman—you forget the disparity of our positions." She quickly weakens, however, after Alf declares, "Josephine, I am a Texan and I love you!"[18]

The couple's plans to elope are foiled by Dick Badegg, a cowboy who scorns civilized conventions and admits to being "one of the wild and wooly sort." He exposes the lovers' plans to Captain Bigbug, who, in a fit of pique, blurts, "Why dam' me it's too tough!" The Captain's ill-advised slip into common vulgarity provides Colonel Longhorn with the opening he needs to force the now twice-disgraced Josephine into marriage. Matters seem desperate as he orders Alf hauled off to prison, but at that moment Little Chilitop steps forward to reveal that many years before, while employed as a dairymaid, she had mistakenly switched two cows—one a steer and one a heifer— belonging to Captain Bigbug and Alf. The heifer and all her subsequent progeny—the source of the Captain's entire fortune—actually belonged to Alf, while only the steer, deprived of its manhood, belonged to Bigbug. Stung by the revelation that the girl he has pursued is, in fact, the daughter of a penniless impostor, Colonel Longhorn renounces his affection for Josephine. He orders Alf, now Fort Worth's richest citizen, released immediately. Alf, newly elevated, is free to marry Josephine, while Bigbug, happily reduced in rank to humble cop and released from his social fetters, can wed Little Chilitop. All, once again, live happily ever after in Texas.[19]

Smith's play, with its full roster of western stereotypes and egalitarian themes, proclaimed with tongue in cheek that in Texas only livestock sported pedigrees. Enterprise and strength of character, on the other hand, separated the men from the mavericks, although a stack of $20 gold pieces and a few improbable twists of fortune never hurt either. Only Colonel Longhorn and Dick Badegg, emblematic of two fading standards—the old class-bound eastern order and the lawless frontier—seemed out of place among the new order of forward-thinking, empire-building Texans. The Colonel at one point proposes that Alf become enlightened to his own jackstraw status by rehearsing a special tune the Colonel has penned. Longhorn explains, "It is a song I have composed for Texans to encourage independence of action and proper thought, and to show them they are all men's equals—excepting mine." Badegg, straight from Hell's Half Acre with his surly disregard for the rules of civility, remains equally out of step, while still acknowledging that his is a dying breed of rascal. He complains at one point, "You all hate my kind don't you? Texas ain't what it used to was [*sic*]."[20]

Only the broad-minded citizens of Fort Worth seem in step with the times as they celebrate the nuptials of Alf and Josephine:

> Let's give three cheers for the Texan's bride
> Who casts all thought of rank aside—
> Who gives up house and fortune, too,
> For the honest love of a Texan true. [21]

On May 10, 1890, the second season of the Spring Palace kicked off with speeches and fanfare before an opening day crowd of four thousand. With better weather than the 1889 season, attendance for the three-week run exceeded expectations, and while directors stopped short of announcing a profit, they were able to pay off all expenses on time. Optimism pervaded the city and a third season in 1891 seemed assured. On May 30, one night before closing ceremonies, a grand finale concert by the Elgin Band and a fancy dress ball had been scheduled. At nightfall, an estimated three to four thousand spectators had already entered the palace or roamed its landscaped grounds and by 10:20, continued arrivals had swelled that number to seven thousand. [22]

Sometime around ten-thirty, a fire whose origin would later be disputed turned the palace into a roaring inferno, burning it to the ground in less than thirty minutes. Because of the quick thinking of such men as Spring Palace president Buckley Paddock, Judge L. N. Cooper, and English civil engineer Al Hayne, the crowd evacuated the structure with little panic. Forty or so people suffered injuries ranging from burns to broken bones, but all eventually recovered. In an ironic twist, Hayne, who had refused to leave the building until assured that everyone else was safely out, became the disaster's one fatality. He died of burns several hours later.[23]

Though firemen and volunteers spent several more days combing through still-smoking piles of debris, no other human remains were ever found, leaving officials to tally the cost of the disaster chiefly in material terms. Weighed against the remarkable escape of so many, the calculating of dollar amounts seemed insignificant by comparison—estimates ran to well over $100,000, with only $15,000 covered by insurance, but few voices complained publicly.[24]

In light of the emotional and physical toll of the disaster, it was somewhat surprising that within a week various influential voices began calling for the rebuilding of the palace as early as 1891. Just days after Hayne's funeral, while many injured were still recovering, a *Gazette* editorial proclaimed its support of such a plan, reminding readers that the palace had "furnished the entire nation with a charming, captivating picture of the state." Sensing perhaps that his remarks might be met with considerable skepticism, the editorialist noted wryly that unless the structure was rebuilt of fireproof materials, "people could only be got to look at it through a telescope."[25]

Though the Spring Palace would never be rebuilt, by late summer 1890 the Chamber of Commerce began to search for a new attraction which could fully utilize the site on the Texas & Pacific reservation, no doubt influenced by a desire to recoup some of the city's financial losses. In a somewhat ironic move, a committee of fifteen influential citizens that included John Peter Smith, A. T. Byers, and T. J. Hurley announced plans to engage the English pyrotechnics firm of James Pain & Sons to stage a dramatization of Edward Bulwer Lytton's *The Last Days of Pompeii*, culminating with the eruption of Mount Vesuvius on the former grounds of the palace. An outdoor extravaganza, billed as a semi-scenic, semi-pyrotechnic exhibition, played almost entirely in pantomime and dance by a cast of more than three hundred, this "scenic" theater was modeled after re-creations of historical disasters which had enjoyed enormous popularity in Great Britain and Europe.[26]

Pain's, an organization that traced its origins to the manufacture of gunpowder in the sixteenth and seventeenth centuries, under the leadership of William Pain and his son James, had moved into the art of pyrotechnics by the 1850s. Over the next forty years, the company added steadily to a reputation built around the scope and artistry of its fireworks displays. In the United States, the firm achieved such success with its pyrotechnic spectacles that James Pain constructed a separate New York factory to supply his American shows and placed its operation under the direction of his son, Henry. First conceived in 1879 for New York's exclusive Manhattan Beach resort, *The Last Days of Pompeii* had, by 1890, been presented in a number of U.S. cities, including New York, Atlantic City, Chicago, New Orleans, and St. Louis.[27]

Despite Pain's solid reputation, some Fort Worth merchants seemed reluctant to back the venture financially, having been literally "burned" once already that year. Their hesitation was perhaps understandable in light of Pain's requirement that cities furnish a start-up investment of $15,000 in the form of fifteen hundred pre-sold "season" box-seat tickets before the firm would begin the necessary construction. By late September, with the Texas State Fair set to begin in Dallas, and with only $7,000 of the required capital raised, members of the chamber committee dug into their own pockets so the money-making scheme could move forward.[28]

By October 2, crews scurrying over the five-acre site once occupied by the Spring Palace had set timbers for a ten-thousand-seat grandstand and begun excavating a miniature Bay of Naples, 275 feet long and seventy-five feet wide, which needed to hold an estimated three million gallons of water. An immense stage stretching the length of the artificial pond gradually took shape along the beachhead opposite the grandstand, backed by the heavy iron and wooden framework needed to support nearly ten thousand square yards of painted canvas backdrop. Fronted along its length by standing set pieces depicting temples, docks, and public buildings, the diorama resurrected the doomed Roman city of Pompeii, resting on the shore of the Mediterranean, with Mount Vesuvius looming ominously in two-dimensional semi-realism in the distance. One reporter called the illusion "so complete [it is] almost impossible to discern where the artificial clouds cease and the natural ones begin."[29]

In advance of the fifteen-day run, originally scheduled to open October 16, agents papered key cities and towns in the state with bills and posters that screamed "Fire, Fire, Fire! Fort Worth In A Blaze of Glory! The Greatest Success Ever Made In Texas—Pain's Gorgeous and Marvelous Spectacle, The LAST DAYS OF POMPEII, THE ERUPTION OF VESUVIUS!" Ads appearing in newspapers pictured charioteers racing at full speed, gladiators locked in mortal combat, and incongruously, dancing girls pirouetting in what appeared to be toe shoes and tutus. Led by local musician Klein Ault, a twenty-piece military band, including leading soloists from across the state,

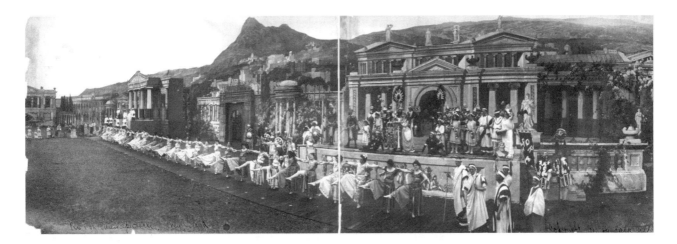

began rehearsing for the event as railroads worked to set up special excursion rates and local hoteliers braced for what they hoped would be another Spring Palace windfall in business.[30]

After delays in completing the artificial bay and amphitheater pushed the original starting date forward two days, *The Last Days of Pompeii* finally opened October 18 before a crowd estimated at between six and seven thousand people, most of whom had paid admissions between fifty and seventy-five cents to witness the event. Acted in pantomime to musical and choral accompaniment, the drama presented in idealized splendor the final hours of Pompeii's existence.[31]

In the opening scene, the audience watched as brightly costumed Pompeiians, oblivious to impending disaster, thronged the marketplace under the aura cast by banks of rainbow-hued lights, giving the scene, what one reporter described as "an atmosphere more ethereal than those which mortals inhabit." The doors to the Temple of Isis were thrown back dramatically to introduce the Egyptian villain of the piece, Arbaces, whose designs on the beautiful heroine, Ione, included disposing of her Christian lover, Glaucus, a wealthy young Athenian. Accompanied by a retinue of city officials and white-robed, pagan priests, Arbaces made his way to the harbor, where Glaucus and Ione made their appropriately heroic entrances, sailing across the miniature bay in a grand procession of galleys and flower-decked barges.[32]

With assorted love triangles, Christians battling the pagan forces of evil, and sudden volcanic doom, the plot had little to do with history, but guaranteed box-office appeal. As the spectacle built toward its pyro-theatrical finale, bevies of harem-costumed Egyptian dancing girls whirled about the stage, gladiators clashed, and circus acrobats tumbled, walked ladders and balanced on tightropes. All the while, Pain's pyrotechnicians tantalized the increasingly edgy grandstand with momentary flashes and distant rumblings from deep inside Vesuvius' painted crater.

The Last Days of Pompeii. The combination outdoor melodrama/pyrotechnic spectacular, presented just months after the destruction of the Spring Palace, attracted nearly 100,000 spectators.

Courtesy, Library of Congress

With each rumble, matters onstage grew correspondingly more tense—after a witch dramatically pronounced a curse on the city, Arbaces denounced Glaucus as a Christian to the authorities, then attempted to seduce Ione.[33]

The drama finally reached its incendiary finale as Arbaces, seeking to dispose of his rival permanently, demanded that all worship at the shrine of the goddess Isis or suffer death. As Glaucus defiantly raised a cross to strike the image of the goddess, Vesuvius suddenly roared to life, raining down symbolic retribution on Pompeii in a carefully orchestrated exhibition of pyrotechnics. Pompeiians scattered in terror, lava cascaded realistically down the sides of the crater, and buildings collapsed artfully into piles of rubble. In the best tradition of theatrical scoundrels, Arbaces met his end crushed beneath a toppling column, allowing Glaucus and Ione to make good their escape by ship across the bay.

Before grandmothers had finished reeling in their seats from Pompeii's calamitous end, a roar from a cannon and a starburst shooting high into the dark sky announced the second phase of Pain's extravaganza—an hour-long fireworks spectacular. Fired from steel mortars, colored rockets exploded against a backdrop of even larger "monster shells," releasing hundreds of brilliants and fire gems high in midair. Flaming gold and silver geysers erupted from the surface of the lake, flying fish and dolphins leapt out of the water, and fiery birds darted back and forth across the surface. The night's festivities concluded with a portrait of Texas governor Sul Ross outlined in fire.[34]

Pompeii's destruction, bolstered by changing features added nightly to the pyrotechnic spectacle, helped to attract ever-larger crowds over the next two weeks. Trains jammed to capacity arrived daily from Dallas and points north, south, and west, while hotel proprietors, initially skeptical of the drawing power of a fireworks show, found themselves hard-pressed to meet the demand for housing. The recently refurbished Fort Worth Opera House, operating under new owner Henry Greenwall, played to mostly empty houses, despite offering several popular blood-and-thunder melodramas, sure-fire draws in previous seasons.[35]

A standing-room-only crowd, the largest of the season, turned out on October 30 to witness Pain's re-creation of the Spring Palace and its subsequent fiery destruction four months to the day after the actual event. Meanwhile, the original supporters of the event, including several who had served previously as directors of the palace, found themselves twice-burned for their trouble. A special benefit performance held November 8 to help defray their personal losses proved anticlimactic, drawing only a fair crowd and leaving members of the committee in the hole despite overall attendance figures estimated at 100,000 for fifteen performances.[36]

Though *The Last Days of Pompeii* would return to the city twelve years later in 1902, the saga of the Spring Palace ended with Pain's pyrotechnic commemoration of the event. Several campaigns between 1890 and 1900 to resurrect the palace as a permanent structure failed to generate the necessary funds, although by 1893, private contributions enabled the city to raise a monument commemorating the sacrifice of Al Hayne near the building's original site. Contributing to the difficulty was a nationwide recession, which by 1890 was already beginning to have an effect, although it did not peak until the financial panic of 1893. Investors remained edgy through much of the 1890s, and by then, the rage for the natural "palaces" had begun to wane. In the absence of the Spring Palace, no other entertainment enterprise managed to focus comparable national attention on Fort Worth until nearly fifty years later during the Texas Centennial, when newspaper publisher Amon Giles Carter partnered with Broadway producer Billy Rose to mount the Frontier Centennial and its own blockbuster centerpiece attraction, Casa Mañana.[37]

THEATER WARS:
1900-1910

"[The performance] was positively ludicrous.
Perhaps that explains the applause."
~*Fort Worth Record*, 1906

In the absence of better fare before the official commencement of any given fall "season," managers of smaller playhouses often fell back on those careless perpetuators of Negro "inferiority," blackface minstrel shows or recycled melodramas offered "at popular prices" by low-budget stock companies. The practice served a dual purpose: pulling in the less-sophisticated, low-end ticket crowd during September, usually a "dead" month on the legitimate circuits, and priming audiences for the major touring combinations and stars, who seldom hit the rails before October. For September 1900, in keeping with the practice, Greenwall's Opera House scheduled two weeks of stock offerings, A. G. Allen's New Orleans Minstrels, and a revival of a popular comedy, *McFadden's Row of Flats*.[1]

The explosion that sank the U.S.S. *Maine* in Havana Harbor sparked the short-lived Spanish-American War, beginning and ending in 1898, and inspired a flurry of flag-waving melodramas, most so patently egregious they quickly disappeared. One, *The Red, White, and Blue,* lasted long enough to make the circuit of Greenwall's Texas houses in the repertoire of the Aubrey Stock Company. To reinforce the slender story line, the stock company fell back on the usual arsenal of technical effects, including a battery-powered wooden cannon set to discharge at a pivotal moment during a battle scene.[2]

Just before the final curtain rang down, as action onstage concluded, the cannon suddenly blew up without warning. The explosion, heard several blocks away, perceptibly jarred the opera house and hurtled jagged fragments of the gun in all directions, ripping through scenery and leaving several bystanders with minor injuries. One four-foot-long, ten-pound chunk of the heavy firing piece catapulted with deadly force into the gallery, striking an audience member squarely in the face. Audience members carried the injured man, unconscious and bleeding, to nearby St. Joseph's infirmary, where he died hours later.[3]

The death of an audience member became just one of numerous dilemmas threatening the continued operation of Fort Worth's opera house as the city entered the twentieth century. By 1900, so many companies and stars had gone over to the Theatrical Syndicate as a matter of self-protection that owners and managers of so-called open door theaters like Greenwall's found it virtually impossible to book a full season of high-quality offerings. In October 1910, a regional scout for the theatrical trade paper *Variety* noted the impact on Fort Worth's theater scene, jotting in his weekly report, "The scarcity of legitimate attractions at Greenwall's . . . is helping vaudeville houses wonderfully." [4]

Greenwall seasons, consequently, remained generally lackluster through much of the century's first decade despite the occasional billings of major shows or stars. Seasons tended to be filled with stock companies or second-rate combinations reprising old standards or presenting inferior new plays. When no replacement for a syndicate attraction could be obtained, the theater was sometimes obliged to go dark for a week at a time.

Citing editorial comments in the *Houston Post,* the *Fort Worth Record* in 1906 euphemistically characterized 85 percent of the offerings at Greenwall's as "Jim-Crow performances." One common ploy of the syndicate required independent managers to pay exorbitant percentages to obtain trust-sanctioned productions. When the play finally arrived in a city, minus the advertised "original New York cast," theatergoers were subjected instead to what the *Record* termed "a lot of cheap actors who make the play ridiculous." One local production falling into this category was the January 1905 staging of *In Louisiana.* Reacting to what he termed "as wretched a piece of dramatization and histrionics as has come this way in a long time" the reviewer concluded,

> People are hungry for amusements. . . . Otherwise such attrac-
> tions would not long remain on the road. It was presented to an
> audience much larger than it deserved, and the people were so good
> natured that they actually applauded. [The performance] was posi-
> tively ludicrous. Perhaps that explains the applause.[5]

Editorials across the state railed against the excesses of the syndicate. When New York City's district attorney initiated anti-trust proceedings against the organization in 1905, the *Fort Worth Record* declared the trust a "theatrical octopus." Calling its leaders "as high-handed and contemptible a lot of scoundrels as ever preyed upon the public," the paper leveled accusations of criminal conduct against Klaw and Erlanger. The *Houston Post* joined the outcry saying,

> The Post is not fully informed as to just what control the New York theatrical cut-throats exercise over the theaters of Texas, but it is evidently sufficient to involve not only the rights of artists, but of the people who patronize the theaters. It would seem that the anti-trust statutes of Texas are being violated in a most audacious manner.[6]

Although the New York anti-trust case was eventually thrown out of court, a 1906 U. S. tour by Sarah Bernhardt produced by upstart syndicate rivals, the Shubert brothers, incited a new round of editorial outrage after managers in Texas and other southern states refused to open their theaters to the aging artiste following threats by Klaw and Erlanger to cut off the South entirely from booking future syndicate attractions. Original plans for Bernhardt's tour had called for stops in Fort Worth, Dallas, Tyler, Waco, Austin, Houston, and San Antonio, but pressure from the syndicate led to the cancellation of several dates.[7]

By late March, the Greenwalls bowed to the same pressure. Bernhardt's American tour manager informed the *Dallas Morning News,* "I made an offer to Mr. [Henry] Greenwall to book Mademoiselle Bernhardt through Texas, but he refused it because he was afraid of losing the Syndicate attractions." Surprisingly, few seemed to blame the Greenwalls for their stance. Squaring off instead against the syndicate's leadership, the *Record* observed simply, "The theater managers of Texas are not to blame. They must do as Klaw and Erlanger say, else they will get no shows." [8]

Even with the Bernhardt appearance canceled, lesser stars loyal to the Greenwalls continued to stop in Fort Worth and other cities on the Texas and southern circuits. Helena Modjeska, Fred Warde, Rose Coghlan, Viola Allen, Stuart Robson, Kate Claxton, and Effie Ellsler, Shakespearean actor Louis James, and James O'Neill, still touring as the Count of Monte Cristo, all continued to appear. Richard Mansfield, despite Phil Greenwall's earlier dictum threatening to bar him from Texas, returned to Fort Worth several times prior to his death in 1907.[9]

Dramatic, comedic, and musical bright spots during the period included a critically acclaimed revival of the tragedy *Francesca Da Rimini* (1902) with an all-star cast led by Otis Skinner and Aubrey Boucicault. Anna Held, diminutive wife of Broadway producer Florenz Ziegfeld toured Fort Worth in *The Little Duchess* (1903), and George M. Cohan and family appeared in *Running For Office* (1904). Chauncey Olcott, who introduced the ballad, *When Irish Eyes Are Smiling* to the world, played the opera house in *Terence* (1905). Dustin Farnum brought *The Virginian* to the city for the first time during the 1904–1905 season, and Texas native Maclyn Arbuckle also proved a popular draw in 1906 as Jim Hackler, *The County Chairman.* Tim Murphy reprised his role as Maverick Brander in a Shubert-produced revival of another political satire, *A Texas Steer,* and Olga Nethersole appeared in *Sapho* (1906), her role as a prostitute so controversial that the actress was briefly arrested on indecency charges in New York.[10]

By the turn of the century, musicals had surpassed melodrama in popularity. One of the more popular was a British import, *Florodora,* which reached Fort Worth in 1901 with its show-stopping feature, the six Florodora girls, accompanied by their male partners, singing "Tell Me Pretty Maiden." *The Wizard of Oz* and *Babes In Toyland,* lavish musicals adapted from children's stories, followed in 1904 and 1905. Also arriving in 1905 was George M. Cohan's *Little Johnny Jones,* with its unabashedly patriotic hit number "Yankee Doodle Boy" and a second rouser, "Give My Regards To Broadway." Cohan's *Forty-Five Minutes From Broadway* followed this in 1906. Franz Lehar's tuneful, romantic operetta *The Merry Widow* played in 1908.[11]

Matching the optimism of turn-of-the-century musicals, there was increasing evidence that Fort Worth was moving beyond its former reputation as the "Paris of the plains" and maturing as a city. Between 1890 and 1910, two universities, Polytechnic College and Texas Christian University, were established in the city, bringing with them play productions staged by campus clubs and dramatic societies. Most training in the fine arts still concentrated on music, elocution, and oratory, however, with few degrees being awarded.

Located just east of the city in Polytechnic Heights, the coeducational Polytechnic College was organized in 1890. In 1914, the school limited enrollment to females and became Texas Woman's College. Through the school's Fine Arts division, students could pursue oratorical training that included "modes of histrionic expression," and "dramatic and oratoric delivery," although theater received no direct instruction. TCU's theatrical tradition can be traced to at least the mid-1890s, when the school was located in Thorp Spring, Texas, and still known as Add-Ran Christian University. In 1896, the school moved to Waco, where it remained until 1910, when a fire destroyed much of its campus. Later that same year, with the promise of both land and money to rebuild, the university relocated to Fort Worth. During 1910–1911, the school's first full term in the city, members of the Dramatic Club staged at least two productions, including J. M. Barrie's *Quality Street*.[12]

The city's growth in size and status, though welcomed by city leaders and the general populace, brought unexpected challenges for the city's opera house. During the two decades since its completion in 1883, Greenwall's had faced little more in the way of competition than the tawdry fare of Hell's Half Acre's variety halls. But in 1905, that situation changed suddenly and dramatically with the completion of the Majestic Theater.

From the 1880s, when Tony Pastor opened the first family-style variety hall in New York, vaudeville had steadily increased in popularity, becoming, by the early 1900s, entertainment's leading growth industry. By the time Interstate Amusement Company completed Fort Worth's first major vaudeville hall in November 1905, three hundred high-class vaudeville houses had opened across the country to support an industry with an estimated worth of $26 million. Vaudeville, unlike legitimate theater, was built around a startlingly diverse catalogue of short, individual acts—a random bill, usually changing weekly, of solos, duos, trios, comedians, tap dancers, acrobats, quick-change artists, contortionists, regurgitators, magicians, dancers, dog-and-pony acts, educated chickens, snake charmers, and lion tamers.[13]

A production of *Quality Street*, staged by the TCU Dramatic Club during the university's first term after moving from Waco to Fort Worth in 1910.

Courtesy, Fort Worth Public Library, Local History and Genealogy

As a separate entertainment form with entire theaters dedicated to it, vaudeville had a relatively short American run—only about fifty years. Its heyday lasted from the 1880s to around 1930, spurred early on by theater owners promoting family-style variety halls. Trying to distance themselves from the sleazy image of dime-a-dance beer halls and honky-tonks, they began incorporating a French term, *vaudeville,* into a sanitized imitation of the male-only variety hall format. The label proved deceptive, however. By 1900, variety halls across the country, including several in Fort Worth's Hell's Half Acre, had begun appropriating the term, leading to new distinctions classifying family-safe bills as "high-class" or "refined."[14]

While Fort Worth remained without a "high-class" vaudeville theater until 1905, vaudeville's steady rise in popularity did not pass unnoticed. Both Greenwall's Opera House, and after 1908, the Byers Opera House, regularly booked attractions showcasing vaudeville acts. Yale's *Devil's Auction,* an "extravaganza" featuring specialty and animal acts, appeared at the opera house at least fourteen times between 1886 and 1908. Nor were the Greenwalls the only local entrepreneurs attempting to capitalize on vaudeville's ballooning popularity. In May 1902, J. Z. Wheat opened the Wheat Roof Garden atop his building at the corner of Main and Eighth. Under a steel-framed portable roof, the summer theater nightly served up food and drink, band concerts, stock companies in popular comedies and operettas, and "high-class vaudeville" between the acts.[15]

Completion of the Interurban Railway between Fort Worth and Dallas in June 1902 led to the creation of another summer vaudeville outlet, Lake Erie Amusement Park, near the Handley station, between Arlington and Fort Worth. Opened around 1903, the park offered boating, swimming, a skating rink, and an open-air theater featuring "vaudeville, illustrated songs, and moving pictures."[16]

Word spread in the summer of 1905 that Missouri-based Interstate Amusement Company, incorporated earlier that year by a group of concessionaires from the 1904 St. Louis World's Fair, intended to construct a chain of vaudeville theaters through Texas. The news may well have been what prompted Henry and Phillip Greenwall to announce their own plans for a new vaudeville circuit to complement their existing legitimate houses. At the time, much of the South and Southwest remained unserved by any wide-reaching vaudeville circuits, making any such venture a potential prize for the right set of investors. A route sketched by Phil Greenwall in mid-July called for acts to play Dallas, Fort Worth, Houston, Galveston, San Antonio, Waco, and Beaumont, although plans for constructing or acquiring additional theaters remained vague.[17]

The Greenwall scheme seems to have collapsed quickly, upstaged by a deal struck two weeks later between Fort Worth attorney William J. Bailey, and H. F. McGarvie, president of Interstate. Over two decades, Bailey had acquired real estate and cattle while serving as city alderman, school trustee, and state senator. Prominent in brokering the lucrative agreement were Fort Worth's Factory Club, created in June 1905 to lure new business to Fort Worth, and the Board of Trade, led by former mayor

For several summers, the Wheat Building, constructed at Main and Eighth in 1902 by J. Z. Wheat, featured the Wheat Roof Garden, offering vaudeville and operettas.

Courtesy, Fort Worth Public Library, Local History and Genealogy

City parks at the turn of the 20th century offered both stock and vaudeville to summer patrons. The Lake Erie Pavilion opened c. 1903 near Handley.

Courtesy, Fielder Collection, Special Collections, University of Texas-Arlington Libraries

Fort Worth attorney William J. Bailey, builder of the first Majestic

Courtesy, Fort Worth Public Library, Local History and Genealogy

B. B. Paddock. To seal the negotiations, the city put up $5,000 in start-up money. On July 27th, Bailey inked a contract with Interstate, allowing construction of the new theater to begin almost immediately at a lot on Jennings Avenue near Twelfth Street behind St. Ignatius Academy.[18]

As the theater went up, Interstate worked hard at heading off potentially damaging comparisons between the Majestic, the name given the new hall, and variety theaters in nearby Hell's Half Acre. Offering reassurances that the new hall would have nothing in common with the Standard or Holland's, two of the Acre's more notorious houses, H. F. McGarvie told reporters,

> the people of [Fort Worth] will think more of us a year from
> now than they do today. By giving high-class, clean, and attractive
> bills . . . we will be given a patronage in keeping with the merits of
> the attractions booked.

Prices ranged from fifteen cents for the gallery to fifty cents for reserved floor seating.[19]

In a time when most vaudeville acts in the south still appeared in saloons or second-rate halls catering to boisterous roughnecks unconcerned with a bill's "decency," Interstate followed the leads of established eastern vaudeville moguls like Tony Pastor, B. F. Keith, and Edward Albee in promoting an atmosphere of beauty, decorum, and quiet. Besides meticulous attention given to interior design and decoration, publicity surrounding the Majestic's grand opening declared the event formal and "de rigueur," an invitation-only event closed to all but an exclusive subscription crowd, "to induce the best people of the city to see our performances."[20]

While designed by the Chicago architectural firm of Keyser and Mooser and constructed by James and Taylor, local firms completed many of the Majestic's interior details and furnishings, including steam heating throughout. In mid-November, the theater's new manager, Charles Fisher, described as "a well-known theatrical man of New York," arrived to sign on local personnel and oversee final details of the grand opening.[21]

Among the first hired was Phillip Epstein, a refugee of the Acre in an era when larger, better bankrolled variety halls often hired well-trained musicians as directors and arrangers for their small orchestras. A violinist and son of English parents who had immigrated to Kentucky, Epstein worked for a number of years as both musician and music director for the Standard, then the city's second-largest theater. During a two-year period after leaving Frank DeBeque's employ around 1903, he operated his own variety hall, the Crown, selling out shortly before taking on the Majestic post. He continued as musical director of Fort Worth's Majestic, except for one short period, until he resigned around 1916 to head his own orchestra, which soon became a fixture of local society events. He went on to serve as musical director of Little Rock's Majestic and Capitol theaters. At the time of his death he had risen to the rank of orchestral arranger for both composer Victor Herbert and legitimate theater moguls, the Shubert brothers.[22]

As workmen began setting in place two newly arrived carloads of chairs and stage scenery, St. Louis interior designer H. E. Croft superintended craftsmen installing decorative relief work. On the curve of the proscenium's sounding board, artisans completed a $5,000 painting, noted variously as "Flower Pickers" and "Cupid Among the Roses" and set in place plaster figures representing "Mirth" and "Music."[23]

The Acre had little that could measure up to the Majestic's amenities, beyond the Standard's well-publicized private carriage entrance, intended more to protect the identities of socially prominent clients indulging lascivious proclivities than to fend off natural elements. From the lobby's mosaic floors and sparkling clusters of crystal lights to the auditorium's ornate proscenium and walls finished in understated tones of old rose, ivory, and gold, every aspect of the new theater's ornamentation was carefully crafted to suggest propriety and respectability. With a seating capacity between twelve and thirteen hundred, the new playhouse was only slightly less intimate than Greenwall's Opera House.[24]

Musician, composer, and conductor Phillip Epstein served as orchestra leader for Hell's Half Acre's Standard Theater in the early 1890s. In 1905, he became first music director of the Majestic Theater, a venue more suited to his talents.

Fort Worth Star-Telegram,
5 March 1956

Unlike Holland's and the Standard, where the adjoining bar was of greater consequence than stage functionality and dimensions, vaudevillians treading the boards of the new Majestic played a space amply suited to most acts working the circuits—thirty-five feet wide, sixty-five feet deep, and above, a fly loft with a drop of fifty-two feet to the stage floor. By its grand opening the theater had twelve complete sets of scenery already in place, with more on the way.[25]

In the days preceding the theater's grand coming out, the *Record* declared the debut the "great event of [the] social season." On opening night, November 27th, 1905, elegantly attired ladies and their well-heeled escorts stepped from carriages and new-fangled automobiles onto a cushioning square of Brussels carpet, assisted by attentive, Waldorf-style, scarlet-coated footmen. The opening night bill served to illustrate vaudeville's underlying eccentricities as much as its charms—superficial doses of science and culture counterbalanced by ample slices of popular music, low comedy, and even the proverbial dog-and-pony show, Professor C. E. Rice's Pony, Dog, and Monkey Circus featuring Jam Robinson, the equestrian baboon.[26]

Next day, the *Record* exulted, "The Majestic, in the language of the stage 'made good.' Good, snappy, clean-talking bits made the hits." With the seasons of two major theaters now in full swing and shows trading places at a fast clip, over the next several weeks the city took on the aspect of a theatrical boomtown. Caravans of performers made their way from Union Station to packed local hostelries. A lion with ambitions of solo billing added briefly to the general air of excitement by bolting from his cage onto the Majestic stage during an afternoon matinee. Stagehands put an end to the big cat's pretensions of stardom by lowering the curtain and cornering the animal before it could escape into the audience.[27]

Each week's vaudeville bill followed a fairly standard formula, opening with an overture by the house orchestra and a full-stage "dumb," or silent act—acrobats, animals, or living tableaus. Acts requiring a full stage alternated with those needing only a small area. The bit working the second slot would often be a two-act, such as harmonizing sisters, two wisecracking young men, or some other turn requiring little space. Headliners, most often comedians or acts that combined singing and comedy, generally appeared in one of two slots—just preceding intermission and at next-to-close, considered the top spot. The bill usually concluded with a second dumb act, since many patrons had, by then, begun exiting. Motion pictures served as a novelty attraction, although by 1913, as their popularity rose, they were increasingly used as bookends to begin and end the show.[28]

Illustrating the formula was the Majestic program for the week of February 15, 1909. Opening the show, the Frey Trio, modestly billed as the "Handsomest Men in

Two views of the first Majestic Theater, the city's first high-class vaudeville house, constructed in 1905 on Jennings Avenue near Twelfth Street by W. J. Bailey. Lessee Interstate Amusement Company operated the hall.

Jennings view, courtesy, Fort Worth Public Library, Local History and Genealogy
Front view courtesy, Star-Telegram Collection, Special Collections, University of Texas-Arlington Libraries.

Vaudeville," demonstrated Greek and Roman wrestling. They were followed by Mr. and Mrs. Jack McGreevy, the "Funny Old Couple"; John and Mae Burke, in another comedy turn, "How Patsy Won the Maid"; and the singing and dancing A. B. C. D. Girls, "bright sunbeams who win all hearts." Claiming top spot on the bill, several years after their last Fort Worth appearance at the Standard, were The Four Keatons and Buster. Performing a family "knockabout" turn entitled "It Breaks Father's Heart to Be Rough," the act had expanded to include Buster's younger siblings, Jingles and Louise. Rounding out the bill was Fred Zobedie, the "world's greatest gymnast and hand balancer."[29]

Admission prices for standard bills ranged from fifteen to seventy-five cents, but special events were occasionally booked at higher prices. Just two months after its grand opening, the Majestic engaged German prima donna Johanna Gadski for a one-night concert at a top price of $3. In November 1907, Minnie Maddern Fiske and George Arliss appeared in *Leah Kleschna,* an event of some note since Fiske had, for eleven years, refused to tour, rather than appear in syndicate-controlled houses. [30]

The names of most performers appearing at the Majestic before 1910 have long since been forgotten, but a significant few in the early stages of their careers went on to become top headliners of vaudeville, movies, and television. Al Jolson appeared the week of April 13, 1908, in an act billed as "The Coast Defender." Already developing the distinctive style that would later bring him fame, Jolson's billing noted that he "appears in blackface, talks a little, whistles some and sings more." In a business where performers constantly tweaked their acts with new material hoping to "hit," he was back just over a month later, this time billed as "The Georgia Cotton Blossom."[31]

Completion of the Majestic and the simultaneous arrival of Interstate vaudeville were at least partly responsible for a burst of theatrical activity across the city between 1906 and 1910. In late spring each year, as Greenwall's and the Majestic shut down for the summer, entertainment shifted to temporary outdoor theaters. Troupes like the Korak Wonder Company, which set up at the corner of Fifth and Throckmorton in the summer of 1906, offered rotating bills of vaudeville and stock. The Airdome Theater, its walls sheets of canvas twelve feet high, opened at the same corner in July 1907, alternating motion pictures and vaudeville acts. Amuzu Park premiered at the corner of Eleventh and Houston in August 1908 with a large stage and seating for two thousand. Taking its place in 1909 was a similar attraction, the Folly Theater.[32]

Fresh real estate development in still-remote areas of the city also led to construction of two new amusement parks, both featuring permanent open-air theaters. Promoters used vaudeville, stock, and orchestra concerts to lure potential homebuyers and drum up business for new streetcar lines. North of the courthouse and west of the stockyards, Sam Rosen developed Rosen Heights and promoted White City Amusement Park, served by the Fort Worth & Rosen Heights Street Railway Company. Opened in April 1906, the park featured Lake Tugo, a seventy-acre man-made lake, and the White Rose Theater, playing vaudeville and stock from spring through fall. The park also boasted a cafe, figure-eight roller coaster, and miniature railroad. Near the site, Rosen had previously operated another summer theater, the Rosen Heights Pike Theater. [33]

White City, top, built by Sam Rosen, opened on the city's north side in 1906 just weeks before the Lake Como Pavilion, bottom, premiered in Arlington Heights.

White City-Courtesy, Quentin McGown
Lake Como-Courtesy, Fort Worth Public Library, Local History and Genealogy

At the city's western boundary, on the bluffs above the Clear Fork of the Trinity, the Arlington Heights Land Company constructed its own streetcar line and amusements pavilion on Lake Como, a lake created during 1890–1891 by the Chamberlin Investment Company, a consortium of Denver businessmen led by H. B. Chamberlin. Lake Como Park, which debuted just weeks after White City in May 1906, featured many of the same facilities—a dancing pavilion, boathouse, roller coaster, and summer theater with free vaudeville acts and concerts by local bands.[34]

In addition to outdoor attractions, within a year of the Majestic's premiere, smaller permanent vaudeville halls had begun sprouting along Main and Houston streets in narrow storefronts. Most ranked no better than small-time or medium-time in vaudeville's peculiar booking jargon, with tickets selling for as little as five cents. At least some of these halls operated under what show people contemptuously termed a "grind" policy of short bills and three, four, or more shows a day. City directories noted the Lyric Theater at 1010 Houston, the Olio Theater at 311 Main,

Vaudeville theaters proliferated following the Majestic's 1905 premiere. The Lyric Theater, right, seen behind the Flatiron Building (foreground) opened in 1907. At 1104 Main, left, several theaters, including New York Vaudeville, the Phillips, the Imperial, and the Hippodrome (pictured) operated between 1907 and 1930.

Courtesy, Fort Worth Public Library, Local History and Genealogy

and One-Cent Vaudeville at 1104–1106 Main. Panther Vaudeville, at 503 Main, followed in September 1908, claiming to be the first city movie house to offer vaudeville acts on the side. Added to the list between 1908 and 1909 were American Vaudeville at 1108 Main, Joseph Aronoff's Lyceum Theater at 1105 Main, and Colonial Vaudeville at 505 Houston. [35]

The escalating competition among local showmen is perhaps best illustrated by just one address, 1104–1106 Main, where in June 1909, One-Cent Vaudeville became New York Vaudeville, before reopening a month later as the Phillips. By January 1910, the marquee had changed yet again to the Imperial, offering both vaudeville and motion pictures. In 1912, the Imperial was, in turn, replaced by the Hippodrome, which, over several years, offered not only vaudeville but stock productions and movies as well. At least two of these Main Street ventures, the New York and Phillips, belonged to Edward H. Phillips, who eventually converted his houses to motion pictures. After moving the Phillips to 710 Main, he opened a second theater, Phillips' Egypt, just one block over at 711 Houston.[36]

Aside from Phillips' halls, most of these early theaters seem to have failed rather quickly. One other exception was the Lyric, operated by Dr. C. W. Kline's Fort Worth Amusement Company, which survived through at least 1910 after premiering at 1010–1012 Houston on March 18, 1907. Priced to attract working-class customers, the Lyric offered a four-act bill at a top admission price of just twenty cents. Two matinees and two evening performances a day also featured moving pictures and illustrated songs sung by Clarence E. Able.[37]

In August 1909, Kline opened a second theater, the Royal, in a building at Fifth and Throckmorton that had once housed the Christian Tabernacle, booking acts for both theaters through C. E. Hodkins' Lyric Circuit. Just three weeks after opening to promising reviews and sell-out crowds, the new theater closed, unable to compete against more established theaters. It reopened in November as a legitimate house, advertising the Royal Company, "the first stock company ever undertaken in Fort Worth." This enterprise, too, lasted only weeks. The theater remained dark until the following year, when Sullivan and Considine, one of the West Coast's leading vaudeville circuits, briefly took over, renaming it the Empress. [38]

The Empress debuted October 17, 1910, but just over two weeks later, S & C abruptly transferred all bookings to Joseph Aronoff's Princess, a theater opened just one week earlier at 1109–1111 Main by Joseph Aronoff, owner of the Lyceum. Described in one press report as a "tidy, trim little theater," the new hall, like its name, stood a cut above many of its theatrical neighbors, equipped with a fairly spacious forty-two-foot stage and both parquet and balcony seating. With the opening of the Princess, Aronoff apparently followed the lead of other local showmen and converted the Lyceum to motion pictures.[39]

Most city theaters opening between 1905 and 1910 focused on vaudeville or movies, but in June 1907, Greenwall's position as the city's preeminent performance hall was further challenged by a new legitimate theater. The Vendome, operated by Jack Schwarz, debuted just across the street from the opera house at Third and Rusk in what had been the Fort Worth Skating Rink. The new theater offered plays performed by rotating stock companies at prices that substantially undercut the larger hall. This fresh test of Greenwall's longtime domination of the city's entertainment market must surely have caused the Greenwall brothers to consider either modern-izing or abandoning altogether their aging Fort Worth facility, but as matters turned out, fate intervened to make the decision for them.

The second week of February 1908 was decidedly blustery as the wind swung sud-denly to the northwest heralding the approach of a norther. By daybreak Friday, under overcast skies, chilling gusts reaching fifty-five miles per hour steadily pummeled the city. Around one o'clock intermittent snow began to fall. Inside the opera house, the afternoon matinee of *Primrose's Minstrels* proceeded more or less uneventfully, interrupted once by the clatter of objects falling into the rigging backstage and jam-ming the main curtain. Stagehands clearing the jam located the cause—several bricks around a key truss had become dislodged at a point where the theater's east wall and proscenium arch joined.[40]

Within hours, Phil Greenwall called in local architect Marshall R. Sanguinet to survey the damage. Sanguinet's inspection revealed that the east wall of the twenty-five-year-old hall had begun to pull away from supporting rods and trusses under the pounding of the recent storm. Greenwall voiced his own suspicions to a reporter, how-ever, that the aging structure had been deteriorating for some time, necessitating more than usual maintenance over the past year. Sanguinet warned that another storm could further destabilize the wall and recommended abandoning the theater.[41]

Acting quickly on the architect's evaluation of the damage, Greenwall announced plans to close the opera house permanently. The decision proved timely. After more high winds on Monday night pushed the wall four inches out of plumb, workmen roped off the building's exterior and posted signs warning pedestrians. Greenwall, meanwhile, cancelled the week's attractions and began emergency negotiations with Jack Schwarz to move what remained of the season into the Vendome. The two theaters quickly reached agreement to shift the remainder of February's shows and one in March into the smaller house, but because of scheduling conflicts, the rest of the season was cancelled. A concert by celebrated pianist Ignace Paderewski was moved to the Christian Tabernacle at Fifth and Throckmorton. Less than a week later, as stagehands hurriedly transferred scenery and stage equipment to the Vendome in preparation for the next week's shows, laborers began tearing out all salvageable fixtures in preparation for razing the opera house.[42]

With the arrival of Henry Greenwall from New Orleans, planning to replace the old structure began almost immediately. Phil Greenwall reassured theatergoers that Fort Worth would remain a part of the Greenwall Circuit, announcing, "By next season Fort Worth will have a new opera house." He stopped short, however, of

Andrew Thomas Byers, North Fort Worth entrepreneur and builder of the Byers Opera House, which opened at Seventh and Commerce in 1908.

Byers Opera House program, 21 September 1908

guaranteeing the completion of a new hall in time for the opening of the new season. Less than a week after abandoning the Third and Rusk site, Greenwall reported being approached by several capitalists interested in funding the project, although final plans for the new theater had not yet been determined. One group, led by E. D. Farmer, brothers George and W. D. Reynolds, and William Brice, proposed spending a total of $100,000 to acquire property and build the new theater on Houston between Tenth and Eleventh. But by April, a second group, largely funded by A. T. Byers, proposed spending $150,000 to build a far more substantial opera house. On April 19th, Phil Greenwall and Byers, a man who had exerted considerable influence on the city's development since his arrival twenty years earlier, announced final agreement to erect a new theater at the corner of Seventh and Rusk with construction to begin immediately.[43]

While design and construction work on the 1883 Fort Worth Opera House had been carried out by several firms imported from St. Louis, the Greenwall-Byers partnership selected Marshall R. Sanguinet and Carl G. Staats, two influential local architects, to collaborate on the design for the new Byers/Greenwall's Opera House. Over the next thirty years, Sanguinet and Staats designed some of Fort Worth's most distinctive buildings, including the Flatiron, Waggoner, and Medical Arts buildings, First National Bank, the Texas Hotel, Monnig's Wholesale Dry Goods, the Fort Worth Club and the *Fort Worth Star-Telegram* building. On May 1st, the Texas Building Company, another local firm headed by James T. Taylor won the contract for actual construction of the theater. One factor in Taylor's selection was his proven ability to finish projects under budget and on time. His firm had just completed the North Side Coliseum, new home of the stock show, forty-five days under deadline. As an added incentive, Henry Greenwall offered Taylor $75 for every day before October 21st the building was completed.[44]

Leased to the Greenwall brothers for ten years, the first five at $10,000 per season and the last five at $12,000, original estimates on the cost of the building had risen to $105,000. By August 30th, with the structure nearing completion, that figure had risen an additional $30,000. Inflating original estimates were such decorative touches as reseda-tinted leather seats furnished by another local firm, Texas Seating Company, and nineteen hundred interior electric lights intended as much for ornamental effect as illumination. The elaborate main drop, an artfully designed steel fire curtain painted by the Lee Lash Studio of New York, depicted cherubs flitting around a scene from Greek mythology—"Psyche Before the Court of Venus." The painting on the fire curtain alone set the budget back $900. With the value of the 150 by 100-foot

lot factored in at $100,000, total estimates of the property's final worth ran as high as $240,000.[45]

In engineering and interior design the Byers/Greenwall's Opera House, modeled on a smaller scale after Klaw and Erlanger's sumptuous New Amsterdam Theater in New York City, seemed to herald the arrival of a thriving new era of theatrical production for the city. Built to last of fireproof materials and lavishly decorated, ironically anticipating the great movie palaces of the 1920s and 1930s, the new theater could easily accommodate the most elaborate road show of the day. Boasting a seating capacity of sixteen hundred, with 675 on the main floor, 375 in the lower balcony, and bench seating for 550 in the upper gallery, it surpassed the defunct Greenwall's Opera House by four hundred seats.[46]

While upper gallery patrons were herded unceremoniously through the Rusk Street side entrance of the new theater, better-heeled theatergoers holding tickets for reserved seating on the main floor or lower balcony entered the main lobby through

The Byers/Greenwall's Opera House, constructed in 1908 at the corner of Seventh and Commerce after the first Greenwall's Opera House was damaged beyond repair.

Courtesy, Jack White Photograph Collection, Special Collections, University of Texas-Arlington Libraries

two sets of double doors facing Seventh Street. Protected from bad weather by a broad, light-bordered metal canopy, playgoers stepped through into a twenty-foot-square, tile-floored outer vestibule containing ticket booth and manager's office. White marble wainscoting wrapped around the walls. Directly ahead, through two more sets of double doors, lay the spacious foyer, flanked on either side by six-foot-wide staircases to the lower balcony.[47]

From street level in the foyer, two main aisles, cushioned with sound-absorbing green velvet-plush carpet descended sharply toward the orchestra pit and the theater's most strikingly unusual feature, a double-arched, trumpet-shaped proscenium. Framing the grand drape, the inner arch measured thirty-five feet in height and width. The bell of the trumpet flared outward twenty-six feet from the inner arch overhanging orchestra pit and the first six rows of seating. The outer arch served as a second frame for both stage and inner arch in a shadow-box effect. Between the curves of

Stage area and audience chamber of the Byers/Greenwall's Opera House, c. 1917. Elaborate decorative work around boxes and proscenium remained intact although the theater had already been converted to vaudeville and motion pictures. In 1919 the theater became the Palace.

Courtesy, Hoblitzelle Collection, Harry Ransom Humanities Research Center, University of Texas-Austin

these inner and outer archways, two tiers of box seating, four on each side, completed the picture.[48]

The novel design of the proscenium arch, at the time the deepest of any theater in the United States, served both as baffle, funneling sound outward from the stage into the hall, and as the theater's central design element. Along the front wall, separating house from stage, an outer perimeter of frosted glass light bulbs created an additional border for the entire stage and box area. Inside the two upper corners of this border, more frosted lights formed two large Texas stars, each encircled by wreaths of oak leaves worked in ornamental plaster. Below these shimmered yet another necklace of lights following the innermost curve of the arch and outlining the grand drape.[49]

Only five years before completion of the Byers/Greenwall, Chicago's recently opened and supposedly fireproof Iroquois Theater had burned during a standing-room-only performance, killing over six hundred people. Progress reports on the

Byers made frequent allusions to the disaster, emphasizing the new theater's state-of-the-art safety features. Many of the deaths in the Chicago fire occurred after theatergoers were either suffocated or trampled in narrow stairwells leading to locked fire exits, effectively trapping all those still trying to escape. The Byers came equipped with a fire curtain that lowered automatically at the first alarm and specially designed exit doors that could be opened from the inside by simply pushing a bar. Exit doors and iron staircases provided ticket holders in the balcony and gallery with direct access to the street. Large skylights, designed to open automatically in case of fire, were strategically installed above the stage area. [50]

Only five months and two days after announcement of a deal to construct the new theater, Byers/Greenwall's Opera House, as it was officially designated, prepared to open on September 21, 1908, nearly thirty days ahead of schedule. Scheduling of the premiere came so early that one local newspaper expressed dismay that prominent members of Fort Worth society might miss the event, since many "still linger[ed] at summer resorts." Another potential hitch in the timing of the gala was the show chosen for the opening, *The Land of Nod,* a lightweight musical comedy without important "name" stars. Already a fixture on the touring circuits, the play had appeared in the city twice in less than two years. Perhaps not accidentally, just blocks away, the Majestic had also scheduled the launch of its fourth vaudeville season for the same night. To ensure the new theater was well filled from pit to dome on such an auspicious occasion, Phil Greenwall needed a sure draw. He found a solution for his problem from an unexpected source—classical composer Richard Strauss.[51]

Strauss had unwittingly launched a national craze and incited outrage when his opera *Salome* opened in New York in 1907. Inspired by the biblical character whose sensual dance before King Herod earned her the head of John the Baptist as a reward, the drama scandalized audiences at its Metropolitan Opera House premiere with Salome's dance of the seven veils. The opera closed after just one performance, but the publicity surrounding the dance merely intensified, launching new careers for dozens of Salome imitators who knew nothing about opera but recognized an opportunity for instant notoriety when they saw one.[52]

As opening night for the new theater approached, the *Fort Worth Record* spotlighted the *Salome* controversy with a full-page spread, complete with oversize photographs of several scandalously unclothed actresses, their well-rounded assets defined by see-through gauze skirts, flimsy brassieres, and ropes of beads and jewels seductively draping bare midriffs. An accompanying headline announced, "Salome Sweeping the World Like an Epidemic." Following the announcement that Marie

Fanchonetti, an actress of minor repute, would perform the dance of the seven veils in Fort Worth, the *Record* reported "extraordinary interest" in the event.[53]

Even with floor seating going for $5 and balcony seating for $2, ticket sales in the week before the premiere remained brisk. Opening night, the new opera house was well filled, although attendance fell just short of the hoped for sell-out. Declaring the theater a "delight to the eye and a joy to the theatergoer," local newspapers applauded the Byers as the "finest, newest, costliest and best appointed structure of [this] nature in the entire southwest."[54]

Reporters wasted little copy on *The Land of Nod*, focusing instead on the gyrations of Fanchonetti as Salome. While allowing that the actress "probably" wore tights beneath her black net skirt, one classed her dance as "nothing more than the kind you see when you slip into the 'Streets of Cairo' when nobody's looking," possibly a reference to circus sideshows. The *Telegram*'s critic was more direct. Calling the performance "weird, savage, and uncanny . . . with the animal barbarism of the days of early civilization," he concluded, "The girl danced with the head of John the Baptist in its ghastliness upon a platter. Why she danced with the grewsome [sic] thing is not explained."[55]

The Byers' first season seemed to mark a turning point in the Greenwall fortunes. Attendance surged as several notable plays and stars toured the city for the first time. Franz Lehar's operetta *The Merry Widow* proved so popular with U.S. audiences that eager American women snapped up *Merry Widow* hats, dresses, and corsets wherever it played. Two other comic musicals, Victor Herbert's *The Red Mill* and George M. Cohan's *Fifty Miles From Boston* starring tiny Edna Wallace Hopper also made first-run appearances. *The Virginian* returned for an encore appearance starring William S. Hart, an accomplished Shakespearean actor who would become better known for his rugged cowboy roles in silent films, and Russian actress Alla Nazimova brought her interpretation of Nora in Ibsen's *A Doll's House*. *Brewster's Millions*, the hit screwball comedy about a man desperately trying to spend one fortune so he can inherit an even larger one, provided the comedy highlight to the season.[56]

Over the next eighteen months, as the Greenwalls basked in the rejuvenation of local interest that followed the opening of the Byers, Interstate had not stood by idly. The circuit continued to expand its vaudeville operations, until by 1910 it boasted seventeen houses in eight states. The circuit's second president, Karl St. John Hoblitzelle negotiated alliances with such well-established vaudeville circuits as Keith and Proctor, the Orpheum, John Hopkins, and Kohl and Castle, improving the overall quality of acts. With the new opera house revitalizing Greenwall interests and the proliferating ranks of small-time vaudeville houses whittling away at its audience base, Interstate decided to close its Fort Worth theater and build a much larger hall.[57]

CHAPTER SEVEN

VAUDEVILLE, SAMMIES, AND THE DECLINE OF LEGIT: 1911-1920

"It reminded one of the halcyon days
of the legitimate stage at the Byers,
so large were the crowds . . ."
~*Record*, November 21, 1915

In the spring of 1910, Karl Hoblitzelle announced that Interstate would begin constructing a new, much larger Majestic at the corner of Tenth and Commerce, two blocks north and east of the Jennings location and just three blocks south of the new Byers. Original plans for the site called only for a three-story office building with retail space for A & L August, a clothing store owned by German immigrant brothers, Alphonse and Leopold August. Interstate persuaded the pair, who had first arrived in Fort Worth around 1886, to add a theater to their plans.[1]

Fort Worth clothier, Alphonse August, builder of the August Building and the Majestic Theater.

Courtesy, Fort Worth Public Library, Local History and Genealogy

While few could have foreseen the collapse of the legitimate circuits within the next decade, construction of the state-of-the-art Byers clearly raised the competitive bar for theatrical productions in the city. Later figures place the second Majestic's seating capacity at just 1,377, while original plans called for a much larger 1,800-seat theater. Announced cost of the structure was $200,000, with another $100,000 lavished on interior furnishings and stage equipment. Like the Byers, the new theater was to be constructed entirely of fireproof materials with a cantilevered, steel-beam support system eliminating the need for posts to bear the weight of the balcony.[2]

Perhaps reflecting a falling out with W. J. Bailey over the move, Interstate abandoned the Jennings Avenue hall following the last show on November 24, 1910, though completion of the new theater was not expected before September 1911, over ten months away. Within days, the Majestic reopened seven blocks north in the Royal/Empress at Fifth and Throckmorton after Sullivan and Considine transferred all their bookings to Joseph Aronoff's newly opened Princess on Main Street. Bargain matinees and giveaways of free tickets and novelty items helped launch the temporary location.[3]

As planning of the new Majestic moved ahead in January 1911, the most heralded production ever to reach Fort Worth played the Byers. *Ben Hur,* a biblical melodrama based on the popular novel by General Lew Wallace, had played to sold-out houses since its New York opening in 1899. One of the largest and most extravagant productions in terms of personnel and stage mechanics ever to be mounted for Broadway, the show featured a cast of over two hundred in addition to horses and camels. Many theaters, including Fort Worth's original opera house, were simply too small to accommodate the production. Dallas, which had constructed a modern opera house in 1901 to replace one that burned in 1900, secured the production three times between 1905 and 1911. Not until two full seasons after completion of the Byers did Fort Worth manage to book the syndicate-produced play.[4]

To prepare for the chariot race, arguably the play's most dramatic scene, crews worked in carefully orchestrated chaos, moving complex stage machinery into place behind the scenes. As the lights went out at the start of the scene, an audible rumbling heralded the beginning of the contest. When the stage brightened once again, the chariots of Ben-Hur and his rival, Messala, each pulled by teams of four horses, already pounded full tilt across the stage, their forward momentum precariously contained on eight separate treadmills set in the stage floor. Concealed behind the outer horses, special collars fastened to iron bars bolted into the floor allowed the animals to surge against the harness without falling or running off the treadmills. The chariots of the duelists, mounted on invisible yokes and fitted with specially designed uneven wheels driven by electric motors, bounced and careened realistically. Dust blown from concealed chambers flew up from beneath the horses' feet and behind the wheels of the chariots.[5]

In the scene's climactic moment, the two chariots locked axles, tearing off Messala's wheel and hurling him to the ground as Ben-Hur's team rushed on to victory. The episode, played out against a moving backdrop, was artful illusion. The horses, treadmills, and Messala's chariot all ran atop an independent section of flooring that allowed the entire platform to be pulled backward as much as fifteen feet as the horses continued to race.[6]

While the grand scale and realistic settings of motion pictures would soon make such mechanical marvels as the chariot race seem ridiculously contrived, *Ben-Hur's* week-long Fort Worth engagement played eight sold-out performances, and, in the words of one critic, "cast a spell" over audiences. The company's pampered equine stars had their own local police detail to keep back admiring crowds as they lounged behind the opera house each night. The show also inspired an enduring local myth. In

1949, as Fort Worth celebrated its centennial, Mamie Greenwall Fain, daughter of Phil Greenwall, recalled that the desire to stage *Ben-Hur* "caused the downfall" of the old Fort Worth Opera House. Fain explained to a reporter, "Our stage was not equal to the heavy production of horses on a treadmill. We had already missed one whole season of *Ben-Hur* and we didn't think it advisable to reconstruct the stage."[7]

Her remarks sparked a widely believed local legend that the floor of the opera house collapsed during the *Ben-Hur* chariot race. Despite well-documented accounts blaming the theater's abandonment on a weakened east wall and the more obvious fact that it had been razed three years before *Ben-Hur*'s first arrival in the city, the story persisted through the remainder of the twentieth century.[8]

Bucking the penchant for haste shown in the building of earlier local theaters, Interstate spent sixteen months on the planning and construction of the new Majestic. Chosen to erect the new hall, described in promotional advertising as "the handsomest and most modern theater in America outside of New York City," was the Chicago firm of H. L. Stevens and Company. Mitchell and Holbeck, also of Chicago, carried out interior decorations, and William A. Corrao Electric Company of St. Louis installed the building's lighting and power systems. Kansas City Scenic Company provided stage equipment.[9]

Karl Hoblitzelle himself was responsible for the Majestic's overall design. As early as 1908, he had begun planning all of Interstate's new theaters, even though he had

Karl Hoblitzelle, president of Interstate Amusement, personally designed the second Majestic in 1911. After selling his theatrical interests during the Depression, his repurchase of the Majestic, Worth, and Hollywood Theaters in 1933 saved those theaters from closing.

Courtesy, Hoblitzelle Collection, Harry Ransom Humanities Research Center, University of Texas-Austin

no formal training as an architect. In his search for the latest design innovations, he regularly visited important new theaters across the country and incorporated features he liked into preliminary sketches. Construction engineers worked from these sketches to complete technical details. One element in the design of Fort Worth's Majestic became a first for any southern or Texas theater—a fully staffed, soundproof nursery and playroom off the second floor mezzanine.[10]

Hoblitzelle furnished the new Majestic with two large reception areas, both to set a tone of elegance and to remedy a common problem in theaters of the time—the crush of arriving and departing patrons. The theater's thirty by sixty-foot outer lobby, entered from Commerce Street on the building's west side, was finished in Italian Renaissance style. French-plate wall mirrors, white Italian marble wainscoting, white marble benches set in arched alcoves, and white, mosaic tile floors conveyed a general sense of openness and light.[11]

The Majestic's lobby decorations included stained glass, French doors, Italian marble wainscotting and benches, and eighteen carat gold-leaf borders and reliefs.

Courtesy, Hoblitzelle Collection, Harry Ransom Center, University of Texas-Austin

Theatergoers passed from the lobby to the first floor's inner foyer through three pairs of French doors. One set of doors gave direct access to the mezzanine by way of a wide, marble staircase. An inner foyer was decorated in a "refined German color scheme" by artisan Karl Horn. Carmine Turkish rugs cushioned the mosaic tile floors. On the opposite wall, five double sets of beveled French doors gave entrance to the auditorium.[12]

The auditorium itself was outfitted for comfort. Ceiling fans kept the atmosphere moving, while a hidden exhaust fan, the largest in Texas, exchanged all the air in the building every two minutes. Widely spaced rows opened onto five steeply pitched aisles designed to insure patrons both a clear view of the stage and easy access to seats. A journalist touring the hall during the final days of construction joked, "[a] man for once in his life can sit behind the biggest creation of women's headgear and not be forced to crane his neck to the breaking point to see the stage."[13]

Like the Byers Opera House, the Majestic was constructed using a revolutionary new system. With no visible posts, the wide balcony seemed to hang precariously in mid-air, its weight supported by what was advertised as the largest single concrete and steel beam in America. Its visible length stretched over eighty feet. Despite reassurances from management, some theatergoers remained skeptical, passing up opening night festivities. One later admitted to a local columnist, "People predicted [the balcony] would fall down, so we waited a few days to see."[14]

With fourteen complete sets designed by Kansas City Scenic Company, four sets of furniture, 144 footlights, and five overhead light strips containing 128 lights each, the theater could handle the complex requirements of the largest road company. If published statistics are accurate, the new house was an easy match for its chief rival, the Byers. At curtain line, the proscenium opening stretched forty-two feet wide and thirty-four feet high, seven feet wider than the Byers. Stage width, eighty-two feet from side wall to side wall, was eight feet wider. The stated height of the fly loft, ninety-three feet from floor to gridiron, would have made it thirteen feet higher than the Byers, although this figure likely reflects the height from floor to ceiling. *Lloyd's Vaudeville Guide,* a well-known trade publication, offered more conservative stage dimensions: width from wall to wall, seventy-five feet; curtain line to back wall, seventy-two feet; proscenium width, thirty-nine feet; and height to gridiron, seventy-two feet.[15]

Personally overseeing final preparations for opening night were Interstate president Karl Hoblitzelle, who had arrived in Fort Worth several weeks earlier, and Arthur C. Best, hired away from the local board of trade to replace T. W. Mullaly as local manager. Harry Gould, treasurer of the first Majestic, was promoted to assistant manager.

As the date approached, workmen began installing the Majestic's new 14 x 31½-foot advertising sign above the Commerce Street entryway. Interstate claimed the structure, with its 1,611 red and white tungsten bulbs, was the largest electrical sign in the south. Above and below a centerpiece of stars, the words, "Majestic Theater, All Vaudeville," flashed out. At night, it could be clearly read six blocks away.[16]

The Majestic's premiere marked not only the opening of Fort Worth's second major theater in just three years but completion of the August Building, the largest office structure in the state. The theater/office complex occupied the entire block

Two views of the Majestic's interior, c. 1911, showing the elaborately decorated proscenium and boxes, right, and audience chamber, left.

Courtesy, Hoblitzelle Collection, Harry Ransom Center, University of Texas-Austin

bounded by Tenth, Eleventh, Commerce, and Calhoun. Drenching rains through much of Monday, August 28th, failed to dampen the spirits of a sell-out crowd of first-nighters. Among guests viewing the proceedings from owner Alphonse August's box was longtime Greenwall's and Byers Opera House manager Phillip Greenwall, who within five years, would be forced to sell out to Interstate.[17]

Seven acts, well-known from previous seasons, made up the opening-night bill. Bursts of applause greeted nearly every new turn with a reviewer reporting, "each [act] was so good it would be hard to pick a headliner." Snaring top billing was Australian mimic and singer Maizie Rowlands, although the Farber Sisters, a pair of singing and dancing comediennes, stole almost as much press wearing skirts with daring side vents "several inches upward from the hems." Motion pictures, by now a regular Majestic feature, capped the evening.[18]

For the next twenty years, the Majestic would remain Fort Worth's most important theatrical venue, showcasing both rising young talent and some of vaudeville's most prominent headliners. While many of those appearing had yet to break into the

Exterior of the Majestic, c. October 1911, with what Interstate claimed was the largest electrical sign in the South.

Courtesy: Southwestern Mechanical Company Photograph Album, Special Collections, University of Texas-Arlington Libraries

Dignitaries and performers aboard a float outside the Majestic, opening day 28 August 1911.

Courtesy, Hoblitzelle Collection, Harry Ransom Center, University of

bigtime, a number eventually parlayed vaudeville stints into successful careers on Broadway, and in nightclubs, radio, motion pictures, and television.[19]

In May 1913, an Oklahoma cowboy named Will Rogers, who had broken into show business around 1900 as a trick roper in a Wild West show, found himself tapped out in Fort Worth, several days shy of payday on his Majestic Theater date. Still three years away from fame on Broadway in the Ziegfeld Follies, Rogers had been living in virtual poverty, sending much of his earnings home to support his wife and children. Billed as "The Famous *Texas* Cowboy," Rogers' easygoing good humor and folksy wit had made him a local favorite. At his entrance opening night, the Majestic crowd spontaneously erupted into wild cheering. The *Fort Worth Record* next day praised him as "one of the rarest comedians on the stage today."[20]

Hearing of Rogers' plight, Rosie Green, half of a song-and-dance act on the same bill, loaned him $60 from her "grouch bag," a small purse many female performers wore strategically concealed inside their corsets for protection against thieves. Rogers paid back the loan at the end of the week but never forgot Green's generosity. To her chagrin, he incorporated the incident into his monologue, bringing it up with such

Cowboy humorist, actor, political commentator, and writer Will Rogers. Vaudeville appearances and his long friendship with *Star-Telegram* publisher, Amon G. Carter, brought him often to Fort Worth between 1910 and his death in 1935.

Courtesy, *Fort Worth Star-Telegram* Collection, Special Collections, University of Texas-Arlington Libraries

regularity that the actress continued to receive unsolicited grouch bags from well-meaning friends and audience members for years. Rogers, meanwhile, rose to national prominence as one of America's most beloved entertainers and public figures, a humorist known for the wit and astuteness of his political observations. Until his death in 1935, he returned often to Fort Worth as both entertainer and guest of close friend Amon G. Carter, publisher of the *Fort Worth Star-Telegram*.[21]

Following Rogers in December 1913 was *Kid Cabaret,* a Gus Edwards musical starring schoolchildren as its chief gimmick. Grabbing top billing were twenty-one-year-old Eddie Cantor and thirteen-year-old Georgie Jessel. Cantor, who would appear twenty-four years later as a headliner in Casa Mañana, returned twice more in 1915—this time as part of a two-act with Al Lee. Mae West, still developing the coquettish persona and tongue-in-cheek sexuality that became her trademark, appeared the week of August 17, 1914, in an act titled, "In a Style All Her Own." The Four Marx Brothers, minus their more familiar alter egos, Groucho, Harpo, Chico, and Zeppo, made several appearances between 1914 and 1917 in a zany comedy skit, *Home Again.*[22]

Other future stars treading the Majestic boards during this period included Fred and Adele Astaire, a brother-sister dance team still in their first year on the vaudeville circuits, and rising young comedian Jack Benny. Twice during the salad days of his career, Benny (real name, Benjamin Kubelsky) was forced to change his stage billing after better-known performers threatened lawsuits. He made his first appearance on the Majestic stage in 1912 in a musical act, Salisbury and Benny. In 1918 he returned as a solo act, billing himself as Ben Benny. A local critic remarking, "[Benny] and his violin furnished quite a lot of fun for the crowd [but] most of the entertainment was [his] jokes and humorous comment."[23]

Probably no more legendary star played the Majestic in the years before World War I than magician and escape artist extraordinaire Harry Houdini. Ads announcing his first local appearance in January 1916 proclaimed him the "Greatest Headliner Ever to Appear Here." Already passing into almost mythic status, Houdini performed his showpiece escape, the Chinese Water Torture Cell, during a weeklong engagement. His ankles securely clamped and bolted to a heavy wooden stock, Houdini was lowered upside down by a winch into a water-filled steel-and-glass chamber. The stock was locked into place, and a curtained cabinet maneuvered around the cell. At each performance, he emerged dripping from behind the screen in less than two minutes.[24]

While completion of the new Byers and Majestic offered clear evidence of a booming local economy, the two halls' tightly spaced theatrical bookings left few openings for other events. With no other building in the city capable of housing large municipal events, around 1911 city leaders began stumping for a municipal auditorium. Construction on the facility finally began at the southwest corner of Fifth and Throckmorton during 1913, following a protracted fundraising campaign. When the eighteen-hundred-seat Chamber of Commerce Auditorium finally made its debut on January 23, 1914, two thousand people turned out for the grand opening. Yet despite this auspicious beginning, the auditorium, with its utilitarian design, largely unadorned interior, and stock painted drops, saw little use beyond lectures and concerts, no competition for the better equipped commercial halls.[25]

Interior and exterior views of the Chamber of Commerce Auditorium, which opened at Fifth and Throckmorton in 1914.

Author's collection

About the same time as the completion of the Auditorium, the Byers Opera House had gone into a sharp decline, partly precipitated by the death of Henry Greenwall on November 27, 1913. During his final years, Greenwall, like many of the remaining independent managers across the country, was forced to make difficult choices simply to stay in business. The fortunes of the few remaining Texas circuit theaters, including Fort Worth's, became increasingly tied to productions originating in Greenwall's New Orleans houses. Between 1910 and 1913, these had stayed afloat chiefly through Greenwall's alliance with the Shuberts. But in 1913, after years of battling for territory, the Shuberts and the syndicate made peace. As part of a new arrangement, the Shuberts agreed to book their attractions exclusively into the syndicate's Tulane Theater, a stonewalling tactic undoubtedly calculated to shut Greenwall out of the first class theatrical market once and for all.[26]

Less than three months later, Henry Greenwall died at age eighty-one. Characterizing him as "the exemplar of the square deal," a champion of independent actors and managers, standing against the syndicate to the last, an obituary appearing in the *Record* used Greenwall's death to vilify what it called the syndicate's efforts to "throttle the southern states."[27]

The death of Henry Greenwall did not have an immediate effect on local legitimate offerings, which had already been declining for several years. Bookings had reached a peak during the 1906–1907 season when 123 plays, musicals, concerts, and other attractions came through Fort Worth. Thereafter, even with Greenwall's considerable sway, the supply steadily dwindled. His loss seemingly created a void that Phil Greenwall and his son Mitchell, who took over management of the Byers around 1914, simply could not fill. In the three seasons following the Byers' grand opening in 1908, bookings reached a peak for the new house—eighty-four offerings during its inaugural season climbed to ninety-one for both 1909–1910 and 1910–1911. That number fell to seventy-seven in 1911–1912, and dropped again to seventy-three in 1913–1914. During 1914–1915, the first full season booked without the manager's influence, the number of attractions plummeted to just forty-one.[28]

Despite a growing scarcity of stellar road offerings, exacerbated for the Byers by its own diminishing returns, a number of important stars made appearances in Fort Worth during the theater's final years. Tiny Maud Adams appeared in 1912 in what would become her signature role, *Peter Pan*. Later that same season, Broadway's most successful comedy duo, Joe Weber and Lew Fields, played the city in *Hokey Pokey*. The 1913 season brought *The Fascinating Widow*, featuring Julian Eltinge, the most celebrated female impersonator of his time, and Viennese-born prima donna

Fritzi Scheff in *The Love Wager.* That same year, Broadway's golden couple, E. H. Sothern and Julia Marlowe, brought a double bill, *If I Were King* and *Romeo and Juliet,* to the opera house. During the 1914–1915 season, two actors who would go on to successful screen careers toured—George Arliss appearing in *Disraeli,* a role which later earned him a best actor film Oscar, and Billie Burke performing in a comic role, *Jerry.*[29]

To fill empty dates when no live fare was available, the Byers increasingly booked motion pictures, a practice that sometimes led to confusion for patrons. Ads for a 1915 performance of *Never Say Die* explained that Nat Goodwin "himself" would appear, while Klaw and Erlanger's production of *The Poor Little Rich Girl* during the same season carried the disclaimer, "This is not a motion picture." At the conclusion of the dismal 1914–1915 season, Mitchell Greenwall announced a first-ever summer season, featuring acts from the Frankel Brothers Vaudeville Circuit and six-reel pictures running continuously each day from noon to 11:00 P.M., a move clearly intended to recoup losses from the regular season. The fortunes of the Byers fared no better during the 1915–1916 season with just forty attractions, nine of those motion pictures. Perhaps foreshadowing the inevitable, the booking of D. W. Griffith's landmark film *The Birth of a Nation,* a reworking of Thomas Dixon, Jr.'s, popular Civil War stage melodrama *The Clansman,* became the most profitable offering of the season. Seven performances quickly sold out, and hundreds of patrons had to be turned away, prompting a second weeklong return of the film in April 1916. A local journalist observing audience reaction noted ironically, "It reminded one of the halcyon days of the legitimate stage at the Byers, so large were the crowds. . . . Women wept at times and [old veterans] who had worn the gray or the blue in the long ago lost control of their emotions."[30]

By 1916, less than three years after the death of his brother and now seventy-six years old himself, Phil Greenwall finally conceded defeat, announcing in large ads what he called "The Birth of a New Policy," for the Byers, a program combining continuous vaudeville acts and six-reel motion pictures. In an open letter published in the *Record* on April 9th, Greenwall's comments seemed more a plea to longtime patrons for support as he assured customers, "I personally guarantee the vaudeville and first-run pictures which will open the summer season." By August, however, the local press carried the announcement that Interstate Amusement Company, owners of the Majestic, had purchased the Byers lease and that W. S. Crosbie, treasurer of the Majestic, would replace Mitchell Greenwall as manager of the house. Whether Phil Greenwall offered the lease to Interstate as part of a buy–out or the Byers' owners lacked confidence in his ability to continue as lessee is unclear.[31]

As part of the new agreement, the Byers continued to operate as a "mixed" house with a combination of feature motion pictures and five "small-time" vaudeville acts, the bill changing twice weekly. To accommodate available stage plays, the Majestic also announced a change of policy, offering legitimate bookings on Mondays and Tuesdays and vaudeville Wednesdays through Saturdays. To prepare for the change, the Byers closed for a facelift. As part of the renovation, workmen painted over the theater's reseda walls and elegant wood trim in shades of Interstate old rose and ivory.[32]

Phil Greenwall's self-imposed retirement lasted a little over a year, although during the interim the Greenwall family continued to operate the Dallas Opera House. Ever the trouper, he announced his intention on August 25, 1917, to resume booking "high class" road shows into Fort Worth after reaching an agreement with W. J. Bailey, owner of the first Majestic on Jennings Avenue. Joining Greenwall in the venture were son Mitchell, serving as manager of the theater, and Albert Weis, Henry Greenwall's long-time partner. The Jennings hall, reopened as the Savoy Theater in November 1911, had often been dark since being vacated by Interstate vaudeville in 1910. It had been leased, with only mediocre success, by a series of resident stock companies. The first, the Lorraine Buchanan Stock Company, opened in January 1911, only to be replaced later that same year by the Charles and Gertrude Harrison Stock Company. Between 1912 and 1917 the theater's lease changed hands repeatedly, operating at various times under the direction of Frank North and Ruth Robison, Albert Taylor, and a local venture attempted by partners Cline E. Hoxworth and Frank G. Bond. For a time in 1912 it had even briefly returned to its status as a vaudeville house under lessee W. W. Woodson.[33]

Shortly after announcing his plans to local newspapers, Phil Greenwall collapsed from the effects of a massive stroke. One day later, on August 26th he died, ending a theatrical career that obituaries traced back over forty-five years to the building of Galveston's Tremont Opera House in 1870, although the *Star-Telegram* gave the date incorrectly as 1890. One month later, press notices announced that Mitchell Greenwall would continue his father's plans for the Savoy, while his sister Mamie, who had previously assisted in local theater operations, would become manager of the Dallas Opera House.[34]

With the advent of World War I, Fort Worth's snaring of not only the U.S. Army's entire 36th Division but three British Royal Flying Corps aviation training fields as well, boosted the local economy and assured a steady supply of customers for the Savoy, Majestic, and other local theaters through the end of the European conflict. Less than three months after the U.S. declaration of war against Germany in April 1917, the army announced Fort Worth as one of the winning bidders among Texas cities vying to become sites for several new military camps classed as cantonments or temporary bases. By mid-July construction was already underway in Arlington Heights just west of the river and downtown, and by August the first troops had begun moving in to Camp Bowie, named after Alamo defender James Bowie. By year's end, the city's population had swelled by 35,000 as soldiers, dubbed Sammies for Uncle Sam, poured into the city.[35]

In an effort to strengthen morale at these emergency cantonments, where soldiers often endured semi-primitive field conditions, the war department began constructing what were called liberty theaters, offering enlisted personnel vaudeville acts, musical concerts, well-known lecturers, and motion pictures. Entertainers making the camp circuit appeared at what amounted to room-and-board rates. To help underwrite expenses of the troupers and salaries for paid theater staffers, civilians were urged to purchase Smileage Books. These coupon books, donated to enlisted men, gained them admission to the liberty theater and other local performance halls, including Majestic Vaudeville, which offered reduced admissions to soldiers at all Majestic Theaters across the state.[36]

Admission to the liberty theater, limited to soldiers and their guests, was twenty cents or a Smileage coupon. The Camp Bowie Liberty Theater was constructed near the Country Club stop of the Fort Worth Transit Company trolley, just north of the corner of Milam Street and Arlington Heights (later Camp Bowie) Boulevard. The theater boasted a forty by forty-foot stage, hinged sidewalls that could be swung open during hot weather, and seating for two thousand. The theater opened March 31, 1918, under the management of Chicagoan Byrne Marcellus and orchestra director Lee R. Smith. Sammies packing the new theater each night quickly shortened the theater's more pretentious "liberty" name to simply "the show shop."[37]

Reflecting Fort Worth's new status as a full-fledged camp town, military police patrolled downtown streets, and the Pershing Theater, named in honor of commander in chief of the U.S. expeditionary force, General John "Blackjack" Pershing, opened for business in September 1917. The show house, located at 1109–1111 Main, occupied the site of the Princess Theater, which had closed following a disastrous fire on Christmas Day 1912. Manager of the new hall was Cullen Bailey, son of Savoy Theater owner, W. J. Bailey. Catering unabashedly to the all-male soldier trade, the theater's bill daily featured the Pershing Beauty Chorus and playlets with such mildly provocative titles as *His Night Out, Wrong Bed, The Ranch Girls, The Girl Question,* and *Up in a Ferris Wheel.* Other local theaters quickly followed suit. At 1010 Houston Street, the Lyric Theater, closed for several years, reopened with ads promising "Twenty-Five People—Mostly Girls." The Lake Como pavilion offered Schutta's Big Musical

Vernon and Irene Castle at the
height of their fame, c. 1915

Courtesy, *Fort Worth Star-Telegram*
Collection, University of Texas-
Arlington Library

Comedy Company, as the Savoy turned over its stage to the 111th Engineers for an old-fashioned minstrel revue.[38]

More soberingly, with increasing frequency newsreels documenting the bleakness of the carnage along the Western Front grabbed top billing from shapely chorus girls and wisecracking minstrel show endmen. Local theaters became the frontline in the push to sell Liberty Bonds with the Byers and Majestic taking out large ads proclaiming one-hundred-percent participation among theater personnel.[39]

As an unlikely part of the new war landscape, the city also acquired its own celebrity in the person of English dancer and stage performer Vernon Castle, who had gained U.S. fame appearing in several Broadway musicals between 1906 and 1914. After he met and married chorus girl Irene Foote, the two formed their own dance team, gaining such popularity with audiences that they set off a national craze for such dances as the turkey trot, fox trot, tango, and Castle Walk. When war broke out in Europe, Castle returned to England and enlisted as a pilot in the Royal Flying Corps; in 1917 he returned to the U.S. as part of a contingent of British flying instructors assigned to Benbrook Field, south of Fort Worth.[40]

Keeping a low profile, the lanky Castle, often accompanied by his pet monkey, Jeffrey, stuck to the training field. He performed only occasionally in a few private homes and for local benefits. On the morning of February 15, 1918, Castle had just lifted off in his Curtiss "Jenny" biplane with a student pilot aboard, when he had to pull up sharply in a half loop to avoid colliding with another aircraft. His evasive maneuver was only partially successful. After clipping the other plane's tail, Castle's aircraft stalled, rolled over, and plunged seventy-five feet, nose first, to the ground. Castle, in the front seat, died instantly, the only casualty of the collision. Because of Castle's quick thinking, his student, the pilot of the other aircraft, and Jeffrey, the monkey, survived. The next day, hundreds crowded into memorial services at Robertson's Undertaking Parlor. Thousands more silently lined downtown streets to watch as Castle's coffin, resting atop a caisson drawn by six horses and draped with a Union Jack, made its way to the T&P Railway Station, escorted by a cortege of two hundred flying cadets and the 133rd Field Artillery band.[41]

By the start of the 1918–1919 season, Cline E. Hoxworth had replaced Mitchell Greenwall as manager of the Savoy, although bookings at the theater failed to improve. Hoxworth promised a turnaround, but the influenza epidemic, which had begun sweeping the country in September 1918, hurt business. By the third week in October nearly a hundred people had died locally, the large majority felled by pneumonia and other secondary complications. Many of the legitimate companies still touring the

Vernon Castle in his role as flying instructor at Benbrook Field, near Camp Bowie, c. 1918.

Courtesy, Fort Worth Public Library, Local History and Genealogy

Vernon Castle's funeral procession makes its way down Lancaster Avenue to the Texas and Pacific railway terminal, February 16, 1918.

Courtesy, Fort Worth Public Library, Local History and Genealogy

country were forced to disband temporarily, a situation that did not improve until the worst of the epidemic had passed several weeks later. By late October the disease reached crisis proportions. As the health department urged citizens to stay home, theaters, churches, and other public gathering places were ordered closed for a week.[42]

While the ban was lifted within days, an embattled Hoxworth found himself mired in the same pit of declining business as his predecessors, the Greenwalls. With stage stars defecting in ever-increasing numbers to the movie studios and eight thousand movie houses nationwide offering them up on handsome platters loaded with cheap admissions, realistic settings, and all-day screenings, there was little left over for the city's one remaining legitimate house. Even the signing of the November 11th armistice marking the end of the war had little effect on the situation. [43]

With the "Great War" at an end, and Fort Worth, like the rest of the country on the verge of the jazz age, touring stars demanding two dollars a ticket for their services seemed hopelessly overpriced. Perhaps reflecting the general malaise afflicting the remaining legitimate circuits across the county, in September 1919 W. J. Bailey abruptly announced plans to rip out the Savoy's stage and convert the theater into a garage, saying he could no longer afford to support a house staff when the theater might be booked only one or two days a week.[44]

The Byers, built at a cost of over $200,000 just ten years earlier, never again operated as a live-performance venue. Hurt, like other local theaters, by the closing of the army base, Interstate abandoned efforts to keep the theater open as a vaudeville house. In 1919, the company sold the lease to Pierre C. Levy, owner of two other local movie houses, the Strand and Hippodrome, and Waco showman E. H. Hulsey. The partners began immediate renovations to convert the former opera house and third-tier vaudeville emporium into a full-fledged movie palace, although Levy promised to book a few legitimate road shows as they became available.[45]

This second remodeling ended for good Fort Worth's theatrical heyday, although the opera house stage was left intact behind the new deluxe screen. When the new theater made its debut on October 19, it opened under the name it would keep for the next fifty-eight years—the Palace. During more than half a century, the Palace passed through a long series of owners, eventually rejoining the Interstate chain,

The Byers Opera House/Palace Theater lightbulb burned uninterrupted from the time the theater opened in 1908 until its razing in 1977. By 2005, ninety-seven years after being set in place, the bulb still burned in a local museum.

Courtesy, *Fort Worth Star-Telegram* Collection, University of Texas-Arlington Library which had long since converted its vaudeville operations to motion pictures. As new generations of movie patrons flowed steadily in and out of its doors, the theater's relatively brief reign as the city's leading performance hall was all but forgotten.

By the time of its final demise in May 1977, the old theater had, in fact, become more renowned for a single item of hardware than for any performer who ever trod the boards of its long-abandoned stage. As part of his routine duties, electrician Barry Burke had installed three carbon electric lightbulbs, then state of the art, in a high-ceilinged corridor just beyond the stage door in September 1908, as the Byers Opera House prepared for its grand opening. Through the ensuing years, two of the bulbs expired routinely and were replaced, but in his comings and goings, Burke gradually became aware that one increasingly antiquated light continued to burn. Several decades passed, with Burke making it a point to check on the bulb periodically. He began telling friends only half-jokingly, "I can't help but feel that when that lamp goes out, I'll go with it." He need not have worried. In a distinguished career, Burke served as stage electrician for both the Greenwall and Byers Opera Houses and then for another three decades managed theaters at several posts around the country for both the Publix and Interstate chains. When he died in 1963, the little bulb still burned on tenaciously. As workmen prepared to raze the theater in May 1977, the light, by then shining sixty-nine years, was gingerly removed by technicians who took care not to disrupt its circuit. At the turn of the twenty-first century it still burned.[46]

Surviving even the second Majestic, the Palace became the last local reminder of what some theater historians have called the "golden age" of the American theater when the great vaudeville and legitimate circuits, following the expanding railroad system, carried an unprecedented array of stellar performers to halls and opera houses all across the country.[47]

THE RISE OF CELLULOID AND THE DECLINE OF LIVE PERFORMANCE: 1920-1935

"This town could do with actors in the flesh."
—Robert Randol

Following the decommissioning of Camp Bowie in 1919 and the subsequent loss of the soldier trade, Fort Worth's fifteen-year theatrical boom, begun with the opening of the first Majestic in 1905, came to an end. The loss of the Savoy, Pershing, and Lyric theaters and the conversion of still others like the Byers Opera House to motion pictures left residents without a ready supply of legitimate offerings for the first time in forty-five years.

The city was by no means completely cut off from theatrical opportunities, however. Interstate's Majestic Theater continued to showcase touring companies and vaudeville through the early 1930s, and in 1927 Paramount-Publix opened a lavish new showplace, the Worth, which was soon drawing crowds with first-run motion pictures and weekly stage revues. Added to these was an upsurge of interest in community theater as a number of individuals and civic organizations emerged with productions that continued live theater in the city.[1]

THE LITTLE THEATER MOVEMENT AND UNIVERSITY PRODUCTIONS

Helping encourage new interest in community-based theater were ambitious stagings of several operas between 1917 and 1929 by Sam S. Losh with the Fort Worth Municipal Chorus and the establishment of Fort Worth's first "little theater." The little theater concept, which had reached America around 1912 after beginning in Europe, advocated simplified realism in stage design and the production of less commercial works in smaller theaters. Massachusetts' Provincetown Players, perhaps the best-known American company, championed unknown playwright Eugene O'Neill and for a time included in its company a Fort Worth man, David Carb. Carb, a Harvard graduate and son of Isidore Carb, a local real estate appraiser and one of the founders of Beth-El Reform Jewish Congregation, had performed in the company's July 1916 production of O'Neill's *Bound East For Cardiff*.[2]

Houston had formed a little theater in 1919, with Dallas following in 1920 and Fort Worth in 1921. By 1930, there were sixty-eight little theaters across the state, most of them, including Fort Worth's, largely dependent on subscribers for financial support, with volunteers taking acting roles and serving as behind-the-scenes technicians.[3]

One of the earliest participants in Fort Worth's little theater was author Katherine Anne Porter, who would later channel the sharp vicissitudes of an impoverished Texas childhood into such twentieth-century masterworks as *Flowering Judas, Pale Horse, Pale Rider,* and 1962's Pulitzer Prize-winning novel, *Ship of Fools.* In 1921, still a struggling unknown, she came to Fort Worth to visit an old friend, Fort Worth reporter Kitty Barry Crawford. Crawford's husband and fellow journalist, J. Garfield Crawford, published the *Oil Journal* locally, and shortly after her September arrival, Porter began writing for the magazine, occasionally contributing articles to the *Fort Worth Record* as well.[4]

When the Vagabond Players, Fort Worth's contribution to the little theater movement, made its modest debut on October 12, 1921, Kitty Crawford and Katherine Anne Porter were in the audience. The play was *Suppressed Desires,* a one-act written by George Cram Cook and Susan Glaspell, two founders of the Provincetown Players. The cast performed from a makeshift stage erected over the horse stalls in Mrs. Lotta Carter Gardner's barn in the 1300 block of Alston Avenue. Players dressed in the

Katherine Anne Porter and Kitty Barry Crawford, c. 1916.

Courtesy, Special Collections, University of North Carolina Libraries

Katherine Anne Porter, Roscoe Carnrike, and Hunter Gardner in the Vagabond Players' 1921 production, *Poor Old Jim*.

Courtesy, Star-Telegram Collection, Special Collections, University of Texas-Arlington Libraries

hayloft, and the seating area could only accommodate 110. Gardner had provided the company, organized and directed by her daughter Rosalind, with $800 start-up money. The opening-night cast featured Rosalind, Marguerite Kerr, and Walker Moore. Others in the company included Gardner's son, Hunter E. Gardner, Jr., and Roscoe Carnrike, a Fort Worth businessman who would serve as Fort Worth mayor from 1945 to 1947.[5]

Shortly after this first production, Porter joined the Fort Worth company, remaining active through the rest of the season. She played Marie in *Poor Old Jim* opposite Carnrike and Hunter Gardner and Columbine in *The Wonder Hat*. In November, she wrote an article on little theater for the *Star-Telegram*, praising the movement's attempts "to free the artist from conventionalized forms, to weave color, music, movement, light [and] the faithful interpretation of human emotions into . . . a four-dimensional art far removed from the mere spectacle of a show. . . ."[6]

In 1923, the Vagabond Players, newly renamed the Fort Worth Little Theater, resumed productions under the leadership of Hunter Gardner. Hoping to improve the artistic quality of productions, the organization secured Alexandria Dean, a graduate of Dartmouth College, to direct some productions. Dean's first staging for the company was *The Romantic Age.* Increased demand for tickets prompted a move to Fort Worth Junior High on Jennings Avenue, but after just one season in the new location, the group disbanded. Finally reorganized in the fall of 1925 with Hunter Gardner as its first paid director, the company shifted productions to a converted bowling alley at 609 West Fourth Street, near the YMCA. It continued there until 1927, when development in the downtown area forced yet another move to the Woman's Club Music Hall, a 238-seat space at 1312 West Tucker Street, just north of the club's main building on Pennsylvania.[7]

Under the auspices of the Woman's Club from 1927–1932, the Little Theater prospered. Though never as large as the Dallas Little Theater, which boasted as many as fourteen hundred members, the company substantially increased its endowment, including in its sponsoring membership such prominent local citizens as W.J. Bailey, Amon G. Carter, Robert Ellison, B.C. Meacham, E.A. "Ed" Landreth, W.C. and W.K. Stripling, W.P. McLean, and John Sparks. Its regular performers included Harry Hoxworth, Clyde and Emma Bell Kraft, Mary Sears, Hunter and Lotta Gardner, Howard Peak, Mary Hartman, William D. Bell, Marguerite Kerr Hamilton, and Cornelius B. Savage. Local musicians, including Brooks Morris and Dot Echols Orum, provided incidental music between acts. At its peak, the organization was producing nine plays a season, had eleven thousand paid admissions, and over seven hundred yearly subscribers. In 1928 the group established a children's theater and in 1929 produced *Beyond the Horizon,* the first Eugene O'Neill play ever staged in Fort Worth.[8]

Following Gardner's resignation in 1929, Cameron King took the reins as producing director from 1929 to 1931. Under his leadership, the company hosted the 1930 state little theater tournament and sponsored a playwriting contest with the Daughters of the Republic of Texas. The winner, *Cannon,* by Margaret Wynne Harrison, was produced by the organization in 1931. King's tenure as director ended in the spring of 1931.[9]

New York native and Yale Drama School graduate Elbert Gruver became director of the organization in the fall of 1931. Gruver's contributions included a production in February 1932 of Maxim Gorky's *The Lower Depths,* but after just one season with the company, he also resigned. His replacement was Blanchard McKee, an Indiana native whose show business credits included stints in both stock and vaudeville. He went on to perform in radio dramas broadcast over the Texas State Network and by 1938 had his own syndicated show, *Neighbors,* originating from Fort Worth's KFJZ.

McKee, who served as director through the end of 1933, attempted to broaden the the-ater's popular base, staging *Naughty Marietta,* the company's first musical production, in TCU Stadium in August 1933.[10]

Later that same year, with a loan provided by board president Marvin Leonard, the Little Theater returned to the downtown area, leasing and renovating a former church at Tenth and Burnett. First vice president Dr. Harry A. Merfeld, rabbi of Beth-El Reform Jewish Congregation, was so enthusiastic about the change that he moved his office into the Little Theater building. The move, undertaken to improve the theater's visibility and double its seating capacity, was tempered by internal bickering and the withdrawal of several board members, including Leonard, who resigned in November. Seth Barwise, elected in Leonard's place, promised changes.[11]

Much of the unrest seemed tied to disagreements over the theater's artistic goals. Audience numbers had declined with the deepening of the Great Depression, but uneven casting, under-rehearsed plays, and a repertoire lacking broad general appeal also hurt the company. The board, however, continued to resist change, opposed to any deviation from the movement's original goal of presenting thought-provoking, noncommercial fare. Adding to these woes, the theater was barred for a time from

Fort Worth Little Theater's ambitious 1932 staging of Maxim Gorky's *The Lower Depths*, directed by Elbert Gruver.

Courtesy, Fort Worth Public Library, Local History and Genealogy

acquiring plays after the company failed to pay royalty fees to a New York dramatists' organization.[12]

At the end of 1933, Blanchard McKee resigned, leaving the company to Robert Nail, a twenty-five-year-old playwright/director who had graduated from Princeton earlier that same year. Nail, a native of Albany, Texas, had joined the company in September as producing director for a new little theater venture, the Workshop, intended as a proving ground for actors and new works, including his own. McKee, meanwhile, formed a rival company, the Community Theater, and moved into the Little Theater's old Tucker Street quarters. The company debuted on February 12, 1934, with the folk drama, *Hell–Bent for Heaven.*[13]

Through 1934 and into 1935, the two groups played against each other. While the Community Theater presented Hatcher Hughes' *Hell-Bent For Heaven,* Noel Coward's *Private Lives,* Somerset Maugham's *The Constant Wife,* and Henrik Ibsen's *A Doll's House,* the Little Theater offered Richard Sherwood's *The Road to Rome,* John Galsworthy's *Old English,* Lawrence Langner's *The Pursuit of Happiness,* Nail's own revue, *The Time of Your Lives,* and Lynn Riggs' *Green Grow the Lilacs.* And although minority actors and patrons would continue to be excluded from most local theatrical organizations for decades to come, Nail solicited actors from the city's African American community and staged an all-black production of Frank DuBose Heyward's *Porgy* in March 1935.[14]

The staging may have led to internal controversy because just days after the production, Nail broke with the company without finishing the season. His exit also seemed to mark a turning point for little theater groups in the city. Though the Depression had been slower to hit Fort Worth than some areas of the country, in 1935 the Little Theater appealed to the Federal Emergency Relief Administration for operating funds. Nothing seems to have come of the request, and through 1936, 1937, and 1938 neither the Little Theater nor the Community Theater mounted seasons. The better-funded Dallas Little Theater, meanwhile, hired Nail in 1936. In 1938, he returned to Albany to write and produce the first Fort Griffin Fandangle, an outdoor drama of West Texas pioneer life that would become an annual event and remain the focus of his creative energy until his death in 1968.[15]

Also contributing to the growth of local theater were the city's two major educational institutions, Texas Christian University and Texas Woman's College. Following World War I, Professor J. Quincy Biggs, head of Texas Christian University's oratory department, reorganized the school's dramatic club as the Footlight Club. Professor Lewis D. Fallis assumed leadership of the club in 1925, after joining the faculty from

Boston's Curry School of Expression. Under his leadership in 1926, the organization took top prize in the state little theater tournament, held from 1920 to 1943 at the Dallas Little Theater. Fallis continued to serve as head of what was then called the department of public speaking until 1952, although he directed his final play, *The Torchbearers,* in 1945. Also directing productions beginning in 1935 was Katherine Moore (Norton).[16]

Texas Woman's College officials sanctioned organization of the Thespian Club in February 1920. The group's inaugural effort was a pair of one-acts, *Pierrot and Pierrette* and *Trifles.* Through the 1920s and 1930s the school at various times offered courses in beginning and advanced play production, the art of acting and directing, and stage dialects, but the Thespian Club, which mounted several productions yearly, remained students' chief dramatic outlet. In the early 1930s, the school began admitting men, although it was not until 1935 that Texas Woman's officially became Texas Wesleyan College.[17]

Until 1922, the school's only performance space was the administration building's third floor auditorium, but during that year the college acquired the old Polytechnic Methodist Church. Over the next three years, with funding from philanthropist Ann Waggoner, the building was renovated. In 1925, it became the Ann Waggoner Fine Arts Building. The fine arts auditorium remained the site of most Texas Wesleyan theatrical performances through the 1990s.[18]

Professor Lewis D. Fallis, headed TCU's Department of Public Speaking and sponsored the award-winning Dramatic Club beginning in the 1920s.

Courtesy, Fort Worth Public Library, Local History and Genealogy

PERMANENT PROFESSIONAL COMPANIES

Simultaneous with the amateur productions of the Little Theater and local universities, a number of businessmen and showmen renewed efforts to establish a local professional theater to focus on legitimate works. The Ritz Theater, opened to great fanfare in September 1924, became the city's first major performance hall since the Majestic took its bow in 1911. Constructed by Harry B. Friedman and bankrolled by a group of investors that included George W. Polk and a trio of Fort Worth law partners, U. M. Simon, William H. Slay, and Mike Smith, the Ritz seemed poised for stardom. Pre-opening publicity touted the new theater as the show house that would "bring back the 'legit.'" The 1,561-seat playhouse went up on a prime lot at the southwest corner of Tenth and Commerce, across from the Majestic.[19]

Lessee for the venture, Azby Choteau, had worked for several years as general manager of Interstate Amusement, proprietors of the Majestic. Choteau tapped Sam Bullman to serve as manager of the new theater and to assemble what became the city's first professional stock troupe since before World War I. The Ritz Players opened

The Ritz Theater, which opened to great fanfare at the corner of Tenth and Commerce in 1924 quickly fell on hard times. Over less than six years, it became the Pantages, Civic, Plaza, and finally the New Liberty in 1930.

Courtesy, Jack White Photograph Collection, Special Collections, University of Texas-Arlington Libraries

September 7, 1924, with Guy Bolton's *Adam and Eva* and through the fall and winter staged a series of recent Broadway successes that rotated weekly. During its first season the company did well—admiring fans trailed company leads Irene Summerly and Howard Miller wherever they went. By the second season, however, ticket sales declined sharply. Bullman moved the Players to the former Royal Theater at Fifth and Throckmorton to make way for Seattle entertainment magnate Alexander Pantages, who took over the Ritz lease in January 1926 and renamed the theater the Pantages.[20]

The opening of the Pantages made Fort Worth a stop on the circuit of the country's largest and most prosperous independent vaudeville circuit for a time. Within six months of taking control, however, the showman dropped vaudeville from his Fort Worth house, shut out by the Majestic's 'name' lineup and solidly entrenched audience base. Taking its place was a rotating format of motion pictures, road shows, and Pantages' own stock company, the Pantages Players. By 1928, facing competition from both the Majestic and a new theater, the Worth, Pantages abandoned his run in the city altogether.[21]

Two more efforts to found permanent stock companies in the Tenth Street hall followed, neither successful. In October 1928, the Pantages became the Civic Repertory, an organization directed by Hunter Gardner, for several seasons a leader in the Fort Worth Little Theater. Just nine weeks into its maiden season, the Civic failed.

Irene Summerly, leading lady of the short-lived Ritz Players, 1924-1926.

Courtesy, *Fort Worth Star-Telegram* Collection, Special Collections, University of Texas-Arlington Libraries

Under director/actor Harry Hoxworth, whose previous local ventures included management of the Savoy Theater between 1916 and 1918, the Plaza Players debuted with unfortunate timing in November 1929, just weeks after the stock market crash. This enterprise, too, collapsed in a matter of weeks. Finally, in 1930 the theater was sold to Leon Lewis, who changed its name to the New Liberty and operated it as a movie house until his death in 1948.[22]

Shortly before the Ritz took its bow in 1924, one of the largest auditoriums ever erected in the city was dedicated in North Fort Worth. From its grand opening, however, the hall came to be associated more with the racist proclivities of its builders than for any stellar performance history. Beginning around World War I, the Ku Klux Klan had begun a troubling resurgence, both in Fort Worth and across the state. By 1923, Fort Worth Klavern No. 101 had become one of the largest chapters in the state and announced its intention in December 1923 to construct a $50,000 hall at 1012 North Main Street near the Fort Worth baseball park. The planned complex included offices, dressing rooms, "standard size" stage, and a 40 by 120 foot auditorium shaped like a "huge oval bowl." Officials of the Klan claimed that the building, designed by architect

The Ku Klux Klan Auditorium, constructed on North Main in 1924 by Fort Worth Klavern No. 101. Just six months after its grand opening, a fire of suspicious origins destroyed the hall. Although quickly rebuilt, membership in the local Klan steadily declined. The building was sold in 1931.

Courtesy, Historic Fort Worth

Earl T. Glasgow, could seat between thirty-six hundred and four thousand. The completed hall was formally dedicated May 18, 1924, accompanied by speeches exalting to "the tenets of the Christian religion, the sanctity of the home, the chastity of womanhood, [and] white supremacy."[23]

The hall's completion seemed, ominously, to usher in a new era of Klan dominance of the city's municipal affairs, with a number of city leaders and local ministers attending the grand opening. In its first months of operation, the Klan Auditorium hosted several events, including an October 18 appearance by legendary escape artist Harry Houdini, giving a lecture demonstration, "Can the Dead Speak to the Living?" Klan leaders, however, showed little evidence of mystical prescience in judging growing community discontent with the organization. On November 6, shortly before a minstrel show was scheduled to take to the boards, arsonists set fire to the hall, burning it to the ground. Death threats signed "the blacks" promised new, more violent acts of retaliation. In defiance of the threats, the auditorium was soon rebuilt, but as various civic leaders increasingly fanned the flames of public sentiment against the Klan's often-brutal tactics, the organization's local membership roster steadily dwindled. In March 1931, facing sharply reduced revenues, the Klan sold the building to Leonard Brothers.[24]

As the Klan continued its decline and various local theatrical companies failed during the 1920s, the Majestic, meanwhile, held on, if not always securely, to its spot as Fort Worth's preeminent theater. Between 1921 and 1927, the hall withstood challenges not only from the Ritz and its successor, the Pantages but from a number of smaller competitors as well. The Rialto, installed at 601 Main in 1921 as a motion picture house by J.S. Phillips and V.E. Hildreth, began serving up vaudeville as a regular weekly feature around 1925. The Hippodrome, at 1104 Main, also continued a program of movies with live stage shows until at least 1930.[25]

MOTION PICTURES

Motion pictures, in fact, increasingly loomed as the most serious threat to the box office of every form of live entertainment in the city. While the Little Theater managed to hang on through the largesse of prominent subscribers, the various attempts to establish repertory companies all failed. By 1924 even Interstate was forced into policy changes to adjust for the business it had lost to film.

To cut expenses, in February of that year the Majestic's seven-act vaudeville bill was pared to six, with performers expected to work an additional Sunday matinee. At the same time, prices were slashed to pre-World War I levels, with weeknight reserved tickets selling for sixty-five and fifty cents and unreserved balcony seats going for just thirty-five cents. By the winter of 1925, Interstate dropped all reserved seats to fifty cents and replaced the theater's longstanding two-a-day venue with its own "grind" policy—three and sometimes four shows a day, with a bill trimmed to five acts playing between motion pictures. The various changes returned the theater to profitability for several more seasons but failed to rescue vaudeville from its eventual fate.[26]

In its final decade as a vaudeville house the Majestic continued to feature not only the industry's top headliners but important rising entertainers as well. Jack Benny returned in 1922, and W.C. Fields, already an established Ziegfeld Follies star, brought "Fields' Family Feud," a skit about a family out for a disastrous Sunday drive, to the theater in February 1923. The *Record* reported, "Fields and his players presented what proved to be one of the most ridiculous and novel farces . . . ever shoved across local footlights."[27]

Singer Eva Tanguay, the industry's highest paid performer during the peak years before World War I, played the theater in April 1924. Husband-and-wife comedy team George Burns and Gracie Allen appeared in 1927, and child performer and future cabaret singer and television comedienne Rose Marie did a turn in 1929. Other important stars making appearances during the 1920s included Harry Houdini, Sir Harry Lauder, the Ritz Brothers, Jimmie Rodgers, Mae West, Bert Lahr, Jack Haley, and Ray Bolger. Bob Hope, who had struggled as an anonymous hoofer for several seasons on the circuits before discovering a knack for stand-up comedy, got his break to the big time during a Fort Worth engagement in 1930.[28]

Nearly six years after the Benbrook Field plane crash that ended Vernon Castle's life, Irene Castle returned to the city in 1923 trying to revive her career after several years' retirement. The one-day Majestic engagement featured vaudeville acts and Castle, with a new partner, in eight dance numbers. Unsure of her draw as a solo performer, Castle wrapped herself in lush stage settings and a succession of ever more elaborate evening gowns. One reviewer quipped, "the twinkling feet of Miss Castle were secondary in the minds of the women to the sartorial splendor of the [gowns]."[29]

Hidden beneath the ornate trappings, the dancer masked still unresolved grief. Between performances, a *Record* photographer snapped an unsmiling Castle laying flowers on a Greenwood Cemetery monument dedicated to her husband and downed Canadian fliers. Later, she sought out Vernon Castle Avenue on Fort Worth's North Side near Oakwood Cemetery. The road, formerly known as Boulevard Street, had been renamed for the flier shortly after his death. Chagrined that the street chosen to honor her husband ran only through a quiet, residential neighborhood, Castle blasted city leaders, calling the road "unworthy of the illustrious name . . . given to it."[30]

Players like Burns and Allen, Hope, and Fields were seasoned veterans of the circuits by the time of their local appearances, but one star-in-the-making began her show business career at the Majestic. Born in 1911, Virginia "Ginger" McMath spent

Young comedian Bob Hope, after several years touring the vaudeville circuits in obscurity, got his break to New York's "bigtime," Palace Theater, following a stint at Fort Worth's Majestic in 1930.

Courtesy, J. Abeles Collection, Harry Ransom Center, University of Texas-Austin several years in Fort Worth after her mother, Lela, married insurance agent John Rogers and moved with him to the city around 1922. The family settled on the near South Side, and Lela took a job as a theatrical reporter and reviewer for the *Fort Worth Record*, a role that put her in frequent contact with performers and local theater managers. By now appropriating her stepfather's last name, Ginger frequently accompanied her mother on trips to the Majestic. Some of the child's earliest contacts with show people came backstage and at the Rogers home, where her mother often prepared home-cooked meals for touring headliners.[31]

One afternoon the youngster encountered Eddie Foy, Jr., and his brother and sisters in the alley behind the Majestic. Experienced troupers, the Foys had long toured with their father, Eddie Foy, Sr., in a family act billed as "Eddie Foy and the Seven Little

Ginger Rogers, c. 1925, about the time the teenaged dancer won an Interstate-sponsored statewide Charleston contest, launching her show business career.

Courtesy, *Fort Worth Star-Telegram* Collection, Special Collections, University of Texas-Arlington Libraries

Foys." Following World War I, when the elder Foy returned to solo billing, several of the children formed a separate act. Foy Jr. indulgently offered to teach Rogers the Charleston, the country's hottest dance craze. Later in the week, when one of the siblings became ill, Foy invited Rogers to join the act for its Friday night performance.[32]

Rogers' Charleston instruction under Foy's tutelage proved fortuitous. In the fall of 1925, Interstate sponsored a dance contest in each Texas city on the circuit to pick a state Charleston champion. Grand prize was four weeks of appearances in the circuit's six Texas theaters, including Fort Worth. At the Fort Worth contest, held in the Texas Hotel ballroom the evening of November 6, 1925, Rogers won handily. Three days later, in the state finals at Dallas' Baker Hotel, she once again took top prize. Following several weeks of rehearsal with two of the runners-up, the fourteen-year-old opened in Waco, in an act billed as *Ginger Rogers and the Dancing Red Heads.* The dancers finally took to the boards of the local Majestic the week of December 12, 1925. Rogers' precocity as a dancer stretched the original four-week booking into a three-year string of vaudeville appearances across the country. In 1930, already appearing on Broadway, she signed her first motion picture contract, an action that led to her pairing in several movie musicals with dancer Fred Astaire and eventual stardom.[33]

In November 1927, Paramount-Publix' million-dollar Worth Hotel and Theater made its grand entrance just east of the corner of Seventh and Taylor. Financed by Houston businessman, Jesse H. Jones, the 2,284-seat movie and live performance hall, largest in the Southwest, was a masterpiece of 1920s art deco extravagance, one of a series of fourteen "deluxe" playhouses erected by the chain across the country. Unveiling of the new facility marked another turning point for the Majestic, ending its sixteen-year run as the city's leading theatrical venue.[34]

Customers stepping inside the Worth found themselves in an Egyptian temple, its entrance defined by ornately decorated pillars with lotus blossom capitals. Wide plaster friezes and crimson-and-gold tapestries in Egyptian-themed motifs topped color-splashed interior walls, watched over by assorted pharaohs and deities. Onstage, Worth management presented a seven- or eight-segment weekly bill that featured musical numbers by the Worth Grand Orchestra under the baton of musical director Hyman Maurice and William "Billy" Muth at the keyboard of the Mighty Wurlitzer Pipe Organ between film shorts, newsreels, and a feature Paramount motion picture. Key components of this nightly entertainment package were the hourlong Publix "unit" shows, live revues sent out over the country from New York.[35]

Produced, written, and directed by Broadway showman John Murray Anderson, the fast-paced shows, sporting catchy titles like "Dixieland," "Fast Mail," "Hula Blues,"

Show Row, West Seventh Street, left, c. 1931, home of both the Hollywood and Worth Theaters. The Worth, with lavish, Egyptian-themed interior motifs, opened in November, 1927 with 2,284 seats, motion pictures, and weekly live revues.

Courtesy, *Fort Worth Star-Telegram* Collection, Special Collections, University of Texas-Arlington Libraries

and "Snapshots," featured as many as thirty performers. The Worth Band, under the direction of a series of tuxedo-clad crooners that included Al Morey, Eddie Stanley, and Lindy Coons, provided musical accompaniment. Students from local dance studios occasionally bolstered the ranks, using backstage breaks to pick up new steps from seasoned troupers. Long after the weekly shows were discontinued, live music remained an integral part of the Worth bill.[36]

By 1929, Karl Hoblitzelle had decided to bow out of show business. He first sold Interstate to Fox Corporation but following the collapse of the stock market in late October, he released that company from its contract. In May 1930, he reached a second agreement with Radio-Keith-Orpheum (RKO) but stayed on temporarily as division manager before finally resigning in February 1931.[37]

Even before Hoblitzelle's final departure, rumors began to circulate that live acts would soon "go out" at the Majestic, though the signs had long indicated vaudeville's days were numbered locally. In September 1928, less than a year after the Worth's high profile grand opening, Paramount-Publix abruptly axed that theater's weekly stage shows, replacing them with the latest technological innovation—talking pictures. Two years later, in early January 1931, RKO followed suit, cutting live performances at the Majestic to just three days a week. Building renovations and the hiring of replacements for retiring music director George Orum and other orchestra members were put on hold. Interpreting the omens, local entertainment columnist Robert Randol predicted, "We would not be surprised to see vaudeville dropped entirely before many weeks."[38]

Like the final episode of a serial cliffhanger, vaudeville dangled from the edge of the precipice for another four months, but within weeks of Hoblitzelle's final exit, RKO moved to phase out all live performance at its remaining Texas theaters. During the first week of May, stagehands and musicians at Majestic Theaters in Houston, Fort Worth, Dallas, and San Antonio were all terminated. For the local theater, the end came officially on May 17th, though Dallas, falling later on the circuit, hosted its final bill on May 21st.[39]

Through the summer that followed, talk persisted, fueled by comments in *Variety*, that RKO would soon construct a stage in the Hollywood, a movie house opened near the Worth on Seventh Street in April 1930. RKO had acquired the property in the spring of 1931 and, lending credence to the rumors, temporarily closed it for renovations. When the theater reopened on August 8, however, it was with motion pictures only. The Majestic, meanwhile, was boarded up and staff members were transferred to the Hollywood.[40]

RKO's profit-driven rush to celluloid, padlocking the stage door against all comers, had one readily apparent consequence: For the first time in nearly fifty years no local theater remained as a permanent home to professional stage performances—all had converted to motion pictures. Assessing the town's theatrical prospects in 1931, Robert Randol, amusements columnist for the *Star-Telegram*, mused glumly, "This town could do with actors in the flesh."[41]

Even so, the outlook was not entirely bleak. Over the next three seasons, road productions sponsored by the New York Theatre Guild, William Morris, and the Shuberts played sporadic one-night stands, with shows sandwiched between movie runs at the Worth or crammed into whatever municipal space had an open date. Several, like the company of *Of Thee I Sing*, George S. Kaufman's Pulitzer Prize-winning musical collaboration with the Gershwin brothers, barnstormed from Central High's stage, actors applying makeup and changing costumes behind makeshift partitions thrown up in the school's gymnasium. Taking to the local boards during the period were such venerable stars as Maude Adams, Otis Skinner, Katharine Cornell, Sir Harry Lauder, Eva Le Gallienne, Billie Burke, and a production of *Earl Carroll's Vanities*.[42]

Sixteen months after the shuttering of the Majestic, on the same day in January 1933, both Paramount-Publix, owner of the Worth, and RKO collapsed into receivership without ever reinstating live performances. Helping avert what very nearly became a complete entertainment debacle for the city was the intervention of Karl Hoblitzelle just as it appeared that three of Fort Worth's most important remaining theaters, the Worth, Hollywood, and Palace, might close their doors simultaneously. Learning RKO intended to shutter all its Texas theaters, throwing hundreds out of work, Hoblitzelle repossessed not only RKO's Texas chain but, in a deal worked out with court-appointed trustees, took over Paramount-Publix houses as well.[43]

Through various austerity measures, including the permanent abandonment of vaudeville, by 1935 Hoblitzelle had consolidated the chains as Interstate Circuit, Inc., and returned them to profitability. As a way to draw patrons back into the theaters, the corporation booked one-night stands by the big bands of Paul Whiteman, Cab Calloway, and Duke Ellington, and to capitalize on the lingering nostalgia for vaudeville, scheduled revival tours headlined by Eddie Cantor, George Jessel, and Dave Apollon. All, however, bypassed the Majestic, playing the larger Worth instead. Hoblitzelle continued the experiment through 1934, bringing live shows to the Worth for an extended fifteen-week trial. Running four nights a week, each unit served up four to five vaudeville acts, snappy production numbers built around a weekly theme, and a full-length, first-run motion picture. Starring in the *Swanee River Revue*, which ran in April 1934, was a young singer, Kate Smith.[44]

Interstate's timely intervention also brought an unanticipated benefit—in December 1933, the Majestic reopened after a twenty-seven-month hiatus, although it was permanently relegated to a bit role, picking up second-run motion pictures and occasional road shows. Even with the loss of status, between 1934 and 1954 the theater welcomed such notables as Helen Hayes in *Mary of Scotland*, Maurice Evans in *Richard II*, Alfred Lunt and Lynn Fontanne in *Idiot's Delight*, Katherine Hepburn in *The Philadelphia Story*, Mae West in *Come On Up*, Ethel Barrymore in *Whiteoaks*, Tallulah Bankhead in *Private Lives*, Judith Anderson in *The Old Maid*, and Cornelia Otis Skinner in *Paris '90*.[45]

The Worth and Hollywood, meanwhile, continued as the city's most high-profile movie houses for several more decades until the advent of multi-screen suburban cineplexes in the 1970s helped finish off downtown theater traffic. The Worth was imploded in October 1972. The neighboring Hollywood closed in 1974, although much of its interior remained, covered over and converted to a bank-processing center in 1979. Not until 1994 did salvagers finally complete the gutting of the corpse to make way for a parking garage, leaving only remnants of the art deco movie house.[46]

AND FORWARD TO CASA MAÑANA

In late 1935, a sequence of unlikely events, replete with screwball plot twists and a cast of eccentrics worthy of a Marx Brothers farce catapulted Fort Worth into the national spotlight, resuscitating its sagging theatrical fortunes. Bewildered Dallas city fathers, guardians of the "official" centennial flame, would be sent scrambling, trying to keep up, as livestock shows, except those showcasing the two-legged female variety, were relegated permanently to second billing.[47]

THE SHOW TO END ALL SHOWS: CASA MAÑANA, 1936-1939

"I've slept through so many [historical pageants]
I'm convinced they're financed by the aspirin people."
~Billy Rose

In June 1936, at the height of pre-opening ballyhoo for the Texas Centennial and its rival exhibition, Fort Worth's Frontier Centennial, a *March of Time* newsreel saluted "the war between the cities." *Fort Worth Star-Telegram* owner-publisher Amon G. Carter was shown marshalling local forces, proclaiming to a cheering crowd, "We're going to put on a show and teach those [Dallas] dudes where the West really begins!" From the centennial grounds thirty-five miles to the east in Dallas, sober-faced executive chairman Robert L. Thornton admonished his Fort Worth rivals, "It's going to take more than legs to attract the intelligence of the American people to an exhibition." Colonel Andrew Jackson Houston, octogenarian son of Texas hero and statesman General Sam Houston, sat studying press reports like a general mapping troop movements. "I don't know whether they're celebrating the birth of the Republic of Texas or the birth of musical comedy," he grumbled.[1]

The melodrama's final player sported a pair of oversized six-shooters strapped to his waist and wore a wide-brimmed, ten-gallon Stetson jammed down uncomfortably over his ears. The persistent swagger in his manner presented an odd contrast to the other men. From his uneasy perch astride a skittish cow pony, he lectured a tough-looking platoon of cowpunchers in an abrupt style that betrayed his Yankee origins. Stabbing the air with an oversized Cuban cigar as if to punctuate the gravity of his mission, he boasted, "This battle between Fort Worth and Dallas is right up my alley. If you people string along with me, I'll make Texas the biggest state in the Union." The cowboys whooped on cue, spooking the horse and nearly unseating its rider, a diminutive New Yorker and sometime Broadway producer named William Samuel Rosenberg—Billy Rose. [2]

How Rose, the fast-talking, chain-smoking son of Russian immigrants from Manhattan's Lower East Side, managed almost single-handedly to tip the lofty Texas

Hoping to make Fort Worth's Texas Centennial festivities competitive with Dallas' Central Exhibition, *Star-Telegram* publisher, Amon G. Carter, convinced skeptical city fathers to hire Broadway producer Billy Rose.

Courtesy, *Fort Worth Star-Telegram* Collection, Special Collections, University of Texas-Arlington Libraries

Centennial Celebration over on its ear became one of the more memorable episodes of North Texas folklore. In the process, Rose helped cement his own reputation as a showman, focused national attention on Fort Worth and the Southwest, and caused the staid *New York Times* to declare his Casa Mañana Revue "a spectacle that has no parallel in our curdled world."[3]

Until Rose's eleventh-hour entrance, Fort Worth, fourth largest of the state's metropolitan areas behind Dallas, Houston, and San Antonio, had resigned itself to a bit role in the centennial drama. In September 1934, in fact, it was neighboring Dallas, a city not even founded until several years *after* the Texas Revolution, that snared the lucrative central exhibition. What Dallas might have lacked in historical provenance, it soon made up in sheer monetary audacity and the single-minded drive of its corporate leadership: Robert L. Thornton, Fred Florence, and Nathan Adams, a triumvirate of the city's most powerful bankers. By June of 1936 as the centennial's grand opening approached, the final price tag of the exposition had ballooned from eight million to an astonishing twenty-five million dollars.[4]

Fort Worth, never even in the running for host city, wangled a modest $250,000 from the State Centennial Commission of Control to stage a "centennial livestock show and celebration," its June 1936 opening scheduled to complement the premiere of Dallas' central exhibition. Yet, even this relatively modest endowment angered some of the state's more vocal historical purists. A commentator for the *Dallas Morning News* huffed derisively that a "memorial to the livestock industry" placed Fort Worth "on parity with San Antonio and its Alamo and Houston, where was fought the Battle of San Jacinto, one of the seven decisive battles of the world."[5]

Such criticism might ordinarily have elicited howls of protest west of the Trinity, but in contrast to Dallas' municipal unity, the Fort Worth exposition was floundering in the clutches of civil unrest, seemingly destined for acrimonious demise. Efforts at planning had been repeatedly hamstrung by the conflicting purposes of two warring

Amon G. Carter persuaded Broadway producer Billy Rose to stage Fort Worth's 1936 Frontier Centennial with an offer of $100,000 for 100 days' work.

Courtesy, *Fort Worth Star-Telegram* Collection, Special Collections, University of Texas-Arlington Libraries

municipal groups. Unable to agree even on a site, city fathers bickered through much of 1935.

Stock Yards Company officials and Mayor Van Zandt Jarvis stumped vigorously to keep the event in North Fort Worth. The fifteen-acre parcel, bound by Exchange Avenue on the south and the stockyards on the east, included the North Side Coliseum, long home to the city's fat stock show, rodeo, and horse show. Opposing this location were several downtown business leaders, who lined up behind newspaperman Amon Carter to promote the much larger Van Zandt tract, two-and-a-half miles west of downtown. The plot, west of the Trinity's Clear Fork, lay between Camp Bowie Boulevard and Crestline Road east of Montgomery Street. In addition to its size, the property had the second advantage of lying along the route of a proposed extension of West Lancaster Avenue.[6]

The city council at first voted in favor of the stockyards location, but the cost of stabilizing the site and acquiring additional land eventually forced a reevaluation of the issue. A second vote several weeks later favored the Van Zandt tract. In an effort to pacify stockyards officials, the council agreed to a fateful splitting of the centennial—livestock events remained on the North Side while other exhibits moved to the Camp Bowie site. Court injunctions followed, seeking to force reinstatement of the council's original choice. Meanwhile, Public Works Administration officials threatened to cut off much-needed federal funding if work on the new complex did not begin immediately.[7]

Not until February 1936 did the city council finally open construction bids for the centennial's permanent buildings—a $1,600,000 municipal center whose major features included a six-thousand-seat indoor coliseum, 2,993-seat municipal auditorium, memorial tower, and permanent exhibit buildings. A pioneer settlement, ranch house, open-air amphitheater, army post, and Mexican village—temporary structures intended strictly for the centennial year—had yet to leave the planning stages. Although the celebration had acquired a new name—Frontier Centennial—City Hall's squabbling gradually pushed back the original June opening date, first to September 1 and then to September 15.[8]

It had become apparent that planners could not finish the new complex in time to compete with Dallas' central exposition, scheduled to be unveiled June 6. As bills and problems mounted, an impatient Amon Carter, with the blessing of the centennial board, began working behind the scenes to provide the Frontier Centennial with a much needed makeover.[9]

Outspoken and given to flamboyant publicity stunts promoting Fort Worth and West Texas, Carter had long resented the naming of Dallas to host the centennial exposition. His friend John Nance Garner, two-term vice president of the United States under Franklin Roosevelt, had once acknowledged, "Amon wants the government of the United States run for the exclusive benefit of Fort Worth and, if possible, to the detriment of Dallas."[10]

With media attention focused on Dallas, Carter needed a larger-than-life attraction with the right man to pull it all together. A "livestock and frontier days exposition" did not even come close to what he had in mind. He phoned Rufus LeMaire, a New York native who, along with his brother George, had spent much of his childhood in Fort Worth. Both eventually returned to the East to enter show business—Rufus working as a theatrical agent and George taking to the vaudeville circuits as half of a blackface comedy duo. With the advent of talking pictures, Rufus shifted his sights west to California, becoming a casting director for Metro-Goldwyn-Mayer.[11]

Though LeMaire declined Carter's offer, he contacted Billy Rose, a rising New York impresario. A relative unknown still in the formative stages of his career in 1936, Rose had long smoldered impatiently in the shadow of his wife, Ziegfeld Follies legend, Fanny Brice. Desperate for his own notoriety after only moderate success as a nightclub entrepreneur, songwriter, and sometime theatrical producer, he had once rented an electric sign rising eighteen stories over Broadway to spell out just two words—"Billy Rose."[12]

Until just after World War I, Rose seemed destined for a steady, if unglamorous, office career. A former New York state shorthand champion and protégé of both John Robert Gregg and financier Bernard Baruch, he had backed into show business almost accidentally. From show business acquaintances, he discovered that songwriters were making thousands of dollars simply churning out formula lyrics to feed the American public's insatiable appetite for new tunes.[13]

Rose abruptly scrapped his career as a stenographer for the uncertainties of the music business. Over the next several years he shared writing credits on a string of popular songs that included "Me and My Shadow," "That Old Gang of Mine," "It's Only a Paper Moon," and "Does the Spearmint Lose Its Flavor on the Bedpost Overnight?" He invested his profits in several moderately successful nightclubs, produced a couple of short-run Broadway revues, and in 1935 finally hit the bigtime with *Jumbo,* a musical circus extravaganza, staged in New York's cavernous Hippodrome Theater. The show, a critical, if not commercial success, drew over a million customers but closed after only 233 performances because of its staggering production costs.[14]

Jumbo, in fact, became an important rite of passage for Rose, demonstrating his flair for bringing together the best talent to realize ambitious creative projects. The show, under the steady hand of stage director John Murray Anderson, fused the libretto of playwrights Ben Hecht and Charles MacArthur with dozens of exotic animals, a large cast of circus greats, the comedic skills of Jimmy Durante, and a memorable score by Lorenz Hart and Richard Rogers. Thrown into the mix for good measure was "King of Jazz" big band legend, Paul Whiteman.

Rose, persuaded by LeMaire and John Hay Whitney, one of *Jumbo*'s key investors, agreed to meet with Fort Worth committee members in early March 1936. After touring the undeveloped Van Zandt tract and learning that the fair proposed commemorating the Battle of the Alamo, he grew increasingly skeptical. "The Americans lost. . . . Why have a celebration?" he reportedly quipped.[15]

Probing further, Rose learned that Dallas' central exposition was top heavy with monumental architecture, historical pomp, and grandiose demonstrations of industrial might. He told Frontier board of control members, "There's only one thing that can compete with twenty million bucks of machinery and that is girls . . . girls, and more girls." Estimating start-up costs at between $1 and $2 million, Rose warned planners not to expect to make money the first year.[16]

Board of control president William Monnig asked Rose about his fee. Rose was blunt: "I would like a flat $100,000."

Monnig managed to stammer, "That's a lot of money."

"That's right," retorted Rose, "but this involves a lot of work."

With Amon Carter guaranteeing the sum personally, the board soon voted in favor of the proposal although it took an additional $25,000 cash advance to persuade Rose to sign.[17]

Rose flew almost immediately to New York to assemble a production staff. His parting comments to the local press avoided mentions of struggling pioneers, martyred patriots, or epic struggles for independence, while including plans for "a mammoth open air dance floor accommodating 3,000 couples." One of his first moves was to scrap many of the Centennial's original "frontier" exhibits and veto any sort of historical pageant. He told members of the Chamber of Commerce, "I've slept through so many of those things I'm convinced they're financed by the aspirin people."[18]

With every new pronouncement, Rose veered further away from Travis and Crockett, Goliad, and the Alamo. He declared his intention to move *Jumbo* lock, stock, and barrel to the wilds of Fort Worth. All two hundred performers, with the exception of comic lead Jimmy Durante, shortly signed on for the trip. He took out ads in *Variety* and *Billboard* comparing himself to legendary showman P.T. Barnum and dismissing the Dallas Centennial Exposition as a "pale carbon copy of the Chicago

World's Fair." By contrast, the Fort Worth show, Rose proclaimed, "will offer to America . . . a Living, Breathing, Highly Exciting Version of The Last Frontier."[19]

Winning the lucrative design contract for the main open-air pavilion and other major structures was Fort Worth architect Joseph R. Pelich. Construction contracts went to three other local firms—Harry Friedman, James T. Taylor, and Thomas Byrne. Rose himself set up shop in the downtown Sinclair Building at the corner of Fifth and Main streets while he awaited construction of a new office in a frontier-style block-house overlooking the entrance to the centennial grounds. He quickly settled into a grueling routine—shuttling twice weekly between Texas and New York via eleven-hour plane flights and putting in twenty-hour workdays.[20]

In one of his early press conferences, Rose informed reporters, "The exposition in Dallas will show the progress of art, education and culture, . . . but my exposition will show just the opposite if possible." Exercising his powers as director-general, he soon banished "educational" frontier life exhibits to the periphery of the fair grounds except for a recreated western street laid out just east of the centennial's front entrance on the corner of West Lancaster and Arch Adams.[21]

By April, an army of laborers had begun laying the groundwork for several large structures devoted entirely to entertainment. To house *Jumbo,* architects designed a circular, 2,800-seat building modeled with a single ring in the style of European

The Frontier Follies building, soon to be renamed Casa Mañana, offered outdoor seating for 4,000, and a 130-foot-wide revolving stage that "floated" backward to reveal a water-filled lagoon.

Courtesy, *Fort Worth Star-Telegram* Collection, Special Collections, University of Texas-Arlington Libraries

indoor circuses. For "The Last Frontier," a musicalized rodeo-Wild West pageant, an open-air pavilion and arena complete with artificial waterfall and mountains, began taking shape. Workers outfitted the Pioneer Palace, built to resemble an old-time variety hall and saloon, with slot machines, an expansive dance floor, and an elevated stage behind the mirrored forty-foot bar.

To house the "Frontier Follies," the exhibition's centerpiece attraction, construction began on a four-thousand-seat outdoor cafe-amphitheater. The structure possessed a number of unique architectural features, including the world's largest revolving stage—130 feet in diameter and weighing 17,000 tons. Richard Bruckner, a Russian immigrant who had previously engineered the machinery for *Jumbo*, designed the complex engineering required for the platform. A complete revolution of the stage, controlled by a 450 horsepower motor, required one minute and forty-five seconds.

The stage itself rested on metal tracks in a tank of water nine feet deep, making it appear to "float" toward or away from the audience. A second, equally powerful motor

Exterior view of Casa Manana's front facade, 1936, left and an aerial view of the theater and showgrounds, right. Key structures include Casa Mañana, upper left; The Last Frontier, upper right; the round Jumbo edifice; and triangular-shaped Pioneer Palace, center.

Courtesy, *Fort Worth Star-Telegram* Collection, Special Collections, University of Texas-Arlington Libraries

drove this action. Surrounding the stage "island" was a manmade lagoon measuring 130 feet by 175 feet and containing 617,000 gallons of water. Pipes mounted along the front rim of the lagoon and at the bottom of the pool shot fountains of water into the air to provide a curtain effect. The central structure of the revolving stage, combining a permanent theatrical set, twin bandstands, and dressing rooms located beneath, weighed a total 4,364,000 pounds.[22]

The rest of the theater was as monumental in scale as its stage. Over thirty blue-and-white Spanish-style arches, each rising nearly thirty feet to the roof, stretched 280 feet around the curve of the building's 320-foot frontal façade. The roofed area supported by the arches sheltered lavish horseshoe boxes and a fifty-foot bar. Patrons walking through this covered promenade re-emerged into the open air on the other side. Before them, in a scaled-down version of a Greek theater, graduated tiers of seating spread out in a wide fan, gradually descending to the water-filled lagoon and stage at the bottom. Tables and chairs placed along each tier permitted customers to

dine in comfort while awaiting the start of the show. Double rows of smaller arches, stacked one on top of the other, framed the perimeter of the outdoor seating area and extended onto the stage setting as well, continuing the design of the immense entryway.[23]

If Billy Rose was not universally well known in 1936, he was rapidly developing a reputation for organizational abilities far beyond his five-foot-two-inch physical stature. For *Jumbo,* Rose had attracted some of the most talented writers, designers, and technicians of the New York theater community. This same staff, virtually intact, followed him to Texas. The list included stage director John Murray Anderson; scenic designer Albert Johnson; choreographers Robert Alton and Lauretta Jefferson; technical wizard Carlton Winckler; and costume designer Raoul Pène du Bois. To create the estimated two thousand costumes needed for the centennial's various shows, he engaged Brooks Costumes, one of New York's oldest and most respected theatrical firms.[24]

Stage director John Murray Anderson with one of Casa Mañana's stars, Ziegfeld Follies dancer, Ann Pennington.

Courtesy, *Fort Worth Star-Telegram* Collection, Special Collections, University of Texas-Arlington Libraries

John Murray Anderson, appointed stage director for all shows connected with the Frontier Centennial, had produced some of the leading musicals of the 1920s and directed the Ziegfeld Follies. Between 1927 and 1928, while working for Publix Theater Circuit, he created a series of flashy unit shows that toured Publix theaters across the country, including Fort Worth's newly opened Worth. Whatever the assignment, Anderson's formula remained the same: visual splendor coupled with a slender story line or theme, comedy, escapism, and ranks of beautiful girls.[25]

Scenic designer Albert Johnson had designed over fifty shows as artistic director of Radio City Music Hall. Costume designer Raoul Pène du Bois, though only twenty-four, already had to his credit both Radio City Music Hall and the 1934 Ziegfeld Follies. Twenty-one-year-old composer Dana Suesse had debuted her "Waltz Rhapsody" at Carnegie Hall when just seventeen. She had several popular hits to her credit, including "You Ought To Be In Pictures," and "Whistling In the Dark." "The Night Is Young and You're So Beautiful," written specifically for the Frontier Centennial, was later recorded by such artists as Bing Crosby and Mario Lanza and became so popular with audiences during 1936 that Rose adopted it as the centennial's unofficial theme song.[26]

To complete his staff, Rose named local musician Hyman Maurice to serve as musical director for all shows. A product of the Warsaw Conservatory, Maurice had immigrated to the United States following World War I after touring as a member of the Russian symphony. In the United States he joined the Publix theater circuit as John Murray Anderson was assembling the first show sent out over the circuit. Maurice was sent to Fort Worth as orchestra director and remained to make the city his home even after the Worth abandoned weekly shows in 1928.[27]

Although the name Frontier Centennial stuck, by late spring the amphitheater housing the Frontier Follies had acquired a glossy new title—Casa Mañana, the House of Tomorrow. With the mechanics of production finally in place, Rose announced open auditions for dancers and showgirls, promising reporters, "There won't be a woman in the show who isn't a looker." The lure of $25 a week in an era of widespread unemployment brought a deluge of applicants that caught even Rose off guard. Several thousand hopefuls descended on the city, some trekking hundreds of miles from surrounding states.[28]

Preliminary tryouts held at the North Side Coliseum were later moved to the Hotel Texas as less suitable candidates were weeded out. The dancers and showgirls eventually assigned spots in the Casa Mañana Revue came from diverse backgrounds and brought with them a variety of youthful ambitions. Many, teenagers too young even to sign their own contracts, had to have their parents sign for them.

One girl, a young mother and dance instructor, age twenty-two, drove the short distance from Weatherford, Texas, to audition. Though she displayed obvious talent, Rose advised her to go home and forget show business. Two years later, while attending the New York debut of Cole Porter's *Leave It To Me*, John Murray Anderson noticed the same girl featured in a show-stopping song-and-dance number, "My Heart Belongs to Daddy." He looked up her name in the program. The girl he and Rose had rejected as hayseed talent was Mary Martin, who went on to star in some of the post-World War II era's most popular musicals, including *South Pacific, The Sound of Music,* and *Peter Pan.*[29]

When dancing auditions failed to produce talent in sufficient quantities, Rose imported twenty-eight dancers and showgirls from New York to bolster the ranks of local talent. Their arrival signaled the beginning of rehearsals for all major shows. Murray Anderson, assisted by choreographers Alton and Jefferson, set a withering pace for Casa Mañana performers in the humid confines of Monnig's Wholesale Warehouse at 1619 Main Street. A few blocks away at the City Recreation Building on Vickery Street, saloon girls from the "Pioneer Palace Revue" and sixty-eight teams of square dancers for "The Last Frontier" practiced cancan routines and clog steps under the direction of Alexander Oumansky, late of the Diaghileff Russian Ballet.

Shortly after his hiring, reporters asked Billy Rose to explain his strategy. His response soon became the official rallying cry of the Fort Worth Centennial: "Let Dallas educate the people. . . . We'll entertain 'em in Fort Worth." In keeping with this pledge, crews began plastering signs and billboards across Texas and several surrounding states. The posters featured a smiling, scantily clad cowgirl astride a bucking horse. At the same time, the centennial's colorful, if specious, official advertising brochure began circulating widely. Beneath overblown text celebrating Casa Mañana's "lovely freight of 250 Eye-Bedeviling Coryphees," topless showgirls paraded across the stage and frolicked nude in the theater's lagoon.[30]

Other publicity tactics included a beauty contest and a daring series of raids that took Rose's crews to the very gates of the fort. The statewide quest for "Texas' Sweetheart Number One," culminated in a pageant held at Fort Worth's Central High School auditorium on May 30. Winner of the contest, nineteen-year-old Borger cashier Faye Cotton, earned a spot in the Casa Mañana Revue and a six-month movie contract. About the same time, workers began putting the finishing touches on a giant neon marquee, 130 feet long and forty feet high atop a building directly opposite the main entrance of the Dallas Exposition. A bucking bronco and flashing letters seventeen feet tall proclaimed the message, "Wild & Whoopee Forty-Five Minutes West."[31]

Sally Rand's appearance in the 1936 Casa Mañana Revue stirred controversy locally while generating national publicity for the Frontier Centennial. After Rose pronounced her fans "dated," Rand performed instead holding a more revealing oversized balloon.

Courtesy, New York Public Library, Billy Rose Theater Collection.

SALLY RAND

1477-83

The coup de grâce, however, in Rose's battle plan was the booking of Sally Rand as Casa Mañana's trophy attraction. After years as a bit player in vaudeville and movies, Rand's ascent to questionable fame began in 1932 when she danced nude behind ostrich-feather fans in a Chicago nightclub. In 1933 she broadened her acclaim with nightly performances in the Streets of Paris, one of the Chicago World's Fair's popular midnight concessions. She disdained the label "stripper," permitting the audience to see only what she wished them to, styling her act "ballet divertissement." "The Rand is quicker than the eye," she became fond of boasting.[32]

While Rand's $1,000-dollar-a-week salary reflected her status as Casa Mañana headliner, Rose announced his intent to take full advantage of his resident cause cèlébre. Just outside *Jumbo*'s main entrance, workers began installing a new concession—Sally Rand's Nude Ranch. Patrons entered "Ranch" headquarters between matched pairs of buxom, red-maned, undraped caryatids, their upstretched arms supporting the roof. Another set of equally well-endowed Aphrodites reclined provocatively atop the roof. Inside, fifteen girls, bare-breasted except for strategically positioned green bandanas, lounged "with nothing to prevent them benefiting from the Texas night air." Rand, who always appeared fully clothed, served as hostess and greeter.[33]

Sally Rand's Nude Ranch, a Frontier Centennial "peep show" featured Rand fully clothed and fifteen bare-breasted cowgirls with "nothing to prevent them from benefiting from the Texas night air."

Courtesy, Dalton Hoffman

Sally Rand's Nude Ranch.
Fort Worth Frontier Centennial.

As the Centennial's opening date drew closer, Rose finally admitted to plans for several other "peep" shows. Dallas officials, who had previously bristled at the mention of such "adult" entertainment, responded by issuing health cards to twenty-four hundred prostitutes operating out of houses near the centennial grounds, loosening enforcement of gambling and liquor control laws, and opening its own "Streets of Paris," modeled after the 1933 Chicago Exposition. Religious leaders in both municipalities mounted protest campaigns, and the *Houston Press* made light of what it impishly styled, "The Battle of the Nudes."[34]

"King of Jazz" bandleader Paul Whiteman with his wife, actress Margaret Livingston. Whiteman had worked previously with Rose in *Jumbo*.

Courtesy, *Fort Worth Star-Telegram* Collection, Special Collections, University of Texas-Arlington Libraries

The lineup of talent booked for Casa Mañana would have been sufficiently impressive even without Sally Rand. One of the biggest "name" stars set to appear was "King of Jazz" bandleader Paul Whiteman and his orchestra. Whiteman's popularity had reached its zenith in the years between World War I and the Depression, a period that saw the decline of ragtime and the birth of the jazz age. Booked to fill Casa Mañana's second bandstand opposite Whiteman was Joe Venuti and his orchestra. The first great violinist of jazz, Venuti had worked as a sideman in several top bands, including Whiteman's, as well as fronting his own group.

Besides Rand, Whiteman, and Venuti, Rose also signed former Metropolitan Opera star Everett Marshall, who had turned to the more lucrative Broadway stage and movies after making his Met debut at age twenty-five. His resonant baritone on such numbers as "Another Mile" and "The Night Is Young and You're So Beautiful" quickly made him a favorite of local theatergoers. Ann Pennington, star for over a decade of both the Ziegfeld Follies and George White's Scandals, was also featured. The tiny

Chorus girls dance onstage in Casa Mañana's opening scene, the St. Louis World's Fair.

Courtesy, Fort Worth Public Library, Local History and Genealogy

dancer, with a purported shoe size of only one and a half, signed to appear as "Little Egypt," the legendary belly dancer whose sensuous numbers scandalized America during the 1904 St. Louis World's Fair. Other performers signed as feature acts included the dance team of Gomez and Winona, comedian Walter Dere Wahl, the Lime Trio, and Gareth Joplin. Replacing Jimmy Durante as the comic lead of *Jumbo* was Eddie Foy, Jr.

On July 17, one day before the Frontier Centennial's official opening, Billy Rose and Amon Carter jointly hosted a preview of the Casa Mañana Revue for over a thousand prominent magazine, radio, and newspaper editors and reporters from across the United States. At the conclusion of the final scene, the invitation-only crowd leaped spontaneously to its feet to give Rose, Murray Anderson, and Carter a rowdy standing ovation. Robert Garland of the *New York World* called the revue "a stage show glorified out of all knowing. I can't tell you the half of it. Casa Mañana is as big as Texas." Even the usually reserved *New York Times* seemed at a loss for words:

> Plenty in the argot of our avenues is the verdict of eyewitnesses
> returned from the scene of the commotion. Gentlemen famed for
> their veracity raise their hands high and solemnly state that in the
> Casa Mañana Mr. Rose presents a spectacle that has no parallel in
> our curdled world.[35]

The commentary of rival Dallas reporters was equally unrestrained in praise of the show. Calling the Revue "staggering," *Morning News* columnist John Rosenfield proclaimed, "The show beggars description.... Two hundred girls and principals and sets larger than life fill the 130-foot stage." He termed the show "Billy Rose's valid bid for international attention," and conceded, "We doubt that anything else so large or sumptuous has risen from the pavements of the world's capitals, let alone the Texas prairie."[36] Jimmy Lovell, *Times-Herald* critic agreed:

> Billy Rose . . . had produced a series of spectacles which
> challenge the use of all the "rave" synonyms in the dictionary . . .
> it is one of the most fabulous affairs which could be offered by
> the most imaginative showman.[37]

Fort Worth Press columnist Jack Gordon rhapsodized,

Never before have there been so many girls on a single stage.
Never before was there a stage large enough to accommodate
them. Never before have such huge stage sets been built. Not once
were so many lights trained on one stage. Here is something to
make Ziegfeld turn in his grave—in sheer admiration.[38]

By opening day, July 18, both performances of the Casa Mañana Revue had sold
out. At exactly 3:30 P.M., President Franklin Roosevelt, fishing off the coast of Maine
onboard the presidential yacht, *Sewanna,* paused long enough to press an electronic
button. By means of an elaborate hookup, the button activated a radio impulse that
traveled via telegraph three thousand miles to Texas. The tiny impulse triggered a
knife, which then severed a ribbon attached to a cowboy lariat, officially opening the
Fort Worth Frontier Centennial. Twenty-five thousand customers poured through the
main gates the first day, paying prices ranging from fifty cents for a general admission
ticket to $1 for the celebration's major attractions, *Jumbo* and Casa Mañana.[39]

At precisely 6:30 P.M., Casa Mañana swung wide its gates to receive first-nighters.
The heat did little to wilt the high spirits of merrymakers who danced to the rhythms

Casa Mañana first nighters await
the start of dinner, July 18, 1936.
Hamburgers went for 40 cents
and a steak with all the trimmings
could be had for $2.00.

Courtesy, Fort Worth Public Library,
Local History and Genealogy

of Joe Venuti's orchestra on the wide expanse of the revolving stage and dined from a menu that offered fare ranging from forty-cent hamburgers and thirty-cent beer to prime rib for $1.50 or a bottle of Piper Heidsieck champagne going for the top price of $7.50. Wine by the glass could be had for as little as thirty-five cents.[40]

At 8:00 maestro Paul Whiteman stepped into position at center stage. At his signal, the two bands swung into the opening fanfare of the Casa Mañana Revue, the "Cavalcade of World's Fairs." Simultaneously Carlton Winckler's battery of spotlights, the strongest ever assembled to that time, sprang to life, and the center of the mammoth stage glided back to reveal the water-filled lagoon. The million-pound structure began a slow revolve, unveiling scenic designer Albert Johnson's fanciful interpretation of the 1904 St. Louis World's Fair. Showgirls and boys dressed as St. Louis belles and beaus strolled arm in arm and a male quartet serenaded the audience with such turn-of-the-century favorites as "Meet Me In St. Louis," and "The Good Old Summertime" as Billy Rose's hand-picked chorus line "enacted at a dizzying pace a dozen romantic, sentimental episodes of the period."[41]

Next came Ann Pennington in her daring impersonation of Little Egypt, her entrance heralded by, "Watch her shake, not a bone in her body, like a bean in a bowl of jelly." Finally, as Everett Marshall crooned "The Night Is Young and You're So Beautiful," beauty contest winner Faye Cotton entered, draped in a $5,000 gold-plated, brass-mesh gown created by New York jewelers Whiting and Davis.[42]

For the Paris Exposition of 1925, the stage revolved repeatedly to reveal such legendary Parisian locales as Maxims, the Moulin Rouge, the Folies Bergère, and the Eiffel Tower wrapped in five thousand miniature lights. Spontaneous applause repeatedly drowned out the music. But it was the third episode, built around the 1933 Chicago Century of Progress Exposition, that many in the crowd had come to see.

As the lights deepened to blue, Sally Rand stepped from a niche within the art-deco curves of a modernistic wall. Rose had pronounced her fan routine "dated," so Rand performed with a huge opalescent balloon specially designed by Goodyear Rubber Company. Her props made little difference—the Rand presence held the audience spellbound, including *Star-Telegram* music critic E. Clyde Whitlock, whose usual copy ran to symphony concerts and chamber music recitals. He reported, "The petite . . . dancer toys with an enormous bubble with charming grace and illusion. The music is hot and jazzy, but never cheap, and the furiously fast-clicking feet of the hordes of dancing girls is exhilarating."[43]

The final scene, listed vaguely as a "Masque of Texas," featured "Indians" decked out in flashy, gold-feathered headdresses and dozens of showgirls and dancers parading past the audience in scanty gold costumes reputed to symbolize Texas under the six flags of France, Spain, Mexico, the Republic, the Confederacy, and the United States. As Everett Marshall sang "Lone Star," Venetian gondolas floated incongruously into the lagoon and Ann Pennington popped out of a papier-mâché "hundred gallon" cowboy hat. Jets of water lit by dozens of rainbow-colored lights erupted from the lagoon, and the combined orchestras of Whiteman and Venuti broke into "The Eyes of Texas," bringing the audience uproariously to its feet singing, whistling, and cheering.

For the next seventeen weeks, front porch sitting became a favored nightly sport as music spilled out of Casa Mañana and washed into surrounding neighborhoods. What investors lost in cash return on their investments, Fort Worth soon made up for in national exposure. In the wake of the media blitz surrounding the premiere, the city became a magnet for high rollers, congressmen, sports figures, and show business luminaries. The guest list of notables included Vice President and Mrs. John Nance Garner, Army Air Corps flying ace Major Jimmy Doolittle, novelist Ernest Hemingway, FBI director J. Edgar Hoover, Broadway producers Earl Carroll and George White, and former heavyweight boxing champ Max Baer.

Despite its popularity, an assortment of problems continued to dog the Frontier Centennial throughout its run. *Jumbo,* presented in a poorly ventilated building where temperatures sometimes soared to 100°, lost $30,000. The addition of fans had little effect. Cast members fainted and after only six performances star Eddie Foy, Jr. suffered the indignity of having his entire part cut as the show's running time was slashed from two hours to just one. The musical was forced to close three weeks early. To help compensate for *Jumbo*'s losses, Rose ordered Casa Mañana's admission price raised from $1 dollar to $1.50. Weekend tickets skyrocketed to $2 dollars. On November 1, Sally Rand quit, exiting with ten of Casa Mañana's best dancers. Furious, he confiscated her V.I.P. pass, only to watch helplessly as she gleefully purchased eleven tickets and paraded the entire party to prime ringside tables.[44]

Revelers continued to jam the amphitheater night after night, with standing-room-only crowds of six thousand for weekend and midnight performances. In Pioneer Palace, business also boomed as patrons tried their luck at nickel slot machines or pressed six deep against the bar to hear Lulu Bates sing "I'm In Love With a Handlebar Moustache" to Tom Patricola. Equally popular were the Tiny Rosebuds, a sextet of lady dancers ranging in weight from a relatively petite 215 pounds to a hefty 340.

By closing day, November 14, the Frontier Centennial had lost $97,000, but few seemed to notice or care. Though Billy Rose was already hard at work on a new project,

Cleveland's Great Lakes Exposition, in March 1937, he and his entire production team signed for an all-new version of Casa Mañana and the Frontier Centennial, renamed for its second year, the Frontier Fiesta. Everett Marshall and Paul Whiteman also agreed to return, but Larry Lee's orchestra replaced Joe Venuti's in Casa Mañana's second bandstand. Other acts accorded feature billing included adagio team Moore and Revel, the Stuart Morgan Dancers, and ballerina Harriet Hoctor.

Plans announced for the 1937 Casa Mañana Revue called for scenes from four best-selling novels: *Wake Up and Live, Lost Horizon, It Can't Happen Here* and, most significantly, 1936's publishing phenomenon, *Gone With the Wind*. Without the publicity potential of a Sally Rand, Rose's team turned to pageantry instead. Raoul Pène DuBois and Brooks Costumes set about the task of creating seven hundred new costumes as crews began assembling sets worthy of a Roman circus. Just one, *It Can't Happen Here,* weighed nine tons and required forty stagehands to maneuver its eleven sections into position.[45]

The Six Tiny Rosebuds, one of the most popular attractions of the Pioneer Palace.

Courtesy, *Fort Worth Star-Telegram* Collection, Special Collections, University of Texas Arlington Libraries

The first signs of trouble emerged as rehearsals got underway. *Press* amusements columnist Jack Gordon flew to Cleveland to see Rose's new *Aquacade,* reporting back, "I'm convinced [he] has moved everything but the mortgage up from the Fort Worth Centennial." Though Cleveland's outdoor amphitheater rested on barges in Lake Erie, a number of its features, including water curtain and moat were carbon copies of Casa Mañana's. Many of the show's acts and musical numbers had simply been reconstituted for Cleveland crowds. Before season's end, this flair for appropriating popular venues to his own use was destined to embroil both Rose and the Frontier Fiesta in litigious controversy.[46]

Rose's casual reuse of numbers might ultimately have been tolerated had it not been for a steadily growing list of other managerial and personal blunders. Amidst persistent rumors that Rose and his Aquacade star, Olympic swimmer Eleanor Holm, were having an affair, the problems inherent with staging two shows simultaneously

Dress rehearsal for *Wake Up and Live* on Casa Mañana's stage, 1937.

Courtesy, Dalton Hoffman

began to take their toll. Several dancers whose parts had been dropped from the Pioneer Palace revue continued on payroll, while in Casa Mañana, choreographer Lauretta Jefferson had choreography for just one of the revue's four scenes. When the show ran long, large segments had to be cut, but not before Brooks Costumes billed the Fiesta $7,500 for costumes completed but never used. The board also found itself contractually obligated to pay the full $3,000 salary of one specialty act whose segment was cut. Yet one week before the June 26 opening date, Rose still insisted on holding most of his production staff in Cleveland.[47]

Opening night, every new revolution of Casa Manana's stage revealed colossal sets, each seemingly designed to surpass its predecessor in outlandish splendor. *Gone With the Wind* featured a three-story, southern antebellum mansion, fronted by white columns twenty-six feet tall. At one point, the structure burst into flame, an effect achieved by the burning of yellow sulfur. Hidden pipes channeled smoke through the mansion's windows. Harriet Hoctor, portraying Scarlett O'Hara, swept in on pointe, leading *Variety* to observe dryly, "in a few minutes on her toes, [she] wipes out a good 600 pages of the original work." Everett Marshall, in his role as Rhett Butler, crooned "Gone With the Dawn," a song touted by Rose as the successor to "The Night Is Young and You're So Beautiful."[48]

For the show's grand finale, *It Can't Happen Here,* Rose's production team shamelessly blended spectacle with a jingoistic display of flag-waving nationalism that had little to do with Sinclair Lewis' original tale. Beneath threatening banners, totalitarian armies of Blackshirts, Brownshirts, and Redshirts, symbolic of fascism, Nazism, and communism, swarmed across the stage. American forces of land, sea, and air massed to engulf them as four miniature battleships steamed into the lagoon firing cannons. Showers of fireworks exploded and Whiteman and Lee's orchestras launched into "The Stars and Stripes Forever." The Symbol of Peace, portrayed by Mary Dowell, daughter of Fort Worth's captain of detectives (later police chief) A. E. Dowell, ascended the four-story chromium-plated staircase, her white satin gown framed by a ten-foot pair of white wings. Twenty-four trainbearers extended the gown's cape until it completely covered the expanse of the gargantuan set.[49]

Other attractions of 1937 paled in comparison to Casa Mañana's epic displays. In place of The Last Frontier, "Flirting With Death" offered a bill of circus-style daredevil acts, while in the hapless *Jumbo* building, Melody Lane showcased eight popular tunesmiths and their best-known works. Among those appearing were David Guion, writer of "Home On the Range;" "Twelfth Street Rag" composer Euday Bowman; and Joe Howard, composer of "I Wonder Who's Kissing Her Now." The Pioneer Palace once again featured its "Honky-Tonk Revue," topped by vaudeville hoofer Pat Rooney, Jr., and his son, Pat Rooney, III.

Rose's 1936 formula alternating fast-paced comedy routines with show-stopping production numbers had helped make the Casa Mañana Revue a consistent money-maker with an average attendance of forty-three hundred a night. By contrast, his shift in 1937 to bookish themes and pageantry fell flat with audiences. Over the first nine weeks, the gate declined sharply—down 45 percent from 1936. Both Everett Marshall and Harriet Hoctor had to endure salary cuts.[50]

On the heels of the Fiesta's mounting financial difficulties came other problems. Dancer Hinda Wassau's "Evolution of the Strip-Tease" in the Pioneer Palace triggered fresh accusations of obscenity from local church leaders and demands from city council that Rose make changes. When the council threatened to close the show permanently, Rose finally obliged, ordering Wassau to perform wearing G-string and brassiere for the remainder of the season. The surge of neoconservatism even spread to Casa Mañana, where modifications in several revealing costumes were ordered.[51]

Casa Mañana's 1937 grand finale *It Can't Happen Here*, featuring the Symbol of Peace, Mary Louise Dowell, whose cape required 24 train bearers to lift.

Author's collection

In September, Rose's tenuous credibility suffered a final blow from a source unrelated to charges of indecency or sagging box office receipts. Mrs. John Marsh, better known as Margaret Mitchell, sued the city, claiming the Frontier Fiesta and Rose had knowingly "pirated" her novel, *Gone With the Wind.* The most incriminating evidence in support of her claim proved to be the scene itself. Besides featuring several of Mitchell's best-known characters, the segment followed the plot of the novel closely. On September 14, in a federal court hearing, Rose's five percent of gate profits was ordered impounded, although the injunction stopped short of seizing sets and costumes.[52]

As Fiesta attorneys scrambled to absolve Fort Worth of any legal blame in the matter, Rose's contract with the city was abruptly terminated. On September 26, one day before a scheduled court hearing and three weeks earlier than originally planned, Casa Mañana and the Frontier Fiesta closed. Not until three months later did Rose and Mitchell finally settle out of court, Rose agreeing to pay the author $3,000 plus an additional $25,000 if any further attempts at plagiarism came to light. In a personal letter to Fiesta board chairman Will K. Stripling at the close of legal action, Mitchell apologized for involving the city in her suit against Rose.[53]

At the conclusion of the 1937 season, crews razed most centennial buildings except for Pioneer Palace and Casa Mañana, but public support for the theater remained strong despite Rose's many faults. To fill the gap left by his departure, the city in 1938 hired Music Corporation of America to produce a scaled-down version of the Casa Mañana Revue. Producer Lou Wasserman and director Paul Oscard mounted an abbreviated four-week season but continued in the established formula of packaging big-name bands with specialty vaudeville acts and nationally known headliners.

Though local auditions once again furnished the dancing corps, an almost spartan economy replaced the opulent sets, and custom-designed costumes of the Centennial and Fiesta years. Simple strands of rainbow-colored lights hung from stage arches served as backdrop for a rotating bill of seven variety acts and four production numbers that changed fortnightly. Oscard choreographed energetic dance turns spotlighting "hot" trends in music and dance with the big bands of Wayne King and Jan Garber providing musical accompaniment. The new austerity led to fears that theatergoers accustomed to Rose's extravagance might stay away, but by opening night, July 29, all four thousand of Casa Mañana's seats had sold out.[54]

Headliners of 1938 included dancer Edna Sedgwick, tight-wire clown Hal Silver, knockabout trio The Three Nonchalants, Horton Spurr, and singer Morton Downey. Downey and Wayne King's band proved so popular with crowds that their contracts were extended for the entire season. The largest crowd in Casa Mañana's three-year history turned out on August 24 to see ventriloquist Edgar Bergen and his wooden sidekicks, Charlie McCarthy and Mortimer Snerd. By closing day, August 27, nearly ninety thousand paid admissions had passed through the turnstiles. Confidence, indeed, ran so high that the theater's permanence seemed assured.

The launch of the fourth season did little to dispel this notion. Under the aegis of New York talent moguls the William Morris Agency and executive producer Lou Wolfson, Casa Mañana opened July 21, 1939, for an extended six-week run. The parade of talent through the summer was impressive: vocalist Kenny Baker from Jack Benny's weekly radio program; comedienne Martha Raye; Bob Burns, the "Arkansas Traveler"; Ziegfeld legend Eddie Cantor; Frances Langford, featured singer of Texaco Star Theater; and eccentric dancer Ray Bolger, fresh from completion of a new movie, *The Wizard of Oz*. The bands of Russ Morgan, Abe Lyman, and Ray Noble all took their turns in the cabaret's bandstand. By the end of the show's first two weeks, attendance surpassed the same period in 1938, and audiences continued to build through the rest of the season.

Growing apprehension that European hostilities would soon expand to America following Germany's invasion of Poland in September 1939 brought a change in public sentiment toward the theater. Just weeks before the scheduled opening of the cabaret's fifth season in June 1940, Music Corporation of America canceled the show, fearing the war scare's nationwide effect on the amusement industry. Local directors attempted to rally support for a bond election to raise the estimated $225,000 needed to make the amphitheater a permanent structure, but several petition drives through the fall of 1941 elicited only a guarded response from the city council. After a coalition of religious leaders complained about the appropriateness of spending city money on an entertainment facility in wartime, in November 1941 the council tabled the matter indefinitely. With the December 7th attack on Pearl Harbor, the United States entered the war, effectively ending all efforts to reconstruct the theater.[55]

Six months later, on May 11, 1942, crews began the orderly destruction of what had once been touted the showplace of the nation. Like mourners, hundreds of spectators showed up to pay their final respects. The crush grew so great that police stationed special officers to discourage souvenir hunters. When the job was completed, only the derelict steel skeleton of the revolving stage remained as a rusting, bleak reminder of what had been for many the Casa Mañana era.

CHAPTER TEN

CHURCH-BASED INITIATIVES
AND FEDERAL GIVEAWAYS:
1936-1945

"At the present time there is no legitimate theatre
in Fort Worth, and no permanent . . . company
operating anywhere in the vicinity of the city."
~1935 WPA report

*J*ust months before the Fort Worth centennial committee announced the hiring of Billy Rose, a 1935 report by the WPA's Federal Writers Project noted pessimistically, "At the present time there is no legitimate theatre in Fort Worth, and no permanent . . . company operating anywhere in the vicinity of the city." With the exception of Casa Mañana's Broadway-style musical revues, which continued to attract audiences through the summer of 1939, the situation would remain virtually unchanged through the end of World War II. The only other local organization with a comparable record of successful stage production during the period was First Methodist's Footlite Club, an improbable alliance of church-based amateur thespians, who became one of the most successful amateur groups of the 1930s and 1940s under the leadership of I.E. McWhirter.[1]

Beginning in 1930, at a time when support for other groups was beginning to wane, members of the club, all active in McWhirter's "Co-Worker" Sunday school class, staged as many as four productions a season in a run that lasted several years past the war into the 1950s. The company, organized by Mrs. Dan Creson and Mrs. Boone Goode, used various directors including McWhirter, Myrtle Dockery, Bill Terry, Everett Morris, and R.E.H. "Dick" Gaedke. Several, like Morris and Gaedke, were also influential in such postwar theatrical organizations as the Fort Worth Dramatic Club, Convair's Wing and Masque Players, and the Greater Fort Worth Community Theater.[2]

In contrast to the Footlite Club's success, the Little Theater mounted no productions for several years following Robert Nail's departure in 1935. There did remain an active core of players, however, who made occasional efforts to revive the movement between 1938 and 1946. Three years after Nail's controversial staging of *Porgy,* Lotta Carter Gardner persuaded the director to make a brief return in an effort to rebuild the company. In August 1938, he staged *Dangerous Corner* in the garden behind Gardner's Lipscomb Street home, but, following this play, no new productions were staged for several seasons.[3]

Not until 1941, under a new board led by president William P. Fonville and vice-president Harrill Bridgess, did the group reorganize as the Fort Worth Community Little Theater. A membership drive gathered over six hundred subscribers, and the season opened in Will Rogers Municipal Auditorium in November 1941 with a production of *The Male Animal* staged by Clyde Godbold. Several productions followed, including *First Lady, Margin For Error,* and *The Bellamy Trial,* directed by TCU instructor Arthur Faguy-Cote and staged in October 1942 in Judge Willis M. McGregor's courtroom in the downtown Criminal Courts Building. After military enlistments severely depleted its acting ranks, the movement lapsed, despite a brief effort to reorganize the company in 1946.[4]

Attempts to establish a permanent local unit of the Federal Theater Project (FTP), also fell apart after just a handful of productions. The FTP, created in the fall of 1935, was designed to provide employment for thousands of laid-off actors, stagehands, technicians, and musicians across the nation. Appointed to head the program, championed by Franklin and Eleanor Roosevelt, was Hallie Flanagan, director of the Vassar Experimental Theater.

While FTP productions in other parts of the country embraced political commentary and various social issues, state Works Progress Administration (WPA) officials claimed more conservative Texas audiences would reject "any new kind of play." Small professional companies set up in Dallas, Houston, and Fort Worth steered clear of controversy, restricting their offerings to such bland fare as historical pageants, marionette shows, and one-acts that initially played without admission fees in parks, schools, and auditoriums. Charles L. Morgan, president of the Fort Worth Theater Guild, served as chairman of the organizational committee for the Fort Worth company. Others on the board included Dr. Frank S. Schoonover, Harry McGown, Mary Hartman, Lotta Carter Gardner, Mrs. James Taylor, and Mrs. C. D. Reimers.[5]

Fort Worth's FTP professional troupe began rehearsals in the spring of 1936 at 1312 West Tucker in a former church previously used as a playhouse by both the Little and Community theaters. The company's inaugural event, a pair of one-acts, premiered April 28, 1936, directed by Richard L. Slaughter. Appearing in *The Dear Departed* were Mable Fletcher, Harry Hearn, Minnie Gladstone, O.H. Glor, and Ann

Barrier. The second production, *Wonder-dark Episode,* also featured Madison Bartlett, Lady Katrin Fine, Johnny Schuller, and Pauline Nobblett. The Fort Worth Theater Guild, a support organization that had survived after the disbanding of the Little Theater, sponsored *Prince of Liars,* a more ambitious three-act production. Staged outdoors at Hillside Park on Maddox Avenue, the comedy's first performance attracted a crowd of five hundred, but after strong winds created problems, remaining performances had to be moved indoors to the Tucker Street playhouse. Following this event, the group mounted no more productions.[6]

Blanchard McKee directed the Town Players, the local FTP amateur group. For a time the company performed in the Vickery Boulevard City Recreation Building. McKee mounted at least two productions, *The Donovan Affair* and *The Barrier,* in the spring of 1936 before the facility was commandeered for rehearsals of Frontier Centennial shows. Amateur players participating in the plays included Bates McClellan, Dick Finnegan, Charles Wilson, Carl Wevat, H.A. Mierding, Elizabeth

The Federal Theater Project, begun in 1935, sponsored both professional and amateur theatrical productions and marionette shows presented at no cost in parks and recreation centers.

Courtesy, WPA "American Hands In Action" photo album, Special Collections, University of Texas-Arlington Libraries

The 2,993 seat Will Rogers Municipal Auditorium, designed by architects Wyatt C. Hedrick and Elmer G. Withers was formally dedicated in December, 1936.

Courtesy, W.D. Smith Collection, Special Collections, University of Texas-Arlington Libraries

Bryan, Jean Morgan, A.B. Waldron, Jr., Marjory Young, Paul Patterson, and Walter Hoyt. Arthur Balfour created settings for the company.[7]

One other important municipal success story emerged from an otherwise lackluster period in the city's theatrical history. On November 16, 1936, two days after the end of Casa Mañana's inaugural season, Will Rogers Municipal Auditorium opened just to the west of the Frontier Centennial grounds with a concert by violinist Jascha Heifetz. Like other centennial buildings, including the outdoor amphitheater, money to complete the 2,993-seat hall and its companion structures, the Will Rogers Memorial Coliseum and Tower, had come from federal funds. Overall design of the complex was by architects Wyatt C. Hedrick and Elmer G. Withers with actual construction, which began in February 1936, carried out by three local firms: Butcher and Sweeney, R.F. Ball, and James T. Taylor. Exterior and interior decorations were all the work of Hedrick's lead designer Herman Koeppe.[8]

The auditorium's curving, monumental front facade, designed in a restrained, late art deco style known as PWA Moderne, consisted of six Indiana limestone piers faced with fluted pilasters. Running across the top of the facade and appearing to rest on the vertical piers was Koeppe's colorful tile mosaic frieze, depicting scenes from the settlement of the West.[9]

Walls of the hall's austere lobby were finished in Texas shell stone ornamented only by fluted molding, black-and-white striped terrazzo floor, and recessed lighting. The auditorium's interior was equally restrained. Among the few ornamental elements were masks of comedy and tragedy on either side of the stage and oblong aluminum screens pierced with plant and sunburst motifs. Interior walls painted in graduated shades of blue complimented the deep blue proscenium arch and crimson grand drape. A patriotic red, white, and blue color scheme embellished the ceiling.[10]

Monumental facade of Will Rogers Municipal Auditorium, capped by Herman Koeppe's mosaic frieze depicting the settlement of the west.

Courtesy, W.D. Smith Collection, Special Collections, University of Texas-Arlington Libraries

The hall's forty by ninety-eight foot stage, fifty foot wide proscenium opening, and forty-nine pipe fly chamber capable of handling drops up to sixty-five feet tall represented a considerable step forward from previous municipal spaces. Designed with the most up to date sound and lighting systems for the time, the hall quickly attracted road show productions that for several years had been staged in the Worth Theater or the auditoriums of Central High, Paschal High, and First Baptist Church. The auditorium remained the city's principal live performance facility for over three decades until the opening of the Tarrant County Convention Center and Theater in 1968 shifted most cultural and theatrical events downtown.[11]

CHAPTER ELEVEN

THE FORT WORTH CIVIC OPERA
AND ITS PREDECESSORS:
1878-2001

"Even in the midst of a beautiful solo, he persisted in sticking up
his ugly mug and prompting the singer in a stage whisper,
audible in all parts of the hall . . ."
~*Democrat,* November 28, 1880

*I*n May 1946 New York's Metropolitan Opera company staged a series of operas
in Dallas' State Fair Music Hall. Two Fort Worth women, Jeanne Axtell and Betty Berry
Spain, attended the presentation of *Madama Butterfly* but discovered that their high-
priced seats were behind a post. Both had additional reasons for feeling disappointed.
Spain had studied voice seriously for several years, including time spent training in
New York and Boston during World War II while her husband, TCU government professor A. O. Spain, served in the U. S. Navy. She gained professional experience singing
for NBC Radio and in the chorus of *One Touch of Venus,* starring Weatherford actress
Mary Martin, before returning to Fort Worth at war's end. Axtell, a talented composer
and pianist raised in California, had married a local man, Herbert G. Axtell.[1]

Days later, Spain recalled the Dallas experience to another friend, Eloise
MacDonald Snyder, wife of Fort Worth surgeon Dr. F. L. Snyder and daughter of
C. Wilbur MacDonald, who had for a number of years served as fine arts dean of the
old Polytechnic College (Texas Wesleyan University). Snyder suggested staging an
opera locally to showcase the talents of area singers and musicians. She, too, had a
serious interest in opera. In 1945, before her husband's illness forced her return to
the city, she had made her debut with the New York City Center Opera as Arsena in
The Gypsy Baron. Socially well connected, Snyder proposed a bolder undertaking—
organizing a permanent opera association. The two women enlisted Axtell to serve as
the third member of the operatic triumvirate. On May 29, 1946, the three women filed
for a state corporation charter under the name Fort Worth Civic Opera Association,
and by July the association had opened its first office in the *Star-Telegram* building on
West Seventh.[2]

While the 1946 founding of an opera association represented a bold step in Fort Worth's relatively short history, opera had long been a part of the city's cultural landscape. There had been at least one previous attempt to establish a permanent organization in the years before World War I, although the history of grand opera in the city extended back over three decades prior to the war. The earliest recorded presentation by a grand opera company came in November 1880 with the arrival of the Tagliapietra Italian Opera Company. One of the sponsors of the event, which was repeatedly postponed after the company's train was delayed, was Walter A. Huffmann, who within three years would finance the construction of the Fort Worth Opera House.[3]

When the troupe finally arrived several days late, the assorted cancellations, persistent gloomy weather, and a steep $1.50 admission price had frozen the resolve of all but the most determined opera lovers—the curtain opened on a half-empty house. The company manager responded by cutting entire scenes, leaving the flustered prompter to guide singers through the wreckage of the libretto.

Next day, a critic for the *Democrat* harrumphed disgustedly, "Even in the midst of a beautiful solo, he persisted in sticking up his ugly mug and prompting the singer in a stage whisper audible in all parts of the hall and confusing even the performers."[4] And while praising the company's principals as "the finest ever [to visit] this section of the state," the reviewer called the decision to eliminate "some of the most beautiful sections of the opera" an "insult to the intelligence of the audience." He warned, "Companies that do not intend to do their best under any circumstances are advised to keep away from Fort Worth."[5]

He need not have worried. Over the next hundred and twenty years, opera would play a significant role in shaping the city's cultural identity. Beginning in the 1880s, several successive civic organizations, including the Fort Worth Musical Union, the Apollo and Municipal Opera choruses, the Grand Opera Association, and the Civic Music Association all played important roles in staging opera in Fort Worth. The Civic Opera Association, its title later changed to the Fort Worth Opera, eventually became the longest continuously active municipal opera association in Texas.[6]

In the beginning, however, touring companies seldom strayed from stock repertoires wallowing in romantic comedy and farce that required little staging. Adah Richmond's Opéra Bouffe Troupe, a forty-member company, had been the first of these troupes to arrive, presenting Planquette's *Chimes of Normandy* and Offenbach's *La Perichole* during a two-night stand in November 1878. The company returned the following season for a performance of von Suppé's *Fatinitza.*[7]

In the twenty-year period between 1880 and 1900, a number of these comic opera companies began making regular stops in the city. Most notable were the companies of Czech manager Maurice Grau and Austrian Heinrich Conreid, each of whom eventually became impresario of New York's Metropolitan Opera House. During a dozen Fort Worth appearances between 1883 and 1902, Grau's various companies played engagements of two to six nights offering a varied mix of popular operettas and comic operas.[8]

Completion of the Opera House in 1883 encouraged an increasing number of nationally known opera singers to adjust their cross-country schedules to include Fort Worth. Such stars as Italo Campanini, Emma Juch, Ernestine Schumann-Heink, Clara Louise Kellogg, and Emma Abbott all made appearances in the city. By far, the most important event of the Opera House's first season was the appearance of Minnie Hauk, who had been handpicked in 1878 by English impresario James Henry Mapleson to sing the title role in Bizet's *Carmen* in both its English and American premieres.[9]

By March 1884, when Hauk performed at both the Dallas and Fort Worth opera houses, she was becoming as well-known for her narcissistic outbursts as her high notes. Following her Dallas appearance, she arrived too late at the Dallas depot to catch the westbound train to Fort Worth. She demanded that the station agent divert a train for her personal use, offering $500 for his trouble. Explaining that all he had available was a switch engine, the agent offered to let the soprano ride in the locomotive's open cab for a mere $250. Hauk declined. Reaching Fort Worth aboard the next regularly scheduled passenger run, Hauk immediately canceled the first night's performance, ignoring the fact that the rest of her entourage and a fifteen-hundred-pound Steinway concert grand piano had arrived without her half a day earlier.[10]

Emma Abbott's popularity was such that between 1878 and 1880, her company, the sixty-member Emma Abbott English Opera Company, had been chosen to open no fewer than thirty-five new opera houses across the country. Officials of the Fort Worth Opera House had tried to secure her services for its premiere in October 1883 but could not meet her price. When she did finally reach the city in December 1885, "large and fashionable" crowds turned out to hear her in Balfe's *The Bohemian Girl* and Thomas' *Mignon*.[11]

By the turn of the century, grand opera presentations, often scheduled together over several nights between November and March helped define a winter "season" for the elite of Fort Worth society. Among the more prominent touring companies to mount full-scale productions in the Fort Worth Opera House and later the Byers

Opera House, were the Aborn English Opera Company and the Henry W. Savage Grand Opera Company. Between 1905 and 1913, these two companies were responsible for the first complete local stagings of *Tannhauser, Carmen, Rigoletto, Lohengrin, Lucia di Lammermoor, Il Trovatore,* and *Pagliacci.* Henry W. Savage, producer of the American premiere of Puccini's *Madama Butterfly* in October 1906, had, by the next season, already mounted a touring version, which reached Fort Worth January 24, 1908. Fortune Gallo's San Carlo Opera also made its first local appearance in 1914, returning to the city periodically for the next three decades.[12]

Phillip Greenwall's announcement in April 1916 that the Byers Opera House would drop legitimate theater in favor of vaudeville threatened the coming season of grand opera. Moving productions to the Majestic, always tightly booked with vaudeville, posed obvious problems, so in late May, a group of prominent Fort Worth businessmen gathered at the Field-Lippman Piano Company on Houston Street to discuss solutions. By meeting's end, the Fort Worth Grand Opera Association had become reality, with dry goods entrepreneur W.C. Stripling chosen as its president. Within days, sixty-six guarantors had pledged $20,000 to assure the appearance of Chicago's C.A. Ellis Grand Opera Company, under the baton of director Cleofonte Campanini, in its only Texas appearance.[13]

From 1916 to 1919 the North Side Coliseum on Exchange Avenue, became the scene of grand opera presentations featuring the Ellis and Chicago Grand Opera Companies.

Courtesy, Quentin McGown

Coliseum, Fort Worth, Texas.

To accommodate the two-hundred-member company, which boasted full chorus, orchestra, and corps de ballet, with principals drawn from the Chicago Opera, New York's Metropolitan Opera, and Milan's La Scala, the fledgling association spent $7,500 remodeling the North Side Coliseum. A wood covering and seventeen hundred seats went down on the arena floor, and an existing stage at the north end of the coliseum was greatly enlarged. To support the troupe's grand-scale scenery, originally constructed for the Chicago Grand Opera House, a grid of battens and over three miles of rope went up. Tickets for each performance sold at a top price of $5 with boxes seating six or eight going for $45 and $60.[14]

By the last week of October, the Grand Opera Association had logged reservations from Texas, Arkansas, and Oklahoma and from as far away as Ohio and Colorado. Opera devotees poured into the city aboard special trains, filling most local hotels to capacity. Before seven o'clock opening night, October 27, an enormous crowd already filled the grounds of the coliseum with lines several spectators wide snaking around the building and spilling onto Exchange Avenue a hundred yards in each direction. To handle the unexpected crush, officials had to delay the opening curtain thirty minutes.[15]

At eight-thirty, over six thousand patrons had shoehorned into the arena, exceeding original attendance estimates by nearly twenty-five hundred and filling the hall to standing room only. Even $1 seats with no view of the stage sold out. The attraction was a dazzling galaxy of operatic talent brought together by Ellis and Campanini, including Geraldine Farrar, one of the Met's principal sopranos; Lucien Muratore, who had served as principal tenor of both the Paris and Chicago operas; Louise Homer, one of the Met's most versatile contraltos; Leon Rothier, the Met's principal bass; and baritone Clarence Whitehill, noted for his Wagnerian roles. Scheduled to perform was Czech soprano Emmy Destinn, but during an ill-timed return to war-torn Europe, she had been placed under house arrest by Austro-Hungarian authorities. Soprano Marie Rappold replaced her.[16]

Matching the brilliance of the performers was the society-box crowd, glittering in an array of sequined lace, charmeuse, taffeta, brocade, and diamonds unmatched in the city's history. Singer Lina Cavalieri, renowned as the most beautiful woman of opera and wife of Lucien Muratore, created a mild sensation as she entered the arena draped in full-length ermine coat, black gown, and diamond headdress. Over the next two nights, at least ten thousand heard performances of *Carmen* led by Farrar and Muratore and *Il Trovatore* featuring Rappold, Homer, and Morgan Kingston. Until the Grand Opera Association finally disbanded in 1919, the coliseum operas remained the highlight of the fall social season.[17]

Metropolitan Opera soprano Geraldine Farrar, one of the stars of the Ellis Grand Opera Company.
Author's Collection

A second round of performances in 1917, this time with Campanini's own Chicago Grand Opera Company, brought two more widely acclaimed divas to the coliseum stage. Nellie Melba sang the role of Marguerite in *Faust,* and rising young singing sensation Amelita Galli-Curci appeared as *Lucia di Lammermoor.* Galli-Curci's final mad scene brought the crowd to its feet for twenty-one curtain calls. Melba's appearance in *Faust* fared less well. The performance came to an abrupt halt when an overhead batten loaded with heavy lighting equipment suddenly crashed to the floor, striking the diva and knocking her unconscious for several minutes. Doctors rushed from the audience to attend her backstage as an understudy hurriedly prepared to go on. Severely bruised but unwilling to disappoint the crowd, Melba recovered sufficiently to return to the stage after a quarter-hour delay.[18]

The nationwide influenza epidemic forced cancellation of the 1918 tour, but in March 1919 the Creatore Company brought *Aida, Rigoletto,* and *Cavalleria Rusticana* to the much smaller Savoy Theater on Jennings. Not until October 1919 did the Chicago Grand Opera finally return to the coliseum, an event that also marked the return of Emmy Destinn. She appeared in Verdi's *A Masked Ball* opposite tenor Alessandro Bonci, along with productions of *Aida,* featuring Rosa Raisa, and *Madama Butterfly* with Tamaki Miura and Clarence Whitehill.[19]

High production costs and Campanini's death finally ended the coliseum operas following the 1919 season, but just one year later the Harmony Club, under the leadership of Mrs. John F. Lyons, scored yet another coup, persuading legendary tenor Enrico Caruso to include Fort Worth on his 1920 cross-country tour.

So great was Caruso's appeal to the general public that by World War I, nearly every American household with a Victrola had a Caruso recording. The announcement of

Legendary tenor Enrico Caruso, whose October, 1920 Fort Worth appearance at North Side Coliseum set off a stampede for tickets.

Courtesy, *Fort Worth Star-Telegram* Collection, Special Collections, University of Texas-Arlington Libraries

his first Texas appearance precipitated a deluge of ticket requests, prompting organizers to continue adding seats to the Fort Worth Coliseum. With just hours to go before the October 19 concert, eight thousand seats had been sold. The fabled tenor sang only three arias in a program that also featured soprano Alice Miriam and violinist Albert Stoessel. After both "Che Gelida Manina" from *La Bohème* and "Una Furtiva Lagrima" from *L'Elisir d'Amore* he responded to "thunderous applause" by singing eight encores, finally closing the evening with the aria most closely associated with him, "Vesti La Giubba" from *Pagliacci*.[20]

As early as the 1880s the Fort Worth Choral Union, which included on its rolls such prominent local singers as haberdasher Nat M. Washer, had staged a number of Gilbert and Sullivan operettas with local talent. The same group was likely responsible for two operettas staged in the Texas Spring Palace in 1889–1890. In the fall of 1905, shortly after the opening of the first Majestic Theater, a local company directed by Rowland D. Williams and Phillip Epstein presented *The Sorcerer* to packed houses. But perhaps the most important promoter of civic opera in the early decades of the twentieth century was Samuel S. Losh.[21]

Born in Perry County, Pennsylvania, in 1884, Losh trained in voice and piano at Germany's Leipzig Conservatory and later taught music at Texas Christian University in Waco. When the university relocated to Fort Worth in 1910, Losh followed, establishing himself as a mainstay of the local music scene over thirty years. He played in the Fort Worth Symphony Orchestra under both Carl Venth and Brooks Morris and served as choir director of Broadway Presbyterian, First Christian, and the Reform Jewish congregation, Temple Beth-El. In 1912, Losh established a new municipal choir, the Apollo Chorus.[22]

Sam S. Losh, c. 1911, shortly after his arrival in Fort Worth as a music instructor for Texas Christian University.

Courtesy, Fort Worth Public Library, Local History and Genealogy

With this chorus, which by 1922 had changed its name to the Fort Worth Municipal Chorus, Losh staged several operas between 1917 and 1929. Favorite principals included Pearl Calhoun Davis, Lillie Bogen Morris, Mabel Helmcamp Neely, Frank Agar, Charles Moore, Walker Moore, J. Oscar Webster, and William J. Marsh, whose tune "Texas, Our Texas," became the official state song in 1929. As its first effort, the chorus performed *Faust* with guest tenor Ellison Van Hoose of the Metropolitan Opera in the title role. An estimated three thousand filled the Majestic Theater for two performances, May 1–2, 1917.[23]

Faust was followed by *The Mikado* (1918), *Aida* (1921), *Cavalleria Rusticana* and *I Pagliacci* (1922), *Il Trovatore* (1924), *Rob Roy* (1925) and *Faust* (1929). With adult principals and students of the Losh Institute of Music and School of Expression, founded in 1924, he also presented *H.M.S. Pinafore* (1926) and *Cavalleria Rusticana*

(1927). A final production, *Rigoletto*, featuring Mrs. Harry B. Friedman as Gilda, Marion Sansom, III, as the Duke, and Allen Rubottom as Rigoletto, was staged in March 1936 at the Community Theater building on West Tucker.[24]

The 1929 stock market crash helped end Losh's run of homegrown operas, but by the late 1930s, some professional companies had resumed touring. Karl Hoblitzelle's reorganized Interstate Circuit sponsored Fortune Gallo's San Carlo Opera Company as a yearly feature in Interstate's Texas theaters for several seasons until World War II disrupted theatrical touring for several years.

Several years after the establishment of the Civic Opera Association in 1946, longtime Fort Worth music critic and teacher, E. Clyde Whitlock recalled of the time, "Fort Worth was ripe for opera." Within a matter of weeks following the official incorporation of the opera association, MacDonald, Axtell, and Spain had managed to enlist an impressive cross-section of the city's prime business and cultural movers.

Eight thousand fans pack the Northside Coliseum on October 19, 1920, to hear legendary tenor Enrico Caruso on what would ultimately be the final concert tour before his death. His only other Texas stop was Houston.

Courtesy, Enrico Caruso Papers, John Hopkins University, Peabody Institute, Archives and Special Collections

Chamber of Commerce president Web Maddox agreed to serve as president of the opera board. Murray Kyger of First National Bank served as treasurer; Clifton Morris of the accounting firm McCammon, Morris, Pickens, and Mayhew became vice president in charge of fundraising, and Brooks Morris, conductor of the Fort Worth Symphony Orchestra since its reestablishment in 1925, served as vice president in charge of educational relations.[25]

In addition to becoming the organization's first business manager, dean of Texas Christian University's School of Fine Arts T. Smith McCorkle provided university facilities for rehearsals and students for the opera chorus. Other TCU faculty members took key roles on the opera's production staff. Dr. Walther R. Volbach, who had come to the United States as a refugee from Germany in 1937, was an ideal choice for stage and artistic director. He had produced more than seventy operas during tenures with municipal opera companies in Germany and Austria. Voice instructor Arthur Faguy-Cote acted as chorus master and associate director.[26]

Cast members of the Fort Worth Civic Opera's first production, *La Traviata* in November 1946. Left to right, George Stephens, Melvin Dacus, James Robinson, and Lou Marcella. Singing the role of Violetta was Eloise Snyder MacDonald, company co-founder.

Courtesy, *Fort Worth Star-Telegram* Collection, Special Collections, University of Texas-Arlington Libraries

Money for the association's first production, *La Traviata,* came from 213 sponsors, but with a bare bones operating budget of just $6,600, the production staff of twenty-four and business staff of six labored without pay. Assisting were still other volunteers, including the 129 members of the organization's advisory board. "There were so few of us that everyone went to meetings even if we were not designated as board members," recalled longtime opera board member Ahdel Chadwick. Budgeted items included orchestra, conductor, stage directors, imported principals, wardrobe mistress, stagehands, and scenery and costume rental, but most other necessities, including stage properties, were donated by local businesses and individuals.[27]

Even at this early stage the association's founders insisted on the most capable personnel available. Spain remembered, "I wanted people that had [performance] experience and people that were good singers [for] building an organization." The task of selecting a qualified ensemble proved more daunting than planners had anticipated. Open auditions held in the old Paschal High School over three nights in

Eloise Snyder MacDonald (Violetta) and Melvin Dacus (George Germont) rehearse a scene from *La Traviata.*

Courtesy, *Fort Worth Star-Telegram* Collection, Special Collections, University of Texas-Arlington Libraries

August attracted singers from several municipal opera companies, but other applicants had more ambition than real ability. Asked to describe the experience some years later, Walther Volbach reminisced, "We suffered every evening from eight until eleven." The final cast, distinctly local in character, represented a broad cross section of the community.[28]

Iwo Jima campaigner and head of the North Texas State Agricultural College voice faculty Melvin Dacus, who would later become general manager of the opera, took the role of George Germont. Another combat veteran, TCU music major George Stephens played the Marquis. Aircraft research engineer James F. Robinson was cast as the doctor, and local radio singer Helen Hunter sang the part of Flora. Other roles went to secretary and First Congregational Church soloist Betty Pecor; New York native and Fort Worth Army Airfield serviceman Lou Marcella; and American Airlines meteorologist Walter Porter. Cast in the lead role of Violetta was opera co-founder Eloise MacDonald Snyder. New York City Center Opera Company tenor Eugene Conley headed the cast as Alfred Germont.[29]

Along with staging the opera, Walther Volbach also conducted early orchestra rehearsals. Eventually, however, Walter Herbert, Frankfurt-born general director of the New Orleans Opera, was brought in to conduct the thirty-six-piece orchestra. Herbert also advised the company on such important matters as repertory, casting, general policy, and rehearsal schedules. TCU music students made up the thirty-five-voice chorus and dancers from Denton's Texas State College for Women formed the corps de ballet. Opening night, November 25, a crowd of nearly three thousand dressed in "Golden Horseshoe splendor" gathered in Will Rogers Memorial Auditorium to witness the Civic Opera's premiere effort. *Dallas Morning News* critic John Rosenfield lauded the production as "the start of something," calling it "a performance of competence and balance."[30]

Rosenfield praised Eloise MacDonald's "impressive technique" as Violetta, though he remained skeptical of Conley's dramatic skills. Calling him "not the best actor nor the worst," he still ranked the guest artist as "one of our better tenors" with a voice that "flowed lyrically over a wide range." Also singled out was "the suave, covered vocal production" of twenty-three-year-old baritone Melvin Dacus, cast incongruously as Conley's father. Conley, who was performing the opera in English for the first time after just one company rehearsal, spent much his time between scenes reviewing the libretto.[31]

With respectable box office receipts from two large if not sold-out houses, the association moved ahead with a second production, *Madama Butterfly*. Except for

Cio-Cio-San, played by New Orleans Opera soprano Tomiko Kanazawa, and Pinkerton, sung by Gabor Carelli, local talent filled roles for the production, staged March 24 and 26, 1947. Other principals included Betty Spain as Suzuki, Melvin Dacus as Sharpless, and Mamie Friedman as Cio-Cio-San's mother.[32]

Walter Herbert continued as guest conductor through the 1948–1949 season, building on the modest first season with productions of *I Pagliacci, The Old Maid and the Thief,* and *Rigoletto* in 1947–1948 and *Carmen, La Bohème,* and *The Bartered Bride* in 1948–1949. Walther Volbach, feeling the pressure of his teaching duties, withdrew as stage director after *La Traviata,* replaced by a series of distinguished professional directors that included Robert C. Bird, Armando Agnini, Glynn Ross, Dino Yannopoulos, Ralph Herbert, Michael Pollock, and William Wymetal. For Fort Worth's centennial celebration in June 1949, Ross directed a restaging of the 1889 Spring Palace production, *The Texas Mikado,* sponsored by the opera association and the Tarrant County Historical Society.[33]

Walter Herbert, guest director of the Fort Worth Civic Opera from 1946-1949, seen here in 1947 with Betty Berry Spain, Opera co-founder, and Tomiko Kanazawa and Gabor Carelli, stars of *Madama Butterfly,* the Opera's second production.

Courtesy, *Fort Worth Star-Telegram* Collection, Special Collections, University of Texas-Arlington Libraries

By 1949, at the urging of its second president, Julian Meeker, the association had also initiated a $25,000 capital campaign to engage its first resident general director. Through an agreement reached with the TCU fine arts department, which helped fund the position, the new director would head a university opera workshop in addition to his duties with the civic opera. In June the association hired Austrian native Karl Kritz, an associate conductor for both the Metropolitan and San Francisco operas with broad European experience. His early professional credits included service as chorus master and assistant conductor of the Nuremberg Opera House from 1927–1933 and as first assistant conductor of the Berlin State Opera House from 1935–1937.[34]

Jeanne Axtell Walker, center, with members of the cast of *The Bartered Bride*, 1949. L-R, Patty Karkalits, Walker, Maurice Harkins, and Betty Bynum Webb.

Courtesy, *Fort Worth Star-Telegram* Collection, Special Collections, University of Texas-Arlington Libraries

An outspoken advocate of opera in English with an aversion to amateurism, Kritz challenged local performance standards during four seasons in Fort Worth. He also introduced innovative and sometimes controversial program formats aimed at attracting new audiences. The strategy limited the stagings of tragic works to just four in four seasons—*Faust, Lucia di Lammermoor, Il Trovatore,* and *Tosca.* Kritz also targeted the city's perceived "western" sensibilities with a 1951 staging of Puccini's *Girl of the Golden West,* based on David Belasco's 1905 melodrama set in the California gold mining camps.[35]

Karl Kritz, an advocate of opera in English, became the Civic Opera Association's first full-time general director in 1949, serving until 1953

Courtesy, Fort Worth Opera Association

Other offerings during Kritz's tenure were a calculatedly upbeat blend of comic opera, operetta, and even a cowboy ballet. The 1950–1951 season featured *Rosalinda,* an Americanized version of Strauss's *Die Fledermaus, The Marriage of Figaro,* and *Shindig,* an original "Texas-ballet," staged by David Preston, head of the TCU ballet department. Two years in a row, Kritz staged popular operettas in conjunction with the annual stock show. *The Merry Widow*'s five-day run beginning in January 1952 featured movie comedians Edward Everett Horton as Popoff and Sig Arno as Nish and drew large crowds even as rodeo events galloped ahead in the coliseum next door. Kritz reprised the event in 1953 with *The Desert Song,* showcasing the talents of another film comic, Sterling Holloway.[36]

At the end of the 1953 season, Kritz resigned to accept a position with the Pittsburgh Opera. He had grown increasingly frustrated by teaching responsibilities and by what he termed local "pick-up orchestras." Throughout his tenure, community leaders had remained resistant to reorganization of the city's symphony orchestra, dormant since 1942. As his replacement, the association next hired English conductor Geoffrey Hobday. Hobday remained for just one season, producing only two operas, *Hansel and Gretel* in January 1954 and *Madama Butterfly* in April 1954. *Madama Butterfly* was distinguished by the presence of Licia Albanese, a leading Met soprano, in the role of Cio-Cio-San, and Eugene Conley, another member of the Met, as Pinkerton.[37]

Still without a full-time managing director, the Civic Opera Association in 1954 embarked on the most ambitious series of productions since its founding eight years earlier. *Salome,* featuring New York City Center Opera stars Brenda Lewis and Walter Cassel opened the season in November 1954. The event, cosponsored by the Dallas Symphony Orchestra and conducted by Walter Hendl, also debuted Fort Worth soprano Sara Rhodes in the final scene of Richard Strauss' 1942 opera, *Capriccio,* believed to be only the second American presentation. The season's two remaining shows, *Carmen* and *Martha,* were both conducted by Walter Herbert.[38]

German-born conductor Rudolf Kruger became the association's third musical director in May 1955. Kruger's long-term vision brought much needed direction and focus to the organization, something it had lacked under Kritz and Hobday. As he completed his twenty-fifth season with the Fort Worth Opera in 1980, the Metropolitan Opera's *Opera News* recognized his achievement, observing: "During his tenure, Kruger has transformed a valiant amateur effort into one of the finest, most stable small opera companies in the United States, [achieving] this with very little money." His hiring ushered in a new era of artistic growth for what had been through its first decade, a company focused principally on local talent.[39]

German-born Rudolf Kruger, shown rehearsing chorus members in 1955, served as conductor and general director of the Opera for 27 seasons (1955-1982). Kruger gave early opportunities to such rising stars as Placido Domingo and Beverly Sills.

Courtesy, *Fort Worth Star-Telegram* Collection, Special Collections, University of Texas-Arlington Libraries

Kruger was born in Berlin in 1916 to Austrian parents but fled the country in 1938 because of the Nazi takeover. Hans Schwieger, conductor of the Southern Symphony Orchestra in Columbia, South Carolina, brought Kruger to the United States in 1939 as his assistant conductor. He subsequently accepted similar posts with both the New Orleans Symphony and the New Orleans Opera House Association, served in the U.S. Army, and worked with the Chicago Light Opera and companies in Jackson, Mississippi, and Mobile, Alabama.[40]

Under Kruger's management between 1955 and 1963 the Fort Worth Opera steadily gained prestige, expanding its repertoire with productions of *Don Pasquale* (1957), *Aida* (1958), *The Magic Flute* (1958), *Manon* (1959), *A Masked Ball* (1960), *Samson and Delilah* (1961), *Boris Godounov* (1961), *The Bartered Bride* (1962), and *Turandot* (1963). Though the opera chorus continued as a volunteer organization for several more years, Kruger began a gradual shift away from other amateur practices that had marked the company's early history. Trained under the more autocratic European conductor-impresario system, the Maestro, as he soon became known locally, exerted complete artistic control in addition to conducting all performances.[41]

The overall effect of Kruger's changes was a new level of professionalism in productions. For principal roles, he recruited singers—some already name stars—from leading American companies. At the same time, he shifted local talent and students from the TCU Opera Workshop to less demanding comprimario (secondary) roles. Where previous directors had reduced orchestrations to compensate for the lack of a permanent orchestra, Kruger, by contrast, insisted on a full complement of musicians for each production.[42]

Within two years, the elevation of standards had brought the city to an important turning point: the Fort Worth Symphony Orchestra was reorganized in 1957 as a seventy-two-member ensemble with TCU music professor Robert Hull as conductor. Automobile dealer Ernest Allen, Jr., and opera co-founder Eloise Snyder became the organization's first president and its organizing director. Meanwhile, Kruger's measured but persistent hand in raising artistic standards was acknowledged in 1958 when the opera board enhanced his title to music director and general manager. Following Hull's resignation, Kruger also served as musical director of the symphony from 1963–1965 and of the Fort Worth Ballet from 1965–1966.[43]

By 1962 the company was operating in the black, thanks in part to a small staff and careful money management by Kruger and opera assistant general manager William Massad. This record continued for nearly twenty seasons until shortly before Kruger retired in 1982. Even by 1981–1982, when the Dallas Opera's four productions cost $2.3 million dollars, Fort Worth offered a comparable series with just four fewer performances for only $655,000.[44]

Though season subscriptions steadily increased, generous underwriting by such individuals as Lura and Fred B. Elliston, Mary D. and F. Howard Walsh, and Elizabeth and Otho C. Armstrong played a pivotal role in the continued well-being of the organization. In addition, a 1963 five-year, $100,000 grant from the Ford Foundation helped the company extend its season from two or three operas to four. Kruger used the yearly $20,000 Ford increments to continue expanding the company's repertoire with productions of Offenbach's *Tales of Hoffmann* (1964), Delibes' *Lakmé* (1965), and *Lohengrin* (1965), the first Fort Worth production of a Wagnerian opera and perhaps the first by a Texas civic opera company.[45]

Over the next fifteen years, grants from the J. Ralph Corbett Foundation, the Texas Commission on the Arts and Humanities, Sears-Roebuck, the Gramma Fisher Foundation, the Martha Baird Rockefeller Fund for Music, and the National Endowment for the Arts further improved both the opera's monetary and artistic footing. The Arts Council of Greater Fort Worth, organized in 1963, remained the opera's largest contributor, providing as much as 20 percent of its annual funding. The various gifts helped finance guest appearances by major artists and funded such milestone events as the first local production of a full-length American opera, *The Ballad of Baby Doe* (1970).[46]

Other operas supported during the same period included *La Rondine* (1971), *The Elixir of Love* (1973), *The Daughter of the Regiment* (1974), *Il Tabarro* and *La Perichole* (1975), *Der Rosenkavalier* (1977), and *Fidelio* (1980). In August 1975 the opera received a $10,000 grant from the National Endowment for the Arts to produce Carlisle Floyd's *Susannah* during the 1976 national bicentennial celebration with Floyd directing. Through such sponsorships the association also inaugurated an educational outreach program through a series of student productions, beginning with *The Bewitched Child* in 1966. By 1977 this program had grown into the Southwestern Opera Theater, presenting performances to thousands of schoolchildren yearly.[47]

In 1969, with a $5,000 bequest from Mrs. George W. Armstrong in honor of her aunt, Mrs. Marguerite McCammon, the opera board also established the biennial Marguerite McCammon Voice Competition. The competition, turned over to the Opera Guild in 1985, had for a number of years provided a scholarship for unpaid opera chorus members. Under guild supervision, the McCammon was first expanded to include Texas residents outside the opera company and in 1991 to a national competition. By then, with additional gifts, the endowment had grown to around $150,000. Among its winners the McCammon included soprano Margaret Jane Wray (1985), bass-baritone Richard Paul Fink (1987), and bel canto mezzo soprano Viveca Genaux (1993).[48]

Throughout his long Fort Worth tenure, Kruger successfully built productions spotlighting leading voices of the Met and New York City Opera. Norman Treigle, Cornell McNeil, Jerome Hines, James McCracken, Luigi Alva, Samuel Ramey, Giorgio

Tozzi, and Eleanor Ross were among those appearing. These appearances became important sources of revenue for the organization, but for lack of what the *Star-Telegram* called "a more realistic budget" Kruger was often forced to be creative in putting together casts.[49]

Coinciding with Kruger's arrival in Fort Worth in the mid-1950s, young American singers were finding it difficult to gain a foothold with opera companies either in Europe or the United States. A resurgence of the arts following the war had left major halls bursting with talent, effectively shutting out many newcomers. Taking advantage of this trend, Kruger became known for his willingness to nurture gifted unknowns. He once explained to an interviewer:

> I always knew that setting out to imitate the Metropolitan was
> not for us. You pay for a great star and get . . . tattered scenery. . . .
> When they are famous, their fee may be ten times as much, but
> they are not ten times as good. . . .[50]

He turned to such rising performers as Ruth Welting, John Alexander, Patricia Wise, Michael Devlin, Gilda Cruz-Romo, and Ashley Putnam, who sang *La Perichole* in 1976, one year before winning first prize in the Metropolitan Opera auditions. In search of talent the local opera could afford on an operating budget less than one-third that of the Dallas Opera, he frequented major American opera centers like New York and Santa Fe. To save money, he met with singers in coffee shops and often stood in the rear of halls with complimentary tickets furnished by artist-acquaintances.[51]

One of his most publicized "discoveries," however, occurred closer to home during a November 1961 Dallas Opera production of *Lucia di Lammermoor* featuring Joan Sutherland and an international cast. Kruger was especially impressed by a twenty-year-old Spanish-born tenor making his United States debut in the secondary role of Lucia's ill-fated husband, Arturo. Dallas critic Rual Askew had also noticed the young singer, calling Placido Domingo a "pure delight . . . whose born instincts for opera mark him as a talent with a future."[52]

Hoping to acquire the young singer before other companies began competing for his services, Kruger offered Domingo the opportunity to play the same opera again the following season, but this time making his debut in the principal role of Edgardo. In an inspired bit of casting, the conductor coaxed legendary Metropolitan Opera soprano Lily Pons out of retirement in Dallas to star as Lucia opposite the tenor, nearly forty years her junior.[53]

The unlikely pairing proved a sensation. Pons, in her final operatic performance, mesmerized audiences, who were unaware they were witnessing the debut of a future superstar. Over thirty years earlier, she had electrified audiences and critics alike during her 1931 Met debut in the same role. Now, close to sixty, she still sang the opera's fabled mad scene a full step higher than written. *Star-Telegram* music editor E. Clyde Whitlock marveled at "the technical mastery with which she sings the part." He concluded, "The voice has the same sweetness, if not quite the same volume as when we first heard it." Though the night clearly belonged to Pons, Whitlock acknowledged Domingo's ability to hold his own in key duets with the charismatic diva, calling his "robust voice, emphatic style and dramatic forthrightness" in the "best traditions of Italian opera."[54]

Domingo returned to Fort Worth eight more times, beginning with an appearance as Don Jose in *Carmen* (1965). He returned as Pinkerton in *Madama Butterfly* (1966); Samson in *Samson and Delilah* (1967); Radames in *Aida* (1967); and Chevalier

Lily Pons during Fort Worth rehearsals of *Lucia di Lammermoor* in November, 1962. Pons had sung the role of Lucia for New York's Metropolitan Opera more than any other soprano.

Courtesy, *Fort Worth Star-Telegram* Collection, Special Collections, University of Texas-Arlington Libraries

Des Grieux in *Manon Lescaut* (1968). Even following critically acclaimed debuts with the New York City Opera (1966), the Met (1968), and La Scala (1969), he continued to appear occasionally in Fort Worth, singing Gustav III in *A Masked Ball* (1970); Rodolfo in *La Bohème* (1971), and Manrico in *Il Trovatore* (1973).[55]

For *Il Trovatore*, Kruger put together a cast that included not only Domingo but a solid lineup of Met singers: Lili Chookasian as Azucena, Louis Quilico as Count di Luna, and Clarice Carson as Leonora. Some weeks later a bewildered box office clerk opened an envelope from Canada. Inside, along with a request for two orchestra seats costing $8 apiece, was a check for $100. The purchaser explained: "I realize your prices are not this high, but I would happily pay $50 a seat to hear this cast."[56]

In 1963, one year after Domingo's local debut, a New York soprano also piqued the interest of area critics during an event sponsored by the Fort Worth Civic Music Association, a group formed in 1930 to provide concerts at reduced subscription rates. Beverly Sills had already performed before area audiences three times, first attracting favorable notice in November 1951, when at age twenty-two, she sang Violetta in a Charles L. Wagner production of *La Traviata*. E. Clyde Whitlock had taken note of Sills' "finished technique" and "soaring and pure [delivery], entirely unforced in the upper register." Sills returned with the same company the next year, singing Micaela in *Carmen*. During Casa Mañana's grand reopening in 1958, she sang the title role in *The Merry Widow*, the new theater's fourth production.[57]

The historic November, 1962 production of *Lucia* featured unknown tenor, Placido Domingo, far left, and Lily Pons, center, in her farewell performance. Others in the cast included Benjamin Rayson, second from right and Joshua Hecht, far right.

Courtesy, Fort Worth Opera

In her debut appearance with the Fort Worth Opera in November 1963, Sills once again sang the part of Violetta in *La Traviata.* Cast opposite her as Alfredo was Met tenor Brian Sullivan. Whitlock praised Sills' mastery of the "coloratura labyrinth" as well as her "warmth of feeling, immediate and personal." Dallas critic John Rosenfield called her simply "a proper candidate for the ideal Violetta."[58]

Kruger recruited Sills during a period in her career when she was finding few roles in major opera houses. Following her 1955 debut with the New York City Opera, she had built a career as a dependable house soprano, but stardom had continued to elude her. Though she rebounded to international attention by 1966, between 1961 and 1963 she had virtually retired from singing as she dealt with the problems of two physically challenged children. She eventually resumed her career, singing wherever she could. Kruger allowed her to sing the parts she wanted during this period, help Sills

Placido Domingo with Raina Kabaivanska in the Fort Worth Opera production of *Manon Lescaut*, 1968.

Courtesy, *Fort Worth Star-Telegram* Collection, Special Collections, University of Texas-Arlington Libraries

Beverly Sills as Constanza with John Alexander in *The Abduction From the Seraglio*, 1966. Sills used Fort Worth appearances to launch several additions to her personal repertoire, including the role, *The Beautiful Galatea*, 1964.

Courtesy, *Fort Worth Star-Telegram* Collection, Special Collections, University of Texas-Arlington Libraries

acknowledged in 1976, saying "Rudy was building shows around me when other people weren't even asking me to sing."[59]

Sills returned to Fort Worth in 1964 to sing Nedda in *I Pagliacci*. Over the next four seasons, she used local opera appearances to launch several additions to her personal repertoire: her debut as *The Beautiful Galatea* (1964) was followed in January 1966 by Constanza in *The Abduction From the Seraglio*. Later that same year came her triumphal appearance as Cleopatra in the New York City Opera production of Handel's *Julius Caesar,* but she returned to Fort Worth in April 1968 to make her debut as *Lucia di Lammermoor.* Her much-anticipated coming-out as Donizetti's heroine "reduced the opening night audience to a howling mob." While critical of the production's "routine" staging and "dreadful" costumes and scenery, *Star-Telegram* music editor Leonard Eureka declared Sills' performance "one of the best I have ever seen."[60]

By the mid-1970s, Sills' rise to the heights of operatic stardom was complete, following several triumphant seasons as the New York City Opera's prima donna and a 1975 Met debut. In 1979, as the diva prepared to retire from the stage, she returned to Fort Worth one last time as Rosina in *The Barber of Seville.* The two performances on March 2 and 4 were underwritten by long-time opera patrons Elizabeth Armstrong, Lura Elliston, and Mary D. Walsh.[61]

By the 1980s, major changes were occurring in the operatic world. Traditional sources of revenue—private donors, foundation grants, and government subsidies—were being eroded, not only by steeply rising production costs but a steady decline in support. At one point, Kruger had observed philosophically to a reporter, "Every time we put up the curtain . . . we lose money. [Donors] are suspicious of something that is here on Friday night and gone on Sunday."[62]

In the rush to find solutions, regional operas across the country began adopting a management model that favored corporate-style executive officers. Unlike old-school conductor-impresarios like Kruger, this new breed of directors concentrated on developing audiences and sources of revenue while leaving conducting to others. Consistent with this trend, in 1982, following Kruger's twenty-seventh season, the Fort Worth Opera executive board reduced his duties and began the search for a new managing director.[63]

The decision to oust Kruger was contentious. His supporters, bitter over his forced retirement, fought back, and in the ensuing political struggle Jack Mastroianni, assistant director of the Houston Grand Opera and already in contract negotiations as the Maestro's replacement, withdrew his candidacy. Some had wanted Kruger to remain with the company indefinitely as advisor and conductor emeritus, but he was retained only through the 1982–1983 season, his twenty-eighth. With his title reduced to conductor/music director, Kruger's duties were limited to preparation of the season's four productions.[64]

In January 1983, the opera board finally announced the selection of thirty-one-year-old Dwight Bowes, manager of Florida's Orlando Opera Company, as Kruger's successor. Bowes, a 1973 graduate of Tulane University, had trained as an actor but had few music credentials. He had served as a director for the New York City Opera Theater, director of education the New York City Opera and the New York City Ballet, and director of productions for the Michigan Opera Theater. At the same time as Bowes' hiring, the board also announced several internal changes, chief among them a reshaping of the general director's role. Although the new director assumed administrative and artistic control, outside conductors would be hired to direct each production.[65]

Turmoil behind the scenes not only slowed the search for Kruger's replacement but seemed to throw a pall over the season's two final productions—both *Don Giovanni* and *Eugene Onegin* were critical disappointments. At the close of the season, in a somewhat belated acknowledgment of Kruger's contributions, the association formally announced the endowment of the Rudolf Kruger Young Artist Fund in May 1983.[66]

As Bowes assumed leadership, few could have foreseen the strife that lay less than two years away for the company. Bowes' previous directing posts and a fresh approach to marketing at first seemed to herald a new direction for the opera. In his two seasons with Orlando, subscription ticket sales had more than doubled. Bowes' debut offering, an opulent staging of Bizet's *The Pearl Fishers*, shared with the Orlando Opera, opened in November 1983. This production, as well as the season's other offerings, *Madama Butterfly*, *A Masked Ball*, and Verdi's *Requiem* were generally well-received by critics and audiences despite another departure from local tradition: All performances were presented in the original languages.[67]

Expectations for the 1984–1985 season ran high. Though predicted jumps in 1983–1984 season ticket sales failed to materialize, the opera association successfully negotiated with the Fort Worth Symphony to become the company's permanent orchestra and charted an ambitious five-production course. The season included several firsts: the southwest premiere of Stephen Paulus' *The Postman Always Rings Twice*, the U.S. stage premiere of Handel's early chamber opera, *Agrippina*, staged at the Kimbell Art Museum, and a lavish, all-new production of *Aida*, coproduced with the Indianapolis and Syracuse opera companies. *Aida* also became the first production to utilize subtitles with a system developed by the Canadian Opera Company.[68]

These artistic successes, as it turned out, came at prices the opera association could not afford to pay. Over twenty-eight seasons, Rudolf Kruger had not only reshaped a well-intentioned municipal institution into one of the country's leading small opera companies but his cautious management had consistently kept it operating in the black. Just four seasons earlier, the organization still maintained a reserve fund of $160,000. But in the midst of Bowes' second season, revelations of massive cost overruns and unpaid bills threatened not only to cancel *Aida* but to bring down the curtain on the association's thirty-nine-year run.[69]

On April 24, just two days before *Aida*'s scheduled premiere, the opera board learned there was no cash to pay principals. Several in the company refused to perform until a number of board members came forward with personal funds to insure the singers' compensation. And although the opera's two performances went on as scheduled, many other opera personnel remained unpaid months later. In an effort to stave off further losses, a triumvirate of board members assumed control over company finances. Draconian budget-cutting measures led to dismissal of the entire permanent staff. Dwight Bowes was eventually rehired but at drastically reduced pay and responsibilities. His remaining tenure with the company was brief—in July, barely two-and-a-half years since his appointment, he resigned.[70]

An internal audit of the company's finances revealed a number of problems. Ticket sales and endowments had not increased as expected, and fundraisers had brought in just $28,000 of the estimated $300,000 needed for the season. Over $100,000 had been spent just on sets for *Aida,* with Fort Worth responsible for one-third of the cost. Cost overruns for this one production, in fact, had mounted to $64,000. Other creditors included the Fort Worth Symphony, owed $89,000, the opera chorus, owed $40,000, and the Tarrant County Convention Center, owed half a season's rent. A second blow came with the discovery of a $220,000 deficit from operas staged during 1982–1983 when the company was without a general director. The final budget shortfall climbed to around $612,000.[71]

In the end, the artistic triumphs of *Aida,* though drawing the largest audiences in ten years, could not offset the production's high cost when stacked with the previous deficit. To prevent the complete collapse of the company, a task force of board members was appointed to restructure the company's finances and find methods for reducing the debt. The 1985–1986 season was cut from the usual four operas to three, a change in the status quo that would remain the new norm through the end of the century.[72]

As the opera association continued to assess its future, thirty-year-old João Mario Ramos, director of development for the Public Opera of Dallas, was named acting director in Bowes' place. A native of Brazil, Ramos held a bachelor's degree in music from Texas Christian University and master's degrees in arts and business administration from Southern Methodist University. In January 1986, following the well-received staging of *I Pagliacci* and *Cavalleria Rusticana* with famed African-American diva, Martina Arroyo, the board named him permanent general director.[73]

By 1987, thanks to gifts from such individuals as Mrs. O.C. Armstrong and organizations like Texas Bank and the Amon Carter Foundation, the opera association had reduced the original $600,000 deficit to just $25,000, with many creditors agreeing to settle for as little as fifty cents on the dollar. Even with such donations and concessions, payments on the debt continued to exact a heavy toll. Each year's operating budget shrank—$790,000 in 1985–1986, $778,000 in 1986–1987, and just $725,000 in 1987–1988 despite the sale of fifteen hundred season tickets. Beginning with *The Mikado* in January 1988, Ramos shifted one production a season to the five-hundred-seat William Edrington Scott Theater on West Lancaster, billing these performances as "intimate" opera. The formula worked well as a once-a-season novelty. Both *The Barber of Seville* (1989) and *The Elixir of Love* (1990) proved popular.[74]

Ramos' announcement that the 1990–1991 season would feature two popular operas, *The Daughter of the Regiment* and *Carmen* along with a staging of Stewart Copeland's 1989 work, *Holy Blood and Crescent Moon,* brought a rush of season ticket requests. With the inflow of cash, the company finally eliminated its five-year deficit but was left with an immediate $80,000 production shortfall. To economize, both *Carmen* and *The Daughter of the Regiment* moved to the Scott Theater, leaving only Copeland's opera to receive full-scale treatment in the Convention Center's John F. Kennedy Theater.[75]

Cleveland Opera's 1989 premiere of the new work had attracted international interest, chiefly due to Copeland's status as drummer and songwriter for the Police, a well-known rock band. Despite generally poor reviews, audiences had flocked to the performances, giving Cleveland an unexpected windfall and encouraging Copeland over the next year to revise and strengthen the score. Eventually, he signed with the Fort Worth Opera for a "re-premiere" of the work in November 1990.

The event's opening night, November 16, drew a crowd of two thousand. Yet even with a large contingent of Copeland fans, less conservative and far younger than the opera's typical patrons, audience counts fell nearly a thousand short of the expected sell out. Nor did the composer's revision of the convoluted work improve his questionable status with critical observers. One reviewer, baldly declaring Copeland an "amateur," urged the opera company to limit itself to "serious, skilled composers, who have gone to the trouble of learning the craft. . . ." The venture into nontraditionalist fare not only proved a commercial disappointment but drew the ire of longtime ticket holders. Within weeks, in response to the complaints, the board forced Ramos out and began the search for a new general director.[76]

Assuming the responsibilities for the interim was Carl O. Johnson, who had previously served as an artistic administrator and production manager with the company. A continued general economic downturn and corresponding drop in support led the opera company to shift all its 1991–1992 productions to smaller theaters. Johnson told a reporter, "We're in a survival mode." The season opener, *The Abduction From the Seraglio,* went on in TCU's Ed Landreth Auditorium, although productions of *H. M. S. Pinafore* and *Lucia di Lammermoor* continued at the Scott Theater.[77]

Not until December 1991, one year after Ramos' ouster, did the opera board finally announce the hiring of William Walker to lead the company as its next general director. A Texan who had grown up and gone to college in Fort Worth, Walker possessed an intimate knowledge of opera gained during a distinguished career as one of the Metropolitan Opera's principal baritones. Over nearly twenty years, he had sung major Italian and French roles, frequently appearing with the company on yearly tour stops in Dallas. Following his retirement from singing in 1980, he had gained business experience working in San Antonio's international real-estate market.[78]

Karl Kritz gave Walker some of his earliest professional experience in 1949 when he enlisted TCU students to sing one summer in the chorus of the Pittsburgh Civic Light Opera. Kritz later cast him as Handsome in the opera's 1951 production of *The Girl of the Golden West.* Intent on a professional singing career, Walker left TCU for New York in 1952. Following service in the Korean War he returned to TCU and resumed occasional appearances in local operas. He played a soldier in *Salome* and Morales in *Carmen.* Rudolf Kruger cast him as Schaunard in *La Bohème* (1956) and as George Germont in *La Traviata* (1957).[79]

As the Fort Worth Opera's newly appointed general director in the winter of 1991, Walker had only limited resources. Important patrons had withdrawn support, grant money was down, and subscription sales had fallen until the revenue accounted for only 20 percent of the company's budget when the national average for similar small companies stood at 30 percent. At the same time, previous seasons' deficits had again soared to over $100,000. The size of the debt, according to Walker "was hurting everyone."[80]

Because of the shortfalls, most productions continued as scaled-back presentations at the Scott or Landreth Auditorium through the spring of 1993. However, a full-scale staging of *La Traviata* sung in Italian returned the company to the Kennedy Theater for the opening of its forty-seventh season in November 1992. The opera proved to be an important turning point for the company, its two performances drawing in three thousand patrons.

Productions for the remainder of the season—*Don Pasquale,* starring Met basso Ezio Flagello, and a double bill of Menotti's *The Telephone* and *The Old Maid and the Thief* were equally well received. Building on this success, Walker announced a "dream season" for 1993–1994 featuring three of opera's most beloved works: *La Bohème, Don Giovanni,* and *Madama Butterfly.* The announcement produced a surge in season ticket sales. By November 1993 when the curtain rose on *La Bohème,* subscriptions had soared to 1,850, up 60 percent from the previous season. Performances of *Don Giovanni,* staged in the smaller Landreth Hall sold out.[81]

Over several seasons, the company's artistic fortunes continued to rise under Walker's leadership. As Rudolf Kruger had done thirty years earlier, Walker sought out rising talent around whom to build productions. "What I want on my stage," he explained "is a brilliantly talented singer performing at the top of his ability with his heart in his hand begging you to love him. That cannot be denied." Among a new

William Walker, general director of the Fort Worth Opera, 1991-2002. Walker, raised in Fort Worth, spent nearly twenty years as one of the Metropolitan Opera's principal baritones.

Courtesy, *Fort Worth Star-Telegram* Collection, Special Collections, University of Texas-Arlington Libraries

generation of singers introduced to Fort Worth during his nine seasons were Jane Thorngren, Louis Otey, Allan Glassman, Robynn Redmon, Paul Austin Kelly, Frances Ginsberg, Bojan Knezevic, Larissa Tetuev, and Olivia Gorra.[82]

Thorngren soon became a favorite of local audiences, appearing as Violetta in *La Traviata* (1992), as Mimi in *La Bohème* (1993), and as Marguerite in *Faust* (1996). She played Rosina opposite Louis Otey's Figaro in *The Barber of Seville* (1996). Otey demonstrated his dramatic range as Germont in *La Traviata* (1992), *Don Giovanni* (1994), and Scarpia in *Tosca* (1995). Tenor Allan Glassman also made several appearances, singing Manrico in *Il Trovatore* (1995) and Don Jose in *Carmen* (1996).[83]

Olivia Gorra's spectacular Fort Worth debut in the title role of *Lucia di Lammermoor* in November 1999 recalled earlier performances with the local company by Lily Pons and Beverly Sills. Gorra's dramatic depth and "extraordinary vocal flexibility" drew glowing notices from area critics and sold out two performances. At each performance, spontaneous cheering from the audience interrupted the soprano's arias. One reviewer called Gorra "a strong candidate to become one of the leading Lucias of the twenty-first century."[84]

Even a massive hailstorm that struck the city on May 5, 1995, failed to dampen the company's prospects. The storm, one of the worst in U. S. history, battered the downtown area with baseball-sized hail just minutes before the opening of the season finale, *Tosca*. Water pouring through the Kennedy Theater's battered roof soaked large areas of the hall and drove the orchestra from the flooding pit. Ignoring the less-than-ideal conditions, several hundred patrons remained for the performance, which went on after less than an hour's delay with only pianist Jing Ling Tam for accompaniment. A day and a half later, over twenty-one hundred returned for a second performance, shifted in the emergency to Will Rogers Auditorium.[85]

The company's rising artistic fortunes also helped spark a return of financial supporters. A May 1994 wine auction chaired by Bil Sullivan-Jones Butner brought in over $200,000 in profits, freeing the company of its remaining deficits. Then in September 1995, in celebration of the company's fiftieth anniversary season, Edgar H. and Rae S. Schollmaier donated $500,000 to establish the Schollmaier Endowment Fund, a gift intended to enhance the company's long-term economic outlook. Fort Worth developer Edward P. Bass, already in the final planning stages of the $60 million Nancy Lee and Perry R. Bass Performance Hall, gave an additional $156,000. The grant was part of $6 million in gifts to various arts organizations, a move Bass hoped would contribute to a revitalization of the arts in the city's downtown area.[86]

The Bass Hall's premiere just over two and a half years later, in May 1998, seemed a harbinger that the opera's long-term financial and artistic woes were finally in the past. In June 1998, for the company's first full production in the hall, Walker selected Puccini's perennial favorite, *La Bohème* with Jane Thorngren reprising her 1993 appearance as Mimi, Glassman as Rodolfo, Otey as Marcello, and soprano Anna Singer as Musetta completed the ensemble. Productions for 1998–1999, *Turandot, Don Giovanni,* and *Tosca,* were each expanded to three performances as the season sold out and subscriptions jumped to a record high of thirty-eight hundred.[87]

But as the opera association prepared to enter its fifty-third season in the summer of 1998, behind-the-scenes discord threatened to erase the substantial artistic and financial gains made during the previous decade. Fallout from the conflict left the company once again scrambling to find funding and its leadership in tatters. The controversy erupted in August following the executive committee's decision not to renew William Walker's five-year contract. Detractors had reportedly clashed with the director over several issues, including his handling of administrative details and his desire to expand the company's repertoire.

Walker initially accepted a two-year severance package, but at the September meeting of the full board, his supporters rallied to vote down the executive committee's original action. Walker was reinstated but over half the executive board, nearly thirty members, and board president J. Stephen Beckman, resigned. Over several months, the schism widened to embrace other issues such as financial responsibility and fundraising. The company's comptroller quit, and Beckman's replacement, Dr. Jack Hardwick, also resigned. Some sponsors withheld funds, most notably philanthropist Rae Schollmaier, who withdrew a pledge to expand the opera's endowment fund by an additional million dollars.[88]

Over the next two seasons, continued robust ticket sales in the new Bass Hall and substantial new contributions from Bank One, Tandy Corporation, and the Sid Richardson and Rosenthal foundations helped insure an uninterrupted production schedule. By the beginning of the 2001 season, for the first time since 1984, the company once again expanded its season to four operas and increased its operating budget from $1.7 million to $2.1 million. William Walker retired at the end of the 2001–2002 season, closing his ten seasons with debuts of three operas new to the Fort Worth repertoire: Leonard Bernstein's *Candide,* Vincenzo Bellini's *Norma,* and George Gershwin's *Porgy and Bess.* To lead the company into the twenty-first century, in July 2001, the company hired Darren K. Woods as Walker's successor.[89]

AN OLD IDEA COMES FULL CIRCLE— CASA MAÑANA: 1958-2001

"The night no longer is so young for some,
but the 'lady' is beautiful. She . . . is a
handsome reincarnation of the original. . . ."
~Jack Gordon

It was a hot afternoon in mid-August 1958, six weeks since the unveiling of Fort Worth's newest showplace, Casa Mañana. Situated just a hundred feet or so from the site of its namesake at the northeast corner of the old centennial grounds, this latest "house of tomorrow" seemed trim, almost diminutive, measured against the grand scale of Billy Rose's four-thousand-seat showplace. Faint echoes of the long-vanished original might have been detected in this structure's curving outer facade and columned, glass-walled entryway, but these, to some, must have seemed a tenuous connection to the past at best. Setting this new theater apart from its ancestor were its circular design and a singularly remarkable roof. Five-hundred-and-seventy-five diamond-shaped aluminum panels, joined together and held in place by gold struts, arched up and over the arena in a gleaming, futuristic, geodesic dome.[1]

On this particular day, the well-dressed crowd had gathered for a performance of Franz Lehar's *The Merry Widow*. The turn of the century operetta, scheduled for just a week's run sandwiched between *The Pajama Game* and *Call Me Madam*, both recent Broadway releases, had proved a surprising hit, selling out all performances. At least part of the show's unexpected appeal could be traced to its redheaded star, an unknown, twenty-nine-year-old soprano from the New York City Center Opera. Beverly Sills' pristine high notes and coquettish warmth as Sonia, the alluring young widow of the title, had readily endeared her to audiences and critics alike.[2]

In the first scene of Act II, a violent Texas thunderstorm passing noisily outside made its presence known just as the orchestra moved into the opening strains of one of the operetta's signature numbers, "Vilia." Without warning, the stage went dark, leaving only a faint glow filtering upward from the pit to illuminate the scene. A momentary stir passed through the crowd, but as Sills, turning slowly at center stage, picked up the haunting refrain, "Vilia, oh Vilia, oh let me be true," the room became hushed, seemingly held in thrall by the serendipitous confluence of art with nature. As the song's final rising notes died away, the lights slowly came back up, as if by design. The audience, released from its spell, broke into tumultuous applause, refusing to let the show continue until Sills had completed two encores.[3]

The moment, a high point of the 1958 season, came, in a way, to symbolize the fortunate conjunction of events that resurrected the spirit of Casa Mañana sixteen years after the razing of its 1936 prototype and nearly two decades after that theater's final season. While efforts to save the popular nightspot had failed, the memory of its impact on the community had never completely faded. With postwar optimism sweeping the country, a bond issue to rebuild the theater gained fresh support in September 1945.

Stopping short of mentioning Casa Mañana, the proposal called for a principal sum of $500,000 "for . . . building . . . and equipping a recreation center and amphitheater"—part of a $1,500,000 bond package to expand and improve the Southwestern Exposition's agricultural and livestock exhibit buildings. On October 2, 1945, voters approved the issue, but for lack of a plan, the bonds for construction of the amphitheater were never sold. Over the next decade they lay dormant, forgotten

Beverly Sills, center, in profile, appearing as *The Merry Widow* in August 1958, consults backstage with director Michael Pollock.

Courtesy, *Fort Worth Star-Telegram* Collection, Special Collections, University of Texas-Arlington Libraries

until 1957 when general manager of the Fort Worth Civic Opera Melvin O. Dacus began exploring ways to promote and raise money for the organization's fall and winter productions.[4]

A product of Paschal High School and TCU, Dacus had been stationed with the U.S. Marines in the Pacific theater during World War II. Following the war, he served briefly as head of the voice department of North Texas Agricultural College (later the University of Texas at Arlington) while doing graduate work in voice at TCU. In 1947, he moved to New York, where he continued professional studies at the American Theater Wing during three seasons in the resident company of the Paper Mill Playhouse in Millburn, New Jersey.[5]

Melvin and Katy Dacus, c. 1955. Both worked in local television until Melvin Dacus became general manager of first, the Fort Worth Opera in 1954, and then of Casa Mañana Musicals in 1958.

Courtesy, Dacus family

Service in the Korean War and a brief stint training as a broker on Wall Street finally brought Dacus to a crossroads. In 1953, he and his wife, Kathryn Peirson Dacus, herself an accomplished singer and graduate of the Juilliard School of Music, made the decision to return to Fort Worth, where both took jobs with WBAP-TV. Dacus also resumed singing in Fort Worth Civic Opera productions, where he met James H. Snowden, a Harvard graduate, local oilman, and president of the opera association from 1952–1958. In 1954, Snowden, overburdened with running his own business in addition to the opera, approached Dacus about becoming the opera's first full-time general manager.[6]

From 1954 to 1957 when not producing and promoting opera, Dacus spent much of his time fundraising. Over coffee one day during the opera's 1956 production of *Rosalinda,* he and comedian Colee Worth discussed the feasibility of opening an outdoor theater modeled on the success of New Jersey entrepreneur St. John Terrell. Terrell, a former carnival fire-eater better known as radio's Jack Armstrong, had, in 1949, discovered a cheap and innovative way to showcase the wave of musicals that had begun flowing from Broadway in the wake of Rodgers and Hammerstein's runaway 1943 hit, *Oklahoma!* Between 1946 and 1957, an unprecedented series of shows, including *Annie Get Your Gun, Kiss Me Kate, South Pacific, Guys and Dolls, The King and I, My Fair Lady, West Side Story,* and *The Pajama Game,* smashed previous box office records.[7]

Using ancient Greek amphitheaters as his inspiration, Terrell carved out a sloping saucer of earth in a Lambertville field, topped it with a circular tent, and christened it the Music Circus. Audiences sat on folding chairs around the stage, but no one ever sat farther back than fifteen or sixteen rows. Although he used a full orchestra, "scenery" was limited to low-profile set pieces that did not obstruct sight lines. Stagehands and actors raced up and down straw-covered dirt aisles in full view of the audience. Far from being put off by Terrell's low-budget productions, patrons lined up by the thousands to purchase single tickets for as little as ninety cents. Over the next eight summers, promoters hoping to match Terrell's success opened at least thirty of the canvas-top theaters all across the country. By 1957, the tents had attracted thirteen million customers for an estimated box office of twenty-five million dollars. [8]

At season's end, with James Snowden's approval, Dacus visited several tent operations, including Terrell's Music Circus in New Jersey. From the showman he learned that private producers were making profits ranging from $15,000 to $100,000 a summer. Snowden, impressed by the figures, thought enough of the idea to begin a search for a Fort Worth site, though no thought had yet been given to building a permanent structure. One location given strong consideration was Forest Park, southwest of downtown on the bank of the Trinity River. Snowden even consulted engineers on the feasibility of installing fans or air conditioning as a way to combat the Texas heat, but eventually, the entire idea was abandoned as impractical.[9]

Snowden remained committed to the idea but evidently rethought plans for a canvas-top outdoor theater. In February 1957, Melvin Dacus presented the opera association's case before the city council, asking members to consider a plan for an indoor sixteen-hundred-seat "arena-type" auditorium, which could be converted to a seven-hundred-seat proscenium theater. Musical comedies would be presented in the theater during summer months to raise money for the opera. A little-used parcel of Amon Carter Square at the corner of University and West Lancaster, near the site of the 1936 Casa Mañana, was pitched as a location. The steel skeleton of the old theater's revolving stage still lay in place near the Frontier Centennial's only other surviving structure, the Pioneer Palace.[10]

The council took no action on the proposal, and over several months, Snowden's repeated overtures to the city manager went largely ignored. But later in the summer, the idea of a new theater for the city gathered renewed momentum with the appearance of an item in a local newspaper. The article concerned the geodesic dome, a revolutionary construction design patented by Richard Buckminster Fuller. Dacus passed the article to Snowden, who, intrigued by the possibilities, had the opera manager gather cost and construction data from Kaiser Aluminum.[11]

While considering the problem of working capital, Snowden remembered the $500,000 recreation center bonds, authorized in 1945 but never sold. Armed with this information and preliminary cost figures from Kaiser, he moved ahead with planning. The finished proposal, titled *Casa Mañana '58*, received its first public airing in local newspapers on November 13, 1957. Two days later, Snowden laid out revised plans before the city council for the construction of side-by-side circular pavilions, each topped by one of Fuller's domes and joined by a common reception area. The main entrance to the new complex would be from University Drive, a few hundred feet south of West Lancaster.[12]

The master plan called for one pavilion to be constructed as a theater in the half-round with seating for thirteen hundred. The other, complete with kitchen and private club, would provide modern banquet and meeting facilities for community events, including some currently relegated to the increasingly dilapidated, wood-frame Pioneer Palace. As authorized by the voters in 1945, the Casa Mañana Center would be built by the city but then leased to Snowden's group for $25,000 annually. The rate would allow the corporation to pay off the $500,000 within twenty-five years at no net cost to the city.[13]

This time, the council voted to study the revamped proposal, and Mayor Thomas A. McCann appointed a committee made up of councilmen Jesse E. Roach, J.J. Lyles, and Gus Jackson. Almost immediately the group encountered opposition from stock show general manager Billy Bob Watt, Sr. During negotiations, Watt repeatedly steered the committee away from the old centennial grounds to more remote locations. Finally, during a showdown in McCann's office, stockshow board chairman Amon G. Carter, Jr., overruled Watt, agreeing to lease the site to the theater group.[14]

Carter's endorsement signaled an important step forward, but several influential business organizations, most notably the Downtown Fort Worth Association and the Junior Chamber of Commerce, voiced further objections to the scheme. The chamber, about to unveil its own $25 million downtown renewal project, had already sketched out preliminary plans for a five-thousand-seat civic center, fifteen-hundred-seat theater, and expanded city hall, all slated for a deteriorating section of the business district south of Tenth Street between Throckmorton and Taylor. In December, president of the chamber Paul Harmon, Jr., requested the council defer any action on the Casa Mañana project by 120 days.[15]

Through it all, Snowden remained adamant that the opera association plan posed no threat to downtown renewal. Moving the amphitheater-recreation center downtown, he insisted, would boost final costs by well over a million dollars and delay hopes for a summer theater season by yet another year. Sentiment for rebuilding a Casa Mañana near the old centennial grounds evidently helped sway the final vote. On January 17, 1958, the city council unanimously approved sale of the 1945 recreation bonds for the Opera Association project.[16]

On February 21, Casa Mañana Musicals, Inc., officially incorporated with Snowden as president, Ernest Allen as vice president, Elizabeth E. Gann as secretary, and Elmer L. Lockwood as treasurer. Melvin Dacus, who had played a pivotal role in the theater's inception and final design, was tapped as the theater's first producer and general manager. Within thirty days, largely through Snowden's personal efforts, the $100,000 needed to capitalize the project was raised through the sale of corporate bonds. The more expansive two-domed plan fell victim, however, to the spike in construction costs since 1945.[17]

The revised design by local architect A. George King returned to the original theater-in-the-round concept, a plan that also increased seating from 1,300 to 1,832. The modification proved fortuitous. Even before its maiden performance, Casa Mañana jumped from the ranks of the chorus to overnight star as the nation's first permanent theater-in-the-round. With an opening tentatively set for June, ground clearing began on March 13, one day after the construction firm of Butcher and Sweeney won the contract with a bid of $508,655. Since the 1945 recreation center bonds totaled only $500,000, the corporation also had to take out nearly $210,000 in additional bank loans to finish out and furnish the facility.[18]

Work on the theater progressed rapidly. By the third week in April technicians had begun assembling and raising the sixty-six-foot-high geodesic dome with the aid of a hundred-foot lift tower set at the center of the theater floor. Each successive tier of aluminum panels was fitted together at ground level like an elaborate puzzle and then hoisted upward until all were in place. The dome's interior surface, fabricated and installed by the E.O. Wood Company, was lined with an asbestos fabric covered by gold-colored aluminum foil sheeting. Meanwhile, in the field behind the new hall, workmen cut apart and hauled away to be sold as scrap the massive steel skeleton of

Casa Mañana founder, James Snowden, with Michael Pollock, who served as stage director from the theater's opening in 1958 through 1965.

Courtesy, *Fort Worth Star-Telegram* Collection, Special Collections, University of Texas-Arlington

the original theater's revolving stage. It had lain neglected and virtually forgotten since 1942—a final ironic footnote to the 1936 centennial celebration.[19]

Dacus began assembling a production staff. Key members included music director, William Baer; choreographers, Joan Mann and Ed Holleman; set designer, Hal Shafer; stage manager, Martha Pulliam; and stage director, Michael Pollock. Baer,

Casa Mañana, with its geodesic dome, goes up at the corner of University and West Lancaster in May, 1958. In the background, the skeleton of the original theater's revolving stage is clearly visible.

Courtesy W. D. Smith Photograph Collection, *Fort Worth Star-Telegram* Collection, Special Collections, University of Texas-Arlington Libraries

Pulliam, and Pollock, like Dacus, had all worked previously with the Fort Worth Opera. Pollock, who remained as director through the theater's first seven seasons, would also became influential in shaping one of Casa Mañana's longest-standing traditions: giving preference to well-qualified if not always well-known talent over the "name" stars favored by many other summer stock operations.[20]

"We think more of our audience than that," Pollock told a reporter shortly before the opening of the theater. "Any group that has a 'name' policy destroys the value of finding new talent." He predicted "the young people you see here will be the favorites of tomorrow."[21]

For its inaugural season the Casa Mañana executive board settled on five shows, shifting opening night from June to July. Selected to launch the theater was a two-week run of Cole Porter's 1953 Parisian tale, *Can-Can*, followed by *Carousel*, *The Pajama Game*, *The Merry Widow*, and *Call Me Madam*. Pollock cast principals in New York

Casa Mañana stage director Michael Pollock, left, with music director, William Baer, and general manager and theater co-founder, Melvin Dacus.

Courtesy, *Fort Worth Star-Telegram* Collection, Special Collections, University of Texas-Arlington Libraries

but auditions held during March and April at the Greater Fort Worth Community Theater building and at universities in several surrounding states filled supporting roles and completed the theater's resident ensemble. Since work still continued on the theater's interior, rehearsals were moved into the nearby Pioneer Palace.[22]

When Pollock toured the facility during the spring, he was one of the first to notice a serious design flaw. A strategic aspect of Terrell's Music Circus was a stage at ground level with surrounding seating angled upward steeply, guaranteeing an unobstructed view from anywhere in the audience. Casa Mañana's floor, on the other hand, was virtually flat, sloping downward only slightly. The most visible consequence of the flaw was the level of the stage—it loomed like a barricade in the center of the hall. Patrons sitting in rows nearest stage action had their sightlines blocked by even the smallest set pieces. Aisle scenes, typically used in arena productions to cover scene changes on the main stage, could be seen by only half the audience because the rise of the stage was an obstruction. Work had progressed too far to change the slope without delaying or canceling the season.[23]

Left, Exterior view of Casa Mañana c. 1958. Right, Casa Mañana's black-tie premiere, July 5, 1958.

Courtesy, Jack White and *Fort Worth Star-Telegram* Collections, Special Collections, University of Texas-Arlington Libraries

Instead, designs were altered to increase the size of the slightly oval stage from its planned twenty-eight-foot width to thirty-two feet. Ten inches below the main stage, carpenters added a two-foot-wide step-down apron, bringing the stage's overall dimensions to thirty by thirty-four feet. Pollock then restaged many scenes, moving all but featured characters to the apron, where they sat or reclined to give the audience a clear view of the action. Moveable platforms were constructed to elevate aisle scenes, main stage scenery was redesigned, and ramps were added at aisles to provide access to the raised stage. [24]

A black-tie premiere, covered by *Life* magazine and attended by many of the city's most prominent citizens, opened the theater July 5, 1958. The guest list also included television celebrities and a half dozen chorus and showgirls from the 1936 Casa Mañana. Heavy rains during the day transformed the still-unpaved parking lot into a sea of mud and led to the discovery of numerous leaks in the domed roof, but most were repaired by showtime. Considering the pioneering nature of the operation, reviewers gave the opening performance, starring Deedy Irwin and Dick Smart,

charitable if not overly enthusiastic reviews. One summed up the effort as "a tolerable *Can-Can* and sometimes a very bright one."[25]

The real star of the evening, taking center stage again nearly two decades after its farewell performance, was Casa Mañana. *Dallas Times Herald* reporter Virgil Miers called the playhouse "an ultra-modern temple of fun . . . a distinguished addition to the permanent Southwestern theater scene," while *Star-Telegram* columnist Elston Brooks proclaimed, "Casa Mañana does indeed sparkle inside with all the brilliance that has been bouncing off the aluminum dome this summer." Jack Gordon, who had covered the unveiling of the 1936 theater, could not resist a sentimental nod to the original's theme song: "the night no longer is so young for some, but the 'lady' is beautiful. She . . . is a handsome reincarnation of the original. . . ."[26]

Other comments, however, focused on technical difficulties still in need of solutions. Staging suffered from Pollock's initial tendency to pose singers "proscenium-style" facing the orchestra pit during musical numbers, while the orchestra was criticized as "woefully incompetent," under Baer's "follow me or else" conducting style. Both problems merely served to highlight an even more glaring, unanticipated problem that nearly closed the theater after just one performance: Contrary to predictions that the dome would provide nearly perfect acoustics, actors could barely be heard.[27]

Casa Mañana had debuted without sound amplification of any sort after experts had assured local planners of the dome's sound reflective capabilities. With construction crews rushing to complete the building, rehearsals for *Can-Can* had to be held in the nearby Pioneer Palace, leaving the theater largely untested. Not until the Saturday opening did the full magnitude of the problem become evident: Actors could be heard only when facing a section, and even then words and phrases were often distorted.

With just two days before the theater's scheduled opening to the general public, Dacus and his staff members scrambled to find emergency solutions. By show time on Monday, five microphones had been placed strategically around the apron and another hung at center stage. After four speakers still proved insufficient, the number was doubled to eight, but even then, sound quality remained an issue. Only constant refinements to the system over several years and new advances in microphone and speaker technology improved sound quality. Changes to the physical plant over several seasons, including the addition of thick velour drapes above the low wall separating concourse from auditorium, also helped.[28]

Adding to technical difficulties, much of the theater's debut season continued to be marred by what one reviewer termed "not enough professional know-how in either the staging or musical departments," though audiences, for the most part, seemed oblivious to the criticisms. *Can-Can* averaged a respectable 70 percent capacity, *Carousel* built to 78 percent, *The Pajama Game* to 91 percent, and *The Merry Widow,* running for just a week, sold out. *Call Me Madam* did almost as well, playing to 94 percent. The five-musical series made a profit of $50,000—too small to recoup start-up expenses but still enough to guarantee working capital for a second season.[29]

The executive board's attempts to keep the theater profitable through the fall and winter were less successful. An abbreviated three-musical series, timed to attract stock show visitors, opened with *Oklahoma!* in January 1959 but did only modest business, wasting valuable properties and leaving the theater with a $5,000 deficit. Replacing musicals through the 1960 and 1961 off-seasons were a series of legitimate plays featuring name stars. Among those appearing were Laraine Day in *The Women;* Ralph Meeker, Eddie Bracken, and Frank McHugh in *Mr. Roberts;* Martha Raye in *The Solid Gold Cadillac;* and Joe E. Brown in *Father of the Bride.* Except for children's productions, the theater finally abandoned efforts to build a year-round season, choosing to concentrate on its summer series.[30]

Casa Mañana's summer musical series continued to expand. From just five offerings in 1958, the season grew to six in 1959, seven from 1960–1964, and eight in 1965. And, in contrast to many other regional summer stock operations, including the Dallas Summer Musicals, the theater banked modest profits throughout its first decade of operation. The profits could be partly attributed to a full catalog of recent and past hits available to summer stock theaters, but the use of rising talent and the absence of elaborate scenery were also factors. The yearly arrival of at least one or two smash hits generally offset occasional losses. *The King and I* in 1959 was followed by *South Pacific* in 1960, *The Music Man* and *Showboat* in 1961, *Gypsy* and *West Side Story* in 1963, *The Sound of Music* and *My Fair Lady* in 1964, and *Camelot* in 1965. High-grossing shows sometimes ran for three weeks to boost earnings, but even with these successes, the theater instituted a patron balloting system in 1963, hoping to eliminate potential money losers.[31]

And though not without its critics, the "star of tomorrow" philosophy soon became a hallmark of the theater's early identity. Such performers as Richard France, Betty O'Neill, Jack Harrold, Colee Worth, Mace Barrett, Deedy Irwin, Gary Oakes, James Hurst, Joy Garrett, Scott Jarvis, and Nolan Van Way developed popular followings without benefit of celebrity billing. The summer musical season also gave work to local professionals. Johnny Sullivan, Geena Sleete, Rose-Mary Rumbley, Erwin Swint, Bill Garber, B.J. Cleveland, Dick Harris, Ned Van Zandt, and Jerry Russell, already active in area university and community theater groups, appeared regularly in supporting roles.

A further sign of the theater's growing prestige came during the 1961 season, when the company was selected to produce *Calamity Jane,* the first try-out of a musical ever staged outside the East or in-the-round. Thanks to its source material, a 1953 movie starring Doris Day and Howard Keel, the show already possessed name recognition and a high-profile score that included the Academy Award-winning tune, "Secret Love." But what worked well on the screen did not necessarily translate to the stage. One critic complained, "When [the show] should rise to a climax, it often merely totters on the brink . . . the characters are colorful legend if as yet the legend is not fully realized." Still, the production represented an important step forward. *Variety* praised Michael Pollock's direction and what it called his "keen sense of spectacle."[32]

The behind-the-scenes production team became an important factor in much of the theater's early success. By the second season, Michael Pollock had assumed the roles of both director and producer, while general manager Melvin Dacus took over marketing and public relations. Answering complaints of a lack of professional know-how, Dacus hired a full-time stage manager and replaced conductor William Baer with Sherman Frank, a veteran of both summer stock and Broadway. One of Frank's first changes was to remove the pit piano to make room for several additional musicians. Costume designer Evelyn Norton Anderson joined the staff in 1961, as did choreographer Ellen Ray and lighting and special effects wizard Jules Fisher.[33]

Michael Pollock was undoubtedly one of the most important forces shaping Casa Mañana's early productions. Pollock took criticism for a proscenium approach to moving players on the round stage, with what one reviewer called "too many immobile backs [and] obvious revolves." Added to this were complaints that the director had replaced "disciplined theater" with a tendency to "gimmick up" shows. Coming under particular fire was 1960's production of *Rosalinda,* which featured Metropolitan Opera stars Ralph Herbert and Thomas Hayward walking through rubberized bars and calling each other Elvis. Whiskey bottles dropped into hands on cue from the overhead light teaser, and when a character requested a chair, one was pulled up from the orchestra pit on a rope.[34]

Pollock's other so-called gimmicks, however, turned weak shows into moneymakers for the theater. Taking a cue from Billy Rose, the director built interest in *Gentlemen Prefer Blondes* by flying in a group of leggy showgirls, purportedly from several New York nightclubs, to Amon Carter Field. The girls were chauffeured to the theater in a caravan of waiting Rolls-Royce automobiles, each driven by eligible millionaires. Jules Styne, the show's composer, directed the overture opening night, and each evening, for the show's big number, "Diamonds Are a Girl's Best Friend," star Emmaline Henry made her grand entrance draped in $5 million worth of gem-stones, transported to Fort Worth under heavy guard by New York jeweler Harry Winston. Uniformed police stood sentry at the head of each aisle throughout the run. Publicity generated by the events gave the theater its strongest opening since the 1958 premiere.[35]

With other shows, Pollock became skillful at using the arena's intimate setting to pull the audience into the action. For a key scene in 1960's *South Pacific,* he enlisted a platoon of Marines, over a hundred men. Dressed in full combat gear, the unit marched across the stage singing "Honeybun." The show did the biggest business of the season, and Richard Rodgers sent a personal representative to view a performance. For 1962's *Damn Yankees,* Jules Fisher set up banks of "stadium" lights around the interior of the theater's dome. To heighten the ballpark effect, Pollock issued seat cushions and breakaway beer bottles to the audience, encouraging them to pelt the umpire and a Mickey Mantle look-alike hired for scenes in Yankee Stadium.[36]

Criticism of the operation gradually diminished as Pollock and the technical staff found innovative ways to tap the permanent arena setting's full potential and get around the absence of large-scale scenery. In 1959's *Annie Get Your Gun,* Indians in ceremonial regalia danced along service catwalks against the shimmering backdrop of the gold dome. Leading lady Deedy Irwin re-created one of Annie Oakley's most famous stunts, sharp shooting as she rode a motorcycle around the theater concourse. Critics were unanimous in their praise of the show, one calling it "a glittering souvenir of turn-of-the-century show business."[37]

When *The Music Man* came available for summer stock in 1961, Casa Mañana became the first theater to secure the rights, though some warned it could never be staged arena-style. For the opening "Rock Island" sequence and "Marian the Librarian," two of the musical's most familiar but problematic numbers, Pollock's design team constructed both a railway car and the interior of the town library using elaborate scrim cut-outs that became translucent when strategically lit. He used similar techniques to even greater effect in 1962's *The Desert Song,* draping the audi-torium's enclosing wall in the sheer fabric. As the hall darkened for the overture, the audience suddenly found themselves surrounded by the full sweep of the desert overhung with stars.[38]

Partly because of such innovative touches, Casa Mañana Musicals operated consis-tently in the black through its first five seasons, one of the few summer stock theaters in the country that could boast such a record. Though profits remained insufficient to repay its original debt, by the spring of 1962 the company felt sufficiently secure to establish an adjunct children's theater and school. Iris Futor Siff, an educational theater expert who had established the Alley Academy for Houston's Alley Theater in 1951, organized the curriculum, served as the first executive director, and gave the school its name—the Merry-Go-Round.[39]

The school opened on September 17, 1962, offering classes in the theater arts and an ambitious program of eight children's plays beginning with *Aladdin and the Wonderful Lamp.* Mason Johnson of Texas Wesleyan College became the school's first dean with Ivan Rider serving as artistic director. Others on the staff included Sharon Benge, Stanley Crow, Mary Lou Hoyle, Olyve Abbott, Johnny Simons, and Virginia Ward. At the end of the first year, Benge, who had earlier founded a similar school for the Greater Fort Worth Community Theater, replaced Johnson as dean.[40]

As the Casa Mañana dome went up during the spring of 1958, cost overruns had raised the facility's final price tag an additional $207,744, an amount financed through

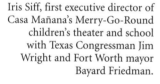

Iris Siff, first executive director of Casa Mañana's Merry-Go-Round children's theater and school with Texas Congressman Jim Wright and Fort Worth mayor Bayard Friedman.

Courtesy, *Fort Worth Star-Telegram* Collection, Special Collections, University of Texas-Arlington Libraries

the borrowing of $210,000. Much of the money had gone toward paving the parking lot and the purchase of the theater's plush red seats. In February 1963, the loan came due, but with only minimal profits to show for the theater's first five seasons, the corporation still owed $196,500. After the banks agreed to extend the deadline, the board launched an emergency underwriting campaign, hoping to raise $60,000 immediately and retire the loans completely within four years. Even though the campaign eventually exceeded the short term goal by nearly $2,000, Michael Pollock had to delay hirings six weeks, until it could be determined if there would be money for a season.[41]

Outwardly revitalized by the crisis, a new, more serious Casa Mañana seemed to emerge. The season featured the premieres of several recent Broadway releases, including *Gypsy* and *West Side Story,* and Pollock's stagings of these shows did much to change the attitudes of Dallas critics, who had dismissed the theater through its first five seasons. The *Dallas Times Herald* lauded *Gypsy* as "responsible theater that puts a pair of becoming long pants on the operation," and *West Side Story* brought new praise for its "more polished, mature approach to show making." The season, chiefly on the strength of these two shows, once again showed a small profit, though there was a drop of $3,000 from the season before.[42]

Then, in the spring of 1964, a second blow fell, jeopardizing the company's already precarious financial situation. On March 26, James Snowden, the theater's founder and financial mentor, committed suicide. Snowden, described by close associates as a modest, almost self-effacing man, had personally signed notes for over $180,000 in loans made to the group. Following an emergency board meeting, an interim management committee composed of Bayard Friedman, James C. Fuller and Charles E. Marshall was appointed to run the theater through the 1964 season. As the long-term effects of Snowden's death were assessed, the 1964 season moved ahead. Acquisition of several recent releases, including both *My Fair Lady* and *The Sound of Music,* turned the season into the most successful to date. Casa Mañana became the first summer stock organization in the country as well as the first theater-in-the-round to stage *The Sound of Music,* and both musicals sold out their three-week runs.[43]

The season also brought the debut appearance of actress Ruta Lee. Her interpretation of the indefatigable heroine of Meredith Willson's *The Unsinkable Molly Brown* was hailed by the composer as the definitive interpretation of the role and helped establish the actress as a local star. Dacus brought her back for 1965's season opener *South Pacific,* and between 1966 and 1972 she appeared five more times. Over three decades, the actress would eventually star twenty-seven times in seventeen different roles ranging from matchmaker Dolly Levi in *Hello, Dolly* to Miss Mona, madam of *The Best Little Whorehouse in Texas*.[44]

The 1964 season drew record crowds and grossed nearly $475,000, but without James Snowden to continue securing the company's outstanding bank notes, the theater's financial situation grew increasingly bleak. On the strength of Snowden's word and signature, lenders had repeatedly extended loan deadlines, but shortly after the seating of a new executive board in September and the election of James C. Fuller as the organization's second president, the banks demanded full payment. With no other recourse, the board decided to shutter the theater permanently if money to clear the debts could not be raised by Thanksgiving.[45]

Ruta Lee's 1964 appearance as Molly Brown in *The Unsinkable Molly Brown* was hailed by composer Meredith Willson as the "definitive" interpretation of the role.

Courtesy, *Fort Worth Star-Telegram* Collection, Special Collections, University of Texas-Arlington Libraries

Mel Dacus, left, Robert Utter, chairman of the "Red Seat" Campaign, and James Fuller, Casa president, symbolically tear up a bank note after donations from individual citizens, school children, and organizations completely erased the theater's debt and saved it from closing in November 1964.

Courtesy, *Fort Worth Star-Telegram* Collection, Special Collections, University of Texas-Arlington Libraries

To meet the deadline, Ice Capades showman Robert Emerson "Rip" Johnson, a long-time Casa Mañana board member, devised a plan to "sell" the theater's 1,832 red seats. Part of the overall strategy called for soliciting an additional $50,000 in larger corporate and individual gifts, but the "Red Seat Campaign" targeted smaller investors, promising each $100 contributor a season ticket and the chance to have a brass nameplate bearing his or her name permanently affixed to a seat. After thirty days, however, the campaign seemed on the verge of collapse, drawing little support from its original target, the local business community. With just a week to go before Thanksgiving, only 40 percent of the seats had sold.[46]

As newspapers, radio, and television reported the theater's plight, deliverance came from an unexpected source. Schoolchildren and scout troops mounted "Save Casa Mañana" campaigns, collecting small change and offering their allowances. Office workers formed company pools to buy seats and then held drawings to see who got the season tickets. Many, citing memories of the original Billy Rose revues, sent in smaller amounts with notes attached, just wanting to have some part in saving the theater. Individual purchasers included Texas senator John Tower and the "King of Jazz," Paul Whiteman, whose big band topped Casa Mañana's headliners during the Billy Rose years of 1936 and 1937.

On Wednesday, November 25, the announced deadline, fewer than two hundred seats remained. Shortly after seven A.M., board members began taking calls over a phone bank set up in the theater lobby, and by noon all remaining seats had sold. But as fast as local radio stations dispatched mobile units to collect the donations, more calls jammed the lines. To handle the surge in demand for seats, several large firms that had previously purchased entire rows offered to resell some so that more donors could participate. By day's end, nearly $70,000 had poured in, pushing the final total to $233,000, and surpassing the original goal of $183,200 by almost $50,000. For the first time in its eight-year history, Casa Mañana was entirely free of debt.[47]

The outpouring of community support not only liberated the theater from its creditors but also applied pressure to city leaders to make other changes. Under a renegotiated lease arrangement, the council agreed to accept a percentage of each season's gross receipts, giving the organization more flexibility to cope with losses from unprofitable shows. With its improved financial picture, the company moved forward with construction of a $30,000 scenery shop and storage area, finally abandoning "temporary" quarters in the ramshackle Pioneer Palace.[48]

The new facility also provided much-needed additional space for the Merry-Go-Round School, which, in its very first year, had seen enrollment balloon from

Sharon Benge, seen with two students, became director of Casa Mañana's theater school in 1964. She went on to found the city's long-running outdoor theater festival, Shakespeare in the Park, in 1977.

Courtesy, *Fort Worth Star-Telegram* Collection, Special Collections, University of Texas-Arlington Libraries

the originally projected 125 students to four hundred. By the fall of 1964, just two seasons after its founding, the school boasted the largest enrollment of any children's drama program in the nation, with classes spilling over into whatever spaces could be found, including the theater's cramped lobby, dressing rooms, rehearsal halls, and concourse.

Despite the school's obvious success, the expense of retaining Iris Siff, who commuted regularly between Houston and Fort Worth, had become an increasing hardship for the debt-plagued theater. In the fall of 1964, Sharon Benge, who had served as dean during the previous season, replaced Siff as executive director. Benge did much to expand the school's curriculum and improve its funding over the next fourteen years. With the help of federal grants, she increased the school's full-time faculty and staff to include a choreographer, fencing master, and composer-in-residence. She also commissioned new plays and musicals from such local writers as Ann Pugh, Betty Utter, and Johnny Simons. Hoping to appeal to a broader age range of students, she changed the name of the school in 1965 to the Casa Mañana Playhouse, offering beginning and advanced acting, movement, stage management, technical direction, lighting design, and creative dramatics. At the same time, she expanded community programs, formerly limited to evening classes and weekend plays, to include daytime performances for area-wide school districts.[49]

Shortly after the seating of a new president and board in September 1964, reports had circulated that Michael Pollock's days as producer-director were numbered. A series of under-rehearsed openings during the 1965 season brought fresh criticism from some local reviewers and gave new credence to the rumors. The *Star-Telegram* was particularly critical of *Roberta*, the season's fourth offering, citing alterations that gave "an uncertain quality to the entire production." His appearance onstage two days into the run to complain about the review angered some board members and earned him a reprimand. At season's end, the board voted not to extend his contract and by early 1966, Melvin Dacus had once again assumed the dual role of producer and general manager.[50]

In the wake of Pollock's dismissal, the Casa Mañana board permanently separated the positions of producer and director. Richard France, Bernard "Buff" Shurr, and Robert Ennis Turoff each assumed directorial responsibilities for varying lengths of time between 1966 and 1973. During the theater's first nine seasons, a series of conductors, including William Baer, Sherman Frank, Boris Kogan, Remi Ghilespi, and Arthur Lief served as the company's music director, but following Lief's resignation in 1967, Joseph Stecko assumed the post. Stecko, who was destined to become the

Joseph Stecko, left, music director of Casa Mañana from 1967-2001.

Courtesy, *Fort Worth Star-Telegram* Collection, Special Collections, University of Texas-Arlington Libraries

theater's most durable figure, would wield the baton over each summer's productions for the next thirty-five years.

For several more seasons the theater continued to post annual profits, though the flow of certifiable blockbusters coming off Broadway had slowed. Some new shows like *Funny Girl,* featuring a strong performance by Linda Gerard, and *On A Clear Day You Can See Forever,* starring local favorite Mace Barrett, did turn profits, but less familiar shows or shows lacking the strong universal appeal of a *Sound of Music* fared less well. Patrons complained about the number of repeated shows and the need for new additions to the repertoire, but then stayed home when the theater produced *Half a Sixpence, What Makes Sammy Run,* and *Little Me,* shows that had enjoyed respectable New York runs. All lost money, as did Tony Award winners *Oliver!* and *George M!* The 1966 production of Frank Loesser's Pulitzer Prize winning musical, *How To Succeed In Business Without Really Trying,* barely broke even.[51]

Confusing the picture still further, the theater's biggest moneymakers continued to be revivals. Ruta Lee's reprise of *The Unsinkable Molly Brown,* chosen to kick off the theater's tenth anniversary season in 1967, shattered all previous records for a two-week run, inspiring Dacus to star her in another revival, the 1968 season opener, *Annie Get Your Gun.* Just three shows later, a revival of *Oklahoma!* became the highest-grossing musical of the season. The production, starring Gary Oakes, also featured Fort Worth singer Betty Lynn Buckley as Ado Annie. Buckley, who had made her professional debut at age fifteen in Casa Mañana's 1963 production of *Gypsy,* went on

Betty Lynn Buckley as Ado Annie with Johnny Sullivan, left and Leonard Drum in 1968's *Oklahoma!* Buckley, a Fort Worth native, went on to a distinguished career spanning Broadway, television, and film.

Courtesy, Casa Mañana Musicals, Inc.

to a distinguished career in television, film, and on Broadway, including roles in *1776,
Pippin,* and *Cats,* for which she won the 1983 Tony Award for best featured actress
in a musical.[52]

Yet another revival, 1968's *A Funny Thing Happened On the Way To the Forum,*
featured the return of exotic dancer Sally Rand. Three decades earlier, her "ballet
divertissement," part of Billy Rose's 1936 Casa Mañana Revue, had stirred controversy
and pulled in record crowds to Fort Worth's Frontier Centennial. Yet, even in the
arena's more intimate setting, the dancer artfully demonstrated the truth of her
trademark boast "the Rand is quicker than the eye," as she performed behind the
same oversized ostrich-feather fans that had first brought her notoriety during
1933's Chicago World's Fair.[53]

Patron calls for new material may have played a role in Casa Mañana's 1969 decision to stage *Hello Sucker,* a new show written by the theater's own musical director
Robert Ennis Turoff and composer Wilson Stone. The production marked the first
time since 1961's *Calamity Jane* that the theater had attempted to stage an untried
work. Revolving around the exploits of Prohibition era New York's fabled "queen of
the nightclubs," Texas Guinan, the musical seemed positioned for an eventual
Broadway try-out with Ruta Lee cast as Guinan. Opening night, critics praised "force-
ful" performances by Lee and co-star Mace Barrett but generally dismissed Turoff's
uneven writing as "heavy on cliché" and "basically bland." *Star-Telegram* reviewer
Elston Brooks noted with a touch of irony, "the show has all the musical comedy ingre-
dients to rocket it to Broadway except one—the rocket never goes off."[54]

Though a critical failure, *Hello Sucker* did well at the box office, a fact that may
have influenced management's decision to try a full season of new shows in 1970. The
move proved disastrous, however, resulting in the theater's first losing season. Out of
eight shows, only two comedies, *Sweet Charity* and *Mame,* starring Betty O'Neill, a
popular leading lady from Casa's early seasons, made money. Even *Man of La
Mancha,* one of Broadway's longest-running hits, failed to earn back its production
expenses.[55]

Partly to blame for the poor showing was a serious miscalculation of Ruta Lee's
popular following. Lee had asked to play *Mame,* but when the theater offered the
role instead to O'Neill, the recently launched Windmill Dinner Theater, located
nearby on North Forest Park Boulevard, quickly stepped forward with a counteroffer.
As Casa Mañana opened its season to small houses and poor reviews, *Peterpat,* starring Lee and Judd Hirsch, played the Windmill stage to sell-out crowds for six weeks.
The production, according to Elston Brooks, "killed Casa at the box office." The

Windmill followed up this success with a production of *The Odd Couple*, featuring Brooks. Once again, the dinner theater drew capacity crowds while the theater-in-the-round did only fair business.[56]

Stung by 1970's dismal box office returns, Casa Mañana made peace with Lee, luring her back to star in 1971's season opener, *Hello, Dolly*, which became the highest-grossing show in the theater's fourteen-year history. *Fiddler On the Roof*, Broadway's most successful musical to date, closed the season with a three-week run, pushing the theater's net earnings to a remarkable $117,000, the most profitable since 1958. The 1972 season promised to be yet another record breaker, stacked with several first run productions and a landmark presentation of George Gershwin's *Porgy and Bess*, unprecedented in the city's history because all but nine of its fifty-two member, mostly black company came from the North Texas area.[57]

Porgy and Bess might have stood alone as the summer's most newsworthy event had the season not been marred by growing labor unrest. A strike of Actors Equity personnel seeking a 17 percent raise closed *The Student Prince* for one performance after the Casa Mañana board refused to defy a federal mandate temporarily capping wage increases across the nation at 5½ percent. Actors Equity, bargaining through the Music Theater Association, maintained that the higher figures were in line because of steeper cost-of-living standards on the East Coast where many actors were based. A compromise agreement seemed to resolve the dispute, but the Casa board elected to drop its troublesome membership in MTA.[58]

Workmen in September completed the transfer and reinstallation of the city's only "Mighty Wurlitzer" pipe organ from its former home in downtown's Worth Theater to Casa Mañana. For a time after the closing of the Worth in November 1971, it appeared that the instrument, one of the few such Wurlitzers remaining in the nation, would be broken down and sold for parts. Fort Worth oilman F. Howard Walsh purchased the organ for $20,000 and persuaded Casa Mañana officials to give it a new home in the domed theater. From the Worth's opening in 1927 through the 1940s, the instrument and its most famous organist, Billy Muth, had remained familiar fixtures of the downtown theater. A September 25 ceremony and concert marked completion of the project.[59]

In February 1973, following six months of negotiations, the Casa Mañana board instructed Melvin Dacus to inform Actors Equity that the company would mount a non-union season for 1973. The action came amidst unresolved union claims that actors were still owed $4,200 in retroactive salaries from the previous summer. In contradictory demands, Equity offered to waive the amount in return for substantial pay increases, even as it continued to insist that all actors on the Casa stage be union. The latter demand ignored the fact that the theater had already operated with Equity sanction for fifteen seasons using occasional non-union players. The executive board, citing Texas right-to-work laws, strongly disputed the claim and an additional mandate that the hiring of principals be limited to New York. Though the amount saved by operating non-union was less than $4,000, one board member, later described by Dacus as "extremely vehement," pressed for a split, declaring "I would rather close the theater and make a library out of it than accede to [Equity] wishes."[60]

With talks stalemated, Equity purchased space in local newspapers threatening to "put [Casa Mañana] out of existence." The large ads, some in the form of a letter to Casa's board of directors, hammered the theater's "substandard" wages while urging the board to "restore professional theater," shrilly declaring the board's refusal to acquiesce to union demands, "a clear and present danger to us." Opening night, patrons had to negotiate a picket line of 150 union protesters led by such prominent actors as Rip Torn, Geraldine Page, and Theodore Bikel. Yet, despite the inflammatory claims, *South Pacific* and *Mame,* directed by the Dallas Theater Center's Barry Hope, played to good reviews.[61]

Promises, Promises and *Cabaret,* directed by the University of Houston's Cecil Pickett, one of the state's most respected drama coaches, also passed critical muster. But after six weeks, the union's unrelenting campaign to close the theater was having an effect. Casa Playhouse director Sharon Benge bitterly recalled, "We found out just how strong a union town this really was." Ticket sales plummeted.[62]

With $53,000 in season revenues already lost by mid-June, the executive board, in a move strongly opposed by producer Dacus and other staff members, voted on June 23 to shutter the theater following the last performance of *Cabaret* on July 14. Calling Casa board members "short-sighted men," union executive secretary Donald Grody professed shock at the decision, but Equity, nonetheless, continued its negative ad campaign against the theater for several more days. The *Star-Telegram* condemned the tactic as "a cold, cruel example of where [the union] stands in this sorrowful affair." On July 16, just two days after the theater's closing, the union and Casa Mañana officials reached an agreement.[63]

Resentment stirred by the boycott continued to affect business into the 1980s. Union rhetoric and the local board's corresponding reluctance to settle its differences with Equity so thoroughly damaged the theater's image that some patrons, even years later, had never returned, either believing the organization guilty of ongoing unfair labor practices or resentful of actors who had supported the strike. The negative

backlash was readily apparent in 1974. The season's first show, *Fiddler On the Roof,* played to half-empty houses, and the second, *A Funny Thing Happened On the Way To the Forum,* did the worst business in company history.[64]

Attendance finally showed signs of improvement by mid-season, propelled by appearances of Nanette Fabray in *No, No Nanette* and Gisele MacKenzie in *Gypsy.* The shows marked a fateful step away from the company's long-time policy of booking relative unknowns. In an even more radical departure, the theater also offered Ann Corio's *This Was Burlesque,* a revue alternating comedy sketches with striptease artists. Opening night, some offended patrons walked out.[65]

Perhaps the most surprising turn of events came at the close of the season when the board of directors, without prior notice, fired Casa Mañana's co-founder and long-time general manager, Mel Dacus. Newly elected president Leon Brachman defended the action as a need to separate the duties of producer and general manager, but a stronger motive driving the change was a diametrical shift away from the theater's original philosophy. Dacus explained, "My desires to use up and coming talent instead of going to the stars . . . plus the strike . . . led to my dismissal."[66]

Prominent Actors Equity union members Theodore Bikel, left, Werner Klemperer, Rip Torn, and Geraldine Page picket Casa Mañana in May, 1973. Protesters claimed that the theater's hiring policies were unfair to union members.

Courtesy, *Fort Worth Star-Telegram* Collection, Special Collections, University of Texas-Arlington Libraries

C. E. "Bud" Franks, hired in 1974
as Casa Mañana's second executive
producer. As part of the theater's
new "star" policy, Franks hired
such well-known performers as
Howard Keel, Van Johnson,
Martha Raye, and Sid Caesar.

Courtesy, *Fort Worth Star-Telegram*
Collection, Special Collections,
University of Texas-Arlington
Libraries

With Dacus' departure, the character of the theater continued its metamorphosis. In November 1974 the board hired C.E. "Bud" Franks. Franks had been born in Fort Worth to Air Force parents but moved with the family to various postings, finally returning to earn degrees at both Texas A & M and Texas Christian University. He later performed as a member of the Casa Mañana ensemble and had managed and directed dinner theaters in both Ohio and Fort Worth before accepting the new post. Also joining the staff was stage director Jack Bunch, a former dancer and choreographer who had previously directed musicals for Ohio's Kenley Circuit.[67]

In his first season with the theater, Franks introduced a full lineup of musical revivals featuring movie and television stars Howard Keel, Van Johnson, Martha Raye, Ruta Lee, Mary Ann Mobley, and Gary Collins. Singers Vicki Carr and Roger Miller also played one-week concert engagements. The shift to high-profile performers and a mixed format produced a jump in season ticket sales, the largest since 1958, and led, over the next five seasons, to bookings of other name entertainers, including Debbie Reynolds, Ken Berry, Chita Rivera, George Maharis, and Anna Maria Alberghetti. The high spot of the 1979 season, however, was a nostalgic revival of *Fiddler on the Roof*, featuring Melvin and Katy Dacus in the lead roles. Besides returning to performing, Dacus had also formed his own production company with director Buff Shurr, mounting plays and musicals for the country's burgeoning dinner theater circuit.[68]

The trend continued through the 1980s with appearances by Arte Johnson, Sid Caesar and Imogene Coca, Phyllis Diller, Ray Charles, Flip Wilson, Betty Buckley,

Former executive producer
Melvin Dacus, along with
his wife, Katy, returned to the
theater in 1979 to star in Fiddler
On the Roof.

Courtesy, Dacus family

and Noel Harrison. But even with the switch to the star system, the organization continued to post significant season losses. With increased competition from television, movies, and amusement parks, and a corresponding decline of summer stock, box office sales could no longer offset production costs and salaries.

After financial crises in 1977 and 1983 once again threatened to close the theater, the Casa Mañana board in 1984 inaugurated the annual Campaign For Casa to offset the company's yearly deficits. Further improving its financial picture, the organization began receiving funding from the Arts Council of Fort Worth and Tarrant County in 1989. At the same time, the company attempted to broaden the scope of its offerings. In 1987 the theater sponsored a national touring company for the first time, presenting *Cats* in the Tarrant County Convention Center's John F. Kennedy Theater. Another break with tradition followed in 1989 when the organization returned to the Kennedy to stage its first proscenium musical, *Peter Pan*, with former Olympic gymnast, Cathy Rigby. In 1990, the theater presented a winter lineup of non-musical plays for the first time since 1961. The comedy series, which included *Noises Off* and *Daddy's Dying, Who's Got the Will?* was performed on the Casa stage, but in the half-round.[69]

By 1990, the domed theater, once a showplace among theaters-in-the-round, had deteriorated badly. The roof leaked, lighting and sound systems were badly outdated, temporary buildings served as administrative offices, and storage space littered the grounds. With year-round legitimate plays, summer musicals, and Casa Playhouse children's productions, nearly 250,000 people used the space annually.

It was hoped in the summer of 1990 that a $20 million bond proposal for renovation of the West Lancaster cultural district would allow much needed expansion and renovation of the aging facility. The master plan, four years in development, called for the refurbishing of Will Rogers Auditorium, Casa Mañana, and the William Edrington Scott Theater. Also hanging in the balance was an additional $30 million in matching funds pledged by several prominent businessmen, including Robert Bass. The measure came before voters on July 10 but was overwhelmingly rejected. Just weeks after the defeat, at the conclusion of the 1990 season, Bud Franks resigned following sixteen seasons as the theater's executive producer.[70]

Van Kaplan, the theater's administrative director, was named as Franks' successor. Since joining the staff in 1981, Kaplan had worked as actor, stage manager, playwright, producer, and fund-raiser. An Indiana native and graduate of Southern Methodist University's professional acting program, he had received additional training from New York's Juilliard School. In his new role as executive producer, Kaplan picked up where Franks had left off, further diversifying the theater's offerings. Over the next

Van Kaplan, seen in 1984, worked as actor, stage manager, playwright, producer, and fund raiser for Casa Mañana over several years. In 1990, he became the organization's third executive producer.

Courtesy, *Fort Worth Star-Telegram* Collection, Special Collections, University of Texas-Arlington Libraries

seven seasons, the number of musicals-in-the-round was reduced to make room for an extended season of concerts and legitimate plays. Among the favorites were Joe Sears and Jaston Williams' *Greater Tuna* plays and appearances by Jerry Seinfeld, Carol Channing, Natalie Cole, Barbara Mandrell, and Anne Murray.[71]

Though continuing to present touring companies in the Kennedy Theater and Will Rogers Auditorium, Kaplan also debuted Casa On the Square in 1991, using a renovated space on the third floor of downtown's historic Knights of Pythias Hall at 110 East Third. The intimate, 124-seat space was an immediate hit with a series of musical revues and comedies that included *Forever Plaid, Ain't Misbehavin,' Shear Madness,* and *Ruthless, the Musical.* Among his other innovations, Kaplan presided over world premieres of two new musicals, *Dodsworth* (1995) starring Hal Linden and *Grossinger's* (1997) featuring Ruta Lee and Gavin MacLeod.[72]

In June 1997, Kaplan resigned to become executive director of the Pittsburgh Civic Light Opera. Hired two months later as Casa Mañana's fourth executive producer was Denton Yockey, former executive director of Galveston's Lone Star Performing Arts Association. Like his predecessors, Yockey, who held degrees from both Indiana University and the University of Georgia, had broad experience as actor, director, and producer. He faced dual challenges in his first year on the job—an ongoing campaign to raise $5.1 million for capital improvements, an outgrowth of the failed 1990 bond election, and the imminent completion of the Nancy Lee and Perry R. Bass Performance Hall in downtown Fort Worth.[73]

Denton Yockey succeeded Van Kaplan as executive producer in 1997. During his tenure, Casa Mañana underwent major changes, including a redesign of the theater's in-the-round configuration.

Courtesy, Casa Mañana Musicals, Inc.

The opening of the $67 million dollar Bass Hall in May 1998 and the resultant shift of public attention away from Casa Mañana presented the organization with perhaps the most difficult dilemma of its forty-year history. While Casa-sponsored productions in the Bass Hall were selling at 74 percent capacity or higher despite ticket prices ranging as high as $67, *Bye-Bye Birdie* and *The King and I,* with tickets priced at just $35, lost $85,000 apiece under the West Lancaster dome in the summer of 2000. With the shift of audience interest downtown, it became increasingly apparent that the heyday of in-the-round production had long since passed. Nor could the theater expect to compete against the Bass Hall's broad range of year-round offerings.[74]

Facing a "join-them-or-be-beaten" dilemma, the board voted in 2000 to end the organization's forty-two year history of summer musical seasons under the Casa Mañana dome. Three shows that season moved to the Bass Hall, with just one, *Gigi,* presented in the round during a six-day September run. Yet even before the opening of the Bass Hall, Yockey had already broached the subject of altering Casa Mañana's longtime in-the-round configuration to the modified proscenium/thrust arrangement originally conceived by the theater's planners in 1957. The company handed to him faced multiple dilemmas. Fewer directors, actors, choreographers, and designers were trained to work in the round, meaning that booking imported productions or coproducing shows with other theaters had become virtually impossible. And, in a throwback to the heyday of live production, audiences increasingly gravitated to proscenium productions mounted with elaborate scenery and technical effects.[75]

Yockey's first proposal in June 1998 was voted down 19-16 by the board of directors. Just three years later, with the Bass Hall's impact as well as its potential increasingly apparent, attitudes on the board shifted. The producer's decision to shift locally produced musicals to the downtown hall, after encountering initial resistance, had proved financially sound, and several of his other innovations were also helping to forge ties with a younger generation of theatergoers. Among these were the launching of the annual Betty Lynn Buckley Awards, honoring high school musical productions, and the Tomorrow Project, introducing new musicals through staged readings and workshops.[76]

With Casa Mañana's ongoing capital campaign to refurbish and expand the existing plant finally nearing its goal in August 2002, the board once again tackled the issue of the theater's future. With only thirty-eight of the sixty directors present, the vote was historic as well as controversial. By the end of the meeting, those present had unanimously approved eliminating the hall's original in-the-round layout in favor of a more conventional stage arrangement. Board members and longtime patrons who favored

Forty-five years after being set into place, workmen dismantle Casa Mañana's round stage in early 2003 as remodeling of the theater begins.

Courtesy, Casa Mañana Musicals, Inc.

Redesign of the theater during 2002-2003 updated the building's cinderblock exterior and added nearly 12,000 square feet of lobby, office, and classroom space.

Courtesy, Casa Mañana Musicals, Inc.

keeping the theater as it was cried foul, threatening petition drives and lawsuits. But to many others the move seemed long overdue, given the building's condition and many out-of-date features.

Over the next year, reconfiguration and renovation of the theater moved ahead quickly. Crews gutted the hall's audience chamber, widening aisles, resloping and increasing the pitch of the floor, and installing a new forty-five-hundred-square-foot proscenium/thrust stage, four times the size of the original round stage. State-of-the-art sound and lighting systems and 1,082 plush new high-back seats completed the makeover. The addition of an 11,400-square-foot wing along the building's eastern facade included a light-filled 46- by 160-foot grand lobby with 24 foot-high glass-and-steel outer walls. Completion of the project provided space for receptions, educational programs, offices, and restrooms without obscuring the building's most significant and striking architectural element, its geodesic dome.[77]

With the acting area pushed to one side, and nearly seven hundred square feet of performance space thrusting out into the hall, the redesigned arena came more to resemble a classic Greek theater in configuration. The seating area, now sloped upward eleven degrees to back rows, gave patrons a virtually unobstructed view of the stage from anywhere in the hall. However, in completing the renovation, planners were left with at least one technical dilemma. Preservation of the dome ruled out the addition of a traditional fly loft and thus limited the company's use of oversize scenery.

On September 20, 2003, forty-five years after the theater's geodesic dome and in-the-round configuration first attracted national attention, the new Casa Mañana made its second debut facing an uncertain future. Summer stock had declined, and the music tents had, for the most part, disappeared. As the trend to musical theater waned, other local theatrical organizations had gradually established themselves. By the turn of the century, such companies as Stage West, Circle Theater, Jubilee Theatre, and Hip Pocket Theater had all grown into well-respected professional and community organizations with solid followings. With the construction of the Bass Hall and the community's expanded entertainment offerings, it remained to be seen if the organization could once again reinvent itself.

CHAPTER THIRTEEN

LOCAL AND UNIVERSITY THEATER: 1945-2001

[The performance] "was pathetic,
believable, [and] heart-rending."
Fort Worth Star-Telegram, May 8, 1955

While the Fort Worth Opera and Casa Mañana Musicals were the two largest and most visible organizations established in the decades following World War II, they were by no means the only forces shaping the city's theatrical fortunes. Significant performance spaces like the William Edrington Scott and John F. Kennedy theaters became part of the landscape as various other clubs and civic organizations helped lay the foundation of what had become, by the end of the twentieth century, a thriving and diverse community of small professional theaters.

The first of these organizations to emerge following the war was the Reeder School, a children's theater academy, which, between 1945 and 1958, developed a national reputation for both its methods and the quality and originality of its productions. Founders of the academy were a pair of local artists, Flora Blanc Reeder and her husband Dickson Reeder.

Flora Blanc, the daughter of Edward Blanc and Martha Elliot King, was born in New York City in 1916. She trained at New York's Art Students' League, and in France, where she met Edward Dickson Reeder, a young Fort Worth artist. Reeder studied in Mexico, Paris, and at New York's Art Students' League. During occasional time at home, he performed with the Fort Worth Little Theater, even illustrating some of its programs.[1]

The couple married in New York in December 1937 and moved to Fort Worth in 1940. Dickson taught art classes at local colleges and worked during the war at Consolidated Vultee, while Flora painted and conducted acting classes for Our Lady of Victory College. The pair performed with the Little Theater and established close friendships with a group of local artists who became known as the Fort Worth Circle, gathering frequently at the Reeders' home for discussion and entertainment.[2]

In the spring of 1945, Flora enrolled in a TCU course exploring the interrelation of the arts, taught by Lorraine Sherley. For a final project, she produced the play *Aucassin and Nicolette* in Sherley's garden, using as actors twenty children enlisted from among Sherley's neighbors and friends. Dick Reeder designed the sets, artist Bror Utter devised the lighting scheme, and Brooks Morris, Jr., planned the music. This impromptu beginning led to the creation of the Reeder-Irwin School in August 1945 with thirty-five students enrolled and Ike Horowitz serving as first board chairman. Flora's friend Zane Irwin led dance classes while other instructors, including Flora, taught drama, painting, and music. Some staff members were paid, but others bartered their skills in exchange for enrolling their children.[3]

Flora and Dickson Reeder in 1968.

Courtesy, *Fort Worth Star-Telegram* Collection, Special Collections, University of Texas-Arlington Libraries.

By 1948 the school had changed its name to the Reeder Children's School of Theater and Design, patterning its curriculum after New York's King-Coit School, which Flora Reeder had attended as a child. Two or three days a week, pupils ranging in age from four to fourteen studied Greek mythology, art, mime, dance, painting, and acting. Every aspect of instruction immersed the children in the study of a single tale from classic literature, moving them gradually over eight months toward a thorough understanding of the story and its time period, music, customs, and dress. The school year culminated in May or June with performances of the play.[4]

Between 1945 and 1958, the Reeders staged thirteen additional plays, using only children as performers. Flora researched music and source material, adapted scripts,

Reeder School students practice mime techniques, c. 1948. Each year's integrated curriculum included art, mime, dance, acting, and mythology, concluding with a student performance of a classic tale.

Courtesy, Reeder School Collection, Special Collections, University of Texas-Arlington Libraries

directed productions, and taught, while Dickson led painting classes and designed the lavish sets and costumes. Horowitz initially arranged for classroom and rehearsal space in Temple Beth-El, at the corner of Galveston and Broadway, but during its first year the school moved to a log cabin behind the William J. Bailey home at 3401 White Settlement Road. The school's first production, *The Rose and the Ring,* was staged in June 1946. In 1953, the school moved to the W.A. Duringer mansion at 1402 Summit. Depending on enrollment, which ranged from fifty to eighty children, productions were typically staged over several nights using as many as three casts. The earliest plays were staged at Paschal High School and on the grounds of the Bailey home, but beginning in 1951 productions moved to TCU's Little Theater. *The Taming of the Shrew* (1957) and *Nala and Damayanti* (1958), the school's final productions, were staged at the Majestic Theater and the Greater Fort Worth Community Theater.[5]

Reeder School productions became known as much for the demanding standards of artistry and authenticity set by the Reeders as for the abilities of the young players

Staff and students in front of the W. J. Bailey log cabin, c. 1948. Flora and Dickson Reeder stand on the back row, second and third from the right.

Courtesy, Reeder School Collection, Special Collections, University of Texas-Arlington Libraries

appearing onstage. In such productions as *Kai Khosru* (1947), *The Happy Hypocrite* (1952), *A Midsummer Night's Dream* (1948, 1953), *The Little Parisian* (1955), and *The Knight of the Burning Pestle* (1956), period costumes, makeup, props, hairstyles, and sets were scrupulously researched by Flora Reeder and meticulously reproduced down to the smallest detail. Artists from the Fort Worth Circle, including Cynthia Brants, Bror Utter, Evaline Sellors, George Grammer, Sam Cantey, and McKie Trotter painted sets using Dickson Reeder's designs while Hans David, Lucas Foss, and David Graham composed original music. An ensemble of professional musicians, directed in the school's first year by Jeanne Axtell, accompanied each performance. Leon Varkas, formerly of the Metropolitan Opera Ballet, assisted Flora Reeder in choreographing *The Tempest* (1949) and *Lady Precious Stream* (1950).[6]

The Reeder School closed in 1958, ostensibly to give the artist couple more time for study and painting. Though the pair eventually tried to reopen the school, the All Church Home, in the meantime, had purchased and razed the Duringer house.

The Reeder School's 1951 staging of *Aucassin and Nicolette* at TCU's Little Theater.

Courtesy, Reeder School Collection, Special Collections, University of Texas-Arlington Libraries

Without a suitable replacement building, Flora taught for a time from the W.E. Chilton home, but no more public productions were attempted. In the mid-1960s, Dr. Bob Barker offered the Reeders a second building on Summit, but the structure's condition made the cost of improvements prohibitive. By the late 1960s, Dickson Reeder's health had declined significantly, and he died in 1970. Not until 1981, more than ten years after her husband's death, did Flora Reeder once again revive the school on a limited scale. She was assisted by D. Jefferson Reeder, Dickson Reeder's nephew, who over the next five years replicated many of his uncle's set designs for a new round of

Flora Reeder with students in *Lady Precious Stream*, 1950.

Courtesy, Reeder School Collection, Special Collections, University of Texas-Arlington Libraries

children's plays reprising Reeder School productions of the 1950s. In 1986, the school finally closed for good. Flora Reeder died in 1995.[7]

The city's two universities also played an important role in the development of new theatrical programs following World War II. Shortly after the end of the war, both Texas Christian University and Texas Wesleyan College had begun a push to modernize and expand their theatrical programs. In 1944, the public speaking wing of TCU's School of Fine Arts was reorganized as the speech-drama department, but facilities remained extremely limited. Instructors of music, art, drama, and music were forced to share cramped offices with the home economics department on the top floor of TCU's administration building. Dean of the School of Fine Arts T. Smith McCorkle, however, had vision. He expanded the curriculum, added a B.A. degree in speech-drama, and in 1945 hired Dr. Walther R. Volbach to head the fledgling drama department.[8]

Volbach, the son of distinguished conductor and composer Fritz Volbach, was born in Germany in 1897. Volbach had directed operas with municipal companies in Berlin, Stuttgart, and Vienna, before he fled Germany with his Jewish wife, Claire Neufeld. In

German transplant, Dr. Walther Volbach headed TCU's Drama Department (1946-1965), served as artistic director during the founding of the Fort Worth Opera, and spearheaded formation of the Fort Worth Theater Council.

Courtesy, *Fort Worth Star-Telegram* Collection, Special Collections, University of Texas-Arlington

the United States, he taught at Marquette University, conducted opera in St. Louis and Cleveland, and served as director of opera at the Cleveland Institute of Music.[9]

Volbach, who took charge of the department in January 1946, was a significant figure not only in the development of the TCU theater program but in a number of other civic theatrical enterprises that laid the foundation for later development of the city's professional theater companies. A taskmaster and perfectionist, he served as artistic director of the Fort Worth Civic Opera Association's first production, *La Traviata*, in November 1946 and in 1952 spearheaded the organization of the Fort Worth Theater Council, the city's first alliance of local theater groups. Under Volbach's direction from 1946 to 1965, the university drama program expanded to a department producing eight or ten plays a year, ranging from classical to contemporary works.[10]

Within three years of his arrival, Volbach was among staff members influential in the planning and final design of the university's $1.5 million fine arts building, completed in late summer 1949. Before that date, all productions had been staged in the administration building's auditorium. Designed by architects Wyatt C. Hedrick, Joseph R. Pelich, and Preston Geren, the three-story fine arts building was the first in the nation to house rehearsal halls, studios, exhibit space, and classrooms for art, music, dance, drama, television, and radio under one roof. The complex, formally dedicated on December 4, 1949, included green room, wardrobe room, scene shop, the 224-seat Little Theater, and Ed Landreth Auditorium, a 1,258-seat hall, featuring a 3,970-pipe organ and acoustics and stage facilities suitable for staging full operas. With the opening of the center, Karl Kritz, a former conductor with the Metropolitan Opera, was jointly engaged by TCU and the Fort Worth Civic Opera to direct local operas and conduct the newly organized university opera workshop.[11]

Speech-drama became an official division of Texas Wesleyan's fine arts department in 1947. Several years later, in the mid-1950s, Dr. Donald Bellah, chairman of the college's Division of Fine Arts, was seeking professional help in staging the school's first Broadway musical. The person recommended to him was Mason Johnson, a Cleburne native, who, for a number of years, had served as stage manager for Dallas' State Fair Musicals and director of that city's Starlight Concerts. Johnson had trained at the University of Texas in the 1940s with famed director, Margo Jones. Following service in World War II, he acted and studied dance at New York's American Theater Wing.[12]

Before officially joining the faculty in the fall of 1958, Johnson had already directed and choreographed several musicals for the college, among them *Brigadoon* (1956) and *Annie Get Your Gun* (1957). Before his retirement in 1987, he had greatly

Mason Johnson brought favorable critical notice to Texas Wesleyan University while raising performance standards in a long series of Broadway musicals between 1956 and 1987.

Courtesy, *Fort Worth Star-Telegram* Collection, Special Collections, University of Texas-Arlington Libraries

enhanced the college's theatrical offerings, bringing on M. Cecil Cole to teach courses in technical theater and to serve as production coordinator. For over thirty years, Johnson's sharp eye in staging, costuming, scenery, and choreography, and his ability to elicit professional-level performances from his student performers boosted awareness of the college and attracted the attention of both critics and influential members of the community. For several years, local oilman and philanthropist A.M. "Aggie" Pate underwrote the cost of staging the musicals.[13]

By 1989 Texas Wesleyan, elevated to university status, had expanded beyond its space in the Ann Waggoner Fine Arts Building. That same year the school obtained

Babs Fulwider, left, and Fort Worth native Joy Garrett in Texas Wesleyan's 1964 musical *Bells are Ringing*. Garrett went on to a career on Broadway and television.

Courtesy, Fort Worth Public Library, Local History and Genealogy

title to Polytechnic Baptist Church and after extensive renovations, the former church reopened in 1990 as the Law Sone Fine Arts Complex.[14]

The city's amateur groups also played key roles in the development of the city's postwar theatrical community. Following World War II, there was an explosion of amateur theatrical activity in the city as a number of religious and civic groups organized theatrical companies. The Fort Worth Dramatic Club, directed by Dick Gaedke, began in 1945. The Fort Worth Theater Guild, organized in 1933 to promote dramatics and support the Fort Worth Little Theater, offered occasional plays as well. Another company, the Arena Players, formed in August 1950 and was led by Mrs. Billy Muth and director Jimmy Hughes. None of these groups survived.[15]

Fort Worth's B'nai B'rith lodge, organized in 1902 by a group of leading Jewish citizens, raised money for charitable causes from its inception. In 1951, under the leadership of President Leo Lipshitz, the group formed the B'nai B'rith Little Theater Guild. For well over a decade the group staged several plays a year from Temple Beth-El Center, Galveston and Broadway, and Ahavath Sholom Center, Myrtle and Eighth Avenue. Herb Slatkin, Dan Gachman, Seymour Spiegel, Joe Shanblum, Frances Goldstein, Lucille Schwartz, and Hilda Lou Cohen rotated director duties.

Regular players included J.B. Daiches, Don Gernsbacher, Eddie Gaines, Joy Spiegel, Fran Prinz, Joe Shanblum, Louise Lipshitz, Melton and Meyer Mehl, Nat Cohen, Lucille Schwartz, Erv Ravinsky, Bernie Goldman, and Dan Gachman. Max Kaye served as the group's backstage technician.[16]

Equally successful were the Wing and Masque Players of Convair Recreation Association (CRA). Convair, which in 1951 was the city's largest employer, with thirty-one thousand on the payroll, funded the conversion of a former food market at 2966 Park Hill Drive into the CRA Playhouse. After constructing an intimate, two-hundred-seat arena space with risers on all four sides of the stage, the group opened October 24 with *Mr. Barry's Etchings*.[17]

The company's roster of actors included Clyde Shrell, Eloise Kelly, Chesley York, Bryant Weickersheimer, Shirley Fritz, Paula Hulsey, Wanda Spradley, Loyd Crader Martin, and Hank Fields. Everett and Murrel Morris, who would later be influential in forming the Greater Fort Worth Community Theater, directed a number of the group's productions. Other directors included E. Stanton Brown and Jerry Ratliff. In June 1967 the company moved into the Wing and Masque Theater in the main building of the General Dynamics Recreation Area, a complex constructed in 1957 along Bryant Irvin Road in West Fort Worth.[18]

By 1952, the city had no fewer than five active theatrical organizations. In an effort to eliminate scheduling overlaps and promote closer cooperation among the various companies, several groups from Fort Worth and surrounding cities met in late fall to organize the Fort Worth Theater Council. Among the council's founding members were Arlington State College's Little Theater, First Methodist's Footlite Club, B'nai B'rith Little Theater, TWC's Thespian Club, the TCU Little Theater, and Convair's Wing and Masque Players. Elected to lead the organization were TCU drama professor, Dr. Walther Volbach, Wing and Masque's Murrel Morris, and TWC speech professor, John Edwards. In May 1953, the council held the first of several annual festivals at TCU's Little Theater, with several companies presenting one-act plays.[19]

Other cooperative ventures followed. In 1954 TCU professor Dr. Edward L. Pross organized Horned Frog Summer Theater on the TCU campus with both students and members of the various community theaters participating. In 1955, under the leadership of president Eddie Gaines, the council embarked on its most ambitious project—a joint staging of Arthur Miller's *Death of a Salesman* with a cast pulled from several local organizations. A capacity audience jammed the Majestic Theater on May 7 to see the production directed by head of TCU's radio-television division, Dr. James Costy. Fran Prinz played the part of doomed salesman Willy Loman, Jean Harrison played his wife, and Alfred Koorey and David Combs played Loman's sons. Supporting players included John Hillerman, Joy Spiegel, J.D. Goodman, Earl Bush, and Donald Hicks. The *Star-Telegram* called it "the best amateur performance that has ever hit the stage here" and Prinz's performance "pathetic, believable, [and] heart-rending."[20]

Death of a Salesman marked a turning point for the city's amateur community. In the decade following the war, acting opportunities had been limited to university theater departments and the few private organizations where membership was closely tied to religious or business affiliations. But within seven months of the production, a new group calling itself the Greater Fort Worth Community Theater had formed.

Destined to become the city's longest-surviving and most successful nonprofessional organization, the Community Theater from its 1956 debut was open to anyone. The company, along with Casa Mañana, served for four decades as an important training ground for aspiring North Texas actors and helped give birth to a vigorous network of small professional theaters.

The group organized in the fall of 1955 at the West Fort Worth ranch of car dealer Ernest Allen. Everett Morris, who along with his wife Murrel had long been active in both Wing and Masque and the Footlite Club, was elected first president. For its first production the company chose *My Granny Van*, by Texas writer George Sessions Perry. The play, directed by Murrel Morris and staged arena-style at Ridglea Country Club, opened January 26, 1956, with Arlington Heights High School student Sandra Faubion in the title role. Rounding out the cast were Harrill Bridgess, Vince Hurley, Jeanne Clark, Lynn Trammell, James Thomson, Pat Stanfield, Oscar Wilson, and Manda Mallon. Other productions of the troupe's inaugural season, *Dial M For Murder* and *The Solid Gold Cadillac*, shifted to the Majestic Theater.[21]

Community Theater productions remained at the Majestic for another year. The company opened its first full season in September with the World War II prisoner-of-war drama *Stalag 17*, featuring a number of players who would become stalwarts of the early group: Erwin Swint, Dick Harris, and Fran Prinz. Stagings of *Anastasia, Oh Men! Oh Women!, A Streetcar Named Desire, Will Success Spoil Rock Hunter?,* and *The Philadelphia* Story followed, but a simmering dispute with Majestic manager Murrel Morris over the scheduling of conflicting events led the company to search for a new theater in 1957.[22]

Fran Prinz, the company's second president, arranged for a move to the old Morgan Theater, a rundown former movie house at 608 North Sylvania, northeast of downtown. Over several months the deteriorating show house was reconstructed as a performance space. At one end of the hall, workmen built a narrow, virtually wingless stage, barely twenty-two feet wide, and installed 212 seats, castoffs obtained at bargain prices from a Dallas church. Because of the cramped conditions, actors dressed in a rented trailer parked at the rear of the building. The company opened September 26, 1957, with a production of *Mister Roberts,* featuring Dan Bridges in the title role.[23]

The company remained at the Sylvania playhouse for over nine years. During its early seasons, the organization relied on volunteers such as Earl Bush, Lynn Trammell, and TCU's Dr. James O. Costy and William "Bill" Garber to direct productions. Many members, including Phil and Bobbie Wygant, Dick Harris, Erin Brown, Erwin Swint, Georgie Harris, J.D. Goodman, Bill Scarborough, and John and Betty Sedwick, were pivotal in keeping the organization afloat, taking roles and working behind the scenes. The organization even added a children's theater school in 1961 under the direction of Sharon Benge, but this program was dropped after just one year with the establishment of Casa Mañana's Merry-Go-Round School.[24]

The old Morgan theater, 608 North Sylvania, became the first permanent home of the Fort Worth Community Theater in 1957.

Courtesy, *Fort Worth Star-Telegram* Collection, Special Collections, University of Texas-Arlington Libraries

In the summer of 1957, shortly after the move to North Sylvania, Bill Garber, who had earlier left TCU, was hired as playhouse manager, becoming the theater's first full-time employee. Garber, a native of Strasburg, Ohio, and a graduate of Wooster (Ohio) College, had come to Fort Worth in 1952 following service in the U.S. Army. As a paid graduate assistant in TCU's drama department from 1952–1957 under Dr. Walther Volbach, he was responsible for staging and directing a number of the university's productions each season.[25]

Garber had been one of the Community Theater's charter members in 1955 and directed several of its early productions, including *The Madwoman of Chaillot.* As the madwoman, he cast Flora Reeder with Dickson Reeder playing the Sewer-Man. The casting of the Reeders proved fortuitous. The pair continued to appear in productions, persuading other influential members of the community to support the group. Although guest directors continued to stage productions each season, by 1959 Garber's title had been enhanced from playhouse manager to director, making him one of the few paid directors of a nonprofessional company in the country.[26]

Players in 1957's *The Heiress,* one of the first productions in the Sylvania Street playhouse, included Bobbi Wygant, left, Betty Cook, and Barbara Graham.

Courtesy, Bill Garber

In January 1966, Fort Worth prepared to unveil the William Edrington Scott Theater, latest addition to the city's growing arts district along West Lancaster Avenue. The Fort Worth Art Center (later the Modern Art Museum) had opened just west of Will Rogers Auditorium in 1954. Plans for the Art Center had originally included a theater wing, but at the time of its construction, no funds were available.[27] Finally completed during 1965, the new hall was funded by a $1.25 million gift from the William Edrington Scott Foundation. Designer of the theater, which included a 493-seat main hall, and 122-seat "experimental theater" was legendary scenic artist Donald Oenslager, whose landmark Broadway productions included *You Can't Take It With You, Born Yesterday,* and *The Man Who Came To Dinner.* During completion of the building, Oenslager worked closely with Fort Worth architect Joseph R. Pelich. Bea Handel, one of the founders of the Dallas Theater Center was hired as managing director.[28]

From its 1954 inception, the Arts Center project had been touted as a means to "unify and strengthen" Fort Worth's cultural activities. Inclusion of the Community

The 1958 Community Theater production of *The Madwoman of Chaillot,* featuring Johnny Simons, left, who would found Hip Pocket Theater in 1977, Edith Tomlinson, Flora Reeder of the Reeder School, Ouida Guthrie, and Joe Lunday.

Courtesy, Bill Garber

Donald Oenslager, right, designer of the William Edrington Scott Theater with architects, Joseph R. Pelich, right, and Dick C. Moore.

Courtesy, *Fort Worth Star-Telegram* Collection, Special Collections, University of Texas-Arlington Libraries

Theater in planning the Scott brought complaints from some, but through the influence of George Quentin McGown, Jr., president of the Scott Foundation and an admirer of the group's productions, the organization was invited to make the new theater its permanent home beginning in January 1966. From 1966 to 1995, the company remained the Scott's major tenant.[29]

The sweeping curves of the theater's white Texas shell-stone exterior and a spacious, mirrored lobby graced by an eight foot Italian chandelier and ten by eighteen foot mural painted by Oenslager, belied the intimacy of the performance hall. Steeply pitched amphitheater seating and baffled walls and ceiling furnished ideal sightlines and acoustics from anywhere in the hall. A thrust stage, when lowered hydraulically, became an orchestra pit, making the entire setting adjustable for both proscenium and open stagings. Following a black-tie grand opening on January 24, 1966, *Auntie Mame* became the first full-length play staged in the theater.[30]

If viewed strictly as a professional venue, the Scott Theater failed to live up to its early promise. Bea Handel left within the year, replaced by Virginia Museum Theater director Robert S. Telford. Few local arts groups made use of the facility although in December 1966, *The Littlest Wiseman,* a Christmas pageant staged since 1961 at McClean Junior High School, moved into the new hall. A gift to the city from F. Howard and Mary D. Walsh, the richly costumed pageant, produced for several years by Flora and Dickson Reeder, brought together such local organizations as the Texas Boys' Choir and Dorothy Shaw Bell Choir. It became an annual event, continuing into the twenty-first century.[31]

The William Edrington Scott Theater, on the right side of the Fort Worth Art Center complex, designed by New York scenic artist Donald Oenslager and local architect Joseph R. Pelich, opened at West Lancaster and Montgomery in January 1966.

Courtesy, W. D. Smith Photograph Collection, Special Collections, University of Texas-Arlington Libraries

The 493-seat William Edrington Scott Theater opened in January, 1966. Interior features included amphitheater-style seating and a mirrored lobby graced with an eight-foot-wide Italian chandelier and murals painted by the hall's . designer, Donald Oenslager.

Courtesy, *Fort Worth Star-Telegram* Collection, Special Collections, University of Texas-Arlington Libraries

Under Robert Telford's leadership in 1969, the Scott hosted the southwest regional finals of the American College Theater Festival. The event, sponsored nationally by such institutions as the Smithsonian and the John F. Kennedy Center for Performing Arts, continued in Fort Worth for nearly two decades. Telford's attempt in 1967 to establish a permanent professional troupe met with less success. The Scott Theater Actors Repertory Company (STARCO) failed after just three seasons, overshadowed by Casa Mañana and the Community Theater. A second company, the

Fort Worth Repertory Theater, organized following his departure, also failed. Not surprisingly, the amateur organization, which in 1980 was renamed the Fort Worth Theater, prevailed, continuing at the Scott for the next twenty-seven years. In recognition of the company's success, Bill Garber's title was expanded once again in 1970 to include managing director of the Scott.[32]

Garber's influence on the development of Fort Worth's theatrical community in the latter half of the twentieth century cannot be minimized. Under his leadership, Fort Worth Theater grew steadily in reputation for over three decades. By the 1990s, the organization counted among its major underwriters Mr. and Mrs. F. Howard Walsh, the Amon Carter Foundation, the Anne Burnett and Charles Tandy Foundation, Tandy Corporation, the Arts Council, and the James L. and Eunice West Charitable Trust. Although attempts to establish a children's academy in 1961 and 1966 were short-lived, in 1990 the Fort Worth Theater School and Kids Who Care, the school's performance company, were established under the direction of Deborah Jung and Lorie Hicks.[33]

Director Carl Tressler with wisemen Maurice Moore, left, Emmett Schumann, and Bill Scarborough in *The Littlest Wiseman*. The nativity play became an annual event, a gift to the city from F. Howard and Mary D. Walsh.

Courtesy, *Fort Worth Star-Telegram* Collection, Special Collections, University of Texas-Arlington Libraries

During 34 years as director of the Fort Worth Community Theater from 1959-1993, Ohio native, Bill Garber, infused local productions with a new level of professionalism.

Courtesy, *Fort Worth Star-Telegram* Collection, Special Collections, University of Texas-Arlington Libraries

At a time in the 1960s and 1970s when Casa Mañana stood as the city's only professional theatrical outlet, Garber steadily raised the quality of company offerings, occasionally hiring, with the help of grants, professional actors such as Fort Worth natives Gayle Hunnicutt and Melvin O. Dacus. Garber also cast a number of individuals who eventually became core founders of Tarrant County's professional theater community. The list eventually included Johnny Simons of Hip Pocket Theater, Rose Pearson and Bill Newberry of Circle Theater, Rudy Eastman of Jubilee Theater, Jerry Russell of Stage West, and B.J. Cleveland of Theater Arlington.[34]

Several of the company's most successful productions, however, resulted from Garber's flair for innovative casting. In 1986, he persuaded Fort Worth socialite George Ann Carter to portray the flamboyant title character in the company's second musical production, *Mame.* And just four years after Neil Simon's comedy of mismatched roommates, *The Odd Couple,* made its Broadway debut, the director cajoled *Star-Telegram* amusements columnist Elston Brooks into playing Oscar Madison opposite Bill Scarborough's Felix Ungar. Another memorable pairing came in 1984 when Garber brought together Melvin and Katy Dacus in Ernest Thompson's poignant drama of aging and familial love, *On Golden Pond.* Dacus, already a local icon from his years with Casa Mañana, was featured in a number of other Scott productions, including *Cat On a Hot Tin Roof* (1983), *Mass Appeal* (1984), and *The Man Who Came To Dinner* (1987). He and Garber teamed for *The Sunshine Boys* in 1988.[35]

Following Garber's retirement in 1993, the company declined. A succession of directors between 1993 and 2001 experimented with works by more recent, less conventional playwrights, such as Jon Klein's 1995 satire *Dimly Perceived Threats to the System.* The strategy alienated some in the theater's traditional audience base and may have contributed to a gradual loss of audience and financial support. Short of funds,

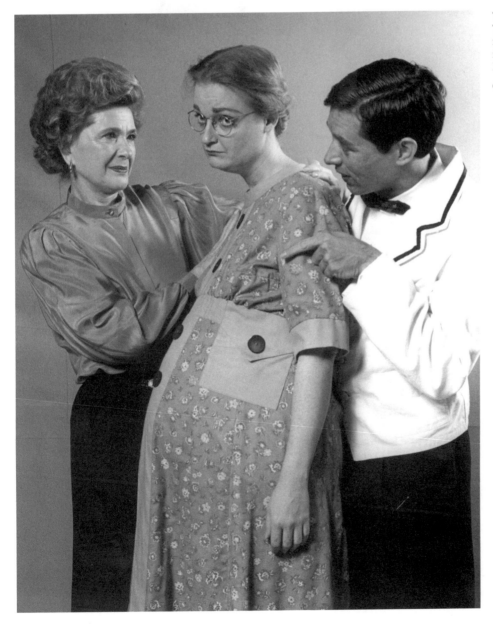

The 1986 Fort Worth Community Theater production of *Mame,* featured George Ann Carter, left, in the title role, with Deborah Brown and Jeff Heald.

Courtesy, Bill Garber

the organization abandoned the Scott in 1996 for Orchestra Hall, a more remote space at 4401 Trail Lake Drive. In 2001, the organization's forty-sixth season, the Arts Council, in a vote of no confidence, slashed its funding by 68 percent.[36]

In July 1966, just six months after the opening of the Scott Theater, ground was broken for the $16 million Tarrant County Convention Center and theater, even as workers continued the task of clearing fourteen blocks of aging structures at the southern end of downtown. Among other buildings targeted for destruction was the final reminder Fort Worth's bygone vaudeville era, the Majestic Theater. Since the 1950s, the former showplace had languished on a decaying side street growing shabby and increasingly forgotten despite late infusions of revenue from such local events as the Cowtown Hoedown, a weekly live-broadcast, country-western show, and plays staged by the recently organized Greater Fort Worth Community Theater.[37]

For a time, the old theater had even seemed poised in the wings for a grand come-back when Dallas businessman and preservationist Herman Goldblatt bought the faded dowager in 1963 and embarked on a yearlong facelift. But the announcement in 1964 that the hall stood within the area needed for the convention center brought attempts at further restoration to an abrupt halt.[38]

A two-year battle between preservationists and the city finally ended with the theater's condemnation, but as the call for demolition bids went out, it seemed for a time that Houdini's spirit might still flutter mischievously in the wings. After a sec-tion of bricks fell away, building inspectors discovered bulges on the south and east walls of the theater, suggesting imminent collapse. As commissioners wrestled with how best to safely demolish the structure, the old show house enjoyed a yearlong reprieve, raising hopes that grass roots efforts might yet save the theater. Finally, however, in September 1966, crews moved in to finish the destruction of Fort Worth's longest standing monument to live performance.[39]

Over the next two years, construction moved ahead on the new convention center and performance hall. Preston Geren, Sr., was chief architect for the project, with erec-tion of both structures carried out by Cadenhead and Childs construction companies. Grand opening of the new complex was on November 21, 1968, with a performance of *La Traviata* by the Fort Worth Opera.[40]

Different from previous Fort Worth performance halls, the convention center the-ater, which was rededicated on May 29, 1969, as the John F. Kennedy Theater, incorpo-rated continental-style seating into the design of its 112-foot-long audience chamber. There were no boxes, and the auditorium's 3,077 red-upholstered seats were set on wide, stair-stepped rows stretching across the full width of the theater's audience

Garber's company of actors included, standing, Jude Johnson, Dick Harris, Gena Sleete, and Erwin Swint; and seated, Bill Scarborough, Jean Harrison, Mary Biedenbender, Grayson Harper, and Tricia Avery. All appeared in 1985's *Morning's At Seven.*

Courtesy, Bill Garber

Wrecking crews raze the Majestic Theater in September 1966 to make way for the Tarrant County Convention Center.

Courtesy, *Fort Worth Star-Telegram* Collection, Special Collections, University of Texas-Arlington Libraries

chamber. The hall's vertically stacked side walls of dark wood paneling were intended to provide acoustical balance, although musicians and the hall's critics complained of a muffled or deadened quality to sound in the theater. The stage, touted as the largest in North Texas at the time of its opening, was 120 feet wide and 50 feet deep, with a 65-foot-wide proscenium opening.[41]

The lobby of the hall, separated from the center's exhibit halls by a relatively narrow concourse, was virtually unadorned, although large plate-glass windows offered views of a landscaped court on the east and Houston Street on the west. Access to balcony seating was by wide, curving staircases at either end of the lobby. Without center aisles or rear entryways, all access to floor seating was through doors arranged along the east and west sides of the hall. The moderately steep pitch of the floor assured good sightlines from any vantage point.[42]

By the 1970s, except for the still-thriving Community Theater, most of the city's amateur groups had folded. Filling the void were a number of small legitimate companies. The Windmill Dinner Theater, a project of Fort Worth real estate man William Harvey, opened in October 1969 in an eight-thousand-square-foot, New England-style red barn at 1800 North Forest Park Boulevard. Plays, produced and directed in

New York by Stockton Briggle, another Fort Worth product, toured Harvey's dinner theaters in Dallas, Houston, and Fort Worth. Structural problems forced the closing of the Forest Park location in November 1973, after just four seasons.[43]

Shakespeare In the Park, founded by Casa Mañana Playhouse director Sharon Benge, began in the summer of 1977 as a way to provide continuing employment for children's theater staff. During its abbreviated first season, the company staged free performances of *A Midsummer Night's Dream* in the WPA-built Trinity Park shelter house on Seventh Street. Casa Mañana withdrew support after the first season, but in 1978, the festival incorporated as Shakespeare In the Park with a board made up of leading citizens and Benge as director. Under her leadership over the next ten years, the organization gained sponsorships and expanded its season to two plays presented over several weeks. Following Benge's departure, the festival continued another fourteen years until rising production costs and declining support ended its run in 2001.[44]

The 3,077 seat Tarrant County Convention Center Theater opened in November 1968 with a performance of *La Traviata*. In 1969, it was renamed in honor of President John F. Kennedy.

Courtesy, Fort Worth Convention Center

But at least one in the number defied any conventional designation, remaining, even in its choice of location, at the fringes of Fort Worth's theatrical establishment. At first ignored by the mainstream press, the Hip Pocket Theater, nevertheless, began to attract sell-out crowds to a small restaurant inside Grissom and Friends, an artisans' compound occupying a former motel on Highway 80, a mile or so west of Las Vegas Trail.

Fort Worth actor/playwright Johnny Simons appeared in Community Theater productions and worked for Casa Mañana before founding Hip Pocket Theater in 1977.

Courtesy, *Fort Worth Star-Telegram* Collection, Special Collections, University of Texas-Arlington Libraries

Called Picnic Theater during its first season, the company made its debut in the summer of 1976, when restaurant owners Lou and George Stevens persuaded Johnny Simons, a local actor/dramatist, to stage the commedia dell'arte classic, *The Three Cuckolds,* as entertainment for customers. Simons, a graduate of Carter-Riverside High School, had worked for several years with the Casa Mañana Playhouse, teaching, directing, and writing plays. In 1964, he became the theater's artistic director. He also acted occasionally in Casa Mañana productions and with the Community Theater. For his TCU master's thesis, Simons had written an autobiographical rock opera titled *The Lake Worth Monster.* Douglas Balentine wrote music for the piece. TCU selected the show, first staged during 1975 in Fort Worth's Modern Art Museum, as the school's entry in the Southwest Regional Finals of the American College Theater Festival, where it took playwriting honors.[45]

The success of *The Three Cuckolds,* which ran outdoors in the Grissom complex through the summer of 1976, inspired a second production inside the restaurant, which had changed owners and been renamed George's Backdoor Restaurant. For this second show in March 1977, Simons reworked *Out Where the West Begins,* a piece originally commissioned by the Texas Bicentennial Commission and presented by Casa Mañana in 1976. Retitled *Cowtown!* and given fresh lyrics by Simons and music by Doug Balentine the show became the Hip Pocket Theater's first official production.[46]

Also playing a key role in the creation of the Hip Pocket Theater was Simons' wife, Diane Rowand Simons. Simons, a graduate of TCU, served not only as the company's costume designer, assistant director, and scenic artist but also its public relations and business manager. She had previously designed costumes for Casa Mañana Playhouse, props for the Fort Worth Opera, and worked as an assistant to the scene designer for Houston's Alley Theater. For several years she was in charge of props for both Community Theater and Casa Mañana Musicals.[47]

In its very first season, the Hip Pocket already exhibited the distinctive style that would set the company apart for the next twenty-five years. Shows were an innovative, sometimes eccentric blend of colorful costumes, physical comedy, multimedia presentations, dance, mime, puppetry, and original music. Simons held no auditions.

Performers, all volunteers, worked regular day jobs and several, who had been professional actors, sacrificed union memberships to return to amateur work. Actors making regular appearances included Cliff Conklin, Peggy Bott, Virgil Phelps, Dick Harris, Jimmie Joe Steenbergen, Ellen Mahoney, Debbie Freed-Cooke, Art Davis, Serena Pfeiffer, and Julie McMahon.[48]

The theater quickly became known for campy, highly original plays and musicals such as the company's tribute to radio melodrama, *Even If You Can Stop The Yellow Claw, My Deadly Tidal Wave Will Still Destroy New York!* Many of these were written or adapted by Simons with music by Balentine, although the company's repertoire occasionally included pieces by playwrights such as Federico García Lorca and Sam Shepard. Simons' works were autobiographical, quirky, and nostalgic, filled with echoes of childhood, Texas, and Fort Worth. The theater's first full season featured *Cowtown!* and *Nova's Shady Grove,* a play about a bar on Lake Worth. Other scripts came from such eclectic sources as *Tarzan of the Apes;* the rock opera *Tommy;* Dickens' *A Christmas Carol;* and *King Kong,* adapted by Simons, Balentine, and others to the theater's distinctive style.[49]

Some of the company's most popular plays were those written by Simons and Balentine together before Balentine's 1991 departure. The collaboration produced *Tarzan of the Oaks* (1979), *Raggedy Farm, Captive Wild Women, Charlie Chan In the House of Tomorrow* (1980), *Return of the Creature* (1981), *Clown Alley* and *Sex Kittens Go To College* (1982), *Old Tarzan* (1986), *Women in Slips* (1987), and *Attack of the B-Girls* (1989). On his own Simons also wrote *A Saga of Billy the Kid* (1982), *Adventures of the Shadow Starring Lamont Cranston and Margo Lane* (1989), *Molemo!* (1990), *Huzzytown* (1993), *Girls From Girdleville Greet Men in BVD's* (1994), and *Daughters of the Zeeack* (1995).[50]

Hip Pocket remained at the Backdoor Restaurant for three seasons (1977–1979), but in 1980 the company moved to a location that became known as Oak Acres. For the next quarter century, this outdoor stage set in a wooded landscape along Las Vegas Trail in far West Fort Worth was the site most closely associated with Simons' productions. At various times, the company also performed from such diverse venues as North Fort Worth's White Elephant Saloon, downtown's Caravan of Dreams, and the Kimbell Art Museum. In 1983 the theater became the first Texas company ever to perform in Scotland's Edinburgh Fringe Festival.[51]

Though city amateur companies had long produced legitimate plays, it took a transplanted Rhode Islander to establish what became the city's first long-term professional legitimate theater. Jerry Russell had worked for NCR (National Cash

Simon's 1983 production of *Elder Oaks* took the Hip Pocket company to Scotland's Edinburgh Fringe Festival. Clockwise from top were featured players John Murphy, Richard Harris, Linda Boydston, and Dana Brinkley.

Courtesy, *Fort Worth Star-Telegram* Collection, Special Collections, University of Texas-Arlington Libraries

Register) Corporation in several cities around the country before transferring to Fort Worth. Enamored of theater since childhood, Russell regularly became involved in local theater companies wherever he lived. By the time he reached North Texas in 1973, Russell had already worked as actor or director in over a hundred productions and soon began performing with both the Community Theater and Casa Mañana. With professional offerings limited to the summer musical series, he considered the possibility of organizing a new company to perform more "adventurous" musicals and legitimate works than those currently available.[52]

Russell quit his job in 1978 and with his savings opened a sandwich shop at 600 Houston Street. By 1979, he had planned an eight-show season, installed sixty-five seats in the storefront next to the shop, and sold seventy-five season tickets. Stage West launched in October 1979 with Edward Albee's two-character dark comedy, *The Zoo Story*. Russell and co-star Joe Berryman played to just 275 people during a modest run, but the production received solid critical reviews. With each successive production, audiences grew—*Rattle of A Simple Man* played to 550, *That Championship Season*, 1100. The musical revue, *Jacques Brel Is Alive and Well and Living In Paris*, was held over repeatedly, finally playing to nearly two thousand.[53]

By January 1981, the theater had gained nonprofit status and a board of directors, although Russell continued as managing director. Still in just its second season, the company moved in June to a nine-thousand-square-foot warehouse at 821 Vickery Boulevard. Even before completion of the 170-seat theater, Russell opened in the smaller Front Room, which also offered preshow dining, with *You Can't Take It With You*. First production in the main space was Furth and Sondheim's musical, *Company*. Over the next ten seasons, Stage West's subscriber list grew to almost eleven hundred and the organization also increased the number and size of its contracts with Actors Equity Association.[54]

Diners in Stage West's Vickery Street location, 1981.

Courtesy, *Fort Worth Star-Telegram* Collection, Special Collections, University of Texas-Arlington Libraries

As part of his plan to develop the company into a major professional regional the-ater, Russell tackled a challenging and wide-ranging repertoire. Contemporary plays included David Mamet's *American Buffalo* and *Glengarry Glen Ross,* Ira Levin's *Deathtrap,* Lanford Wilson's *5th of July,* Peter Shaffer's *Equus,* Brian Clark's *Whose Life Is It Anyway?* and Alan Ayckbourn's *The Norman Conquests* and *Absurd Person Singular.* Into the mix were added musicals such as *Stop the World (I Want To Get Off),* *Pump Boys and Dinettes,* and *Three Penny Opera,* and classic works by Shakespeare, Molière, Chekov, Shaw, Wilde, Pinter, and Coward. The company also staged works by emerging regional and ethnic writers such as Ntozake Shange (*For Colored Girls Who Have Considered Suicide/When the Rainbow Is Enuf*), James McClure (*Lone Star/Laundry and Bourbon*), and the world premiere of *Little Lulu In A Tight Orange Dress* by John Moynihan.[55]

By 1988, the theater was attracting twenty-five thousand patrons annually, but projected rerouting of Interstate 30 led to the abandonment of the Vickery location in 1991, just three seasons later. While the search continued for a permanent location, the organization spent two years in downtown's Caravan of Dreams, where season sub-scriptions climbed to over thirteen hundred. Productions during the period included August Wilson's *Fences,* the world premiere of Claudia Allen's *Ripe Conditions,* regional premieres of *The Promise,* by Hispanic playwright Jose Rivera, *Tales of the Lost Formicans* by Constance Congdon, and Stephen Wade's *Banjo Dancing.*[56]

Following a capital campaign that raised $300,000, in 1993 Stage West purchased and began renovating the TCU Theater at the corner of West Berry and University.

Stage West founder Jerry Russell, with Jim Covault, the theater's longtime artistic director, in 1990's *A Walk In the Woods.*

Courtesy, *Fort Worth Star-Telegram* Collection, Special Collections, University of Texas-Arlington Libraries

The 1989 Stage West production of *Moonshadow* with Jim Covault, left, David Poynter, Todd Anderson, and Jane Milburn.

Courtesy, *Fort Worth Star-Telegram* Collection, Special Collections, University of Texas-Arlington Libraries

Unanticipated problems boosted the final cost of reconstruction to $175,000, but the new space finally opened October 19, 1993, with Kander and Ebb's musical revue, *And the World Goes Round.* Over the next five seasons the company staged productions by Edward Albee (*Who's Afraid of Virginia Woolf*), Tony Kushner (*Angels in America, I & II*), and Terrence McNally (*Lips Together, Teeth Apart* and *Master Class*), August Wilson (*Two Trains Running* and *Joe Turner's Come and Gone*), Jeffrey Hatcher (*Scotland Road*), Brian Friel (*Dancing At Lughnasa*), and the American premiere of Alan Ayckbourn's *The Time of My Life.*[57]

In 1998, Jerry Russell retired after nineteen seasons as managing director. The company continued under the leadership of Diane Anglim, but two years after Russell's departure, the dissolution of Shakespeare In the Park, impending war, and sharp reversals in the economy combined to exacerbate the company's long-standing debt.

Hoping to improve its financial situation in the late 1990s, Stage West merged with Shakespeare In the Park to form Allied Theater Group, but following the September 2001 destruction of New York's World Trade Center, support from the Arts Council and other sources dropped off. In the economic downturn resulting from the disaster, Shakespeare In the Park closed. With the loss of its partner, Stage West, heavily burdened by unpaid loans remaining from its 1993 move, made the decision to sell its building and regroup in the little-used Scott Theater.[58]

Two years after the beginning of Stage West in downtown, another theater took shape in Southwest Fort Worth. The idea to found a new professional theater followed performances of Oliver Hailey's tale of small town Texas, *Who's Happy Now,* produced by Rose Pearson and Bill Newberry in the Scott Theater's Scott II space in 1979. The play was an immediate hit, extended several times and eventually moved to the Kell Street Cafe in the Westcliff Shopping Center near Texas Christian University. After a second production of *Bus Stop*, Pearson and Newberry decided to look for a permanent space.[59]

During the summer of 1981, the pair renovated a former Mexican restaurant at 3460 Blue Bonnet Circle near TCU, added seventy-three seats and turned a tortilla-making booth into the theater's technical center. Circle Theater premiered September 10, 1981, with a champagne opening of *The Great American Backstage Musical*, although curtain time had to be delayed for over an hour after costumes failed to arrive on time. The company remained at its original location until 1987, when the city, trying to coax new life into the near South Side, offered to assist with a move to Magnolia Centre, a renovated Masonic lodge on Magnolia Avenue. In its new, more spacious quarters, Circle Theater added seating and staged more technically challenging productions such as Michael Frayn's farcical play-within-a-play, *Noises Off*.[60]

By 1984, the Centre's owners had decided to convert it to other uses. Aware that Circle needed a new space, the Bass Foundation contacted Newberry and Pearson,

Circle's *Hysterical Blindness and Other Southern Tragedies That Have Plagued My Life Thus Far* by actor/playwright Leslie Jordan with music and lyrics by Joe Patrick Ward, featured Jordan, bottom row, with Steven D. Morries, Terry D. Seago, and Ricky Pope, (top row, left to right); and Jeff Heald, Lois Sonnier-Hart, Darla Robinson, and Dayna J. Fowler (middle row)

Courtesy, Circle Theater, photo by Rose Pearson, founding director

suggesting that the company follow Rudy Eastman's Jubilee Theatre downtown. With the inducement of a $50,000 endowment from the Amon Carter Foundation, the theater raised $100,000 to fund the move. In March 1994 the company opened in the basement of the Sanger Lofts at 230 West Fourth Street with Larry L. King's *The Golden Shadows Old West Museum* starring Melvin Dacus. Circle improved its financial footing with the move, picking up new audiences and expanding its list of season subscribers.[61]

While Circle Theater occasionally presented works by established writers and found commercial success in plays like the Gothic thriller, *The Woman In Black,* the organization found its permanent mission in presenting contemporary works by such writers as Joe di Pietro, Mike Foley, Vince McKewin, and Wendy Kesselman. The theater formed working relationships with writers William Mastrosimone, who worked with the theater on its early production of *The Woolgatherer,* and actor/playwright Leslie Jordan, who became popular with local audiences during the run of his *Hysterical Blindness and Other Southern Tragedies That Have Plagued My Life Thus Far.* The theater also focused on works by several Texas writers, among them Robert Shenkaan,

The 2000 Circle Theater production of Larry L. King's *The Dead Presidents' Club* featured left Kit Hussey as Calvin Coolidge; Bill Jenkins as Richard Nixon; R. Bruce Elliott as Lyndon Johnson, and Loring Stevenson as Harry Truman.

Courtesy, Circle Theater, photo by Rose Pearson, founding director

Oliver Hailey, Horton Foote, and Del Shores. Shows by Larry L. King, including *The Golden Shadows Old West Museum, The Night Hank Williams Died,* and *The Dead Presidents Club,* proved popular with audiences.[62]

An earlier experiment in returning live theater to downtown had far less success compared to other local companies. The Caravan of Dreams, opened in the 300 block of Main Street by Ed Bass and Decision Teams, Ltd., in September 1983, was an amalgam of theater, restaurant, karate studio, cactus garden, film studio, grotto and rock cave, and library under one roof. The project, which became better known for its eclectic nightclub offerings, attempted to establish a permanent theatrical repertory company but faltered with less commercial offerings by such writers as Brecht and Greek tragedian Aeschylus. After 1988, several companies including Stage West and Jubilee Theatre used the theater space as temporary quarters, but the *Dallas Morning News* described the theater as "a murderously limited facility" with little space or street presence. The final vestiges of the original project closed in 2001.[63]

CHAPTER FOURTEEN

VOICES OF CHANGE:
THE EMERGENCE OF MINORITY THEATER:
1885-2001

"Nothing like this had ever happened before."
~Rudy Eastman, founder of Jubilee Theatre

*O*n a May afternoon in 1913, a black man shot and killed two men, one of them a white Fort Worth policeman, and wounded several other people. As word of the shooting spread, a crowd of white men and boys gathered near the city's prosperous black business district along Jones near Eighth and Ninth Streets. Perhaps fearing additional bloodshed in the charged atmosphere, white authorities, in a controversial move, ordered black merchants and shopkeepers to shut down their businesses and go home.[1]

Among those forced to evacuate were twenty members of a traveling black minstrel troupe, who had earlier pitched a tent near the train yards along Jones Street with plans for two weekend performances. With the area deserted and virtually undefended, the performers retreated to the only shelter they could find—their special rail car. The fact that the car had been moved to a siding may well have saved the actors' lives. Through the night and into the next day, mobs raged virtually unchecked through area, smashing windows, looting, and destroying businesses.[2]

The incident and its aftermath starkly document the suspicion, bigotry, and racism that stifled the progress of Fort Worth's black citizenry for much of the twentieth century. Like most southern communities, Fort Worth had, through the years, enacted Jim Crow ordinances intended to restrict or exclude persons of color from elections, schools, businesses, housing, and entertainment. Consequently, in an era otherwise dominated by live shows, opportunities for black performers remained limited, except for those who managed to obtain bookings in black-owned halls and lodges. For the average black citizen, access to theaters was restricted to side entrances, upper balconies, and occasional "special" performances, such as the "colored" amateur night sponsored by the Byers Opera House in 1917 and what was disparagingly called a "Negro jig show" offered by the Majestic at the end of 1932.[3]

Until after World War I, African-American performers appeared in white-controlled local theaters only rarely and then most often in the context of the ubiquitous minstrel show, performing in cartoon like segments featuring so-called "black" behaviors and scenes of southern plantation life. One artist to suffer particular indignity was opera singer Sissieretta Jones, dubbed the "Black [Adelina] Patti" by exploitive white promoters. Jones, who made at least thirteen appearances at the Byers Opera House between 1901 and 1912, was compelled to sing her arias between acts of the Black Patti Minstrels, an all-black vaudeville company. The 1937 Frontier Centennial featured black Fort Worth composer Euday Bowman playing his "Twelfth Street Rag" but countered this with the appearance of the "Cabin Kids," a quintet of black children who sang "plantation songs" in Casa Mañana's *Gone With the Wind* episode. Local pundits dubbed the youngsters, "musical pickaninnies."[4]

Other black performers of note made occasional appearances at such venues as the Worth, Majestic, and, after 1936, Will Rogers Municipal Auditorium. Ethel Waters, reprising her role in the original Broadway production of the Moss Hart-Irving Berlin revue, *As Thousands Cheer*, took to the Majestic boards in March 1933. Nine months

Fort Worth educator, Professor Isaiah M. Terrell became one of the first to promote theatrical presentation in Fort Worth's African–American community.

Courtesy, Fort Worth Public Library, Local History and Genealogy

Lillian B. Horace was influential in establishing I. M. Terrell High School's department of dramatics and drama club.

Courtesy, Fort Worth Public Library, Local History and Genealogy

later, in December, the theater booked Marc Connelly's Pulitzer Prize winning biblical drama, *The Green Pastures,* featuring noted black actor, educator, and lecturer Richard B. Harrison. Two years earlier, Harrison had originated the role of The Lord on Broadway, yet despite his stature, he and a cast of over one hundred had to be placed in the homes of prominent black citizens during the play's two-day Fort Worth engagement after white hotels refused to accommodate the all-black company. In April, 1931, opera singer Marian Anderson, the first female black artist to perform in New York's Carnegie Hall, had received similar treatment. Her Fort Worth appearance was shifted to Mount Gilead Baptist Church after she was denied access to white venues.[5]

Relegated to the back row of Fort Worth cultural life by exclusionary segregationist policies, the black community, of necessity, turned inward for many of its entertainments. Yet because white newspapers gave little coverage to such events, only a handful of these can be documented. In 1885, three years after the opening of Fort Worth's first all-black public school, pupils under the direction of principal Isaiah M. Terrell, staged an evening of "comedies and songs" in Germania Hall. An event in 1901 also had close ties to ongoing efforts aimed at improving educational opportunities for the city's poor and minority populations. Between 1898 and 1901, the Free Kindergarten Association, organized by some of Fort Worth's most influential white clubwomen had opened two free kindergartens, one of them at Eleventh and Calhoun, in the heart of the city's "colored" district. An April fundraiser for the kindergartens advertised a "negro minstrel jubilee" featuring a cast made up of local black talent. The program, staged in the Worth Hotel under the musical direction of Professor Armstead D. Davis, a local barber and musician, followed a traditional minstrel show format with comedy sketches, song and dance numbers, and a cakewalk performed by several couples. Featured performers included William Agery, Mary Carter, Ophelia January, Carrie Thornton, Chester Johnson, John Tutt, Mary Blocker, and the Texas and Pacific colored quartette.[6]

A musical-dramatic performance of the *Queen Esther* cantata in March 1906, under the supervision of Professor I. M. Terrell, once again brought favorable notice to the city's African-American schools from the local press. The performance, declared "an excellent entertainment" that "would have done credit to amateur singers anywhere" was staged in Fort Worth's city hall and featured a chorus of students supporting a cast of adult soloists. Among those singled out for particular notice were Charles W. Crouch as Mordecai, James W. Pratt as Haman, and Mrs. Eloise J. Lightfoot as Zeresh. Taking the role of Esther was twenty-year-old soprano, Lillian B.

The I. M. Terrell Dramatic Club, organized in 1922, performed an original operetta, *The Stolen Princess,* as its first production.

Courtesy, Fort Worth Public Library, Local History and Genealogy

Jones, a young teacher, who, through her work over the next four decades as writer, clubwoman, church worker, and educator, would play a pivotal role in the promotion and development of theatrical activities and training in Fort Worth's black community.[7] Lillian B. Jones Horace, who moved to Fort Worth from Jefferson, Texas, at age two, did undergraduate study at Prairie View Normal, Bishop College, and Simmons University before returning to teach in Tarrant County schools around 1905. After accepting a position as English teacher and dean of girls for I.M. Terrell High School in 1911, she pioneered Terrell's department of dramatics. With her encouragement, the school's first theater club was established in 1922, with Miss E.M. Benton serving as director and sponsor. Students performed Benton's original operetta, *The Stolen Princess,* as their first production.[8]

Hazel Harvey Peace built on Horace's earlier work. In the late 1920s, after joining the faculty of I. M. Terrell, she became cosponsor of the English Dramatic Debating Society with Mrs. M.L. Livingston. Peace, a graduate of Howard University, had done graduate studies at both Ohio and Columbia universities and while studying for her master's degree at Columbia took courses in play production. For over two decades, she provided the spark for both I. M. Terrell's drama and debating programs, promoting tournaments and theater productions and persuading Alpha Kappa Alpha, the country's oldest Greek letter sorority for black women, to sponsor these activities. In the 1930s, when Fort Worth's Junior League began touring local schools with children's productions, Harvey convinced that organization to include black schools in their regular performance itinerary.[9]

Several other teachers and performers emerged from Fort Worth's African-American community. During the 1920s, Mabel Hallowell Echols offered classes in dramatic expression from her studio at 1108 Galveston Avenue. She herself gave readings and impersonations for concerts, recitals, and house parties. In the 1930s, Mrs. W.E. Humphrus conducted a school of dramatics that regularly furnished 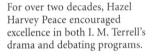 actors for plays performed in colored halls, schools, and recreation centers. Dramatic soprano Manet Harrison Fowler, a product of Tuskeegee Institute and the Chicago College of Music, gained fame as an early director of Mount Gilead Baptist Church choirs and undoubtedly took part in many of the community's cultural events. After moving to New York, Fowler founded the Mwalimu Center For African Culture during the Harlem Renaissance of the 1920s.[10]

Through the 1930s, Bennye Reeves conducted a dancing school and presented annual revues described by the city's only black newspaper, the *Fort Worth Mind,* as "the greatest events of the year." The 1933 program offered Tennessee magician and contortionist Odis E. Hannah, and such scenes as "From Dixie to Broadway," and "Theater in New York City" that featured Reeves and "dancing rockets" ensemble members J. Winzelle Sims Jr., Fergus and Reba Maddox, Jessie Robinson, Emma Watson, Clarence Lillian Flint, Martha Miller, Thelma Martin, Johnnie Mae Mosley, and Cliserine Taylor.[11]

For over two decades, Hazel Harvey Peace encouraged excellence in both I. M. Terrell's drama and debating programs.

Courtesy, Fort Worth Public Library, Local History and Genealogy

Minority cultural and theatrical events remained closely tied to the African-American community's major social and religious institutions—schools, churches, clubs, and fraternal organizations. The State Grand Masonic Temple, built at 401 East Ninth in 1907 to serve as headquarters for Texas' black Masons, was furnished with a fifty-by-hundred-foot third-floor ballroom and hosted community events such as the "Grand Concert and Style Show" staged in the hall in April 1922. The event featured music by Singie Smith and his Jazz Boys, sketches by Messrs. Moore and Thompson, and songs performed by John Henry Jackson, Frank Clemons, and Miss Will Ester Smith. In acknowledgement of Fort Worth's standing in state Masonic activities and the largesse and influence of politician, banker, and fraternal leader William M. McDonald, the city's first black millionaire, The Prince Hall Masonic Mosque, designed by architect H.L. Spicer, was completed in 1924 at 2213 East First Street. In its heyday, the Mosque, with seating for three thousand, hosted performances by a number of leading black performers and musicians.[12]

Although primarily a movie house, the Grand Theater, opened around 1937 at 1110 Fabons Street, occasionally staged amateur and vaudeville nights.

Courtesy, Fort Worth Public Library, Local History and Genealogy

Other influential organizations also sponsored theatrical events. The Log Cabin Players of Marshall's Wiley College brought performances of *The Little Minister* to I. M. Terrell in 1951 with funding provided by the City Federation of Colored Women's Clubs, while the touring *Tropicana Review,* backed by the national black men's fraternity, Phi Beta Sigma, made a February 1953 stop at the City Recreation Building.[13]

Black churches played an especially critical role in community theatricals, offering religious edification while providing an artistic outlet for members through the presentation of Bible-centered plays. Congregations such as Jerusalem, New Bethel, and Mount Gilead Baptist churches and East Annie Street Christian Church sponsored their own dramatic clubs, mounted productions, and occasionally offered their facilities to outside performance companies. Productions were shared not only with other churches but with the wider community as well. In December 1936, Mount Gilead presented *Passion and Triumph,* a drama by nationally known New York pastor and civil rights activist Dr. Ralph Mark Gilbert. Staged in the City Recreation Hall and featuring a hundred-voice choir, the play attracted audiences from both white and black churches, though white patrons were offered separate, reserved seating for each performance. Gilbert himself directed and played the lead role of Jesus. The 120-member cast included Felix Wright as Judas, Floyd Mebane as Nicodemus, and Ross Stanford as Pontius Pilate.[14]

Accounts from surviving issues of the *Fort Worth Mind,* though incomplete, chronicle an expanding network of small amateur theatrical groups within the black community in the decade before World War II. And though such organizations as the Dixie Park, Lake Como, Smarter Set, and Northside Dramatic clubs failed to survive, they nevertheless laid important groundwork for the establishment in 1972 of the landmark Sojourner Truth Players. Among the earliest recorded local companies were the Utopian Dramatic and Versatility Club and the Century of Progress Dramatic Club, both active in the early 1930s. The Century of Progress Club met at the "club rest," 1408 Louisiana Street, home of Charles F. and Maelene Norfleet. Charles Norfleet, a porter for Northern Texas Traction Company, served as manager for the group. Other company members included Frances Kelley, Myrtle Faye Peterson, Lorenzo and Glenera Jenkins, L. Williams, and John Odom. Norfleet later served as president of another organization, the Globe Entertainers Dramatic Club.[15]

In the early 1960s, the Playhouse Guild offered several plays, including at least two staged in Carroll Peak Elementary Auditorium. Reverend Mose Laderson, pastor of East Annie Street Christian Church, was director of the group. An April 1960 Fort Worth production of *Anna Lucasta* featured Jean Tucker in the title role with other principal roles filled by Grady Toliver, Bobbie Simmons, Lonnie Trim, Joan Holbert, and Laderson's wife, Mildred. A third organization, established sometime in the mid-1930s but little documented, was the Fort Worth Negro Little Theater (NLT). The NLT stands apart from other black companies in the coverage it received from local white newspapers after forming a brief yet unprecedented alliance with the whites-only Fort Worth Little Theater (FWLT) in 1935.[16]

Minority actors, writers, directors, and technicians continued to be shut out of participation in many local amateur and professional theatrical organizations for several years after passage of 1964's sweeping Civil Rights Act. Of all productions mounted by local, predominantly white companies before the late 1960s or early 1970s, only one featuring a majority of black players taking leading roles is recorded. In March 1935, the FWLT scheduled as one of its final productions, the folk-drama *Porgy*. The play, written in 1925 by DuBose Heyward, a white southerner, and then dramatized in 1927 with his wife Dorothy, was uncommon for its time. Heyward's bittersweet study of the crippled street-beggar Porgy and his courtship and subsequent loss of Bess to Crown offered psychologically complex, sympathetic portraits of its central characters as well as the other Negro residents of Charleston, South Carolina's waterfront tenement, Catfish Row. Since casting of the drama required more than thirty black actors, the FWLT's director, Robert Nail turned to the local African-American community.

The final cast represented a broad cross-section of that community. Emma Lillian Greenwell, Milton C. Scott, Ruby Williamson, Demaris V. Scott, and A. Maceo Johnson were all teachers in the city's segregated, black schools. A number of students were recruited from those same schools, including Charles "Farina" Waters, Laura Elizabeth and Lionel Cooper, and Lewis Robinson. Eugene C. Askey worked as a janitor for the Fort Worth and Denver City Railway, Vernon Gray and Alphonso Jordan were each employed as porters in white-owned businesses, and Mutelle Flint was married to Clarence W. Flint, a local dentist. Robert Nichols and C.L. Parks sold policies for Atlanta Life Insurance, Idelle Enge served as a caseworker for the Tarrant County Board of Relief, and Bennye LaFrancelle Reeves, worked for the Works Progress Administration.[17]

Others supporting players in the cast included Clotee N. Wallis and Ruben Juan Curtis. Alphonso Jordan starred as Porgy to Emma Lillian Greenwell's Bess; Idelle Enge played Black Maria; Frank M. Carter appeared as Crown; Hovey Don Moore played Sportin' Life; and Maceo Johnson acted the part of Alan Archdale. The play's week-long engagement in the FWLT building on West Tucker Street ran March 24–29, 1935.[18]

Renowned acting coach Ella
Gerber directs Eugene Edwards,
Sportin' Life, during rehearsals
for Casa Mañana's 1972 production of *Porgy and Bess*. The event
marked the first time a black cast
had been featured in the theater.

Courtesy, *Fort Worth Star-Telegram*
Collection, Special Collections,
University of Texas-Arlington
Libraries

It would be thirty-seven years before another white-controlled theater would feature a predominantly black company. Casa Mañana, the city's only professional theater from 1958 until the late 1970s, had only occasionally cast black actors and then usually in small roles or for performances of Kern and Hammerstein's 1927 musical, *Showboat*, another play ahead of its time in its sympathetic portrayal of interracial marriage and southern black characters. It was not until 1972's production of George Gershwin's *Porgy and Bess*, however, that black professionals finally received top billing. Because of the show's operatic length and vocal demands, double casting became necessary: Leonard Hayward and Robert Mosley alternated as Porgy, while Phyllis Bash and Janette Moody split duties as Bess. Eugene Edwards sang the role of Sportin' Life and Charles Homes, Jr., appeared as Crown.[19]

While Casa Mañana's presentation of *Porgy and Bess* did not succeed in fully integrating local theater groups, the production, nevertheless, marked a turning point in the city's theatrical history. Just two years earlier, Melvin Dacus' abortive attempt to integrate the theater's resident ensemble had brought a backlash of protest from white patrons, and, in 1971, the board returned the ensemble to its previous, all-white status. Commenting on the about-face, one journalist observed cynically, "If Casa is bending to these objections, it should make for some interesting casting in *Showboat*."[20]

As rehearsals continued in the summer of 1972 for *Porgy and Bess*, a group of activists and church leaders prepared to inaugurate a new company. The Sojourner Truth Players (SJT) were named after famed abolitionist and civil rights pioneer,

Porgy and Bess marked the first time an African–American cast had appeared in Casa Mañana.

Courtesy, Casa Mañana Musicals, Inc.

Isabella Baumfree, who took the name Sojourner Truth in midlife. The company had its origins in the Junior Debs, a group of high school women who took their idea for a theatrical group to community leaders. The organization was destined to become what one of its founders, Rudy Eastman, later called "the fountainhead of black theater in Fort Worth." Among those involved in the company's development were Eastman, a Fort Worth history teacher; Erma Lewis, a leader in the Southside's Bethlehem Center; Paul Sims, pastor of Community Christian Church; Dr. Ralph Stone, of TCU and University Christian Church; and Opal Wilcox, a Texas Woman's University student.[21]

SJT made its official debut in August with a production of James Baldwin's *The Amen Corner,* performed in the annex of Community Christian Church at 1801 E. Vickery. Despite cramped conditions—the building had no wing space, air-conditioning, or dressing rooms and seated just seventy-eight—audiences flocked to the performances, coming, in Eastman's words, "because nothing like this had ever happened before." By 1975, the organization had broadened its outreach to include both the adult theater and a children's drama and dance program, funded by the Department of Health, Education and Welfare's Emergency School Act.[22]

For well over a decade, SJT continued to produce several plays each season, occasionally collaborating with such local writers as Hip Pocket's Johnny Simons, who wrote *Down To the Roots* for the company. The organization remained at its Vickery location for five years, but after a fire destroyed Community Christian's annex in 1977, the group moved to the Harmon Field Recreation Center while mounting a fund-raising campaign to obtain a permanent space. In June 1980, the company formally opened the Sojourner Truth Cultural Arts Center in a renovated store front at 1101 Fabons Street.[23]

Sojourner Truth eventually folded in the mid-1980s following a second fire, but Rudy Eastman, one of the company's founding members, had already left in pursuit of what he called "a different kind of theater." Shortly after his graduation from Waco's Paul Quinn College in 1966, Eastman accepted a position teaching history at Fort Worth's Como High School. Active in theatrical productions since grade school, he served as cosponsor of the school's drama club and eventually added drama to his teaching responsibilities. When Sojourner Truth organized in 1972, he was quick to become involved, directing several of the organization's productions over nine seasons. In 1981, eager to focus on "pure art" that "reflect[ed] the African-American

Sojourner Truth Players' 1981 production of *The Green Pastures*, featuring Gaylord Savannah as the Lord.

Courtesy, *Fort Worth Star-Telegram* Collection, Special Collections, University of Texas-Arlington Libraries

Teacher, writer, producer, director-Rudy Eastman became Fort Worth's most influential voice for minority theater in the last quarter of the 20th century, helping found both the Sojourner Truth Players and Jubilee Theater.

Courtesy, *Fort Worth Star-Telegram* Collection, Special Collections, University of Texas-Arlington Libraries

experience," Eastman broke away to found the Jubilee Players, a company mirroring in its name its founder's philosophy of "focusing on the celebration of theater and the black culture as opposed to the struggle."[24]

Jubilee, like SJT, began in the annex of Community Christian Church in 1981 with a production of *Mojo String*. Though audiences came, the company struggled to pay its rent and after just six months had to abandon the location. For the next five years, the organization survived as a gypsy troupe, rehearsing in fellowship halls and community centers and performing in church basements, upstairs at the White Elephant on Exchange Avenue, and Stage West's Front Room on Vickery.[25]

During this same period, Eastman officially incorporated Jubilee Theatre as a nonprofit organization with the help of such longtime supporters as Darwin and Muriel Mendoza, who maintained the theater's office in their home for several years, and Gloria Abbs, who served as house manager and assistant director. A major turning point came in 1986–1987 when the company received a $15,000 matching grant from the Amon Carter Foundation and produced a hit show, *Negroes In Space*.[26]

With the profits from *Negroes In Space* added to financial support from patrons and the Carter Foundation, Eastman leased a storefront at 3114 East Rosedale in January 1987. The building, across the street from Texas Wesleyan University, was in the heart of Polytechnic Heights, an old, working-class white neighborhood that over two decades had become predominantly African American. In the flux the area had declined, but Eastman remained hopeful that by putting down roots he might find time to write shows with the potential to attract audiences from both the white and black communities. After renovations to install a twenty-two by eleven-foot stage and seating for eighty, Jubilee Theatre opened its first permanent home in August 1987, remaining there for the next six seasons.[27]

The 1990s brought momentous changes for both Jubilee Theatre and downtown Fort Worth. In 1991 with approval of the Jubilee board, Eastman finally left teaching to become the theater's full-time artistic director. Meanwhile, businessman Edward Bass had approached a number of theaters, including Jubilee, about relocating to the downtown area as part of the city's efforts to revitalize the area. With Bass's help and $40,000 raised through patron fund drives, Jubilee reopened at 506 Main Street in 1992. The move into the heart of downtown nightlife brought new audiences into the theater. With the hiring of Benjamin Espino as managing director in 2000, the company's financial situation also improved, freeing Eastman to write and produce.[28]

During its first two decades, Jubilee Theatre created performance opportunities for area minority actors and offered regional students chances to gain professional experience. Members of the regular company through the years included such performers as Robert Rouse, Mary Keaton-Jordan, Steven Griffin, Blake Moorman,

Jubilee Theatre's first permanent space opened at 3114 East Rosedale in 1987, with *The Blues Ain't Nothin'.* Cast members included Robert Rouse, left, Meretta Savannah, and Jim Ponds.

Courtesy, *Fort Worth Star-Telegram* Collection, Special Collections, University of Texas-Arlington Libraries

God's Trombones, one of Jubilee's most popular shows, debuted in 1990, with, top row, left to right, Darren Ray, Blake Moorman; middle row, Antoinette Watts, Janice Jeffrey, May Allen, David Patterson, Coletta Strickland; bottom row, Steven Griffin, Bessie Richards.

Courtesy, Jubilee Theatre

Grover Coulson, Jim Ponds, and David Patterson. In the theater's uncertain early years, Eastman sought out local volunteers to write for the company, but after becoming increasingly disappointed with the quality of scripts, he began writing some of the group's material himself. As finances improved, he added productions by established playwrights, and occasionally commissioned scripts by such African-American writers as Diane Tucker, Silas Jones, Rudy Gray, and Eugene Lee.[29]

Black music was at the core of many of Jubilee's most memorable shows. Some of Eastman's most innovative scripts were written in close collaboration with two Fort Worth natives, musician Joe Rogers and writer/musician Douglas Balentine. Balentine gave the theater two of its most successful productions, *Negroes In Space* and *God's Trombones*. Eastman's partnership with Rogers, begun in 1988, produced over fourteen years such works as *Midnight Walker, The Book of Job, Bessie Smith: Empress of the Blues, Travelin' Shoes, Coop DeVille: Time Travelin' Brother* (a sequel to *Negroes in Space), The Tempest,* a Motown-flavored version of the classic Shakespearean tale, and *Alice Wonder,* inspired by the Lewis Carroll children's tale.[30]

In many ways, the experiences of Fort Worth Hispanics closely parallel that of the African-American community. Latino performers, like their black counterparts, experienced prejudice and appeared only occasionally on local stages without achieving permanent inroads. And even though African-American and Hispanic influences had long been a part of Fort Worth's cultural landscape, theatrical companies featuring Hispanic performers, playwrights, and themes did not begin to emerge more prominently until late in the twentieth century.

Performances by Hispanic artists on local stages can be traced to at least the late 1870s. Perhaps the first to be documented by the local press was the September 1879 engagement of Laura, May, and Birdie Carrera playing in *Adelaide, the Smuggler's Daughter* at Evans Hall. In 1884, George Holland's My Theater, at the time the town's most notorious variety theater, featured aerialist Juan Zamora on its rotating bill. Two decades later, Zamora had improved his lot considerably, appearing with other family members in 1908 at the city's high-class vaudeville house, the Majestic. City directories record at least two other variety theaters with Hispanic performers. In 1886–1887, A. Gonzales was listed as a performer for the Fashion Theater, 1616 Main, while in 1894–1895, Adolph Gonzales (possibly the same person) served as a comedian

The Rose Theater, c.1928. Under the management of Marie and Addison Burkhalter in the 1940s, the hall, renamed the Marine Theater, became a showcase for Spanish language movies and such well-known entertainers as Lydia Mendoza, Pedro Infante, Sara Garcia, and Cantinflas.

Courtesy, Latin Arts Association of Fort Worth

for Andrews Pavilion Theater at Twelfth and Jones. Lula Gonzales worked as a musician in the same theater.[31]

The Mexican Opera Company made a stop at the Fort Worth Opera House in 1887, and the Mexican National Band, touring Texas during 1889, was one of several musical organizations featured in the Texas Spring Palace. California actor and environmentalist Leo Carrillo, whose career would eventually span vaudeville, motion pictures, and television, performed his comedy monologue from the Majestic stage in 1909.[32]

Marie and Addison Burkhalter, far left, in 1953.

Courtesy, Latin Arts Association of Fort Worth

Marie Burkhalter, center, white collar, with Mexican stars, Sara Garcia, left and Emma Roldán, right, at the Marine Theater in February, 1953.

Courtesy, Latin Arts Association of Fort Worth

The first female star of Tejano music, guitarist Lydia Mendoza, one of several important Latino performers to appear at the Marine Theater.

Courtesy, Latin Arts Association of Fort Worth

More than three decades after Carrillo's final Majestic turn, a local showman finally made a deliberate attempt to serve the city's growing Latin minority. Local Hispanics had few opportunities to experience live theatrical performance, outside traditional religious festivals and plays staged occasionally as fundraisers by students of the Northside's San José School. This changed in 1942, when Addison and Marie Burkhalter, both Anglos, took over management of the Marine Theater. Originally constructed as a movie house at 1440 North Main, the theater opened around 1918 as the Roseland during a period when North Fort Worth's population was still predominantly white.[33]

Under the Burkhalters' management, the theater quickly became a showcase for both Spanish-language movies and live stage shows catering to Fort Worth's rapidly

Local Tejano performers such as the group pictured, were also featured regularly on the Marine stage during the 1940s and 1950s.

Courtesy, Latin Arts Association of Fort Worth

expanding but underserved Hispanic neighborhoods. Patrons regularly filled the theater to see mariachi groups, Mexican dance troupes, and such important performers as Tejano guitarist Lydia Mendoza, Mexican comedian and movie star Cantinflas, the "granny of Mexican cinema" Sara Garcia, and one of Mexico's most beloved actors and singers, Pedro Infante. Because most local hotels barred Hispanics, performers frequently stayed in private homes during their Fort Worth engagements. The Marine remained an important platform for Latino acts until the early 1960s when television's growing popularity brought a corresponding decline in business, forcing the Burkhalters to end the live shows and finally close the theater.[34]

Efforts to revitalize North Fort Worth in the 1990s brought a resurgence of local interest in Hispanic culture. As early as 1990, Michael Muller, producing director of Shakespeare In the Park, scheduled an alternative to the usual pair of Shakespearean presentations, staging Frederico Garcia Lorca's tragedy *Blood Wedding*. As part of Stage West's 1993–1994 season, Jerry Russell included Calderon de la Barca's 1629 comedy, *A House With Two Doors Is Difficult to Guard* from Spain's golden age of theater. But it took Fort Worth native Lynda Rodriguez to furnish opportunities on an unprecedented scale for local Hispanic actors and writers with her pioneering work in creating theater programs expressly by and for the city's Hispanic population.[35]

Rodriguez, a graduate of Texas Wesleyan with a master's degree from Texas Woman's University, began working as outreach director for Fort Worth Theater (FWT) in 1992. Over several seasons with the organization, during which she created drama-based arts classes for Metro Opportunity High, a campus for at-risk teens in North Fort Worth, she became increasingly interested in promoting a Latino series as part of FWT's seasonal offerings. With the cooperation of FWT's managing director Brynn Bristol, she produced and directed Luis Santiero's *Our Lady of the Tortilla* in 1996. The comedy, in what was probably a first for any local theater, not only portrayed Hispanic themes but featured in lead roles a number of local Latino actors, including LeVonna Anderson, Cristela Carrizales, George Rodriguez, and Eddie Zertuche.[36]

Our Lady of the Tortilla's success sparked a second production, the off-Broadway comedy hit *El Grande de Coca Cola,* directed by Bristol and Jay Adkins, and once

Fort Worth Theater's 1999 Hispanic Series production of *The Grapes of Wrath* featured, left to right, Emma Cordova, Keith Smith, Henry Rios, Yvonne Duque, Alex Sandoval, Eddie Zertuche, Michael Gomez, Brian Torres, and Stephanie Bravo. Kneeling is George Rodriguez. Child actors are Brent Hametner and Catharine Gonzales.

Courtesy, Lynda and George Rodriguez and photographer, John Gabriel

again featuring a cast of local Hispanic actors, including Rodriguez. For three seasons following this pair of successes, FWT's Hispanic Series became an annual event. Several directors, among them Rodriguez, staged adaptations of such major works as John Steinbeck's *Of Mice and Men* and *The Grapes of Wrath* and Shakespeare's *Much Ado About Nothing,* as well as the first Fort Worth presentations of Josefina Lopez' *Real Women Have Curves* and Ray Bradbury's *The Wonderful Ice Cream Suit.* The series also produced a bilingual version of *La Bella Durmiente* (*The Sleeping Beauty*), written by local children's author Ann Pugh, with Sara Herrera featured in the title role. [37]

In April 1999, Fort Worth's first annual Hispanic Playwright's Festival (HPF) showcased the works of local writers Marisa Villareal, Robyn Medina Winnett, Henry Rios, Rob Bosquez, Robert Neito, and Alejandro Sandoval II in a series of short scenes and monologues. Just one year later, the HPF officially became a competition festival, with five writers submitting three one-acts and three full-length plays. With the added sponsorship of the Latin Arts Association, the festival expanded yet again in 2001 to include fourteen new works by twelve Hispanic writers from across the nation.[38]

The success of the Hispanic Playwrights Festival inspired other experiments in Latin theater. Teatro Main Street, a theatrical company founded by Robyn Medina Winnett, opened at 1541 North Main in 1999. About the same time, the scarcity of Latin-focused scripts led Rodriguez to take the Hispanic Series in a new direction.

As part of ongoing efforts to revitalize the city's North Side, Fort Worth officials announced plans in 1998 to purchase and restore the long abandoned Marine Theater and other important buildings in the Marine Commercial Historic District along North Main. A number of local Latino artists, including Robert Cortez and Pete Escamilla, and Fort Worth city councilmen Jim Lane and Louis Zapata were responsible for bringing the project to fruition. In acknowledgement of its long history, the restored theater, which reopened in October 2000, was renamed the Rose Marine, combining two previous names. The Latin Arts Association was created in 1999 to serve as caretakers for the hall, which by the early years of the century had joined the National Register of Historic Places.[39]

Over several years the arts association helped establish the theater as Fort Worth's premiere venue for Hispanic culture and performance. In addition to live performance, its varied programs included classes for both children and adults and Teatro de la Rosa, the city's first professional Latino company, offering support and opportunities to emerging writers and performers.[40]

CHAPTER FIFTEEN

ANGELS
TAKE FLIGHT

"Perhaps [in this hall] we'll see . . .

the pentimento of our dreams"

~Fort Worth Star-Telegram, **1998**

By the late 1970s, the growing prestige of the Van Cliburn International Piano Competition was attracting music critics, composers, and conductors to the city from many countries across the globe. To many local arts leaders, it seemed increasingly apparent that in beauty, quality of sound, and accommodation of important events, Fort Worth's three major performance spaces, Ed Landreth Hall, Will Rogers Auditorium, and the John F. Kennedy Theater, could not match the standards set by performance halls in other regions of the country and the world.[1]

Over the next decade, a number of feasibility and acoustical studies led by renowned acoustician Dr. Christopher Jaffe at the behest of Robert M. and Sid R. Bass determined that only Will Rogers Auditorium possessed enough of the qualities for possible upgrading. However, in the late 1980s, when plans for a potential renewal of the city's cultural district along West Lancaster began to develop, a scheme was formulated to raze the existing hall behind the 1936 auditorium facade and construct a new, multi-purpose, state-of-the-art performance hall. Although funding for the transformation was to come from both private and public sources, the plan was overwhelmingly defeated in a July 1990 city bond election.[2]

With the failure of the bond election, organizers turned to a new strategy. Under the guidance of such prominent civic leaders as Edward P. Bass, Sid W. Richardson Foundation executive director Val Wilkie, and others, Performing Arts Fort Worth, Inc., was organized in the fall of 1992, as the first step in erecting a world-class hall built with private funds. Following the selection of Martin C. Bowen as president and chief executive officer and David M. Schwarz as design architect, a team studied theaters and performance halls across Europe and the United States before concluding that New York's Carnegie Hall most closely fit the vision of Fort Worth planners.[3]

Once a design focus for the hall had been achieved, physical planning began. Joining architects for the interior design of the hall, David M. Schwarz/Architectural Services, Inc., were theater consultants Fischer-Dachs Associates, cost consultants Donnell Consultants Incorporated, program architects Calloway Johnson Moore, P. A., Architect of Record HKS, Inc., acoustic designers Jaffe Holden Scarbrough Acoustics, Inc., and contractor Linbeck Construction Company. A major goal of planners was to construct a facility blending classic architectural elegance, state-of-the-art technology, and the rich acoustics typical of world-class halls.[4]

Sparking the drive to raise the estimated $60 million needed to complete the hall was the gift of a 40,000-square-foot downtown lot by Fort Worth philanthropists Nancy Lee and Perry R. Bass. The relatively small space, just one city block square bordered by Commerce, Calhoun, Fourth and Fifth streets, became the catalyst for other donations. Founding gifts of $18 million from the Sid W. Richardson Foundation and $10 million from the Burnett Foundation were followed by gifts of over $1 million by each of twenty-three individuals and corporations, including other members of the Bass family, Mary D. and F. Howard Walsh, Linda R. and Thomas M. Taylor, Rosalyn and Manny Rosenthal, and the Mabee, Amon G. Carter, Kimbell Art, and Ryan foundations. By 1998, donations exceeded $78 million, allowing for enhancements to original plans for the hall and the creation of a children's education program. Final cost of the hall was estimated at $67 million.[5]

At the official groundbreaking, June 1, 1995, the name Nancy Lee and Perry R. Bass Performance Hall was unveiled before several thousand donors. Over the next two years and eleven months, the hall rose, its most striking external features, a ninety-one-foot-tall grand façade of creamy Texas limestone blocks flanked at the building's northeast and northwest entryways by twin copper-faced domes. As the hall neared completion in the winter of 1998, Hungarian sculptor Márton Váró began the complex installation of two monumental stone angels on the broad vertical spaces of the façade, framing a central balcony parapet and four arching glass windows.[6]

The angels, chiseled from one hundred blocks of Texas Cordova Creme limestone quarried near Austin, had a combined weight of 293,048 pounds. Each form, draped in flowing robes, was attached to a concealed seventy-foot-tall, steel-reinforced, solid concrete wall. Designed to create the illusion of animate beings flowing from the architecture, the figures began at their bases as simple bas relief, appearing to lean outward over the sidewalk as they emerged, rising forty-eight feet into full body sculpture, arms raising gilt trumpets. Behind each herald, pairs of wings rose gracefully upward thirty feet, fanning outward into an eighteen-foot arc. Varó, who trained at the Ion Andresscu School of Fine Arts in Cluj, Romania, before coming to the United States on a Fulbright Scholarship in 1988, spent nearly three years completing the figures, working mostly alone at three locations in Texas and California.[7]

With no fronting grand plaza as in New York's Lincoln Center, the 183,500-square-foot Bass Hall remained intimately integrated with surrounding downtown buildings. Patrons entered the hall through doors at the building's northeast and northwest corners, under the corner domes. Facing each entryway, Italian marble grand staircases rose to upper levels of the hall, and wrapping around the audience chamber, east and west grand foyers merged into the central promenade of the grand lobby in a series of barrel-and-groin vaults, its decorative touches combining restrained elements of classical and contemporary design.[8]

Front facade of the Nancy Lee and Perry R. Bass Performance Hall with its pair of monumental angels chiseled from Texas limestone by sculptor Márton Váró.

Courtesy, Nancy Lee and Perry R. Bass Performance Hall

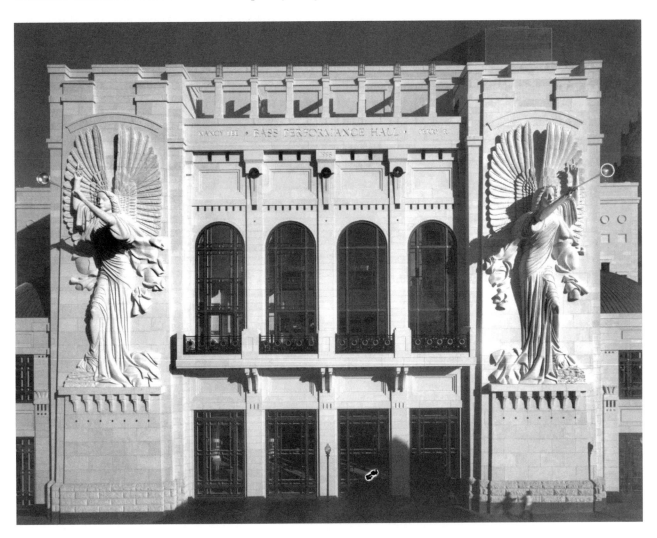

A muted scheme of grays and creams continued the color of exterior walls. Ceiling murals under the twin domes combined natural and mythic elements in designs created by Fort Worth artists Scott and Stuart Gentling and executed by muralists of New York's EverGreene Painting Studios. The Gentlings, educated at Tulane University and the Pennsylvania Academy of the Fine Arts and known for their critically acclaimed 1986 folio, *Of Birds and Texas,* used universal and native Texas motifs to depict man's opposing natures. On the east dome, golds and reds of an early morning Texas sky glowed above a painted tapestry of Texas red bay laurel branches symbolizing man's logic, harmony, and reason. Under the west dome darkly menacing clouds loomed in an angry red sunset over intertwining Texas mustang grapevines, suggesting passion, intuition, and emotion.[9]

The interior of the 2,056-seat, horseshoe-shaped audience chamber, which continued the color schemes of the exterior and lobby, sought to recreate the intimate, tiered seating arrangement of classical opera houses built during the nineteenth and early twentieth centuries. Ninety-six feet long and eighty-four feet wide at orchestra level, the chamber rose nearly ninety feet in five seating tiers—floor level, divided into orchestra and parterre, box tier, mezzanine, lower gallery, and upper gallery. Balcony parapets wrapped around the orchestra level below to form a grand court at each level of the hall. Fluted columns, spaced at intervals along back walls of each level, aligned precisely with those on other levels, lending further symmetry and elegance to the chamber.[10]

More than ninety feet overhead was the chamber's most striking feature, the eighty-foot-diameter Rosenthal Great Dome. The dome and its central oculus provided mythical resolution for the hall's two central motifs. Creating the illusion of a window open to the heavens, white clouds drifted across an azure midday sky, glimpsed through the ribs of the dome's gilded vault. A pair of eagles drifted on air currents beneath the clouds. Silver-gray feathers of a pair of wings encircled the oculus, completing the exterior metaphor of angelic guardians.[11]

The stage, 115 feet wide by 57 feet deep with a 58–foot proscenium opening and average wing space of 28½–feet on either side, also possessed a number of unique features. A massive, 44–ton acoustic ceiling with its own self-contained fire, electrical, and lighting systems could be deployed over the stage and precisely adjusted by three motors to reflect and disperse sound properly for concerts. Addition of rolling wooden shell towers surrounding the performance space beneath the ceiling turned the stage into a "hard box." At the time of the hall's premiere, no similarly complex system for control and dispersal of sound existed in any other performance

hall in the country. An adjustable series of four-thousand-pound gold-leafed, airfoil-shaped plaster sound reflectors, suspended at the front of the stage, stretched the full width of the proscenium, providing additional sound control.[12]

Controlling and shaping the acoustics of the audience chamber were other features, designed under the oversight of Dr. Christopher Jaffe and Jaffe Holden Scarborough Acoustics. Heavy masonry and concrete walls, layers of thick insulation, and dead air space between the dome and roof sealed off the audience chamber from external noise. Curtains hidden in recesses along the wall of the chamber could be deployed for theatrical and amplified events.[13]

Formal dedication and "Lighting of the Hall" on May 1, 1998, ushered in a six-week-long Grand Opening Festival that showcased the city's major performing organizations. A black-tie opening night gala followed on May 8, attended by state officials and members of Fort Worth society. Highlighting the opening program, "Let The Angels Play," were appearances by actress Carol Burnett, opera singer Frederica von Stade, pianist Van Cliburn, and performances by the Fort Worth Symphony, Fort Worth-Dallas Ballet, Fort Worth Opera, and the Texas Boys Choir. Inaugural productions over the next three months included a concert by Metropolitan Opera star Denyce Graves, the Fort Worth Opera's performances of *La Bohème*, a concert appearance by Fort Worth native Betty Buckley performing with the Fort Worth Symphony, the world premiere of Joe Sears and Jaston Williams' *Red, White and Tuna*, and Andrew Lloyd Webber's *Phantom of the Opera* in its first Fort Worth appearance.[14]

Press coverage analyzed every detail of the hall's design and construction, speculating on its ability to finally unite the city's major performance organizations in a single venue. One local journalist noted, "This great hall . . . inspired by the grand halls of Europe, is a testament to . . . community pride, a confirmation of our fervent wish to be reminded through music, dance, and drama of humankind's Divine spark [and] indomitable spirit."

"Perhaps," she reflected, "[in this hall] we'll see . . . the pentimento of our dreams, like a shadowy etching painted over by a world rushing forward." Less tentative in its praise, the *Dallas Morning News* declared it simply, "the last great hall of the 20th century."[15]

With the close of the millennium and the dawn of the twenty-first century less than three years away, Fort Worth's theatrical and cultural history had come literally and figuratively full circle. Completion of the Bass Hall marked a symbolic rite of passage for the city, returning it to its cultural beginnings. Within three blocks of the Hall, both Evans Hall and the Fort Worth Opera House had gone up between 1876 and 1883. Around the footprints of those original halls, a cosmopolitan city had emerged with a broad range of companies and theatrical offerings, a tribute to the collective efforts and vision of succeeding generations of philanthropists and citizen activists.

AUTHOR'S NOTE

This volume is devoted to the history of the dramatic arts in Fort Worth during the nineteenth and twentieth centuries, a period covering approximately 130 years, from around 1873 through 2001.

As much as possible, the book follows chronological order. However, several subjects called for a different treatment. One is the history of the city's various minority performers and theaters. Since this topic has never received the coverage it deserves (and still may not here, given the current scarcity of original documents), I thought it would be better served in its own chapter, where a full history could be traced through the entire span of the time period. A similar method has been used in following the course of the early variety theaters and in relating the histories of the city's two longest surviving theatrical institutions, the Fort Worth Opera and Casa Mañana Musicals. Rather than spreading segments of these unique histories over several chapters, I have instead chosen to keep the entire course of each organization's development within its own chapter.

Some liberties have also been taken with noteworthy milestones in the progress of a number of local theatrical organizations when those events could not be made to fit neatly into the chronological parameters of the study. A prime example is the 2003 redesign of Casa Mañana, doing away with the theater's longtime in-the-round performance configuration. To leave readers without closure seemed illogical.

The inclusion of certain other events and institutions may seem a misapplication of the broader term "theater," but I have allowed the study's limits to be shaped both by past trends in show business nationwide as well as the city's own colorful and sometimes eccentric history. For instance, Enrico Caruso's 1920 Fort Worth appearance, while only a concert, is included, partly in acknowledgement of Caruso's semi-legendary status and partly because his performance capped a groundbreaking series of grand opera presentations in the city between 1916 and 1919. Nor can the ribald variety acts performed by entertainers of questionable repute from the stages of the Centennial, the Standard, and Theatre Comique, three of Hell's Half Acre's most notorious saloon/theaters, be described as "dramatic presentations," but tales of the Acre and its denizens remain central to Fort Worth's heritage.

Similar yardsticks might also be applied to Casa Mañana's flashy musical revues of the 1930s and vaudeville, which from 1905 through the early 1930s remained the driving force in the city's entertainment engine. Each was less about theater in the traditional sense than about entertainment. However, Casa Mañana's construction in 1936 brought unprecedented national attention to Fort Worth. The immense popularity of vaudeville in the first quarter of the twentieth century led to the construction of several local theaters, most importantly the first Majestic, completed in 1905, and the second Majestic, opened just six years later, in 1911. Additionally, memories of the first Casa Mañana, which was razed in 1942, led to the creation of the second Casa Mañana, one of the city's most enduring theatrical organizations.

Because of the need to set working limits, much has been left out: circuses, Wild West shows, symphony (except as the evolution of the Fort Worth Symphony relates to city operas), dance, nightclubs, the public schools, and all except a few significant amateur groups. Omitted as well are most presentations by the city's highly regarded service and charitable organizations. Notable exceptions are the Junior League's plays for minority children in the pre-Civil Rights Act era between 1932 and 1964 and F. Howard and Mary D. Walsh's enduring gift to the city, *The Littlest Wiseman*, which has remained an important annual event for four decades.

The most troubling omission for some will be those fondly remembered downtown and neighborhood theaters whose primary function was the presentation of motion pictures. Only those that began as live performance houses or which prominently featured "mixed" bills on a regular basis during a significant period in their histories are included. Most important of these are the Byers Opera House, converted to the Palace Theater in 1919; the two Majestic Theaters; the Ritz, which in its second or third life became the New Liberty; the Worth; and the North Side's Roseland/Marine Theater. Many others like the Hollywood, one of the city's most lavish movie houses, receive only slight mention or none at all. Those who enjoyed those theaters may argue that movie houses, too, are historically significant, but the fact remains: This work's focus is the actors, showmen, musicians, directors, organizations, theaters, and auditoriums which helped shape the development of live theater in the city.

JAN L. JONES
FORT WORTH
2005

ACKNOWLEDGMENTS

In the completion this project, I owe a great debt of gratitude to a list of individuals and organizations that has steadily grown over the twenty-five years since I first began collecting information about the city's theatrical heritage. Among the first to sit down with me for interviews around 1980 were several generous people who are now gone: Melvin O. Dacus and Michael Pollock, both of whom participated in the opening of Casa Mañana; and amusements columnists Jack Gordon and Elston Brooks, who, between them, had personally witnessed most of Fort Worth's theatrical events since 1930.

Since 1980 many others have given generously of their time, not only sitting down for interviews, but guiding me in the right direction, helping me with editing and correcting, offering advice, and providing information and materials. Fort Worth writer Ann Pugh prodded me to begin this volume, offering material from her own files. I am especially indebted to Kim Dacus Reynolds, Brent Dacus and Brent's wife Debbie Dacus, all of whom shared not only their memories of Melvin and Katy Dacus but also lent important family documents and photographs.

Others who played pivotal roles in completion of the project include Bill Garber, retired managing director of Fort Worth Theater; Diane Rhodes, marketing director; Bill Massad, Ahdel Chadwick, and Dr. John Forestner, board members of the Fort Worth Opera; Sharon Benge, former director of both Casa Mañana's theater school and Shakespeare In the Park; Mrs. Hazel Harvey Peace and Margie Major, retired staff members and teachers at I. M. Terrell High School; Cathy Hernandez, executive director of the Latin Arts Association; the late Rudy Eastman, founder of Jubilee Theater; Rose Pearson and Bill Newberry, founders of Circle Theater; William Walker, retired managing director of the Fort Worth Opera; Jerry Russell, founder of Stage West; Lynda Rodriguez, founder of Fort Worth Theater's Hispanic Series and the Hispanic Playwrights Festival; George X. Rodriguez, actor and director for both the Hispanic Series and the Playwrights Festival; Denton Yockey and Kristin Campbell of Casa Mañana; Joy Spiegel of B'nai B'rith Little Theater; Ruth Kruger, widow of Rudolf Kruger; Lynn Conley, Don Fearing, and Terry Simons of the Bass Performance Hall; Joy Langley, booking coordinator of Will Rogers Memorial Center; and Betty Tanner of the Fort Worth Convention Center.

Many other individuals and educational institutions provided invaluable assistance in locating photographs and historical documents: Max Hill, Ken Hopkins, and Tom Kellam, archivists with the Fort Worth Public Library's Genealogy and Local History division; Susie Pritchett of the Tarrant County Historical Commission; Hollace Weiner, archivist, Congregation Beth-El, Fort Worth; Brenda McClurkin, Blanca E. Smith, and Kit Goodwin, archivists, University of Texas-Arlington Library's Special Collections; Lewis Sherwood, archivist, Texas Wesleyan Library's Special Collections; Catherine Ritchie, archivist, Dallas Public Library; Steve Wilson, University of Texas, Harry Ransom Center for the Humanities; Beth Alvarez, archivist, Hornbake Library, University of North Carolina; the New Orleans Public Library; Rosenberg Library, Galveston; Texas Christian University Library; the Center For American History, University of Texas, Austin; Jim Wheat, Dallas historian; Nancy Buckman, Auckland, New Zealand, great-niece of William Fife Sommerville; Fritz Volbach, nephew of Dr. Walther Volbach; John Deeker, chairman, Pain's Fireworks, England; Cathy Spicer of First Methodist Church; Fort Worth historians Dalton Hoffman, Scott Barker, and Dr. Richard Selcer; and Joseph K. Dulle, president White Elephant Enterprises, Fort Worth.

NOTES

CHAPTER ONE

1. *Fort Worth Daily Standard*, 19 January 1877, 4.

2. *Tri-Weekly Gazette*, 30 December 1872, quoted in Federal Writers' Project, Fort Worth and Tarrant County, Texas, 1849, hereafter cited as FWP-FWTC.

3. Buckley B. Paddock, *Early Days In Fort Worth, Much of Which I Saw and Part of Which I Was*, Fort Worth: n.p., n.d., 6–7, 9.

4. *Dallas Herald*, 15 July 1876, 1.

5. Sheldon Gauthier, "Fort Worth City Guide" in FWP-FWTC, n. d., 47, 19250–19251.

6. *Fort Worth Democrat*, 8 February 1873, 3; 22 March 1873, 3.

7. *Daily Standard*, 12 June 1877, 4; 15 June 1877, 4; 30 June 1877, 4; 23 July 1877, 4; *Fort Worth Star-Telegram*, 30 October 1949, 42; FWP-FWTC, 18004–18005, 18013–18014.

8. Correspondence between B. B. Paddock and Emmie Paddock, 28 February 1873; 2 March 1873, B. B. Paddock Papers, University of Texas-Arlington Library, Special Collections, GA 194, Folder 4. According to the 1878 city directory, the Masonic Hall was located at the corner of Jones and Belknap. Whether this was its location in 1873 is unknown.

9. *Democrat*, 16 January 1874, 2; 8 March 1873, 3

10. "Texas Facts and Fancies," *Austin Weekly Democratic Statesman*, 16 November 1876, 3.

11. *Democrat*, 12 October 1876, 4; 16 January 1877, 4; *Star-Telegram*, 10 February 1921 (eve.), 7. Anecdotal accounts suggest that the Adelphi and the first Theatre Comique (there were two) may have stood a few doors off the corner of Weatherford and Houston.

12. *Democrat*, 21 July 1876, 4.

13. *Democrat*, 9 August 1876, 4.

14. Ibid.

15. *Democrat*, 16 August 1876, 4; 12 October 1876, 4.

16. David Bowser, "Jack Harr's Vaudeville and San Antonio's 'Fatal Corner'" in *Watering Holes of Texas*, compiler and coauthor, Richard Selcer, Texas A&M University Press, 2004, 67; *Democrat*, 19 September 1876, 4; *Daily Standard*, 21 September 1876, 4; 27 September 1876, 4. Will Burton appears in city directory for 1877 and possibly 1883–1884.

17. *Weatherford Exponent*, 9 June 1877, n.p.; 31 May 1879, n.p.; 16 May 1880, n.p.; *Democrat*, 17 December 1880, n.p.; 26 January 1881, n.p.; *Fort Griffin Echo*, 17 May 1879, n.p.

18. Gauthier, *Fort Worth City Guide*, n.d., 47; *Fort Worth Star-Telegram*, 13 December 1914, 11; *Standard*, 11 October 1876, 4; 12 October 1876, 4.

19. *Standard*, 12 October 1876, 4.

20. Description of Theatre Comique, no source, no date, FWP-FWTC, 47; *Democrat*, 1 October 1876, 4.

21. Description of Centennial Theater, n.s., n.d., FWP-FWTC, 18010–18012.

22. *Fort Worth Telegram*, 17 February 1907, sec. 1, 12.

23. *Fort Worth Record*, 30 December 1906, 3, part 1.

24. *Democrat*, 30 September 1876, 4; 18 October 1876, 4; 28 October 1876, 4; 29 October 1876, 4; *Standard*, 18 November 1876, 4; 21 November 1876, 4; 5 January 1877, 4;

25. *Democrat*, 15 February 1873, 3; *Standard*, 9 November 1876, 4.

26. *Standard*, 30 October 1876, 4; *Democrat*, 31 December 1876, 4.

27 *Standard*, 9 November 1876, 4; 30 October 1876, 4; 29 January 1877, 4; 7 March 1877, 4; 31 March 1877, 4; 14 January 1877, 4.

28 *Democrat*, 18 October 1876, 4; 29 October 1876, 4. While Joe Lowe is listed as the Centennial's proprietor in later city directory, in these early newspaper accounts, the Centennial is described as "his [Leer's] theater."

29 *Democrat*, 18 October 1876, 4; 29 October 1876, 4; 16 January 1877, 4. While certainly not conclusive, the comment "the old theater Comique" suggests that Leer may have either operated the Comique Saloon as Theatre Comique or operated a previous Theatre Comique near his saloon. In either case, it seems likely that Theatre Comique had existed previous to its 1876 incarnation and was moved from its original location to Main Street.

30 *Fort Worth City Directory*, 1877; Richard Selcer, *Hell's Half Acre*, Fort Worth: Texas Christian University Press, 1991, 77; *Democrat*, 16 January 1877, 4; 10 January 1878, 4. The 1878–79 directory locates Leer's stable on the southwest corner of Houston and Seventh. In the same directory Leer is also listed as "undertaker," selling supplies from the Houston St. location.

31 Joseph G. Rosa and Waldo E. Koop, *Rowdy Joe Lowe, Gambler With a Gun*, Norman: University of Oklahoma, 1989, 8, 97–105.

32 Ibid., *Democrat*, 1 October 1876, 4; 28 October 1876, 4.

33 Fort Worth City Council minutes, 14 November 1876; Selcer, *Hell's Half Acre*, 76–77.

34 *Democrat*, 26 November 1878, 4.

35 David Copeland, *Hell's Half Acre: Fort Worth's First Amusement Center, 1873–1889*, 11–12, unpublished dissertation Fort Worth Public Library, Local History and Genealogy, hereafter cited as FWPL-LHG. Fort Worth City Council Minutes, Book A, 8 April 1873, 8; 13 October 1873, 40; Minutes of the Criminal Docket of the County Court, 1878–1879, Book 168, University of Texas-Arlington Library, Special Collections.

36 Rosa and Koop, *Rowdy Joe Lowe*, 114; *Democrat*, 27 August 1878, 4, 29 August 1878, 4; 4 October 1878, 4; 1 December 1878, 4.

37 *Democrat*, 7 December 1878, 3.

38 *Democrat*, 31 December 1878, 4.

39 Ibid.

40 *Democrat*, 15 January 1879, 4; 21 March 1879, 4.

41 Rosa and Koop, *Rowdy Joe Lowe*, 120, 151–168.

42 *Democrat*, 2 August 1879, 3, 4 September 1879, 4. The Apollo Garden appears in the 1878–1879 directory, but only under saloon listings; it is acknowledged as a variety theater only in the later newspaper account. This suggests that the saloon expanded its operations after the printing of the directory. When the city's next directory was issued in 1882, both the Apollo Garden and the Centennial had disappeared from all listings.

43 *Fort Worth Daily Gazette*, 4 December 1885, 8. In city directory after 1877, Leer is never listed as owner or proprietor of a variety hall or saloon. However, in 1885–1886, he made several appearances before the city council when operating licenses for these establishments came up for renewal. These appearances, along with the *Gazette's* reporting of the location of his theater as the corner of Second and Main, seem to indicate that he owned a part interest in some of these establishments. Between 1882 and 1885, city directories list George Bird Holland as proprietor of both My Theater and later, Theatre Comique (presumably the same theater), both at the corner of Second and Main. My Theater actually opened in 1880 according to the *Daily Democrat*, 2 January 1880.

44 *Star-Telegram*, 10 February 1921, 7; *Record*, 10 February 1921, 2.

CHAPTER TWO

1 J. Frank Norris, *Inside History of First Baptist Church, Fort Worth and Temple Baptist Church, Detroit*, n.p.: n. d., 85. The book contains the full text of several of Norris' sermons, which were copied verbatim by church stenographers as Norris spoke.

2 Ibid., 85-87.

3   *Star-Telegram*, 10 February 1921, 7; *Fort Worth Daily Register*, 2 June 1897, 8.

4   Norris, *Inside History of First Baptist Church*, 87. The date of Holland's conversion is based on Norris' recollection that the event occurred six years before Holland's death in 1921.

5   FWP-FWTC, 19248-19251; Jones, *United Confederate Veterans*, 2; *Democrat*, 21 July 1876, 4; 7 November 1879, 4; *Star-Telegram*, (eve.) 10 February 1921, 7.

6   *Democrat*, 7 November 1879, 4; 16 December 1879, 4; 18 December 1879, 4. This possibility is bolstered by the fact that Holland is listed as a clerk working for Herman Meyer in the 1878-79 directory, when ads in the *Democrat* clearly identify him as proprietor of My Theatre.

7   *Fort Worth City Directory*, 1882; *Democrat*, 7 November 1879, 4; 16 December 1879, 4; 2 January 1880, 4; 14 January 1880, 4; 16 January 1880, 4; 14 July 1880, 4.

8   *Star-Telegram*, 10 February 1921, 7; *Fort Worth City Directory*, 1877, 1878-79, 1882, 1883, 1885-1886; *Democrat*, 2 January, 1880, 4; 13 January 1880, 4; 15 August 1880, 4. Based on its ads, which ran regularly beginning in August 1879, My Theater opened sometime that same year at Houston and Weatherford. The *Star-Telegram* ran a copy of one of Holland's New York ads, along with a photograph of the showman in his Confederate uniform, as part of his obituary.

9   Mack Williams, *In Old Fort Worth*, Fort Worth: Mack Williams, 1986, 81.

10 *Democrat*, 18 December 1879, 4; *Record*, 10 February 1921, 2; *Star-Telegram*, 10 February 1921, 7; interview with E. H. Keller, FWP-FWTC, 505. Records of the variety theaters at the corner of Second and Main remain extremely muddy, complicated no doubt by the 1876 fire that destroyed the county courthouse along with many municipal records. Holland's or anyone else's role in the Adelphi and first Theatre Comique is supposition. The 1878-79 directory lists Geo. B. Holland as a clerk for H. Meyer & Co., although this last situation might be entirely logical if a previous theater he owned had gone out of business or if he had yet to open My Theater at the time the directory went to press.

11 *Fort Worth City Directory*, 1883-1884, 1885-1886; report of Fort Worth City Director, 1883-1884, FWP-FWTC, 16414.

12 *Democrat*, 2 October 1881, 1, 4; 4 October 1881, 4.

13 *Democrat*, 9 October 1881, 4 (two separate articles); 9 November 1881, 4; *Fort Worth Telegram*, 17 February 1907, sec. 1, 12.

14 *Fort Worth City Directory*, 1886-1887, 1888-1889; Fort Worth City Council minutes, 3 December 1885. Leer's reemergence evidently followed the issuance of the 1885-1886 city directory. By the 1886-1887 directory, Theatre Comique had vanished, leaving only Fashion Theater. Leer still resided in the city but had no business interests listed. Fashion Theater continued to operate through 1888, although John Ashmore became its proprietor. W. E. Graves lived in Fort Worth for several years, working as a bartender for at least two different saloons. The 1890 city directory shows him employed by the Occidental.

15 The evidence that My Theatre and Theatre Comique are the same theater is circumstantial but substantial. City directories for 1883-1884 and 1885-1886 show both theaters located at the same address, the corner of Second and Main. George Holland is listed as proprietor of the first My Theatre in 1883-1884 and then of Theatre Comique in 1885-1886. Several employees specifically named in city directories also overlap the two theaters between 1882 and 1886. These include stage manager Charles Knight, bartender Joseph Tiffee, and William Sands, listed first as doorkeeper and then as ticket agent; variety actress Mary Knight (possibly a relative of Charles Knight), and variety performers James and Rose LeClair and Fred Spicer. Knight had stage managed for Holland since at least 1882.

16 *Gazette*, 8 April 1886, 3; Fort Worth City Council minutes, 3 June 1885; 10 August 1885. The *Gazette* article is somewhat ambiguous in its wording but lists those appearing before the city council with petitions to operate variety theaters as John T. Leer, W. E. Graves, and George Holland. The article observes, "The first two applied to institutions already in operation and the last to one which it was proposed to open near the foot of Houston street." Leer had been engaged to run Theatre Comique, possibly as early as June 1885. He received the requisite operating license for a variety theater 3 June 1885, although the name Theatre Comique does not appear in connection with his name until the 10 August council meeting. Since he also expanded its operation to include a dance hall in December 1885, it seems unlikely that he would try to open an additional theater. Graves, as the proprietor of the smaller Fashion Theatre, also seems unlikely to diminish his resources by opening a second theater. Even if the names are not listed in their proper order, this still leaves Holland as the individual with the resources and motivation

to open a new theater. As it turned out, other factors, including a city council election in April 1886, which changed the balance of power on the council significantly, worked against all of the variety operations. Holland did not receive a permit for a new theater, and Theatre Comique closed down for good sometime in 1886. It was not until 1891 or 1892 that Holland finally opened another variety theater in the city.

17 *Gazette*, 15 November 1885, 8; 4 December 1885, 8; *Star-Telegram*, 30 October 1949, Automobile Section, 23.

18 *Gazette*, 13 November 1883, 6; 15 December 1883, 8.

19 Tarrant County Court Criminal Docket, Book 169, 1878-1879, case nos. 713, 846; Book 170, 1882-1883, case nos. 1744, 1800; Book 177, 1886, case no. 3724. The euphemism "disorderly house" was used by law enforcement to describe both bordellos and places such as saloons, dance halls, and variety theaters where customers engaged in loud, crude, or raucous behavior.

20 *Fort Worth City Directory*, 1883, 1885-1886, 1886-1887, 1888-1889, 1890; *Gazette*, 28 December 1886, 8.

21 *Gazette*, 10 September 1890, 2; *Register*, 18 November 1899, 2; Selcer, *Hell's Half Acre*, 204-210.

22 City of Fort Worth Ordinances, Book A, Ordinance 224, passed 7 April 1880; Ordinance 227, passed 20 April 1880; Book B, Ordinance 322, passed 4 April 1884. The Fort Worth Opera House, a respectable producer of "legitimate" entertainment had opened in 1883. The wording of the ordinance allowed authorities to deal with problems in either the opera house or a variety theater, although variety theaters, in common parlance, were sometimes referred to as "opera houses." The ordinance clearly sought to prohibit disruptive behavior in any theatrical setting.

23 City Council Minutes, 19 February 1884, 6 July 1886, 7 September 1886. Ordinance 357, passed in January, 1885, raised the bond proprietors were required to file from $250 to $300. The last time Holland applied to operate a variety theater was April 1886. His license request was denied and he did not refile.

24 City Council minutes, 7 April 1886; *Gazette*, 8 April 1886, 3.

25 *Gazette*, 15 April 1886, 8; 5 May 1886, 8; 12 May 1886, 8; 18 May 1886, 8; 20 May 1886, 8. John Leer was fined at least three times between 7 April and 15 April for continuing to operate without a license. He demanded a jury trial, but lost and was assessed a fine of $10.

26 *Gazette*, 2 June 1886, 8.

27 *Gazette*, 19 June 1886, 8; 20 May 1886, 8; 28 December 1886, 8; City Council Minutes, 1 June 1886, 7 September 1886, 7 December 1886; Tarrant County Court, Criminal Docket, Vol. 9, 1886-1887, case no. 3724. After 7 December 1886, no person appeared before council to obtain a license for Theatre Comique. Theatre Comique appeared in the 1886-1887 directory but disappeared by the issuance of the 1888-1889 directory. The term "under execution" in connection with the sale of a part interest in Theatre Comique indicates the enforcing of a legal judgment against a debtor who either cannot or refuses to pay. Whether the judgment was actually against Holland is open to supposition without surviving court records.

28 City Council minutes, 6 September 1887; *Fort Worth City Directory*, 1886-1887, 1888-1889, 1890, 1892-1893; *Gazette*, 7 August 1890, 2; 3 September 1890, 2; 7 September 1890, 2.

29 *Gazette*, 9 August 1890, 8; 6 August 1893, 2; 31 August 1893, 2. Based on these articles, People's Theater opened on Main sometime between 1887 and 1890. Bill Deering was approved on 5 August 1890 as a special policeman to this theater, although the hall does not appear in city directories until 1899, under the proprietorship of C. W. Hurley. On 7 September 1890, (p. 2) the *Gazette* reported that "Mr. Andrews" (J. D. Andrews, who coincidentally opened Andrews' Pavilion Theater at the corner of 12th and Jones during the same year) bowed to public pressure and closed "the variety theater, corner of Second and Main." The 7 August 1890 *Gazette* suggests that three variety theaters remained in operation, although only Andrews' Pavilion is listed in the 1890 city directory. There is no surviving 1891-92 city directory. The theft of the Farmers and Merchants' Bank silver shipment actually occurred in 1889.

30 *Fort Worth City Directory*, 1890, 1892-1893, 1894-1895, 1896-1897, 1899-1900, 1905-1906. By January, 1906, Dave Houghton was operating the Star.(*Record*, 19 January 1906, 5).

31 Selcer, *Hell's Half Acre*, 204-210.

32 City Council minutes, 15 July 1890, 18 July 1890, 12 August 1890, 19 August 1890, 26 August 1890, *Gazette*, 7 August 1890, 2; 16 August 1890, 8; 25 August 1890, 2.

33 Ibid.

[34] City Council minutes, 2 September 1890; *Gazette*, 25 August 1890, 2; 3 September 1890, 2. One of the two variety theaters indicated by city council minutes was People's Theater. The other theater may have been Fashion Theater on Main Street or the Gem Theater, a theater located at 1404 Main according to the 1912-1913 city directory. The only reference to it is in a short local item in the *Gazette* (9 August 1890, 8). J. D. Andrews obtained a second theater permit for the corner of 12th and Jones, but not until 12 August. City directories are not helpful in this instance, listing only Andrews' Pavilion Theater (12th and Jones).

[35] *Gazette*, 4 August 1893, 8; 14 August 1893, 2; 15 August 1893, 2; 17 August 1893, 8; 22 August 1893, 8; 31 August 1893, 8; 2 September 1893, 6; 6 September 1893, 6. In 1892, Holland had been arrested in front of his own theater after getting into a fist fight with another man (*Gazette*, 27 March, 5). Following Holland's 1893 arrest, Chief Maddox told a *Gazette* reporter that managers of other variety halls and bawdy houses imported new "hostesses" unknown to local law enforcers. All the new arrivals claimed to be married, making them exempt from the ordinance description of "loose or immoral women."

[36] *Register*, 2 June 1897, 8.

[37] *Star-Telegram*, 12 October 1934, 11; *Fort Worth City Directory*, 1892-1893, 1894-1895, 1901-1902, 1902-1903; Selcer, *Hell's Half Acre*, 237; Dora Davenport Jones, *Additions and Corrections to the History of the Robert E. Lee Camp 158, United Confederate Veterans, Fort Worth, Texas*, 2-9, Tarrant County Historical Commission, Fort Worth Texas.

[38] Newspapers for much of 1896 did not survive, making it difficult to pin down a precise date for the opening of the Standard.

[39] Gerald Bordman, *Oxford Companion to the American Theater*, 2nd edition, Oxford University Press, 1992, 538, 690-691; Albert F. McLean Jr., *American Vaudeville as Ritual*, University of Kentucky Press, 1965, 30-31; *Fort Worth City Directory*, 1899-1900, 1901-1902, 1902-1903, 1904-1905, 1905-1906; *Record*, 26 November 1905, 3; *Fort Worth Telegram*, 8 February 1906, 5; 11 February 1906, Sec. 3, 9. By 1904, even the last holdout, George Holland, had changed the designation of his theater, now located at 115 E. 13th, to vaudeville. The term "legitimate" generally applied to theaters showing plays acted by professional actors, but not including bills of variety, vaudeville, or other short acts. Phil Epstein closed the sale of the Crown to J. N. Brooker on 3 February 1906.

[40] Williams, *In Old Fort Worth*, 83-85.

[41] *Star-Telegram*, 12 October 1934, 11.

[42] *Fort Worth Record-Telegram*, 3 January 1931; interview with Frank Debeque, 1922, formerly filed in the Hell's Half Acre file but now missing; FWPL-LHG, typescript by Dallas historian, Jim Wheat; "Debeque vs. Ligon," *South Western Reporter*, Vol. 286 (29 September -17 November 1926), 752-754.

[43] *Dallas Daily Herald*, 5 October 1886, 5; 5 September 1887, 3; *Dallas Daily Times-Herald*, 6 February 1892, 5; 22 April 1892, 5; 2 June 1892, 1. Frank Debeque, in a 1926 probate case filed against the estate of Maggie DeBeque, testified that Maggie's true name was Mawhorn. See the previous endnote.

[44] *Register*, 30 September 1901, 2; 3 October 1901, 7; *Telegram*, 11 February 1906, Sec. 3, 9; *Star-Telegram*, 12 October 1934, 11; Douglas Gilbert, *American Vaudeville: Its Life and Times*, New York: Dover Publications, 1968, 188-190.

[45] *Telegram*, 11 February 1906, Sec. 3, 9; *Star-Telegram*, 12 October 1934, 11; Williams, *In Old Fort Worth*, 85; Gilbert, *American Vaudeville*, 188-190.

[46] Ephraim Katz, *The Film Encyclopedia*, New York: Thomas Y. Crowell, 1979, 1155; Anthony Slide, *The Encyclopedia of Vaudeville*, Westport, Connecticut: Greenwood Press, 1994, 356; *Star-Telegram*, 12 October 1934, 11.

[47] Slide, *Encyclopedia of Vaudeville*, Ibid., 352; *Telegram*, 4 March 1906, 4; *Record*, 6 March 1906, 3.

[48] Buster Keaton with Charles Samuels, *My Wonderful World of Slapstick*, New York: Da Capo Press, 1960, 11-35; *Star-Telegram*, 12 October 1934, 11; Interview with Frank DeBeque, FWPL-LHG. The Keaton family performed many variations on their basic "knockabout" act; there are no actual records detailing what version appeared at the Standard. The family most likely performed at the theater sometime between 1897 and 1908, although Keaton maintained in his autobiography that the family never played anything but so-called bigtime circuits. The week of 15 February 1909, the Keatons appeared at Fort Worth's Majestic billing themselves as *The 4 Keatons and Buster*.

49 *Record*, 17 October 1905, 10; 18 October 1905, 12; 9 December 1905, 12; 16 December 1905, 1; 17 January 1906, 6. Proprietors of variety theaters arrested in the crackdown included Edward Dinwiddy, George Turner, Maggie DeBeque, Phil Epstein, and Ida Carico. "Actresses" received a 20 percent kickback on every alcoholic beverage sold. An 1890 ordinance prohibited variety theaters from selling or giving away liquor, but because of a loophole, patrons could still obtain liquor from nearby saloons or so called "beer gardens." An 1893 ordinance prohibited dancing in variety theaters and made it illegal to operate a variety theater within the corporate limits of the city. Those with business interests in the Acre tended to view Hell's Half Acre as a self-contained entity already outside these limits and ignored city ordinances. The ordinances did serve as a deterrent for those proprietors who might otherwise have tried to set up shop in the city's main business district along or west of Main Street and north of Eleventh Street.

50 City Council Minutes, Book R, 18 December 1905; *Telegram*, 7 December 1905, 3; 16 December 1905, 1; 19 December 1905, 5; 10 January 1906, 12. *South Western Reporter*, "Debeque vs. Ligon," 750.

51 *Telegram*, 16 December 1905, 1; *Record*, 10 January 1906, 12; 16 January 1916, 5. People's Theater, while not mentioned in city directories after 1900, is one of the theaters named specifically 16 January 1906 as a target of the police crackdown. One possibility is that People's leased or bought George Holland's location at 115 E. 13th after Holland closed.

52 *Telegram*, 9 January 1906, 2; 17 January 1906, 2; 18 January 1906, 5; 27 January 1906, 5; 31 January 1906, 5; 8 February 1906, 5; *Record*, 11 February 1910, 8. The Crown Theater was sold by owner Phil Epstein in February, 1906 to J. N. Brooker (*Fort Worth Telegram*, 8 February 1906, 5). Newspaper accounts published in the *Record* in 1910 recount the battle to close the variety theaters in 1906 and establish that all the city's variety theaters, except the Standard, closed down at that time.

53 *Record*, 23 December 1906, 5.

54 *Record*, 24 December 1906, 3, 4; 27 December 1906, 4; 10 February 1907, 10.

55 *Record*, 5 February 1910, 12, 6 February 1910, 10, 11 February 1910, 8; *Telegram*, 17 February 1907, 12; *Star-Telegram*, 12 October 1934 (morning), 11; *Press*, 8 October 1934, 4.

CHAPTER THREE

1 *Record*, 2 April 1911, 11; *Star-Telegram*, 21 February 1936, 19; Tarrant County Deed Book, Volume H, 190, no. 4280; FWP-FWTC, 16672–16673.

2 *Record*, 2 April 1911, 11; *Star-Telegram*, 21 February 1936, 19; FWP-FWTC, 16672–16673.

3 *Record*, 2 April 1911, 11; *Star-Telegram*, 21 February 1936, 19; Frank C. Condon, "A Lady Who Tells Her Age," *Colliers*, 26 January 1935, 19–20.

4 Weldon B. Durham, *American Theatre Companies, 1883–1930*, New York: Greenwood Press, 1987, 159–163; Daniel Frohman, *Daniel Frohman Presents*, New York: Lee Furman, 1935, 262–264; William Winter, *The American Stage of Today*, New York: E. F. Collier & Sons, 1910, n. p.; Foster Hirsch, *The Boys From Syracuse: The Shubert's Theatrical Empire*, New York: Cooper Square Press, 2000, 24–25, 31; Condon, "A Lady Who Tells Her Age," 19–20; *Record*, 2 April 1911, 11; *Star-Telegram*, 21 February 1936, 19; *New York Times*, 21 October 1942, 21.

5 Ibid.

6 *Record*, 2 April 1911, 11; 8 April 1911, 5.

7 *Record*, 2 April 1911, 11; *Star-Telegram*, 21 February 1936, 19; *New York Times*, 21 October 1942, 21; FWP-FWTC, 16672–16673. Biographical accounts of Robson's life vary widely on the "facts." The reliability of these accounts is hard to determine, since Robson furnished colorful, yet sometimes conflicting, versions of her life to interviewers.

8 *Democrat*, 16 November 1876, 4.

9 Interview with John Swayne, FWP-FWTC, 489–490; *Standard*, 9 November 1876, 4.

10 David Naylor and Joan Dillon, *American Theaters: Performance Halls of the Nineteenth Century*, New York: John Wiley & Sons, 1997, 14; Oscar G. Brockett, *History of the Theater*, 6th ed., Boston: Allyn & Bacon, 1991, 453–456; Mary C. Henderson, *Theatre In America*, New York: Harry N. Abrams, 1986, 142.

[11] *Democrat,* 7 November 1876, 4; 19 November 1876, 4; Brockett, *History of the Theater,* 455.

[12] *Standard,* 16 December 1876, 4; 19 December 1876, 4; 22 December 1876, 4; Bernard Sobel, *A Pictorial History of Vaudeville,* New York: Bonanza Books, 1961, 200; Gilbert, *American Vaudeville,* 14.

[13] *Standard,* 13 January 1877, 4; 17 January 1877, 4. *Our American Cousin* was sometimes presented under the name *Dundreary,* a title widely adopted by acting companies after President Abraham Lincoln was assassinated while viewing the play in 1865.

[14] *Democrat,* 29 January 1877, 4; 4 April 1877, 4; Joseph Gallegly, *Footlights On the Border: The Galveston and Houston Stage Before 1900,* The Hague, Netherlands: Mouton & Co., 1962, 97–98, 111.

[15] *Galveston Daily News,* 9 March 1875; *Standard,* 9 March 1877, 4; *Democrat,* 8 March 1877, 4; 9 March 1877, 4.

[16] Ibid.

[17] Seasons of Evans Hall, 1876–1881, compiled by the author. A copy is found in the Tarrant County Historical Commission, Tarrant County Court House, Fort Worth, Texas.

[18] *Democrat,* 10 January 1879, 3; 11 January 1879, 3.

[19] *Democrat,* 2 December 1879, 4; 4 December 1879, 4; 5 December 1879, 4; Don Russell, *The Lives and Legends of Buffalo Bill,* Norman: University of Oklahoma Press, 1960, 28–29, 34–35, 259.

[20] *Democrat,* 5 December 1879, 4.

[21] *Democrat,* 24 March 1881, 4.

[22] *Democrat,* 25 March 1881, 4. The identities of Booth and Dryden, mentioned as the lessees of the hall cannot be determined from extant records such as city directories.

[23] The conclusion that no theatrical season was held during 1881–1882 is based on a study of city newspapers between September 1881 and May 1882. No theatrical announcements appeared in the *Democrat* during that period.

[24] FWP-FWTC, 19432; *Democrat,* 30 December 1881, 4; Fort Worth City Directory, 1883–1884; Sanborn Fire Map of Fort Worth, 1885, FWPL-GLH. Texas Wesleyan University (not to be confused with the later Texas Wesleyan College, established as Polytechnic College in 1891) had opened in 1881. The 1883–84 Fort Worth city directory lists Deutscher Verein Hall at the southeast corner of Throckmorton and Seventh. The Sanborn map shows its location in the middle of the block, along Seventh. A fire on 15 October 1887 destroyed most of the buildings in that block, including Deutscher Verein Hall. A later hall was renamed Germania Hall.

[25] *Democrat,* 19 January 1883, 4. City newspapers between July 1882 and late January 1883 did not survive, so no record exists to show the full extent of theatrical bookings at the hall during the 1882–1883 season.

[26] Report of the Fort Worth City Director, 1883–1884, FWP-FWTC, 16414; *Democrat,* 16 January 1883, 4; 22 January 1883, 4.

[27] *Galveston Weekly News,* 19 August 1883, 1; Naylor and Dillon, *American Theaters,* 21; *Galveston Daily News,* 30 November 1882, 1; 16 December 1882, 1; *Dallas Weekly Herald,* 18 October 1883, 4. In 1896, a trade journal ad for the McElfatrick firm included only a partial listing of the firm's design and construction work: seventy-one theaters in an area stretching from New York to Nebraska.(*Julius Cahn's Official Theatrical Guide,* 1896, p. 54).

[28] *Gazette,* 9 September 1883, 4; *Galveston Daily News,* 10 January 1883, 1; *Dallas Weekly Herald,* 18 October 1883, 4; David Byrne Blackwood, *The Theatres of J. B. McElfatrick and Sons, Architects, 1855–1922,* Vol. 2 (unpublished Ph.D. dissertation) University of Kansas, 1966, 243; Naylor and Dillon, *American Theaters,* 21; "Theatrical History of Fort Worth," *Bohemian,* Vol. 3, No. 2, Christmas, 1901–1902, 69. Blackwood's second volume is an appendix of statistics and demographic information for over 40 McElfatrick theaters, all taken from *Julius Cahn's Official Theatrical Guide,* 1896. *Cahn's Guide,* a trade publication intended for the use of producers, managers, etc., contained important listings of seating capacity, stage dimensions, available equipment, lighting capabilities, and prices. These seating capacity estimates correspond to estimates found in *The Bohemian.* Seating diagrams for the lower floor, parquet, and balcony circles appearing in *The Bohemian* suggest that these areas combined seated approximately 780 spectators. This meant that the upper gallery alone contained over 430 seats, an additional stress to exterior walls and bracing. Dimensions and capacity found in the *Daily Gazette,* 9 September 1883, while interesting for comparison, were somewhat overestimated, placing the theater's seating at 1,500.

29 Ibid.

30 *Gazette,* 9 September 1883, 4.

31 Ibid.; Brockett, *History of Theater,* 436, 448; Blackwood, *Theaters of J. B. McElfatrick,* 243.

32 Blackwood, Ibid. *Gazette,* 12 August 1883, 4; 19 August 1883, 5; Blackwood, 243.

33 Ibid. In *Cahn's Guide,* as cited by Blackwood, the width of the stage is listed as the width of the proscenium opening, generally accepted as being the same width as the visible performance area of a stage.

34 *Gazette,* 27 July 1883, 4.

35 Ibid.

36 *Gazette,* 27 July 1883, 4; various ads and reviews appearing in the *Gazette* throughout the 1883–1884 season. Newspapers for October 1883 failed to survive. The only evidence that some acts appeared are lists appearing in the *Gazette* during July, 1883.

37 *Gazette,* 15 August 1883, 4; 10 September 1883, 4; *Galveston Daily News,* 11 October 1883, 1; *Dallas Weekly Herald,* 18 October 1883, 4. Surviving *Gazette* ad announcing the grand premiere from the files of the Tarrant County Historical Commission, Tarrant County Court House, Fort Worth, Texas, n.p., n.d. *Gazette* issues for October did not survive. Accounts of the opening come from both the *Galveston Daily News* and *Dallas Weekly Herald.*

38 *Dallas Weekly Herald,* 1 November 1883, 1.

39 *Dallas Weekly Herald,* 22 November 1883, 1; *Gazette,* 9 November 1883, 6.

40 *Gazette,* 14 November 1883, 6.

41 *Daily Gazette,* 16 February 1884, 6; 28 June 1888, 8.

CHAPTER FOUR

1 *Gazette,* 27 December 1887, 8; *Galveston Daily News,* 18 April 1888, 8; Gallegly, *Footlights on the Border,* 136.

2 *Gazette,* 13 October 1888, 3. Maddern, who eventually married producer and publisher Harrison Grey Fiske and continued to tour as Minnie Maddern Fiske, appeared at Galveston's Tremont Opera House and Houston's Pillot's Opera House in October 1882, and again at Pillot's in January 1884.

3 *Gazette,* 27 July 1883, 4; 14 November 1883, 6; 7 January 1886, 8; 19 January 1886, 8; 23 January 1886, 8; 1 February 1886, 8; 17 April 1886, 8; 6 June 1886, 3; 21 July 1886, 8; 29 July 1886, 8; *Star-Telegram,* 5 November 1933, 8. Fort Worth City directories never list Max Elser as manager of the opera house although he is named as manager in two different *Gazette* articles during 1883. The 1885–1886 directory lists Charles Benton as lessee and manager while still maintaining a residence in Dallas. Agnes Benton, his wife, is listed as opera house business manager, boarding at the Pickwick Hotel. The 1888–1889 directory is the first to list George Dashwood as both lessee and manager, although newspaper accounts in 1886 make it clear that he had already taken over management by then. Mrs. Benton (not her husband) had her lease extended to three years in January 1886 by the directors of the opera house; six months later the Bentons resigned. Whether the Bentons left of their own accord or were forced out over some disagreement remains unclear. A February 1883 *Gazette* news item mentions Charles Benton as supervising the remodeling of Gray's Opera House in Houston for its grand reopening. Then, in July 1886, Benton announced that he had been offered theaters in New York and San Francisco and would accept one of these positions. A *Gazette* account covering the Fort Worth appearance of actress Lotta Crabtree mentions manager Dashwood, (14 February 1889, 5). By September, the opera house had been purchased by Henry Greenwall, although Dashwood remained with the organization for at least another season. By the 1891–92 directory, there is no more mention of him.

4 Gerald Bordman, *The Oxford Companion To American Theater,* 2nd ed., New York: Oxford University Press, 1992, 380, 483, 584, 682–683; David Dempsey and Raymond P. Baldwin, *The Triumphs and Trials of Lotta Crabtree,* New York: William Morrow, 1968, 111–112, 143, 224–225; *Gazette,* 14 February 1889, 5.

5 *Gazette,* 11 January 1887, 8, 1 February 1888, 8.

6 Roger A. Hall, *Performing the American Frontier, 1870–1906,* New York: Cambridge University Press, 2001, 128–131.

[7] Ibid. Gallegly, *Footlights On the Border,* 119; Gerald Bordman, *American Theatre: A Chronicle of Comedy and Drama, 1869–1914,* New York: Cambridge University Press, 1994, 220; Brockett, *History of Theater,* 459–462; *Gazette,* 9 November 1885, 8; 10 November 1885, 5; 26 October 1890, 15.

[8] *Gazette,* 5 January 1889, 8; 16 January 1889, 8; Gallegly, *Footlights On the Border,* 137.

[9] *New Orleans Times-Picayune,* 28 November 1913, 12–13; Sue Dauphin, *Houston By Stages: A History of Theatre in Houston,* Burnet, Texas: Eakin Press, 1981, 24; C. Richard King, "Texas Theatrical Impresario," *East Texas Historical Journal,* October 1966, 128; John Kendall, *The Golden Age of New Orleans Theatre,* Baton Rouge: Louisiana State University Press, 1952, 584–585, 588; Hirsch, *The Boys From Syracuse,* 24; Gallegly, *Footlights On the Border,* 77–78; Brockett, *History of the Theater,* 508.

[10] Brockett, Ibid., 462; Gallegly, Ibid., 77–78, 197–209; King, Ibid., 134. Not only did companies appear fairly consistently in Fort Worth and Dallas after performing in Galveston and Houston, they also were booked in an order consistent with the coastal theaters, once again indicating a plan for coordination.

[11] Dauphin, *Houston By Stages,* 13, 20; Kendall, *Golden Age of New Orleans Theater,* 584–585; Claudia Anne Beach, *Henry Greenwall, Theatre Manager,* Ph.D. dissertation, n.p., Texas Tech University, 1986, 60–67, 99; *The Israelites of Louisiana, Their Religious, Civic, Charitable and Patriotic Life,* New Orleans: W. E. Myers, n.d, 111. Published sources disagree as to when Greenwall took over management of the Dallas Opera House. Charles Benton is still mentioned as manager in mid-October 1883 as both Dallas and Fort Worth prepared to open new opera houses (see *Gazette,* 10 July 1883, 4; 22 July 1883, 4; 27 July 1883, 4; 15 August 1883, 4; 10 September 1883, 4). The *Fort Worth Daily Gazette* referred to him as "Manager Greenwall of Dallas" (30 October 1885, 6). Henry W. Barton in *A History of the Dallas Opera House* (M. A. Thesis, Hardin College [SMU], 1935, 7) maintains that Greenwall "successfully handled its affairs for over thirty years." If this is true, a more accurate date might be 1883–1884, since Greenwall died in 1913. Joseph Gallegly provides a complete record of many of the seasons of the Galveston and Houston theaters in *Footlights On the Border.* By comparing these with existing records of the Fort Worth Opera House, it becomes clear that the Greenwall brothers exerted a great deal of influence on state bookings. For instance, in 1885, only five acts out of at least thirty booked for the season did not originate at Greenwall-controlled theaters.

[12] *Dallas Morning News,* 5 September 1886, 3; Charles B. Myler, *A History of the English-Speaking Theater in San Antonio Before 1900,* Ph.D. dissertation, University of Texas, 1968, 229; Kendall, 590–591

[13] Ibid. *Gazette,* 30 October 1885, 6; 5 November 1885, 5.

[14] *Gazette,* 17 April 1886, 8; 18 May 1886, 3; 6 June 1886, 3.

[15] *Dallas Morning News,* 5 September 1886, 3; Brockett, *History of the Theater,* 458; Bordman, *The Oxford Companion to American Theater,* 55, 92–93; Gallegly, 127–128 Booth appeared in Dallas on 25 February 1887.

[16] *Gazette,* 19 February 1888, 8.

[17] *Dallas Morning News,* 28 June 1890, 2; 29 June 1890, 11; 30 June 1890, 1; 18 July 1890, 2, 30 July 1890, 6; Mary Greenwall Fain, *The Greenwall Opera House,* Mary Daggett Lake Papers, Series II, Box 2, folder 7, FWPL-GLH; Williams, *In Old Fort Worth,* 57–58; Tarrant County Deed Records, Volume 69, 419. Sallie Huffman, Walter Huffman's widow, is named in court house deed records as president of the Fort Worth Opera House Company.

[18] *Dallas Morning News,* 28 June 1890, 2; 29 June 1890, 11; 30 June 1890, 1; 18 July 1890, 2; 30 July 1890, 6; Williams, *In Old Fort Worth,* 57–58.

[19] *Dallas Morning News,* 18 July 1890, 2; Tarrant County Deed Records, Volume 69, 419. News items regarding the purchase of the opera house in the *Fort Worth Daily Gazette* did not survive. Accounts in the *Dallas Morning News* indicate that the opera house was part of what was referred to as the "Huffman estate." The announced purchase price of $40,000 changed to $39,000 on the final deed, filed on September 2, perhaps indicating that additional negotiations lowered the price even further after an assessment of the building's condition. The *Morning News* set the original construction costs for the structure as $53,000 in 1883, a figure that agrees fairly closely with figures that originally appeared in the *Fort Worth Daily Gazette* (see chapter 3, note 28). Land values were listed at $20,000 by the *Morning News.*

[20] *Gazette,* 7 November 1890, 5; 26 December 1890, 6; 27 September 1891, 13; *New York Clipper,* 10 October 1891, n. p.; Beach, *Henry Greenwall,* 131.

21 Beach, Ibid., 125; *Gazette,* 2 September 1890, 2; *Star-Telegram,* 17 August 1917, 10.

22 *Gazette,* 1 October 1890, 2; 6 September 1891, 5; 13 September 1891, 5; 27 September 1891, 13; Bordman, *American Theatre,* 97.

23 *Gazette,* 9 December 1890, 2.

24 Taken from various *Gazette* ads, 14 November 1891, 8; 5 February 1892, 8; 17 October 1892, 8; 17 November 1892, 8; Bordman, *American Theatre, 1869–1914,* 299, 305.

25 Bordman, Ibid., 267, 335; *Gazette,* 17 March 1892, 5.

26 Interview with Barry Burke, FWP-FWTC, 6074.

27 *Gazette,* 17 January 1895, 2, 6.

28 Ibid.

29 Theater scrapbook, Julian Umbenhour Theater Collection, Box 30, Tarrant County Historical Commission; Greenwall Opera House program, *Cyrano de Bergerac,* 23 March 1899, Box TT11, Hoblitzelle Interstate Theater Collection, Harry Ransom Center For the Humanities, University of Texas, Austin, hereafter referred to as HITC-HRC; FWP-FWTC, 6074.

30 Ibid. The undated incident more than likely occurred 23 March 1899. *Cyrano de Bergerac* did not make its American debut until October 1898, starring Mansfield. Reasonably successful shows in the 19th century customarily began touring within months of a New York or Chicago debut. Between fall 1899 and spring 1906, Mansfield toured in other plays, appearing at Greenwall's 14 February 1902 in *Beaucaire* and again on 3 March 1905 in *Ivan the Terrible.* He died in August 1907.

31 *Gazette,* 12 November 1892, 8; 20 February 1894, 2.

32 Cornelia Otis Skinner, *Madame Sarah,* Boston: Houghton-Mifflin, 1967, 280–282; *Gazette,* 24 January 1892, 8; 27 January 1892, 8; 29 January 1892, 2.

33 *Gazette,* 1 February 1892, 8; 2 February 1892, 2.

34 Kendall, *Golden Age of New Orleans Theater,* 587–588; M. B. Leavitt, *Fifty Years in Theatrical Management,* New York: Broadway, 1912, 564–565; Bordman, *Oxford Companion to American Theatre,* 664; Brockett, *History of Theater,* 508.

35 Kendall, Ibid.; Leavitt, Ibid.; Beach, *Henry Greenwall,* 150; *Gazette,* 19 February 1893, Sec. 2, 1.

CHAPTER FIVE

1 "Al Hayne, Hero of 1893 [sic] Fire, Not Fireman, Say Residents," undated *Star-Telegram* article in the Spring Palace file of the FWPL-GLH, Fort Worth and Tarrant County Collection. The survivor and eyewitness, attorney T. J. Powell, went on to become mayor of Fort Worth (1900–1906).

2 B. B. Paddock, *Early Days in Fort Worth, Much of Which I Saw and Part of Which I Was,* 28; E. D. Allen, *Descriptive Story of the Texas Spring Palace,* Fort Worth: Texas Printing and Lithographic Co., 1889, 8–9; Edward J. Smith, "The Karporama of Texas" in *Texas' Spring Palace City Fort Worth, A Parody of H.M.S. Pinafore* (souvenir libretto and promotional brochure), Fort Worth: The Texas Spring Palace, 1889, 48, in the collections of The Tarrant County Historical Commission, Tarrant County Court House, Fort Worth, Texas.

3 Paddock, Ibid., 27–28. *Gazette,* 3 June 1890, 4; *Dallas Morning News,* 30 May 1889, 1. An editorial following the Palace's demise reveals that the structure was intended to be permanent. More than likely, lack of time and the need to hold down costs influenced the final decision to build it out of more combustible materials. Once its framework was completed, the decorating of the Palace was finished in only thirty days. According to the *Handbook of Texas,* the Denver, Texas and Fort Worth Railway acquired control of the Fort Worth and Denver City in 1888. The new DT and FW became part of the Union Pacific, Denver and Gulf Railway Company in 1890.

4 Allen, *Descriptive Story of the Spring Palace,* 7–8; Paddock, Ibid., 28

5 Allen, Ibid., 9; Paddock, Ibid., 28; Smith, "The Karporama of Texas," 34. The word "karporama," employed to describe the murals created for the Spring Palace, was evidently based on Smith's explanation, a word coined specifically for the Fort Worth exhibition, combining Greek terms, *karpos,* meaning fruits, and *rama,* a view.

6   *Dallas Morning News,* 30 May 1889, 1; 31 May 1889, 2.

7   *Dallas Morning News,* 1 June 1889, 4; 6 June 1889, 1; 14 June 1889, 2; "Notes from Old Newspapers," found in Texas Spring Palace file, Tarrant County Historical Commission, Tarrant County Court House, Fort Worth, Texas, 1, 3–4; FWP-FWTC, 30242.

8   (Hecker obituary) *Elgin* (Illinois) *Daily Courier,* 1 February 1917, n. p.; E. C. Alft, "Man of the Century: Joseph Hecker," *Elgin Daily Courier-News,* 27 July 1974, n. p.; E. C. Alft, *Elgin: Days Gone By,* Carpentersville, Illinois: Crossroads Communications, 1992, 187–188.

9   Bordman, *Oxford Companion to American Theatre,* 291.

10 Ad for *Grand Inauguration Night Fort Worth Opera House, Gazette,* n. d., n. p. in the files of the Tarrant County Historical Commission, Tarrant County Court House, Fort Worth, Texas. The Fay Templeton Star Alliance appeared 21–24 March 1881. *H. M. S. Pinafore* was one of several plays performed by the group.

11 *Gazette,* 15 May 1886, 8; 26 May 1886, 8; *The Handbook of Texas Online,* s.v. "KREISSIG, HANS," http://www.tsha.utexas.edu/handbook/online/articles/KK/fkr3.html (accessed February 20, 2006).

12 Correspondence with Nancy Buckman, great-niece of William Fife Sommerville, 2 December, 2001; Fort Worth City Directory, 1888–1889; *Gazette,* 28 April 1888, 8; 12 May 1888, 8.

13 Fort Worth City Directory, 1883–1884, 1885–1886, 1886–1887; FWP-FWTC, 8049; Edward J. Smith, *The Capitalist, or The City of Fort Worth,* 1888, Halbower-Umbenhour Collection, Box 35, Tarrant County Historical Commission, Tarrant County Courthouse, Fort Worth, Texas, hereafter cited as H-UC, TCHC; *Star-Telegram,* 24 April 1949, sec. 1, 11. Issues of the *Fort Worth Gazette* for May-July 1889 (except for the Thursday weekly edition) did not survive—most accounts come from the *Dallas Morning News,* which provided a daily calendar of events at the Palace, but did not provide the in-depth coverage of a local newspaper.

14 Smith, *The Capitalist.*

15 Ibid., 6–7.

16 Ibid., 11.

17 *New York Times,* 28 June 1889, 1; Allen, *Descriptive Story of the Texas Spring Palace,* 3, 7; Paddock, 27–28.

18 Edward J. Smith, *Fort Worth, Texas, a Parody of H.M.S. Pinafore,* 12.

19 Ibid., 4, 22.

20 Ibid., 4.

21 Ibid., 4, 15.

22 *Gazette,* 28 June 1890, 1; *Dallas Morning News,* 11 May 1890, 1; 2 June 1890, 5.

23 *Gazette,* 3 June 1890, 6; 5 June 1890, 8; *New York Times,* 31 May 1890, 1; *Dallas Morning News,* 31 May 1890, 2; 1 June 1890, 9.

24 *Gazette,* 5 June 1890, 8; *Dallas Morning News,* 31 May 1890, 2; 1 June 1890, 9.

25 *Gazette,* 3 June 1890, 4; 5 June 1890, 8.

26 *Gazette,* 24 September 1890, 2; 27 September 1890, 2; Alan St. H. Brock, *A History of Fireworks,* London: George G. Harrap & Co., 1949, 104–105.

27 Brock, Ibid., 105–107; *Fort Worth Evening Mail;* 17 December 1885, 2.

28 *Gazette,* 24 September 1890, 2; 27 September 1890, 2; 3 October 1890, 2; 13 October 1890, 2.

29 *Gazette,* 3 October 1890, 2; 19 October 1890, 15.

30 Ibid. *Gazette,* 12 October 1890, 16; 24 October 1890, 2; 29 October 1890, 2.

31 *Gazette,* 19 October 1890, 2; 21 October 1890, 2.

32 *Gazette,* 6 October 1890, 2; 19 October 1890, 15; 21 October 1890, 2; Program, *The Last Days of Pompeii,* furnished to the author by John Deeker, chairman, Pain's Fireworks, England.

33 Program, *Last Days of Pompeii; Gazette,* 19 October 1890, 15; 21 October 1890, 2; 28 October 1890, 2; 29 October 1890, 2.

34 *Gazette,* 14 October 1890, 1; 19 October 1890, 2.

35 *Gazette,* 10 October 1890, 2; 21 October 1890, 2; 24 October 1890, 2; 26 October 1890, 15.

36 *Gazette,* 8 November 1890, 2; 9 November 1890, 2.

37 *Star-Telegram,* 11 September 1902, 16.

CHAPTER SIX

1 FWP-FWTC, 15088.

2 Bordman, *American Theater, 1869–1914,* 430; *Fort Worth Register,* 13 September 1900, 4; records of Oakwood Cemetery Association, Fort Worth, Texas.

3 *Register,* Ibid.

4 *Variety,* 15 October 1910, 27; *Telegram,* 13 February 1906, 12.

5 Hirsch, *The Boys From Syracuse,* 55–56; *Record,* 15 January 1905, sec. 1, 4; 18 February 1906, 9. The *Record*'s allusion to "Jim Crow performances" undoubtedly expresses a racist perception of the time that blacks lacked the education and more refined theatrical tastes of their white "superiors." With the passage of Jim Crow laws, blacks could be legally restricted to segregated seating in the upper gallery of most theaters.

6 *Houston Post* quoted in the *Fort Worth Record,* 18 February 1906, 9.

7 *Record,* 15 July 1905, 1; 24 December 1905, 8; 28 December 1905, 3; 18 February 1906, 9.

8 *Record,* 1 July 1906, sec. 2, 3; *New Orleans Daily Picayune,* 11 March 1906, n. p.; *Dallas Morning News,* 21 March 1906, n. p.; Henderson, *Theater in America,* 26.

9 Surviving records indicate Mansfield returned to Fort Worth at least twice more: in *Beaucaire* (14 February 1902), and *Ivan the Terrible* (3 March 1905).

10 Bordman, *American Theater, 1869–1914,* 457, 522, 551.

11 Stanley Green and Kay Green, *Broadway Musicals Show By Show,* 5th edition, New York: Hal Leonard Corp., 1996, 6, 8, 10–13; Bordman, *American Theater, 1869–1914,* 519, 733.

12 *Bulletin of the Polytechnic College School of Fine Arts,* 1910; *Bulletin of the Texas Woman's College,* 1916, 1918, Texas Wesleyan Library, Special Collections, Texas Wesleyan University, Fort Worth, Texas; Colby D. Hall, *History of Texas Christian University: A College of the Cattle Frontier,* Fort Worth: TCU Press, 1947, 285, 289–290; Jerome A. Moore, *Texas Christian University: A Hundred Years of History,* Fort Worth: TCU Press, 1974, 193; Add-Ran Christian University (precursor to Texas Christian University) commencement program 1895, in the collection of the author; *The (TCU) Skiff,* 15 May 1936, 2. The 1895 Add-Ran commencement program mentions "Entertainment provided by Dramatic Club." That same year the university moved to Waco. In 1902, trustees changed the institution's name to Texas Christian University.

13 Gilbert, Ibid. *Record,* 28 November 1905, 3.

14 Gilbert, Ibid., 3–5; Brockett, *History of the Theater,* 421–422, 461.

15 Records of opera house seasons, 1883–1916, compiled by the author; *Register,* 21 May, 1902, 1, 5; 25 May 1902, 10; 27, May 1902, 3 . M. B. Leavitt's *Spider and Fly,* which toured the city several times from 1891 onward, *McFadden's Row of Flats,* and Charles H. Hale's *Greatest Twelve Temptations* (28 January 1895) all featured vaudeville acts prominently. J. Z. Wheat, proprietor of the Stag Saloon, purchased the building at the corner of Eighth and Main in 1902. He operated the Roof Garden for several summers until the city's need for additional office space induced him to add a story, in the process doing away with the summer cabaret.

16 *Register,* 19 June 1902, 8; *Record,* 18 July 1905, 5; 30 July 1905, 4; FWP-FWTC, 20664–20665.

17 *Record,* 13 July 1905, 5; 14 July 1905, 5; 27 July 1905, 5; *The Story of Karl Hoblitzelle,* unpublished manuscript, Box 1, Chapter I, p. 32, HITC-HRC. *Variety* (16 April 1910, 9) mentions that the Ehrlich Brothers of Shreveport controlled eleven theaters by 1910, although it does not specify when this chain began or where the theaters were located. Interestingly, Interstate closed its Shreveport theater, perhaps because of competition from an already-established entity.

18 Ibid.; "W. J. Bailey" in *Makers of Fort Worth,* Fort Worth Newspaper Artists Association, 1914, n. p.; *Record,* 15 July 1905, 5, 28, November 1905, 3, Fort Worth City Directory, 1890.

19 *Record,* 27 July 1905, 5; 16 November 1905, 12.

20 Ibid. Don Hinga, *Forty Years In Community Service: The Story of Karl Hoblitzelle and the Development of Interstate Theaters*, Dallas: Stellmacher and Son, 1946, 2–4.

21 Ibid.

22 Gilbert, *American Vaudeville*, 32–33; *Telegram*, 6 September 1908, 2; *Record*, 30 May 1924, sec. 2, 1; *Star-Telegram*, 30 May 1924, 7; *Arkansas Gazette*, 30 May 1924, 18. See also chapter 2, note 39. Fort Worth Federal census records for 1900 seem to suggest that both Epstein and his wife, who listed her profession as "actress" were employed in Frank DeBeque's Standard Theater. During the 1908 season, Epstein was based in Little Rock, but returned the next year and remained for the next seven years.

23 *Record*, 16 November 1905, 12. Among several local firms contracted to complete the theater were Ellison's Furniture, which provided carpet and furnishings; fixtures and electrical wiring by A. J. Anderson and J. G. Carlile; heating and plumbing by Van Zandt and Ackley; and draperies by Parker-Lowe Dry Goods Company.

24 Ibid.

25 Ibid. Surviving newspaper accounts, the only records remaining, do not indicate whether stage measurements represent dimensions or the actual proscenium opening and visible playing space seen by the audience.

26 *Record*, 16 November 1905, 12; 24 November 1905, 12; 26 November 1905, 3; 28 November 1905, 3.

27 *Record*, 28 November 1905, 3; 22 December 1905, 7; 27 January 1906, 6.

28 Marian Spitzer, "The Mechanics of Vaudeville" in *American Vaudeville As Seen By Its Contemporaries*, Charles W. Stein, ed., New York: Alfred A Knopf, 1984, 173–176; Hinga, *Forty Years of Community Service*, 6.

29 Majestic Program, Week of 15 February 1909, Box 39, H-UC, TCHC.

30 Gadski appeared 8 February 1906; Fiske appeared 14 November 1907.

31 Majestic programs, Box 29, H-UC, TCHC.

32 *Record*, 2 October 1906, 5, 7; 21 July 1907, sec. 3, 1; 23 July 1907, 4; 6 September 1908, sec. 1, 5; 19 May 1909, 4; 1 August 1909, sec. 2, 2.

33 *Record*, 5 January 1905; 5; 5 March 1905, 12; 15 July 1905, 5; 22 July 1905, 3; 31 December 1905, 7; 15 April 1906, sec. 3, 9; 31 March 1907, sec. 3, 5; 8 August 1909, sec. 2, 7; FWP-FWTC, 3798–3799.

34 Ibid. *Beautiful Arlington Heights*, Fort Worth: Arlington Heights Realty Company (c. 1905), FWPL-GLH; *Gazette*, 12 May 1890, 5; 12 August 1890, 4; 23 August 1890, 4; 19 April 1891, 10; 25 April 1891, 4; 9 February 1892, 2; 10 July 1892, 2; 12 November 1894, 2; 13 November 1892; 2; *Register*, 7 May 1897, 4; 23 May 1897, 9; 16 July 1899, 7; *Record*, 18 July 1905, 5; 27 May 1906, 6. News accounts of Arlington Inn, which opened 9 July 1892 and burned 11 November 1894, contain frequent mention of concerts and dances, but not of theatrical performances. No substantial pavilion on Lake Como seems to have existed before 1906. After the inn's destruction, boating was the only activity still mentioned in news accounts. Not until 1897 did the Polytechnic Street Car Company announce plans to construct a band pavilion, tables, and seats in a grove of trees near the inn's original site.

35 Joe Laurie, *Vaudeville: From the Honky-Tonks to the Palace*, New York: Holt, Rinehart, Winston, reissued by Kennikat Press, Port Washington, New York, 1972, 237, 243, 487; Sanborn Fire Map, Fort Worth, 1911; *Record*, 1 October 1908, 12; 4 October 1908, sec. 2, 5; 11 July 1909, sec. 2, 5; Fort Worth City Directory, 1905–1906, 1907, 1909. Fire maps reveal that some of these theaters had frontages of only 37 feet and only a narrow platform to serve as a stage. Based on ads, the Lyric opened 18 March 1907, Panther Vaudeville opened 28 September 1908, and the Lyceum opened 7 March 1909.

36 *Record*, 17 March 1907, sec. 4, 5; 12 June 1907, 9; 1 October 1908, 12; 4 October 1908, sec. 2, 5; *Star-Telegram*, 24 August 1909, 8; *Record*, 5 September 1909, 4; 2 January 1910, sec. 2, 3; 30 January 1910, sec. 2, 4–5; 5 September 1910, sec. 2, 7; Fort Worth City Directory, 1907, 1909, 1910–1911, 1912–1913, 1916. Some theaters did not survive long enough to make it into city directories. Based on ads once again, New York Vaudeville opened around 6 June 1909, and the Imperial operated from January 1910 through at least March of 1912 before becoming the Hippodrome. E. H. Phillips opened the second Phillips and Phillips Egypt around 1911, continuing in business until at least 1916.

[37] *Record,* 17 March 1907, sec. 4, 5; 29 March 1907, 10; 4 October, 1908, sec. 2, 5; 28 March 1909, 3; *Star-Telegram*, 12 September 1909, 3; 3 January 1911, 4; *Variety*, 16 April 1910, 9. Clarence E. Able, a local singer, appeared in several area theaters. Ads for the Lyric disappeared in 1910; however, it reopened to capitalize on the soldier trade during World War I. It and a neighboring motion picture theater, the Blue Mouse, were razed to make way for the larger Capitol, also a movie theater, in 1924.

[38] *Record*, 28 March 1909, 3; 20 June 1909, 14; 29 August 1909, sec. 1, 6; 31 August 1909, 5; 14 November 1909, sec. 2, 4; 21 November 1909, sec. 2, 5; Royal Theater program, 1909–1910 season, H-UC, TCHC.

[39] *Record*, 11 October 1910, 7; *Variety*, 15 October 1910, 27; 5 November 1910, 28; Fort Worth City Directory, 1910–1911; Sanborn Fire Maps, Fort Worth, 1911.

[40] *Telegram*, 17 February 1908, 1; *Record,* 18 February 1908, 3.

[41] Bordman, Ibid., 422; *Telegram*, 17 February 1908, 1, 7.

[42] *Telegram*, Ibid., 18 February 1908, 1, 3; 21 February 1908, 1, 22 February 1908, 8; *Record*, 18 February 1908, 3; 19 February 1908, sec. 1, 3; sec. 2, 3; *Star-Telegram*, 6 July 1952, 12. Cecil Meadows, last surviving member of the Greenwall pit orchestra, told music critic E. Clyde Whitlock in 1952 that the west wall had begun collapsing. This seems to be a mistake on Meadows' part, since all other accounts refer to the east wall. Shows moved to the Vendome were Blanche Walsh in *The Kruetzer Sonata*, Al Wilson in *Metz in the Alps*, Max Figman in *The Man On the Box,* and the comic opera, *Woodland*. Paderewski's concert took place at the Christian Tabernacle on 12 March 1908. The Grocers and Butchers' Association had previously leased the Vendome for the month of March in preparation for a "Pure Foods Show."

[43] *Record*, 18 February 1908, 3; 18 March 1908, 8; 19 April 1908, sec. 1, 10; *Telegram*, 21 February 1908, 1. It was Byers' underwriting of the project that enabled the second group to propose a substantially larger and better constructed theater. Other subscribers mentioned by the local press included C. I. Dickinson, W. G. Newby, G. H. Colvin, A. J. Long, F. M. Long, Sam Levy, Charles Swasey, Tom Burnett, A. J. Roe, R. F. James, J. M. Vincent, George Lettler, N. McGinnis, C. A. O'Keefe, Edwin Bewley, First National Bank, and Farmers and Mechanics National Bank.

[44] *Land of Nod* program for grand opening of Byers Opera House, 21 September 1908, n. p., H-UC, TCHC.

[45] *Record*, 2 August 1908, 9; 30 August 1908, sec. 2, 6; *Telegram*, 16 September 1908, 5. The worth of the Byers is based on figures estimating both costs of construction and purchase of property, plus overruns and projected figures for fixtures and stage machinery.

[46] *Telegram*, 2 September 1908, 1. Seating capacity figures found in old city records dated 11 February 1915 and published in the *Fort Worth Press* (15 February 1965) lists the Byers capacity at 1,607, almost identical to originally published figures.

[47] *Record*, Ibid., 22 September 1908, 3. Original plans, according to the *Record* (19 April 1908, sec. 1, 10) called for the theater to front on Rusk Street.

[48] *Record*, 2 August 1908, 9; 30 August 1908, sec. 2, 6; 22 September 1908, 3; Sanguinet and Staat's line drawing of house detail; Sanguinet and Staat's rendering of lower and balcony floor plans in *Land of Nod* program, H-UC, TCHC.

[49] Sanguinet and Staat, Ibid. *Record*, 2 August 1908, 9; 30 August 1908, 6; *Telegram*, 2 August 1908, 6; photograph of Byers Opera House stage, labeled Palace-Ft. Worth, Hoblitzelle Interstate Theater Collection, Box TT1–9d; Harry Ransom Humanities Research Center, University of Texas, Austin. Various accounts disagree on the width of the proscenium opening. Both the *Telegram* and *Record* in early articles give the proscenium dimensions as 25x35. These dimensions were based on a standard publicity release published 2 August 1908. An almost identical article appeared the same day in the *Dallas Morning News*. A later article, written by Lester Colby of the *Telegram* gives the width emphatically as 35 feet (16 September 1908, 5). The latter seems more likely, since the first row of the main floor contained 18 seats, each 22 inches in width, and two aisles at least the width of two more seats. The proscenium opening, on architect's plans of ground floor seating and in a surviving photograph, is shown to be *as wide* as the first row of seats.

[50] *Record*, 2 August 1908, 9; Chicago Fire Marshall, Annual Report, 1903, Municipal Reference Collection, Chicago (Illinois) Public Library; Bordman, *Oxford Companion to American Theatre*, 257.

[51] *Record*, 30 August 1908, sec. 2, 6.

52 *New York Times*, 23 January 1907, 9.

53 Davis, *The American Opera Singer*, 166; *Record*, 30 August 1908, sec. 2, 6; 20 September 1908, sec. 2, 4.

54 *Dallas Morning News*, 22 September 1908, 1; *Record*, 13 September 1908, sec. 2, 4; *Telegram*, 16 September 1908, 5; 22 September 1908, 3: Jerry Flemmons, *Amon: the Life of Amon Carter, Sr. of Texas*, Austin: Jenkins Publishing, 1978, 127, 137–138.

55 *Record*, Ibid.; *Telegram*, 22 September 1908, 8.

56 Bordman, *Oxford Companion to American Theater*, 327, 351, 613; Bordman, *American Theater, 1869–1914*, 601.

57 *Record*, 6 May 1906, 6; 26 August 1906, sec. 3, 3.

CHAPTER SEVEN

1 *Star-Telegram*, 11 May 1910, 1; 27 August 1911, 5, 6, 7. Majestic theater programs and office stationery, Box 39, H-UC, TCHC; Alphonse August in *Makers of Fort Worth*, n. p.; Alphonse August folder in Founders File, Congregation Beth-El, Fort Worth, Texas. Interstate statistics are based on figures presented by Hoblitzelle in August 1911, subtracting the new Majestic from the count for 1910.

2 Ibid. *Star-Telegram*, 24 August 1911, 12; 27 August 1911, 5, 6, 7; *Record*, 9 October 1910, sec. 2, 4; 16 October 1910, sec. 2, 3–4; 3 November 1910, 25; 5 November 1910, 28; 24 November 1910, 8; 17 September 1911, sec. 2, 5; 22 October 1911, sec. 2, 5; 30 October 1911, 10; 14 March 1912, sec. 2, 5; *Variety*, 15 October, 1910, 27; 5 November 1910, 28. Old city records dated 11 February 1915 were found in 1965 by L. G. Larson, city building inspector, and later reported by the *Fort Worth Press*, (*Press*, 15 February 1965, n. p.). These figures list the Majestic's seating capacity as 1,377.

3 *Star-Telegram*, 24 November 1910, 8; 27 November 1910, 3; 13 January 1911, 4.

4 *Dallas Morning News*, 24 January 1911, 4; Robert E. and Katharine M. Marsberger, *Lew Wallace: Militant Romantic*, New York: McGraw-Hill, 1980, 458–459, 464–465.

5 Benjamin E. Smith, "The 'Ben-Hur' Chariot Race," *St. Nicholas*, November 1900, 45–49; *Star-Telegram*, 22 January 1911, 17.

6 Smith, Ibid.; Marsberger, Ibid., 459; *Star-Telegram*, 22 January 1911, 17; 31 January 1911, 4.

7 *Star-Telegram*, 31 January 1911, 4; 1 May 1949, sec. 1, 4; interview with Olan Clyde "Tex" Eddleman, whose father, a policeman, was assigned to the detail guarding the horses each night.

8 *Star-Telegram*, 6 July 1952, 12 (interview of former opera house personnel by E. Clyde Whitlock); Fort Worth theater records between 1899 and 1908 when the opera house was razed are well-documented. Although newspapers for one period in October-November 1902 were lost, the missing shows can be documented through comparison of shows appearing at the Dallas Opera House and through surviving programs. However, Mrs. Fain's 1949 remarks (see previous note) make clear that Klaw and Erlanger's *Ben-Hur*, the only production authorized by Wallace, did not arrive in the city prior to 1911.

9 *Star-Telegram*, 11 May 1910, 1; 27 August 1911, 5, 6.

10 *Star Telegram*, 27 July 1911, 1; 16 August 1911, 5; 20 August 1911, 3; 27 August 1911, 6–7; Souvenir post cards of Majestic interior, Box 22, Folder 4B, HITC-HRC.

11 Ibid. The published width of the lobby was 30 feet x 60 feet. However, Sanborn fire maps of the period (1911) record the building's Commerce Street entrance as 38 feet. The discrepancy may be explained by the added width of the ticket booth, a narrow office on the north side of the lobby.

12 Ibid.

13 Ibid.

14 Ibid. *Star-Telegram*, 24 August 1911, 12; *Record*, 29 August 1911, 8; *Fort Worth Press*, 29 December 1964, 17.

15 Ibid. Herbert Lloyd, *Vaudeville Trails Thru the West: Orpheum-Pantages-Interstate and Ackerman and Harris Circuits*, 1919, 89–90. Lloyd's guide provided vaudevillians traveling various circuits

with precise technical specifications and dimensions of theaters. Fly loft dimensions are particularly difficult to interpret, since there were always several feet of open space between gridiron and ceiling. Lloyd's figure for stage depth, 72 feet, a marked contradiction with the locally published figure of 32 feet, seems either a misprint or includes all backstage areas, including those not visible to the audience.

[16] *Star-Telegram,* 27 July 1911, 1; 20 August 1911, 3; 27 August 1911, 5–6.

[17] *Record,* 16 August 1911, 5; 29 August 1911, 8; *Star-Telegram,* 29 August 1911, 12. Tenth Street ended at Commerce. A broad passageway stretching between Commerce and Calhoun ran along the north side of the theater.

[18] *Record,* 29 August 1911, 8; *Star-Telegram* 29 August 1911, 12.

[19] Majestic playbills and programs, 1908–1954, Box 39, H-UC, TCHC.

[20] Gilbert, *American Vaudeville,* 293; *Record,* 4 May 1913, sec. 2, 4; 5 May 1913, 7; Majestic playbill, Box 39, 5 May 1913, H-UC, TCHC. The incident more than likely occurred the week of 5 May 1913, when Green and Rogers appeared together on the same Fort Worth bill, although comments in the press suggest Rogers may have made earlier local appearances.

[21] Gilbert, *American Vaudeville,* Ibid.

[22] Bordman, *Oxford Companion to American Theater,* 465. *Kid Cabaret* played the week of 29 December 1913; Cantor and Lee appeared the week of 4 January 1915 and again the week of September 4th. The Marx Brothers appeared the weeks of 27 September 1914, 24 January 1916, and 21 October 1917.

[23] *Star-Telegram,* 23 April 1912, 14; 1 October 1916, 23; Jack Benny and Joan Benny, *Sunday Nights At Seven: The Jack Benny Story,* New York: Warner Books, 1990, 12-15; Bordman, *Oxford Companion to American Theater,* 20. The Astaires appeared the week of 1 October 1916. Benny also appeared the weeks of 1 September 1918 and 3 December 1922.

[24] *Record,* 9 January 1916, sec. 2, 4; 10 January 1916, 8; Kenneth Silverman, *Houdini!!! The Career of Ehrich Weiss,* New York: Harper-Collins, 1996, 165–167. Houdini made a second Majestic appearance in 1923.

[25] *Record,* 24 January 1914, 4; 5 October 1919, 16; *Press,* 20 January 1963, 19A; postcards mentioning the Auditorium's seating capacity, rental rates, and showing several views of both exterior and interior from the collection of the author.

[26] *Times-Picayune,* 28 November 1913, 12–13; Beach, Henry Greenwall, 215–216.

[27] *Record,* 28 November 1913, 2. In listing the manager's accomplishments, the obituary credited Greenwall with the idea for the booking system that eventually allowed the Syndicate to gain control of major routes and shut out independent managers and producers.

[28] *Record,* 18 April 1915, sec. 2, 5. Exactly when Mitchell Greenwall took over management of the opera house is uncertain. Phil Greenwall's obituary (*Star-Telegram,* 27 August 1917, 10) mentions that he had been in ill health for three years. Mitchell Greenwall's name appears as manager in at least one article announcing plans for the 1915 season.

[29] Maud Adams appeared 31 October 1912, Weber and Fields on 27 February 1913, Fritzi Scheff on 17 March, Julian Eltinge on 8 October, E. H. Sothern and Julia Marlowe on 20 December.

[30] *Record,* 21 November 1915, sec. 1, 19.

[31] *Record,* 9 April 1916, sec. 1, 6; sec. 2, 12. According to his obituary (*Record,* 27 August 1917, 1) Greenwall was born 6 November 1839.

[32] *Record,* 5 August 1915, 10; 3 September 1916, sec. 2, 9; 10 September 1916, sec. 2, 7.

[33] *Star-Telegram,* 21 May 1916, sec. 2, 11; 13 August 1916, 23; 26 August 1917, 15; 27 August 1917, 10; 16 September 1917, 12; *Record,* 5 January 1911, 5; 2 September 1913, 3; 27 August 1917, 1; FWP-FWTC, 15091; programs for the Savoy Theater, n.d., in the files of the Tarrant County Historical Commission, Tarrant County Court House, Fort Worth, Texas.

[34] *Star-Telegram,* 27 August 1917, 10; 16 September 1917, 12; *Record,* 27 August 1917, 1.

[35] Bernice B. Maxfield and William E. Jary, Jr., *Camp Bowie Fort Worth, 1917–1918: An Illustrated History of the 36th Division in the First World War,* Fort Worth: B. B. Maxfield Foundation, 1975, 2, 4–6, 9.

[36] *Star-Telegram,* 30 December 1917, 7; 4 February 1918, 2; 17 March 1918, 14; 31 March 1918, 7; 14 April 1918, 16; map of Camp Bowie cantonment, c. 1918, FWPL-GLH. Several streets within

Camp Bowie were named after Texas revolutionary heroes. Shortly after the war, most streets west of Montgomery were renamed and new streets were added to make way for new housing. Based on extant maps of the base and the naming of the trolley stop, Milam Street was located somewhere in the vicinity of present-day Carleton and Western avenues, both of which terminate just south of River Crest Country Club's main building.

[37] Ibid.

[38] *Record,* 26 December 1912, 1; 27 December 1912, 1; *Star-Telegram,* 24 February 1918, 30; 10 March 1918, 14; 16 March 1919, n. p.; 21 March 1919, 5; 7 April 1919, n. p.; 12 April 1919, 30; *Camp Bowie Texahoma Bugler,* 15 September 1917, 5; 26 October 1917, 4; 9 November 1917, 3; FWP-FWTC, 8839, 8873. The Pershing continued to operate for at least two years following the war, but the Lyric's ads disappeared quickly.

[39] *Star-Telegram,* 12 December 1917, 3; 9 January 1918, 3; programs for the Savoy Theater, n.d.

[40] *Star-Telegram,* 16 February 1918, 1; Bordman, *Oxford Companion To American Theater,* 130; Maxfield and Jary, *Camp Bowie,* 51–52.

[41] *Star-Telegram,* 17 February 1918, 1.

[42] *Star-Telegram,* 20 October 1918, 22; 1 December 1918, 13.

[43] *Star-Telegram,* 1 December 1918, 13.

[44] *Star-Telegram,* 7 September 1919, sec. 2, 12.

[45] *Record,* 15 October 1919, 3; 19 October 1919, 9; *Star-Telegram,* 7 September 1919, sec. 2, 12. E. H. Hulsey had previously operated a successful movie house in Waco, Texas.

[46] *Fort Worth Press,* 2 August 1951, 16; 31 March 1968, 9B; *Star-Telegram,* 8 May 1977, 3D.

[47] *Press,* Ibid; *Record,* 15 October 1919, 3; 19 October 1919, 9; *Star-Telegram,* 7 September 1919, sec. 2, 12.

CHAPTER EIGHT

[1] *Star-Telegram,* 7 September 1919, sec. 2, 12.

[2] Hollace Ava Weiner, *Beth-El Congregation Centennial, 1902–2002,* Fort Worth: Beth-El Temple, 2002, 6,9, 14; Isidore Carb folder, Beth-El Congregation archives, Fort Worth, Texas; Brockett, *History of the Theater,* 544–547; Travis Bogard, *Contour In Time: The Plays of Eugene O'Neill,* New York: Oxford University Press, 1972, Appendix II.

[3] Brockett, Ibid; *Handbook of Texas Online,* s. v. "Little Theater Movement," htttp://www.tsha.utexas.edu/handbook/online/articles/LL/kpl 1.html (accessed 20 November 2004).

[4] Joan Givner, *Katherine Anne Porter: A Life,* New York: Simon and Schuster, 1982, 147–159, 526 (fn 43, 46).

[5] Givner, Ibid., 124–131, 158–159; *Star-Telegram,* 11 September 1921, 4; 23 June 1929, sec. 2, 2; 11 December 1933, 18; *Fort Worth Press,* 6 February 1968 (Roscoe Carnrike obituary).

[6] Ibid., Givner, 159. *Fort Worth Record,* 9 November 1921, 2 ; 11 December 1921, sec. 3, 13; *Star-Telegram,* 13 November 1921, sec. 2, 10; 23 June 1929, sec. 2, 2; Fort Worth Little Theater Program, *The Pursuit of Happiness,* 1933, 12, in the collection of the author. In 1978, Givner interviewed Kitty Crawford, who died in 1982 at age 93. Lotta Carter Gardner's home, located at 1320 Lipscomb, served as Little Theater offices, and the address frequently appeared on Little Theater programs. The barn, in which many early productions were performed, was located at the rear of the property, bounded on the west by Alston. Other plays produced by the group during its first year included *The Sweetheart Game, For Distinguished Service, The Florist Shop, Overtones, The Four-Flushers, Investigation,* and *Clarence.* Katherine Anne Porter returned to New York in 1922.

[7] FWP-FWTC, 6412–6413, 18025; *Record,* 21 October 1923, 8B; 23 June 1929, sec. 2, 2; *Star-Telegram,* 21 October 1925, 3; 12 October 1941, sec. 2, 10. Little Theater Program, *The Pursuit of Happiness,* 12. The group continued to refer to itself occasionally as the Vagabond Players through at least 1924.

[8] Ibid. Kenneth MacGowan, *Footlights Across America,* New York: Harcourt, Brace and Co., 1929, 86, 278, 360–361; *Press,* 21 February, 1928, 10; *Star-Telegram,* 16 December 1928, sec. 1, pt. 2, 1;

24 February 1929, sec. 4, 14; 16 June 1929, society, 8; 23 June 1929, sec. 2, 2; Little Theater program, *Michael and his Lost Angel*, 5 December 1927, Box 1, Little Theater Programs, FWPL-GLH. Dot Echols Orum played in the orchestra of the Majestic Theater for many years under the baton of her husband, conductor George Orum. Brooks Morris organized the Fort Worth Symphony Orchestra in 1925.

[9] *Star-Telegram*, 1 September 1929, society, 8; 25 February 1931, 6; 26 April 1931, sec. 2, 6; 12 October 1941, sec. 2, 10; FWP-FWTC, 18025–18026. Dates for various directors are based on analysis of the Fort Worth Library's collection of Little Theater programs as well as reports found in local newspapers. For a brief period in 1928, Hunter Gardner served as managing director of the Civic Repertory Company that performed from the former Ritz Theater on Commerce Street. After the failure of that company, he returned to the Little Theater, but left permanently in 1929 to act and manage professionally. From 1932–1942, he appeared in a number of Broadway plays. Following World War II, he had a brief, but evidently unsuccessful career in television. He committed suicide 16 January 1952 in California (*Star-Telegram*, 17 January 1952, 20).

[10] Obituary for Elbert Gruver, *Dartmouth College Alumni Magazine*, (January 1963), Little Theater clip file, Fort Worth Public Library; *Fort Worth Little Theater and Community Playhouse Magazine*, Vol. 3, No. 1 (October 1931), 1; "Neighbor McKee," *Newsweek* Vol. 21 (7 June 1943), 92–93; *Star-Telegram*, 20 October 1970, 10A (Blanchard McKee obit.); FWP-FWTC, 18025–18026. Elbert Gruver, a New York native, eventually authored an influential text on stage management and supervised a number of important Broadway productions, including *Mr. Roberts* and Dylan Thomas' *Under Milk Wood*. Blanchard McKee's program *Neighbors*, was picked up for national syndication by New York's WJZ and WOR in 1943.

[11] *Star-Telegram*, 26 November 1933, society, 7; 12 October 1941, sec. 2, 10; *Little Theater Magazine*, Vol. 5, No. 3, (11 December 1933), 8–9; FWP-FWTC, 18026–18027. Some news accounts mention a debt of $7,500. Whether this full amount was loaned by Leonard or whether it also included previous outstanding debt is unclear. Rabbi Merfeld began devoting so much time to the Little Theater that in December 1933, the temple board demanded that he "move his office to the Temple and have regular office hours. . . ."(Minutes of the board, Beth-El Congregation, 4 December 1933).

[12] Ibid. *Star-Telegram*, 1 October 1933, society, 8; FWP-FWTC,18026–18027.

[13] *Star-Telegram*, 24 September 1933, society, 5; 17 September 1933, Society, 5; 1 October 1933, society, 8; 7 January 1934, sec. 4, 5; 14 January 1934, 5; 4 February 1934, sec. 4, 4.

[14] *Star-Telegram*, 29 April 1934, society, 11; 12 December 1934, 3; 7 May 1935, 19; Fort Worth Little Theater Program, *The Pursuit of Happiness*. For details of the FWLT production of *Porgy*, see chapter 14.

[15] *Star-Telegram*, 7 May 1935, 19; 31 August 1935 (eve.), 2; 26 April 1936, society, 11; 12 October 1941, sec. 2, 10; 30 October 1949, Community Life, 42; *Handbook of Texas Online*, s.v. "NAIL, ROBERT EDWARD, JR," http://www.tsha.utexas.edu/handbook/online/articles/NN/fna5.html (accessed February 20, 2006).

[16] Jerome A. Moore, *Texas Christian University: A Hundred Years of History*, Fort Worth: TCU Press, 1974, 193; The (TCU) *Skiff*, 15 May 1936, 2; TCU Theater Arts, twenty-fifth anniversary program, *The Imaginary Invalid*, 1969, 7, from the collection of William Garber, Fort Worth, Texas.

[17] Ibid., The *TXWOCO*, 1920. *Fort Worth Magazine*, (March 1961), 10; *Bulletin of Texas Woman's College*, 1927, 1933, 1934; *Bulletin of Texas Wesleyan College*, 1936, 1947, 1953.

[18] Ibid., The *TXWOCO*, 1922. *Bulletin of Texas Wesleyan College*, 1935; *Texas Wesleyan University: A Centennial Album*, Fort Worth: Texas Wesleyan University, 1990, 10, 38.

[19] *Star-Telegram*, 7 September 1924, 7; 5 January 1930, sec. 1, part 2, 8; *Press*, 5 October 1924, 2; *Record*, 3 August 1924, 4B; 31 August 1924, 10B; 7 September 1924, 8B; 8 September 1924, 4; Ritz Theater program, *She Walked In Her Sleep*, 8 February 1926, H-UC, TCHC.

[20] Ibid. *Star-Telegram*, 1 January 1926, 4.

[21] Bordman, *Oxford Companion to American Theater*, 535; *Record*, 1 January 1926, 4; 2 January 1926, 4; 23 June 1926, 4. The Pantages' no-vaudeville policy went into effect 26 June 1926. Pantages had announced his intentions to construct a theater in the city as early as 1921, but later canceled those plans.

[22] *Star-Telegram*, 23 September 1928, sec. 4, 10; 22 September 1929, 13B; 17 November 1929, 10B; 5 January 1930, sec. 1, part 2, 8; 13 March 1985, 14A; *Press*, 22 November 1964; FWP-FWTC,

2552–2553. Following Lewis' death, the Liberty continued to operate as a movie house until 1956. Its last years were spent as a homeless shelter. Like its neighbor the Majestic, it eventually fell to the wrecker's ball to make way for the Tarrant County Convention Center.

[23] *Tarrant County Historic Resources Survey: Fort Worth Near North Side, West Side and Westover Hills,* Historic Preservation Council For Tarrant County, Texas, 1988, 72–73; *Star-Telegram,* 2 December 1923, 8; 19 May 1924, 1. The Klan auditorium actually opened in March 1924.

[24] Victoria and Walter L. Buenger. *Texas Merchant: Marvin Leonard and Fort Worth,* College Station: Texas A&M Press, 1998, 63–64, Tarrant County deed records, Vol. 1134, 66; Vol. 1808, 211; 10 March 1931; *Star-Telegram* 12 October 1924, 7B; 20 May 1927, 1. In the 1930s the hall saw use as a warehouse for Leonard Brothers and became the Fox and Fox Boxing Arena. In 1946, it became the Ellis Pecan Company.

[25] *Fort Worth Press,* 5 October 1926, 2; *Record,* 9 November 1921, 14; 23 March 1922, sec. C, 8; *Star-Telegram,* 2 January 1926, 4; 5 January 1930, sec. 1, pt. 2, 8. As the theater was being constructed, the *Press* reported seating of the Worth at 2,500; however, figures published after its opening place the capacity at just 2300.

[26] *Star-Telegram,* 15 February 1924, 2; *Fort Worth Press,* 5 October 1926, 2; *Record,* 1 February 1925, Sec. B, 8; 8 February 1925, sec. B, 6.

[27] Partial season list of the Majestic, compiled from newspapers and programs by the author; *Record,* 26 February 1923, 3.

[28] Ibid., partial season list; William Robert Faith, Bob Hope: *A Life in Comedy*, New York: G. P. Putnam's Sons, 1982, 61-65; 78-80; Bob Hope and Pete Martin, *Have Tux, Will Travel*, New York: Simon and Schuster, 1954, 74-79; correspondence with Marie Boren, secretary, office of Bob Hope 27 July 1993. Hope appeared the week of 28 July 1929 in a unit show, *WLS Showboat,* sponsored by Chicago radio station WLS. He returned in a solo comedy routine, "Keep Smilin'," 27-29 June 1930. Faith's biography inaccurately places Hope's breakthrough performance to the big-time in 1929; Hope, however, was still playing the regional Interstate Circuit through 1930. In his autobiography, Hope credited the mentoring of Interstate manager Bob O'Donnell during his 1930 Fort Worth appearance as the turning point of his vaudeville career. Ironically, shortly after Hope finally played New York's Palace in 1931, the vaudeville industry collapsed. The Palace closed as a strictly vaudeville theater on 16 November 1932.

[29] *Record,* 7 November 1923, 1, 2.

[30] Ibid.; *Near North Side, West Side and Westover Hills, Fort Worth: Tarrant County Historical Resource Survey, 1988,* 4; Fort Worth City Map, C. H. Rogers, 1919. As if in retort to Castle's snub, the street was renamed Boulevard around 1923. Later a street near Benbrook Field in southern Tarrant County was designated Vernon Castle.

[31] Ginger Rogers, *Ginger: My Story,* New York: Harper-Collins, 1991, 38–49.

[32] Ibid. The exact date of the incident is unknown, but it may have occurred the week of 16 August 1925, when the Four Foys, led by Eddie Foy, Jr., were appearing at the Majestic.

[33] Ibid. *Star-Telegram,* 16 August 1925, 4; 6 November 1925, 6; 13 December 1925, 6, 7. Rogers remembered the Foy act having five siblings while the press reports only four. This may indicate a different appearance by the Foys or just Rogers' own forgetfulness. The Charleston did not become well-known until around 1923.

[34] *Star-Telegram,* 27 November 1927, sec. 1, pt. 2, 1, 10–11. Published accounts in 1927 give a seating capacity of 3,000. The more conservative figure comes from accounts prior to the theater's razing in October 1972. A directory of local theaters published by the *Star-Telegram* (4 August 1931, 8) lists operators of the Worth as Paramount-Publix.

[35] Ibid, *Star-Telegram,* 24 October 1971; Worth Theater Program for the week of 16 June 1928, Box 38, H-UC, TCHC. Paul Forster was the theater's original organist. By 1928, Billy Muth had taken over. Descriptions of the Worth's interior are based on photographs documenting the sale of theater fixtures just before its razing. Photographs of the interior published at the time of its premiere in 1927 have disappeared from the *Star-Telegram* collection, although they can still be viewed on microfilm.

[36] Ibid. John Murray Anderson and Hugh Abercrombie Anderson, *Out Without My Rubbers,* New York: Library Publishers, 1954, 97–102; interview with Mrs. Gloria Petta Kies, retired dancer and performer, 29 March 2002, Fort Worth, Texas; *Jewish Monitor,* 27 January 1928, 8; 4 May 1928, 12; 1 June, 1928, 12; 29 June 1928, 7. The Worth originally had both a pit orchestra and a band that played for the live shows from the stage.

37 Unattributed newspaper article in scrapbook, Box 38, H-UC, TCHC; *Star-Telegram*, 16 February 1931, 7; Hinga, *Forty Years of Community Service*, 12.

38 *Star-Telegram*, 25 September 1928, 6; 29 June 1930, 5; 9 January 1931, 8; 14 January 1931, 4; 15 January 1931, 22; 19 April 1931, 4–5; 20 September 1931, 4C; *Press*, 2 January 1931, 12. Comments in Randol's column indicate that other Texas RKO theaters maintained a three-shows-a-day schedule. Fort Worth's Majestic adopted a four-shows-a-day policy because acts were booked for only three days.

39 *Star-Telegram*, 7 May 1931, 5; unattributed newspaper article, Box 38 H-UC, TCHC.

40 *Star-Telegram*, 2 May 1931, 4; 4 August 1931, 8; 7 August 1931, 25; unattributed newspaper article in scrapbook, Box 38, H-UC, TCHC.

41 *Star-Telegram*, 20 September 1931, 4.

42 *Press*, 6 January 1933, 6; FWP-FWTC, 2552–2553. With Broadway largely dark, many actors returned to the classics: Adams and Skinner appeared together in *The Merchant of Venice*, 15 January 1932; Cornell starred in *The Barretts of Wimpole Street*, 17 February 1934; Le Gallienne offered *Hedda Gabler*, 9 April 1934; Billie Burke appeared 27 November 1931 in *The Vinegar Tree*. *Earl Carroll's Vanities* played 25 January 1933.

43 *Star-Telegram*, 9 March 1967, 15A; Hinga, *Forty Years in Community Service*, 12. The Worth and Hollywood continued as the city's most high-profile movie houses for several more decades until the advent of multi-screen suburban cineplexes in the 1970s helped finish off downtown theater traffic. The Worth Theater was imploded in October 1972. The neighboring Hollywood closed in 1974, although much of its interior remained, covered over, and converted to a bank processing center in 1979. Not until 1994 did salvagers finally complete the gutting of the building to make way for a parking garage, leaving only remnants of the art deco movie house.

44 Ibid. *Star-Telegram*, 14 April 1933, 14; 28 January 1934, 5. Eddie Cantor and George Jessel appeared on 22 March 1933. They were followed by Paul Whiteman on 26 April, Cab Calloway on 29 April, and Duke Ellington on 8 October. Kate Smith was featured 18–21 April 1934.

45 *Star-Telegram*, 8 February 1933, 12; 21 February 1933, 8; *Press*, 8 February 1933, 7; unattributed newspaper article in scrapbook, Box 38, H-UC, TCHC. Although the Majestic opened briefly for what was described as a 1932 New Year's Eve "Negro jig show" (*Press*, 4 January 1933, 5) and a weeklong engagement of The Weavers (24 February-2 March 1933), it remained essentially closed until December 1933. The first live show under this new arrangement was the original Broadway company of *The Green Pastures*, 15–16 December 1933. Helen Hayes appeared 13 April 1935 and 19 April 1938; Evans appeared 29 January 1938; Lunt and Fontanne played 6 February 1939; Hepburn appeared 2 January 1941; West toured 17 January 1947; Barrymore appeared 20 February 1939; Bankhead appeared 6 January 1950; Skinner played 27 November 1952.

46 *Star-Telegram*, 1 October 1972, 10A; 2 October 1972, 4A; 13 December 1994.

47 FWP-FWTC, 16664–16665, 18028.

CHAPTER NINE

1 * For a complete account of the Frontier Centennial and Casa Mañana, 1936–1939, see Jan Jones, *Billy Rose Presents Casa Mañana*, TCU Press, 1999. *Time*, 8 June 1936, 12–13 (ad display); 22 June 1936, 83 (ad). *March of Time* newsreel, "Texas," released around 19 June 1936.

2 Ibid.

3 Ibid.

4 Darwin Payne, *Big D: Triumphs and Troubles of an American Supercity in the Twentieth Century*, Dallas: Three Forks, 1994, 166–168; Kenneth B. Ragsdale, *The Year America Discovered Texas: Centennial '36*, Texas A & M Press, 1987, 46, 77–86.

5 Minutes, Fort Worth City Council, 23 October 1935; *Star-Telegram*, 26 July 1935 (eve.), 1; 1 December 1935, 8; 11 February 1936, 1; *Dallas Morning News*, 21 July 1935, 1, 4.

6 *Star-Telegram*, 11 November 1935, 4; 15 November 1935, 1; 3 December 1935, sec. 2, 1; 11 February 1936, sec. 2, 1; 13 February 1936, 2; J'Nell Pate, *North of the River: A Brief History of North Fort Worth*, Fort Worth: TCU Press, 1994, 20–24. Even with the proposed acquisition of 26 acres west of North Main, total acreage of the North Fort Worth site would have reached only forty acres and would have required the construction of an underpass to cross North Main.

Acquisition of the Van Zandt tract was also dependent on heirs lowering the asking price for the property.

7   *Star-Telegram,* 1 December 1935, 8; 3 December 1935, sec. 2, 1; 4 December 1935, 1; 8 December 1935, 8; 10 December 1935; sec. 2, 1; 15 December 1935, 7.

8   *Star-Telegram,* 28 January 1936, 1; 11 February 1936, 1; 15 February 1936, 1, 2; 5 March 1936, 1.

9   *Star-Telegram,* 11 February 1936, 1. Board chairman Monnig was in favor of rescinding all contracts for the building of the Will Rogers Memorial Coliseum, Auditorium, and Tower. Other city council members persuaded him that this would unfairly jeopardize other aspects of the local celebration.

10 Alva Johnston, "Colonel Carter of Cartersville," *Saturday Evening Post,* 26 November 1938, 8.

11 Rufus LeMaire (obituary), *Star-Telegram,* 4 December 1950, 1, 4. LeMaire (real name Rufus Goldstick) and his brother George had performed in amateur theatricals at the Majestic as young men.(unattributed article, Box 32, H-UC, TCHC; *Record,* 23 December, 1923, Sec. B, 7). Rufus Lemaire's most prominent client was actor George Arliss (scrapbook, Box 32, H-UC, TCHC).

12 Billy Rose, *Wine, Women and Words,* New York: Simon and Schuster, 1948, 15.

13 Stephen Nelson, *Only a Paper Moon: The Theater of Billy Rose,* Ann Arbor, Michigan: UMI Research Press, 1987, 5–7.

14 Ibid., 13–23, 29–46.

15 Maurice Zolotow, *Billy Rose of Broadway* (unpublished manuscript) File MWEZ+nc25518, Billy Rose Theater Collection, New York Public Library, 297; Rose, *Wine, Women and Words,* 75; *Star-Telegram,* 7 March 1936, 15; 10 March 1936, 1.

16 Ibid., Zolotow, 302–305.

17 Ibid., 304–305.

18 *Star-Telegram,* 9 March 1936, 1, 4; 10 March 1936, 1, 10 April 1936, 1; *Fort Worth Press,* 9 March 1936, 1; 19 March 1936, 8; 10 April 1936, 14.

19 *Billboard,* 14 March 1936 5; *Variety* 11 March 1936, 38.

20 *Press,* 1 April 1936, 1; *Star-Telegram,* 3 June 1936, sec. 2, 1; 9 June 1936, 24; *Time,* 8 June 1936, 13.

21 Robert Randol, *Star-Telegram,* 7 July 1936 (eve.), 14; *Press,* 1 June 1936, 1, 5.

22 Official programs, Casa Mañana, 1936, 1937.

23 Taken from various accounts including Casa Mañana programs, 1936, 1937; *Star-Telegram,* 12 April 1936, 1; 14 April 1936, 1; 17 April 1936 (eve.), 1, 4; *Press,* 1 April 1936, 9; 14 April 1936, 1.

24 John Murray Anderson, *Out Without My Rubbers,* 161–162.

25 Earl Conrad, *Billy Rose: Manhattan Primitive,* New York: World, 1968, 105–106; *Press,* 1 June 1936, 8; official program Casa Mañana, 1936.

26 Official program, Casa Mañana, 1936.

27 Hyman Maurice 1942 obituary (n. d.), Box 32, H-UC, TCHC. Maurice's real name was Maurice Hyman.

28 Unattributed article, Women's Division Scrapbook, 1936, Tarrant Collection, Fort Worth Public Library.

29 Mary Martin, *My Heart Belongs,* New York: William Morrow, 1976, 54–56; Anderson, *Out Wthout My Rubbers,* 166; interview with Beth Lea Clardy, former Casa Mañana showgirl, October 1985, Fort Worth.

30 Fort Worth Frontier Centennial tri-fold advertising brochure, "Wild and Whoopee!" 1936, in the collections of the Center For American History, University of Texas, Austin.

31 Interview with William E. Jary, Fort Worth historian and advertising executive, October 1980; *Variety,* 20 May 1936,1, 54; 27 May 1936, 63; *Star-Telegram,* 31 May 1936, 1. Jary, as a young employee of Corn Sign Company, did much of the planning for the sign.

32 *Time,* 31 July 1933, 20; Bordman, *Oxford Companion to American Theater,* 567.

33 Interview with Mary Wynn Wayman, former *Star-Telegram* reporter, Fort Worth, July 1996; *Press,* 1 July 1936, 1; 9 July 1936, 9; Nelson M. Davidson, *Pencil Trails: The Texas Centennial*

Exhibition in Dallas and Texas, Dallas: Dealey and Lowe, 1936, 10; *Variety,* 22 July 1936, 1; *Press,* 23 July 1936, 12; *Star-Telegram,* 14 July 1936, 198.

34   Ragsdale, *The Year America Discovered Texas,* 287–288; Payne, *Big D,* 169–70; undated article reproduced in a half-page display of articles from across the state, *Star-Telegram,* 9 June 1936, 9; 9 August 1936, 3.

35   *Star-Telegram,* 2 August 1936, 11; *New York Times,* Drama section, 26 July 1936, 2.

36   *Dallas Morning News,* 18 July 1936, 1,12; 19 July 1936, 12.

37   *Dallas Times-Herald,* 19 July 1936, sec. 3, 13.

38   *Press,* 18 July 1936, 7.

39   *Star-Telegram,* 19 July 1936, 1; *Dallas Morning News,* 19 July 1936, 12.

40   *Star-Telegram,* 19 July 1936, 6; Casa Mañana menu, 1936, Tarrant Collection, FWPL-GLH.

41   Bob Vollmer, "Flashback To Fame: The Biggest Summer Texas Ever Had," (source and page unknown), 1946, Center For American History, Austin, Texas.

42   *Star Telegram,* 1 June 1936 (eve.), 9; 7 July 1936, 9.

43   *Press,* 2 July 1936, 3; E. Clyde Whitlock, *Star-Telegram,* 19 July 1936, 7.

44   *Press,* 3 November 1936, 12; interviews with Mrs. Wilby Lingo Goodman and Janice Nicolson Holmes, former Casa Mañana dancers, October 1985, Fort Worth.

45   *Press,* 13 May 1937, 6; *Star-Telegram,* 11 June 1936 (eve.), 22.

46   Jack Gordon, *Press,* 31 May 1937, 1, 6; John E. Vacha, "Biggest Bash: Cleveland's Great Lakes Exposition," *Timeline,* March/April, 1996, 18–22.

47   Memos from James North to Amon Carter outlining Rose's indiscretions, 8 July 1937, 10 July 1937; second undated memo from several days later, Box 17, Folder 11a, Amon Giles Carter Papers, Texas Christian University, Fort Worth, Texas.

48   *Variety,* 30 June 1937, 60; *Press,* 17 July 1937, Women's Division Scrapbook, 1937, Tarrant Collection, Fort Worth Public Library, hereafter cited as WDS; *Star-Telegram,* 17 June 1937 (eve.), 17.

49   Ibid. *Star-Telegram,* 11 June 1937, (eve.), 22; 30 June 1937, 1.

50   Memo from general manager James F. Pollock to James North, 30 August, 1937, Box 17 Folder 11a, Carter Collection.

51   *Star-Telegram,* 26 July 1937 (eve.), 17; *Press,* 27 July 1937 (WDS).

52   *Star-Telegram,* 15 September 1937, 9; 15 September 1937 (eve.), 1; *Press,* 15 September 1937, (WDS, 1937); *Variety,* 22 September 1937, 13.

53   Richard Harwell, ed., *Margaret Mitchell's Gone With the Wind Letters, 1936–1949,* New York: Macmillan, 1976, 195–196; Finis Farr, *Margaret Mitchell of Atlanta,* New York: William Morrow, 1965, 176–177.

54   *Variety,* 13 July 1938, 43; 19 July 1938, 44; 3 August 1938, 43.

55   *This Month In Fort Worth,* March 1940, 14; May 1940, 5; June 1940, 14; July 1941, 10; August 1941, 15; Fort Worth City Council Minutes 8 October 1941, 15 October 1941, 5 November 1941.

CHAPTER TEN

1   *Star-Telegram,* 11 February 1934, society, 4; 2 June 1936, 7; 20 August 1935, 17 (Robert Randol's column); FWP-FWTC, 16664, 18028.

2   Ibid., *Star-Telegram,* 27 November 1938, sec. 1, 5; 18 October 1942, sec. 1, 7; 7 March 1943; 23 October 1949, sec. 1, 13; I.E. McWhirter Papers, including assorted programs and ticket books, First Methodist Church, Fort Worth, Texas.

3   *Star-Telegram,* 6 August 1938, society, 6; 9 August 1938, 4.

4   Ibid., *Star-Telegram,* 30 October 1942, 5, 42. Program, *Margin For Error,* 17 February 1942; program, *The Bellamy Trial,* 29–31 October 1942, in the collection of the author; programs for *The*

Male Animal, 4 November 1941 and *First Lady,* 16 December 1941, Box 18, Flora and Dickson Reeder Collection, University of Texas-Arlington, Special Collections; department memoranda from C.M. Thelin, acting director of public works, City of Fort Worth to J. D. Price, manager of Will Rogers Memorial Auditorium and Coliseum, 16 December 1946, 18 December 1946, considering the request of the Fort Worth Community Little Theater to renovate the Pioneer Palace for play performances, FWPL-GLH.

5　Hallie Flanagan, *Arena: The History of the Federal Theatre,* New York: Benjamin Blom, 1940, 93–94; *Star-Telegram,* 14 May 1935 (eve.), 21; *Press,* 6 March 1936, n. p.

6　Ibid., Flanagan; *Star-Telegram,* 9 April 1936, 8; 26 April 1936, society, 11; 14 May 1936, 21; 2 June 1936, 7; 20 July 1935(eve.), 1; FWP-FWTC, 16664–16665, 18028.

7　*Star-Telegram,* 9 April 1936, 8; 14 May 1935, 21; 2 June 1936, 7; 20 July 1935 (eve.), 1.

8　*Star-Telegram,* 22 September 1936, 1; 17 November 1936, 8; 20 December 1936, Amusements, 12; *Press,* 17 November 1936, 7; Judith Singer Cohen, *Cowtown Moderne: Art Deco Architecture of Fort Worth, Texas,* College Station: Texas A & M Press, 1988, 122, 124; Informational Data, Will Rogers Memorial Center in Will Rogers clip file, FWPL-GLH. Although the hall opened on November 16, its formal dedication came with a municipal concert held on December 23. Various sources, including "official" statistics issued by the Center describe the hall as having as few as 2,964 seats and as many as 2,993.

9　Ibid., Cohen, 124–125.

10　Ibid., 133, 135.

11　Informational Data, Will Rogers Memorial Center; *Star-Telegram,* 20 October 1968, sec. 5H; Interview with William Massad, former assistant general manager and public relations director of the Fort Worth Opera, 4 February 2004.

CHAPTER ELEVEN

1　Harold Gene Blackwelder, *The Fort Worth Civic Opera Association, 1946–1953,* unpublished M.F.A. thesis, Texas Christian University, 1965, 135.

2　Norwood P. Dixon, *The Story of the Fort Worth Opera Association,* Fort Worth: 1979, 7 (informational pamphlet prepared by the Opera Association); interview with William Massad; interview with Ahdel Chadwick, longtime board member Fort Worth Opera, 12 February 2004; telephone interview with Betty Berry Spain Klein, 29 February 2004; FWP-FWTC, 18360–18361; Fort Worth City Directory, 1905–1906; *Star-Telegram* 22 December 1984, 1E (Eloise M. Snyder obituary); NBC Radio transcripts of performances by Betty Spain provided to author by Thomas Garber, New York.

3　*Democrat,* 25 November 1880, 3, 4; 28 November 1880, 2, 3, 4.

4　*Democrat,* 28 November 1880, 3.

5　Ibid.

6　Interview with William Massad, Fort Worth, Texas, February 2004. In fall 2005, the Fort Worth Opera commenced its fifty-ninth season.

7　*Democrat,* 12 November 1878, 4; 12 December 1879, 4.

8　*Democrat,* 23 April 1887, 8; 24 April 1887, 8; David Ewen, *Encyclopedia of the Opera,* New York: Hill and Wang, 1971, 146, 281; Bordman, *Oxford Companion to American Theater,* 305.

9　Peter G. Davis, *The American Opera Singer,* New York: Anchor Books, 1997, 87, 93–97; Gallegly, *Footlights On the Border,* 133–134. Campanini played the Opera House 24–25 February 1889; Emma Juch appeared 19–20 December 1890; Schumann-Heink, a Wagnerian specialist, sang the first of several Fort Worth engagements 5 December 1907. The London premiere of *Carmen* occurred 22 June 1878 at Her Majesty's Theatre. Mapleson brought the same company, including Hauk and Italo Campanini as Don Jose, to New York's Academy of Music, 23 October 1878.

10　*Gazette,* 14 March 1884, 6.

11　Leslie Orrey, ed., *The Encyclopedia of Opera,* New York: Charles Scribner's Sons, 1976, 117; Davis, *The American Opera Singer,* 70; *Gazette,* 22 July 1883, 4; 19 December 1885, 8; 20 December 1885, 8. Not surprisingly, Abbott returned to the city several more times—1–2 January 1886; 6–7 January 1888; and 20–21 December 1889.

[12] Ewen, *Encyclopedia of Opera*, 396, 618. On 17–18 March 1914, the San Carlo Opera presented performances of *Lucia di Lammermoor, Il Trovatore,* and *La Traviata* at the Byers.

[13] *Record,* 9 April 1916, sec. 2, 12; 31 May 1916, 3; *Star-Telegram,* 30 May 1916, 9; 31 May 1916, 9; FWP-FWTC, 19410, 29926. Elected vice presidents of the organization were Ben J. Tillar, L. Jackson, and William Monnig. R.E. Harding served as treasurer, Sam S. Losh as secretary, and T. H. Wear as manager. Chosen as directors were such prominent members of the community as John P. King, Amon G. Carter, Ben E. Keith, Leon Gross, Mrs. J.F. Lyons, Mrs. T.H. Wear, Sam Levy, and H.C. Meacham. In the official program of the 1916 season, sixty-nine final guarantors are listed.

[14] *Record,* 15 October 1916, sec. 2, 1, 4; 21 October 1916, 5; 4 October 1919, sec. 1, 10; FWP-FWTC, 30187; program for Ellis Opera Company productions of *Carmen* and *Il Trovatore,* 1916, FWPL-GLH, Miscellaneous Programs, Box 2,1905–1939; seating and price diagram of North Side Coliseum, TCHC.

[15] *Record,* 15 October 1916, sec. 2, 1, 4; 27 October 1916, 1, 2; 28 October 1916, 1, 5.

[16] Ibid. Ewen, *Encyclopedia of the Opera,* 226, 310, 466, 599, 745. Attendance figures are based on both newspaper ads and seating and price diagram. Louise Homer had previously appeared at the Byers in a concert tour, 29 October 1914.

[17] *Record,* 28 October 1916, 1; FWP-FWTC, 29926–29927.

[18] *Record,* 25 October 1917, 1, 6; 26 October 1917, 1, 6.

[19] *Record,* 1 November 1918, 1; 27 October 1919, 1; FWP-FWTC, 29926–29927. Ads for the operas, 27–29 October 1919, announced Destinn's appearance in *La Bohème,* but *A Masked Ball* was substituted. Campanini, already ill in October, did not conduct for the 1919 tour. He died in December.

[20] *Record,* 19 October 1920, 1; 20 October 1920, 2; Davis, *The American Opera Singer,* 240. Caruso's tour also included Houston, 22 October 1920. His efforts to accommodate an adoring public may have actually contributed to his demise. Just nine months later on 2 August 1921 he died from complications related to purulent pleurisy.

[21] *Record,* 16 December 1905, 4. For a complete account of the Spring Palace operettas, see Chapter Five.

[22] *Star-Telegram* (eve.), 3 June 1943, 1; 4 June 1943, 16; 6 June 1943; FWP-FWTC, 29926, 30185, 30215; list of Losh productions in 1927 program for *Cavalleria Rusticana,* Samuel Losh Papers, FWPL-GLH.

[23] Taken from various newspaper accounts, 1918–1929 and surviving programs in the Samuel Losh Papers; *Record,* 29 April 1917, sec. 2, 4; 30 April 1917, 8; 1 May 1917, 7; 2 May 1917, 8; *Star-Telegram,* 31 March 1918, society, 14; FWP-FWTC, 19410.

[24] Ibid., surviving programs, Samuel Losh Papers; *Star-Telegram,* 13 July 1924, 7B; 8 March 1936, music section, 6; 11 March 1936, 10. Some sources, including the FWP, incorrectly place *Faust* in 1914, but the *Record* (30 April 1917, 8) states the production "never [before] has been attempted by a local organization." Dates and locations of other productions: *The Mikado,* Chamber of Commerce Auditorium, 1–2 April 1918; *Aida,* First Baptist Auditorium, 25–26 May 1921; *Cavalleria Rusticana, Pagliacci,* Majestic Theater, 5–6 May 1922; *Il Trovatore,* First Baptist, 20–21 May 1924; *Rob Roy,* First Baptist, 24–25 March 1925; *H.M.S. Pinafore,* Masonic Home and School, 27 May 1926; *Cavalleria Rusticana,* Shelton Hall, Woman's Club, 6–7 April 1927; *Faust,* 6–7 March 1929, Civic Theater. *Rob Roy* (1925) was presented "under the auspices of" Azotos Temple, Dramatic Order of Knights of Khorassan, 175. *Aida* (1921) was "presented by" Moslah Temple Shrine Band and Patrol.

[25] *Star-Telegram* (eve.) 23 July 1946, 19; 30 July 1946, 15; 24 November 1946, sec. 2, 12; Dixon, *Story of the Fort Worth Opera,* 7; Blackwelder, *The Fort Worth Civic Opera Association,* 38, 105, 138.

[26] *Press,* 9 August 1946, 16; Dixon, *Story of the Fort Worth Opera,* 7–8.

[27] Dixon, 8; *Star-Telegram* 24 November 1946, sec. 2, 12; interview with Ahdel Chadwick, Fort Worth, Texas, 12 February 2004; Fort Worth Civic Opera Association income and expense statement, 1 October 1946 to 15 May 1947, in Blackwelder, *Fort Worth Civic Opera Association,* Appendix, n. p. Chadwick also served as accompanist for Betty Spain during Spain's concert appearances.

[28] Telephone interview with Betty Spain Klein, co-founder of the Fort Worth Opera, Santa Fe, New Mexico, February, 2004; Blackwelder, *Fort Worth Civic Opera Association,* interview with Dr. Walther R. Volbach, 129.

[29] *La Traviata* program, 1946, FWPL-GLH; Davis, *American Opera Singer,* 443.

[30] *Dallas Morning News,* 26 November 1946, sec. 2, 6; *Star-Telegram,* 26 November 1946, 23. Herbert's comments are found in a questionnaire in Blackwelder, *The Fort Worth Civic Opera,* 104.

[31] Ibid. *Star-Telegram,* 1 December 1946, sec. 2, 12.

[32] Dixon, *Story of the Fort Worth Opera,* 8; Blackwelder, *The Fort Worth Civic Opera,* interview with Volbach, 129.

[33] Fort Worth Opera Association, *Celebrating Fifty Years of Excellence,* (Fiftieth anniversary commemorative program), Fort Worth Opera Association, 1996; Fort Worth Civic Opera Casts and Technical Personnel, E. Clyde Whitlock Papers, FWPL-GHL; Fort Worth Opera Scrapbook, 1949, FWPL-GLH. Walter Herbert, who conducted nine Fort Worth productions, became the founding general director of the Houston Opera in 1955. Glynn Ross went on to found the Seattle Opera; Wymetal managed the Pittsburgh Civic Light Opera from 1947–1968; Agnini and Yannopoulos had both staged productions for the Metropolitan Opera. Pollock worked for the New York City Center Opera and became, in 1958, the first director of Casa Mañana. Ralph Herbert made his Met singing debut in 1955, before turning to a career as both producer and director of operas. See chapter five for details of the 1889 production of *The Texas Mikado.* Originally entitled *The Capitalist,* the operetta had been performed as one of the entertainment offerings of the Texas Spring Palace.

[34] *Star-Telegram,* 11 April 1949, 12; 24 April 1949, sec. 1, 11; 4 May 1949, 21; 26 June 1949, sec. 2, 12; 29 August 1949, 16; 10 November 1949, 21; Blackwelder, *Fort Worth Civic Opera,* 65, 106.

[35] *Star-Telegram,* 10 November 1949, 21; *Lucia di Lammermoor* was staged 26 and 28 November 1951; *Il Trovatore,* 24 and 16 April 1952; *Tosca,* 4 and 6 March 1953.

[36] *Press,* 26 January 1952, 6; 31 January 1952, 15; *Star-Telegram,* 26 November 1952, 12; 1 February 1953, sec. 2, 10.

[37] Blackwelder, *Fort Worth Civic Opera,* 106; E. Clyde Whitlock, compilation of Fort Worth Opera seasons, 1946–1959, n. p.; E. Clyde Whitlock Papers, FWPL-GLH; *Star-Telegram* 4 October 1953, sec. 2, 12; interview with William Walker, former general director of the Fort Worth Opera, April 2004, Fort Worth, Texas.

[38] *Celebrating Fifty Years of Excellence,* 10; Whitlock, Fort Worth Opera seasons, 1946–1959, n. p.; *Star-Telegram,* 5 September 1954, sec. 2, 5; 30 October 1954, sec. 2, 10. *Martha* was substituted for a planned production of Nicolai's *Merry Wives of Windsor.*

[39] Deborah Seabury, "A Lot From A Little: A Visit With Rudolf Kruger," *Opera News* (15 March 1980), 32; interview with Ruth Kruger, widow of Rudolf Kruger, Fort Worth, Texas, March, 2004.

[40] *Star-Telegram,* 2 October 1955, sec. 3, 21; 8 November 1981, 1,4D; 5 January 1991, 36 (obit.); Rudolf Kruger curriculum vitae in vertical files, Fort Worth Public Library, Local History and Genealogy.

[41] Seabury, "A Lot From A Little," 35; George Heymont, "A Painful Process," *Opera News* (November 1987) 13; Fort Worth Opera Repertory, 1946–2004, various programs, Fort Worth Opera Association; *Fort Worth News-Tribune,* 28 November 1975, 11; interview with William Massad.

[42] Ibid.

[43] Ibid. *Star-Telegram,* 21 July 1957, sec. 3, 16; 13 October 1957, sec. 3, 1–2; 16 June 1963, 5. Though the city had previous symphonic groups organized by C. D. Lusk and Carl Venth, Brooks Morris is credited with founding and conducting Fort Worth's modern symphony in 1925. Loss of members during World War II forced its "temporary" disbanding in 1942.

[44] Interview with Massad; *Dallas Morning News* 19 June 1983, (Metro West Edition) People, 1, 4. Figures come from the 1981–1982 annual report of Opera America. Dallas' costs per performance broke down to $183,000, while Fort Worth's costs averaged only $82,000.

[45] Interview with Kruger; interview with Massad; Dixon, *Story of the Fort Worth Opera Association,* 10–11; Fort Worth Opera *La Traviata* program explaining conditions of the grant, 13 November 1963. Besides extending its season, a further condition of the bequest required that the company increase its operating budget by a total of $20,000 within five years.

[46] Dixon, *Story of the Fort Worth Opera,* 10–11; Fort Worth Opera Repertory 1946–2004, various Opera Association programs. In 1962–63 before formation of the Arts Council, $45,000 of the opera's $75,000 budget had to be raised through public solicitation. By just five years later, the Arts Council was providing $70,000—48% of the opera's $148,000 budget (Arts Council of Greater Fort Worth, Allocations to Funded Organizations, 1967–68).

[47] Ibid.

[48] Telephone interview with Dr. John Forestner, president of Fort Worth Opera, 1996–1998, 26 May 2004. In 2003, the winner of the competition was awarded $7,000. This was expected to rise shortly to $10,000.

[49] Interview with Kruger; *Star-Telegram*, 20 July 1975, 6F; Seabury, "A Lot From a Little," 33. McCracken performed *Otello* in 1967 though suffering from a high fever that left him virtually unable to stand. When efforts to locate a replacement failed, he insisted on completing the engagement. The set was rearranged so the tenor could lean or recline while singing.

[50] Ibid., Seabury, 33; Davis, *The American Opera Singer*, 488.

[51] Ibid. Seabury; interview with Kruger; interview with Bill Massad; *Star-Telegram*, 7 January 1983, B1; *Fort Worth News-Tribune*, 7 June 1985, 8A. Budget figures are based on the comparison of Dallas and Fort Worth performance budgets published in annual reports of *Opera America*, 1978–79, 1979–80, 1980–81, 1981–82.

[52] Ibid. *Dallas Morning News*, 17 November 1961, sec. 4, 6 ; interview with Kruger; interview with Massad. The Dallas review by Rual Askew incorrectly listed Domingo's age as nineteen.

[53] Interview with Massad; interview with Kruger; *Star-Telegram*, 27 November 1962, sec. 2, 4; 8 November 1981, 4D. Some sources list Pons' birth date as 12 April 1904; others list it as early as 1898.

[54] Ibid., *Star-Telegram*.

[55] Ewen, *New Encyclopedia of Opera*, 191; *Celebrating Fifty Years of Excellence*, 12–14.

[56] Seabury, "A Lot From a Little," 32; *Celebrating Fifty Years of Excellence*, 12–14; *Il Trovatore* program, Fort Worth Opera Records, FWPL-GLH, Series IV, Box 2.

[57] *Fort Worth Magazine*, November 1947, 29; "Civic Music Brings Symphony and Concert Stars At Bargain Prices," December 1957, 28; *Star-Telegram*, 11 November 1951, sec. 2, 15; 9 November 1952, sec. 2, 16; 19 August 1958. First president of the Civic Music Association was W.K. Stripling.

[58] Fort Worth Opera *La Traviata* program, 13 & 15 November 1963; *Star-Telegram*, 14 November 1963, 6; *Dallas Morning News*, 15 November 1963, sec. 3, 8.

[59] *Star-Telegram*, 21 November 1976; Ewen, *New Encyclopedia of Opera*, 643; Davis, *The American Opera Singer*, 492–493

[60] *Star-Telegram*, 22 January 1966, 3; 6 April 1968, 12A; interview with Leonard Eureka, former *Star-Telegram* arts critic, Fort Worth, Texas, October 2003. Sills' Fort Worth debut as Lucia was tune-up for a planned fall 1969 New York City Opera debut in the same role.

[61] *Barber of Seville* program, 1979; Davis, *The American Opera Singer*, 495–498; interview with Massad.

[62] George Heymont, "A Painful Process," *Opera News*, November 1987, 13; interview with Massad.

[63] Heymont, Ibid., 13–14; Seabury, "A Lot From a Little," 34; *Star-Telegram*, 7 January 1983, 2; interview with Massad.

[64] Interview with Massad; interview with Kruger.

[65] *Star-Telegram*, 7 January 1983, 1–2; 13 March 1983, 1–2F.

[66] Interview with Kruger; interview with Massad; *Star-Telegram*, 7 January 1983, 1–2; 14 March 1983, 4B; 26 April 1983, 7C; *News Tribune*, 7 June 1985, 8A. The Kruger Young Artist Award became part of the Marguerite McCammon Competition, given to a promising runner-up (usually second or third place) in the competition.

[67] Ibid., 7 January 1983, 1–2.

[68] *Star-Telegram*, 11 November 1984, 1, 2E; 14 May 1985, 1, 5C. *Agrippina* was made possible by a grant from the Anne Burnett and Charles D. Tandy Foundation.

[69] Interview with Massad. In 1980, the company spent only $110–115,000 on salaries, with Massad receiving $27,000 and Kruger, $44,000.

[70] Ibid. *Star-Telegram*, 14 May 1985, 1, 5C; 10 January 1987, 1, 15A; *News-Tribune*, 10 May 1985, 1, 24A; 20 September 1985, n. p.; 31 January 1986, 16, 24A.

[71] *Star-Telegram*, 10 January 1987, 1, 15A; 14 May 1985, 1, 5C; *News-Tribune*, 10 May 1985, 1, 24A; 7 June 1985 1A, 20B; 5 August 1985, 4; interview with Massad. More optimistic early estimates

placed the debt at only $300,000, but by October 1985, the figure had already grown to $516,000 (*News-Tribune*, 11 October 1985, 14A).

[72] Ibid., *News-Tribune; Star-Telegram*, 14 May 1985, 1, 5C; 10 January 1985, 1, 15A; 85; interview with Massad. A previously scheduled production of Puccini's *Girl of the Golden West* had to be canceled.

[73] *Star-Telegram*, 15 November 1989, sec. 5, 1,10. Arroyo, relegated to minor roles with the Met following her 1958 debut, made her presence spectacularly known in 1965 when she substituted for Birgit Nilsson as Aida. From then on, the Met was forced to give her leading roles.

[74] *Star-Telegram*, 10 January 1987, 1, 15A; 14 February 1988, sec. 7, 1, 6–7; 12 March 1988, sec. 4, 10; 14 January 1989, 20; 13 January 1990, 14 December 1990, sec. 1, 22; *Fort Worth Business Press,* 14–20 September 1990, 11. The December 1990 article reports $925,000 for 1985–86; $750,000 for 1986–87.

[75] Ibid., *Business Press. Star-Telegram,* 11 November 1990, sec. 6, 1.

[76] *Star-Telegram*, 17 November 1990, 28; Fort Worth Opera Association executive committee minutes, 18 December 1990; interview with Massad. The decision to terminate Ramos is mentioned only circumspectly, but Massad reports that the board was disappointed with the artistic quality of shows. He received three months full salary and then $1,000 monthly through 30 June 1991.

[77] *Star-Telegram,* 23 April 1991, 6E.

[78] Interview with Walker; *Star-Telegram,* 15 November 1991, 1A.

[79] Ibid. Fort Worth Civic Opera Casts, E. Clyde Whitlock papers. Walker's *Carmen* appearance came in 1955. That same year he played Antonio in *The Marriage of Figaro* and Schaunard in *La Bohème.*

[80] Ibid., Walker. *Star-Telegram,* 19 July 1993, 3F; Fort Worth Opera Association, Income and Expense Summary for period ending 31 May 1991. Income from various fund-raisers, including the annual opera ball, were down $39,000. Contributions from foundations, businesses and other sources had declined by $95,000.

[81] *Star-Telegram,* 21 November 1992, 1E; 29 August, 1993, n. p.; *Dallas Morning News,* 23 November 1993, 1, 4C.

[82] Interview with Walker.

[83] *Star-Telegram,* 12 November 1994, 18A; 14 January 1995, 16A.

[84] *Star-Telegram,* 6 November 1999, 12A.

[85] *Star-Telegram,* 6 May 1995, 24A; 8 May 1995, 3B; 12 November 1994, 18A; 14 January 1995, 16A.

[86] *Star-Telegram,* 26 September 1995, 11, 16A. Additional gifts eventually pushed the endowment fund to $800,000 (*Star-Telegram,* 19 September 1998, 1A). Newspapers reported the wine auction tally at just $200,000. According to Walker, the final figure was the substantially higher figure, $286,000.

[87] *Star-Telegram,* 19 September 1998, 1, 17A.

[88] *Star-Telegram,* 25 September 1998, 1A; 8 January 1999, 6E; 13 February 1999, 1, 5A. Walker's five-year contract extended originally through the 1998–1999 season. The new three-year contract, including 1998–1999, went through the 2001–2002 season.

[89] *Star-Telegram,* 13 February 1999, 1, 5A.

CHAPTER TWELVE

[*] Note: a number of newspaper references in this chapter are found only in the Casa Mañana Scrapbook Collection, Fort Worth Public Library, Genealogy and Local History. Because of mislabeling or unavailability to the author from any other source, some of these articles have no page numbers. These are hereafter cited as CMS+year.

[1] *The Story of Casa Mañana Musicals* (advertising booklet), Fort Worth: Casa Mañana Musicals, Inc., 1966, 11–12.

2   *Star-Telegram,* 18 August 1958, 12 (eve.); 19 August 1958, 15; 19 August 1958, 22 (eve.).

3   Interview with Melvin O. Dacus, general manager-producer of Casa Mañana Musicals, 1958–1974, Fort Worth, Texas, 23 September 1980.

4   Ibid., Dacus. Ordinance 2378, City of Fort Worth, September 5, 1945; *Star-Telegram,* 14 November 1957, 2.

5   Interviews with Kim Dacus Reynolds, Brent Dacus, and Debbie Dacus, daughter, son, and daughter-in-law of Melvin O. Dacus (hereafter cited as Dacus family) October 2003, January 2004, Fort Worth, Texas; "A Man of Parts," *UTA Magazine,* Vol. 2, September 1979, 16; *Star-Telegram,* 5 January 1947, sec. 2, 8; 4 October 1953, sec. 2, 18; Casa Mañana program for *Carousel,* 21 July-2 August 1958, n. p.; *Fort Worth Magazine,* September 1958, 17.

6   Interview, Melvin Dacus; interviews, Dacus family; *Star-Telegram,* 18 February 1951, sec. 2, 12; 4 October 1953, 18; 26 March 1964 (eve.), 1.

7   Ibid., Melvin Dacus.

8   Gordon Allison, "Music Circus," *Theatre Arts* Vol. 35, June 1951, 89; David Dachs, "Ten Years of the Music Tents," *Saturday Review,* Vol. 41, 31 May 1958, 37–38.

9   Interview, Melvin Dacus.

10 *Star-Telegram,* 13 February 1957, 20 (eve.); Fort Worth City Council Minutes, 13 February 1957. Council minutes do not detail the precise location on Amon Carter Square. However, later publications announcing the plan do.

11 Ibid.

12 Interview with Melvin Dacus; *Fort Worth Press,* 13 November 1957, 3; *Star-Telegram,* 17 November 1957, sec. 2, 10; *Casa Mañana '58,* unpublished brochure released to the press and presented to Fort Worth City Council by the Fort Worth Opera Association, November 1957; Fort Worth City Council Minutes, 15 November 1957.

13 Ibid., *Casa Mañana '58.*

14 City Council Minutes 22 November 1957; interview with Melvin Dacus. One alternate location proposed by Watt was the northwest corner of the stockshow grounds near the Fort Worth Art Center.

15 City Council Minutes, 15 November 1957, 22 November 1957, 4 December 1957; *Star-Telegram,* 12 January 1958, 1; 23 February 1958, 4; interview with Melvin Dacus. The Chamber presented its urban renewal plan to the city council on 10 January 1958. Ultimately, the Tarrant County Convention Center and John F. Kennedy Theater, a project that consumed fourteen city blocks, moved farther east between Houston and Commerce and was not completed until 1968.

16 *Press,* 19 November 1957, 3; 5 December 1957, 3; 15 December 1957, 20; 24 December 1957, 23; Fort Worth City Council Minutes, 17 January 1958, 28 February 1958; interview with Melvin Dacus; interview with James C. Fuller, former president of Casa Mañana Musicals, Inc., 7 August 1980. Formal issuance of the bonds was not completed until the February 28 council meeting, with the bonds actually dated 1 March 1958.

17 Casa Mañana Musicals, Inc., Executive Committee Minutes, 26 February 1958.

18 *Star-Telegram,* 13 March 1958, 14; Pat Record, "Mr. Casa Mañana, Alias Melvin Dacus," *Fort Worth Magazine,* Vol. 40, May 1964, 17; interview with Dacus. Several sources place the loan for cost overruns at $200,000, but Dacus placed the actual figure at around $210,000.

19 *The Story of Casa Mañana Musicals,* 11; ad for E.O. "Gene" Wood Co., in *Call Me Madam* program, 1958; *Star-Telegram,* 1 May 1958, 2.

20 Interview with Michael Pollock, producer-stage director of Casa Mañana Musicals (1958–1965), Austin, Texas, 14 July 1980; *Star-Telegram,* 11 June 1958, 8; sec. 2, 10; *New York Times,* 6 September 1959, sec. II, 9.

21 Ibid., *New York Times; San Diego Union-Tribune,* 16 November 2003, B7, (obit.).

22 *Star-Telegram,* 23 March 1958, 10; *Press,* 12 March 1958, 19; interview with William Garber, director of Fort Worth Community Theater, 1956–1993, Fort Worth, Texas, 12 March 2001.

23 *Star-Telegram,* 5 October 2003, 7D.

[24] Interview with Pollock; interview with Melvin Dacus; *Fort Worth Magazine,* Vol. 34, May 1958, 15. Dacus attributed the design misstep to a city ordinance restricting the pitch of aisles in city-owned amphitheaters and auditoriums.

[25] *Star-Telegram,* 6 July 1958, 1; "Stage Struck Texas," *Life,* Vol. 45, 22 December 1958, 122; *Dallas Times Herald,* 6 July 1958 (CMS, 1958); interview with Elston Brooks, amusements editor, *Fort Worth Star-Telegram,* Fort Worth, Texas, 16 December 1980.

[26] *Star-Telegram,* 6 July 1958, 1; sec. 2, 10; *Times-Herald,* 6 July 1958 (CMS, 1958); *Press,* 6 July 1958, 1.

[27] *Dallas Morning News,* 7 July 1958, sec. 2, 5; *Times Herald,* 5 August 1958 (CMS, 1958); interview with Pollock.

[28] *Morning News,* 22 July 1958, 10; *Press,* 7 July 1958, 8, 13; interview with Pollock; interview with Brooks.

[29] *Star-Telegram,* 7 September 1958, sec. 2, 5; Minutes of the board of directors, Casa Mañana Musicals, Inc., 19 February 1959.

[30] *Star-Telegram,* 8 March 1959, sec. 2, 17; Minutes of executive committee, Casa Mañana Musicals, 19 February 1959.

[31] *Star-Telegram,* 12 January 1964, sec. 2, 7.

[32] *Denton Record-Chronicle,* 2 June 1961; *Variety,* 29 May 1961 (CMS, 1961) .

[33] *Morning News,* 22 July 1958, 10; *Star-Telegram,* 26 December 1958, 9;11 June 1961, sec. 2, 15; various Casa Mañana programs, 1958–1963; Minutes of Casa Mañana executive committee, 30 March 1959; interview with Pollock. Also serving as music director before 1967 was Arthur Lief, who had conducted a number of Broadway Shakespearean revivals. For several seasons, the theater made additional revenue renting Evelyn Norton Anderson's creations to other theaters.

[34] *Morning News,* 27 August 1958, 9; *Times Herald,* 19 March 1961(CMS, 1961); 29 June 1963 (CMS, 1963); *Star-Telegram,* 12 July 1960, 13; 14 July 1963, sec. 2, 11.

[35] Interview with Melvin Dacus; interview with Pollock; *Morning News,* 28 May 1960, sec. 3, 7; 30 May, 1960, 14.

[36] Ibid. "Honeybun," from *South Pacific,* music by Richard Rodgers, lyrics by Oscar Hammerstein, II, book by Joshua Logan, 1949.

[37] *Morning News,* 19 August 1959, sec. 3, 5; *Press,* 18 August 1959, 21.

[38] Interview with Pollock.

[39] Interview with Sharon Benge, professor and Program Director for Drama, Texas Woman's University; former executive director, Casa Mañana Playhouse, Fort Worth, Texas, 18 June 2001; program, *Sound of Music,* May 1964, 25; *Handbook of Texas Online,* s.v. "SIFF, IRIS FUTOR," http://www.tsha.utexas.edu/handbook/online/articles/SS/fsi44.html (accessed February 21, 2006).

[40] Ibid. Program, *Damn Yankees,* 13–25 August 1962, n. p.

[41] Interview with Dacus; *Star-Telegram,* 3 February 1963, sec. 2, 19; 10 February 1963, sec. 2, 15; 3 May 1963, (eve.) 7. Based on figures released to the press, profits remained only marginal, averaging $2,900 during the first five seasons (*Press,* 10 February 1963, 15B).

[42] *Times Herald,* 19 June 1963 (CMS, 1963); 8 September 1963 (CMS, 1963).

[43] Interview with Fuller, interview with Brooks; *Star-Telegram,* 26 March 1964 (eve.), 1; *Press,* 26 March 1964, 1.

[44] Interview with Melvin Dacus; interview with Ruta Lee, actress, Fort Worth, Texas, 7 July 1980.

[45] Financial records, Casa Mañana Musicals, Inc.; interview with Fuller; interview with William O. Jary, former advertising executive, Casa Mañana Musicals, Inc., 15 October 1980. Members of the new executive board included Mrs. Amon Carter Jr., Sam Weatherford, III, Charles Anton, L.R. Sarazan, and Robert Utter.

[46] Letter from James C. Fuller to members of the board of directors, 15 September 1964; telephone interview with Rob Johnson, son of Rip Johnson, Houston, Texas, 12 April 2005; *Star-Telegram,* 26 November 1964, sec. 3, 5; 29 December 1989, sec. 1, 23 (Rip Johnson obituary).

[47] Interview with Melvin Dacus, *Star-Telegram,* 17 November 1964, 8; 22 November 1964, sec. 2, 7; 24 November 1964, 1; 26 November 1964, 1.

[48] Interview with Dacus; Casa Mañana program, *The Sound of Music,* May 1964, 25. From 1958 to 1964, the agreement called for a flat rental rate of $28,000 each year, an amount the theater was unable to pay in either 1963 or 1964 until the Red Seat Campaign provided additional funds. As the theater's finances declined once again after 1974, even the percentage amount was often not paid. The Pioneer Palace, originally constructed in 1936, was torn down in 1965.

[49] Interview with Benge; telephone interview with Ann Pugh; materials provided to author by Ann Pugh; *Fort Worth Magazine,* vol. 41, September 1965, 33. Faculty members included William Garber, director of Greater Fort Worth Community Theater; Mrs. John E. Dieb, a former president of the speech-drama department of the Fort Worth Junior Woman's Club; TCU instructor Bill Sapp; Mrs. Lawrence Curtis; Mrs. Tom J. Abbott; and Daniel Nevot, fencing instructor for Dallas' Hockaday School and St. Mark's Boys School.

[50] *Star-Telegram,* 29 September 1964, 9; 6 July 1965, 10; 7 July 1965, 9 (eve.); 8 October 1965, 1 (eve.); 10 October 1965, sec. 2, 7; 12 July 1966, 7; *Dallas Morning News,* 8 July 1965, 21A; minutes of the board of directors, Casa Mañana Musicals, 14 July 1965. The *Dallas Times-Herald* (9 September 1964) reported that some board members wanted to reduce Pollock's title to director, thus limiting his pay to summer months. Pollock's skill as a director proved a hard act to follow: In 1978, the *Star-Telegram* selected the ten best productions of Casa Mañana's first twenty seasons. All but one were directed by Pollock (*Star-Telegram,* 24 September 1978, 1H).

[51] *What Makes Sammy Run* made its debut in 1966; *Funny Girl, On A Clear Day You Can See Forever,* and *Oliver!* in 1967; *Half A Sixpence* in 1968; *Little Me* and *George M!* in 1970.

[52] *Star-Telegram,* 2 June 1967 (CMS, 1967); *Dallas Morning News,* 24 May 1967 (CMS, 1967).

[53] *Dallas Morning News,* 17 July 1968, 18A; financial records of Casa Mañana Musicals, Inc. Rand, at age 70, appeared once more in 1974 when Casa did a second revival of *Forum.*

[54] Interview with Lee; *Dallas Times-Herald,* 21 May 1969 (CMS,1969); *Star-Telegram,* 19 May 1969, 10A. Though a critical failure, the show attracted good crowds. Encouraged by the response, the theater invited writers and composers in the fall of 1969 to submit other unpublished scores for possible production. Of twenty scores submitted, however, none was good enough to justify the expense of development.

[55] *Star-Telegram,* 9 June 1970, 10A; 18 August 1970, 8A; financial records, Casa Mañana Musicals, Inc.

[56] Interview with Lee; interview with Brooks.

[57] *Dallas Morning News,* 19 September 1971, 1C; *Star-Telegram;* 27 August 1972, 1G; 11 February 1979, 1C.

[58] *Star-Telegram,* 28 July 1972, 1; 29 July 1972, 1; 3 August 1972 (CMS, 1972); interview with Melvin Dacus. The theater agreed to pay the actors an additional 4.8 percent on condition that ticket prices remained unchanged through the end of the 1972 season.

[59] "Casa, New Home of Worth Wurlitzer," *Fort Worth,* Vol. 48, August 1972, 12–13; *Star-Telegram,* 26 September 1972, page 4A. Among those attending the 1972 concert was Muth's family. Muth himself had died in 1949. Following the renovation of Casa Mañana in 2002, the organ was moved into storage.

[60] Interview with Dacus; minutes of Casa Mañana executive board, 6 February 1973; 5 March 1973; 14 March 1973; 22 March 1973; *Star-Telegram* 4 May 1973, 11A.

[61] *Star-Telegram,* 4 May 1973, 19A; 22 May 1973, 1; 17 July 1973, 1A, 10A.

[62] Interview with Benge.

[63] Minutes of the executive board, 23 June 1973; *Star-Telegram,* 24 June 1973, 1; 28 June 1973, 9D; 16 July 1973, 10A; 17 July 1973, 1A, 10A. By terms of the agreement, Equity made concessions to Texas right-to-work laws, allowed the hiring of some non-union performers and dropped a requirement previously demanded that the theater conduct interviews of principals only in New York. Casa Mañana agreed to take no recriminatory action against union members who participated in the strike and raised performers' weekly scale from $175 to $185 (Casa Mañana/Actors Equity tentative agreement, 16 July 1973, Casa Mañana business records). For 1974, the theater raised ticket prices seventy-five cents.

[64] Interview with C.E. "Bud" Franks, general manager-producer, Casa Mañana Musicals, 1974–1990, Fort Worth, Texas, 14 August 1980; *Star-Telegram,* 15 June 1974, 1; 31 July 1974, 4D (eve.).

[65] Interview with Melvin Dacus.

⁶⁶ *Star-Telegram*, 8 October 1974, 1, 14A; interview with Melvin Dacus; interviews with Dacus family.

⁶⁷ Interview with Franks; minutes of the board of directors, Casa Mañana Musicals, 26 November 1974; *Press*, 7 March 1975 (CMS, 1975).

⁶⁸ *Star-Telegram*, 1 June 1975 (CMS, 1975); 1 October 1975 (CMS, 1975); interviews with Dacus family; "A Man of Parts," 16. Under the "star system," the theater posted initial profits of $28,528 for 1974 and $20,186 for 1975 (*Star-Telegram*, 11 February 1979, 1C).

⁶⁹ *Star-Telegram*, 12 October 1977, 4B (eve.); 31 May 1984, 1B; 17 July 1984, 20A; Casa Mañana news release announcing a change of policy to include proscenium touring shows, 20 April 1987, FWPL-GLH; Casa Mañana *Oklahoma!* program, 1989, 34; Arts Council information provided by Flora Maria Garcia, president, Arts Council of Fort Worth and Tarrant County. Published newspaper reports set losses at $10,000 in 1979; $106,000 in 1980; $208,000 in 1981; $118,000 in 1982; and $150,000 in 1983, 1988, and 1989.

⁷⁰ "Casa Mañana Renovation," *Man of La Mancha* program, July 1990, 38; *Star-Telegram*, 11 July 1990, 1; 29 August 1990, 2; *Dallas Morning News*, 11 July 1990, 21A. Passage of the issue would have also provided a five million dollar endowment fund for Casa, Will Rogers Auditorium, and the William Edrington Scott Theater. In December 1990, Bud Franks was named executive director of the San Diego Civic Light Opera.

⁷¹ Casa Mañana program, *Brigadoon*, July 1993, 38–39; *Star-Telegram*, 29 August 1990, 2; 17 June 1997, 1.

⁷² Ibid.

⁷³ *Star-Telegram*, 17 June 1997, 1; 27 August 1997, 1B

⁷⁴ *Star-Telegram*, 22 September 1998, 6B; 3 June 2001, 3D. In September 1998, Yockey reported to the Casa Mañana board a net loss of $209,434 for the season, but anticipated a revenue surplus of $203,581 for the 1999 season.

⁷⁵ *Casa Mañana '58* (presentation brochure prepared for Fort Worth City Council and potential investors), *Star Telegram*, 16 October 2002, 1; 5 October 2003, 5D.

⁷⁶ *Star-Telegram*, 16 October 2002, 1.

⁷⁷ *Star-Telegram*, 5 October 2003, 7D; additional figures provided to author by Casa Mañana Musicals, Inc.

CHAPTER THIRTEEN

¹ *Handbook of Texas Online*, s.v. "REEDER, EDWARD DICKSON," http://www.tsha.utexas.edu/handbook/online/articles/RR/fre44.html (accessed February 21, 2006). "Dickson Reeder" in *Beyond Regionalism: The Fort Worth School (1945–1955)*, Wilma Jo Mitchell, ed., Albany, Texas: The Old Jail Art Center, 1986, n. p.; interview with Flora Blanc Reeder by Gerald Saxon, associate director of libraries, University of Texas-Arlington, Reeder Collection, 1994; *Star-Telegram*, 24 April 1934, society, 11; 9 May 1970, 4A (Dickson Reeder obituary); 2 February 1988, sec. 4, 1.

² Ibid., Saxon, interview with Flora Blanc Reeder.

³ Ibid. *Star-Telegram*, 5 August 1945, sec. 2, 8. Reeder Collection, Box 18, program folder. There were many instructors over the years. They included Jane Crawford Jenkins, Sue McCleery, John Walsh, Mrs. Peter Gimber, Dorothy Whitman, Marguerite Cardwell, Joyce Rogers Shrake, and Sallie Wilson. Susan Tonetti served as business manager. Board members included Mrs. R. E. Harding, S. B. Cantey III, Edwin E. Bewley, Jr., Mrs. Albert Evans, Jr., Andrew P. Fuller, Sallie Gillespie, Mrs. Walter R. Humphrey, Sue McCleery, Robert Nail, W.R. Nail, J. Olcott Phillips, Rhinehart Rouer, Anne Ryan, and Mrs. James H. Snowden (*Star-Telegram*, 26 September 1948, sec. 2, 8; 14 October 1951, sec. 2, 9; 23 May 1954, sec. 2, 10).

⁴ Ibid., Saxon. *Star-Telegram*, 26 September 1948, sec. 2, 8; 2 February 1988, sec. 4, 1.

⁵ Ibid., Saxon. Fort Worth City Directory, 1937–38; *Star-Telegram*, 23 May 1954, sec. 2, 10 ; 18 October 1978, B1; *Press*, 8 April 1954, 8. Bailey's home later became the Elks Club lodge.

⁶ Ibid., Saxon. *Star-Telegram*, 26 September 1948, sec. 2, 8; *Handbook of Texas Online*, s.v. "REEDER SCHOOL," http://www.tsha.utexas.edu/handbook/online/articles/RR/kkrl.html (accessed

February 21, 2006). Color transparencies and slides of various productions, Box 16; programs, Box 18, Reeder Collection; Marcelle Hull, "A Retrospective of The Reeder School of Theater and Design," *The Compass Rose,* Vol. VII, Fall, 1993, 4–5.

7 Ibid., Saxon; Hull, "A Retrospective of the Reeder School of Theater and Design, 4–5. *Star-Telegram,* 27 September 1995, 21A (Flora Blanc Reeder obituary). The second Reeder school produced *A Midsummer Night's Dream* (1981, 1982), *Aucassin and Nicolette* (1983), *The Tempest* (1984), and *Nala and Damayanti* (1986).

8 Colby D. Hall, *History of Texas Christian University: A College of the Cattle Frontier,* Fort Worth: TCU Press, 1947, 285, 289–290; Moore, *Texas Christian University,* 193; *Skiff,* 11 August 1944, 4; 11 January 1946, 1; interview with Mrs. Esther Winesanker, widow of Dr. Michael Winesanker, TCU professor of musicology. Dr. Winesanker, like Volbach, was recruited by Dean McCorkle. He came from the University of Texas in 1947, his assigned task to build the university's music department. He shared office space with Volbach for several years.

9 Telephone interview with Fritz Volbach, nephew of Dr. Walther Volbach, San Francisco, California, 9 September 2004*; Press,* 9 August 1946, 16.

10 Interview with Winesanker; interview with Garber; *Press,* 1 January 1953, sec. 2, 17; 1 May 1953, 9; *Skiff,* 21 February 1947, 4; *TCU Faculty Bulletin,* 3 March 1965, n. p.; 24 March 1965, n. p., TCU Library, Fort Worth, Texas, Special Collections. Dr.Volbach retired in 1965. He was succeeded by Dr. Jack Cogdill.

11 Interview with Volbach; Moore, *Texas Christian University,* 193; *Star-Telegram,* 4 December 1949, sec. 1, 17*; Skiff,* 23 September 1949, 5. Ed Landreth Hall's pipe organ was constructed and installed by Moeller Organ Company of Hagerstown, Maryland.

12 "Realistic 10-year Growth Plan Next Stop for College," *Fort Worth Magazine,* March 1961, 10; *Bulletin of Texas Wesleyan College,* 1947, 1953; *Star-Telegram,* 14 September 1958, sec. 2, 13; telephone interview with Cathey Cady, former Johnson student and Johnson's assistant director, 1968–1985, Fort Worth, Texas, 21 September 2004.

13 *Star-Telegram,* 7 April 1957, sec. 2, 16; 23 February 1958, sec. 4, 6; 2 October 1989, n. p. (Mason Johnson obit.); *Temple Daily Telegram,* 22 April 1979, 11. Before becoming a staff member, Johnson directed *Brigadoon, Annie Get Your Gun,* and *South Pacific* (1958). He may also have had a hand in 1955's *Finian's Rainbow,* although his name does not appear in news accounts.

14 Ibid., *The TXWOCO,* 1922. *Bulletin of Texas Wesleyan College,* 1935; *Texas Wesleyan University: A Centennial Album,* Fort Worth: Texas Wesleyan University, 1990, 10, 38.

15 *Star-Telegram,* 23 December 1936, society, 1; Fort Worth Dramatic Club program, *Lombardi, Ltd.,* 1945, miscellaneous program file, FWPL-GLH; Fort Worth Theater Guild Program Magazine, *The Time of Your Life,* 23 June 1947, FWPL-GLH.

16 Hollace Weiner, *Beth-El Congregation Centennial Fort Worth, Texas, 1902–2002,* Fort Worth: Beth-El Temple, 2002, 3–4; "History of B'nai B'rith in Fort Worth," Max Kaye Notebook 1; various programs and fliers in Max Kaye notebooks 2, 4, 5, 9, Congregation Ahavath-Shalom Library, Fort Worth, Texas; interview with Joy Spiegel, widow of Seymour Spiegel, 28 January 2004, Fort Worth, Texas; *Star-Telegram,* 29 November 1953, sec. 2, 15.

17 *Star-Telegram,* 21 October 1951, sec. 2, 17; 25 October 1951, 10.

18 Interview with Garber; *Star-Telegram* 1 January 1953, sec. 2, 1; 7 April 1957, sec. 3, 4; 4 January 1967, 2F.

19 *Star-Telegram,* 1 January 1953, sec. 2, 18; 1 May 1955, sec. 3, 17; 2 September 1956, sec. 2, 8.

20 Interview with Garber; *Star-Telegram,* 8 May 1955, sec. 2, 17. John Hillerman, a Denison native who had also played Bernard in the Theater Council's 1955 production of *Death of a Salesman,* went on to a successful professional career, appearing as a regular in several television series and in such movies as *Paper Moon, The Last Picture Show, Blazing Saddles,* and *What's Up, Doc.*

21 Ibid., Garber; *Star-Telegram,* 4 December 1955, sec. 2, 7; 18 December 1955, sec. 2, 12; 22 January 1956, sec. 3, 15. Ridglea Country Club opened in 1954.

22 Ibid., Garber; *Star-Telegram,* 16 September 1956, sec. 3, 14.

23 Ibid., Garber; *Star-Telegram,* 22 September 1957, sec. 4, 9.

24 Interview with Benge; interview with Garber.

25 Ibid., Garber. Various Community Theater programs in the collection of Bill Garber.

26 Ibid., Garber. *Star-Telegram*, 23 January 1966, special section on the Scott Theater, 4.

27 *Star-Telegram*, 8 October 1954, 2; 23 January 1966, Scott Theater special section, 2.

28 *Star-Telegram*, 23 January 1966, Scott Theater, 2; 25 January 1966, sec. 2, 2; interview with Garber.

29 Ibid., Garber. *Star-Telegram*, 25 January 1966, 1, 4; 16 April 1967, 1, 3G.

30 Ibid., Garber. *Star-Telegram*, 15 August 1965, sec. 7, 3; 23 January 1966, Scott Theater section, 2, 5; 25 January 1966, 1; sec. 2, 1, 2. The first theatrical production in the space was Edward Albee's *The Sandbox*, a one-act staged for the grand opening.

31 Ibid., Garber. *Star-Telegram*, 10 November 1966, C1; 7 December 1966, B4.

32 Ibid., Garber. *Star-Telegram*, 16 April 1967, 1, 3G; various issues in clip files of FWPL-GLH.

33 Ibid., Garber. Various Community Theater/ Fort Worth Theater programs, 1983–1993.

34 Ibid., Garber.

35 Ibid.

36 *Star-Telegram*, 1 March 2002, 1B. Fort Worth Theater's loss of funding came well before the national events of September 2001 that forced the Arts Council to cut contributions to other groups because of declining donations.

37 *Fort Worth Press*, 10 December 1957, 21; *Dallas Morning News*, 7 November 1964, sec. 1, 8. Interview with William Garber. Cowtown Hoedown was broadcast by radio station KCUL.

38 *Star-Telegram*, 29 November 1963, 14; *Press*, 3 March 1966, 3; *Dallas Morning News*, 7 November 1964, sec. 1, 8.

39 *Star-Telegram*, 3 August 1965, 9; 18 April 1966, 18; 10 September 1966, 2A.

40 *Press*, 11 July 1966, 1; 5 August 1966, 3; *Star-Telegram*, 31 May 1966, 1; 2 August 1966, 9; 10 September 1966, 2A; 20 October 1968, 5H; 2 November 1968, 3F; 10 November 1968, 10A.

41 *The Tarrant County Convention Center*, Fort Worth: Tarrant County Convention Center, 1968, n. p. descriptive booklet in TCCC clip files, FWPL-GLH; *Star-Telegram*, 10 September 1967, 6G; 19 May 1969. Distance from the front edge of the pit to the rear wall was under 100 feet, based on newspaper accounts.

42 Ibid., *The Tarrant County Convention Center*.

43 *Press*, 3 September 1969, 15; *Star-Telegram*, 5 October 1969, G1; 4 November 1973, 2A ; 1 December 1974, K1.

44 Interview with Benge.

45 "The Theatre Smorgasbord: Hip Pocket Theatre," *Fort Worth Magazine*, June 1978, 41–42; *Star-Telegram*, 4 March 1967, 6A; 15 July 1977, 3B; 23 July 1979, E1; 10 June 2001, 1, 3D.

46 *Star-Telegram*, 20 June 2001, 1, 4–5D.

47 *Star-Telegram*, 23 July 1979, E1.

48 Ibid. *Star-Telegram*, 22 March 1994, 1B; 20 June 2001, 1, 4–5D; *Dallas Morning News*, 20 July 1991, 7C.

49 Hip Pocket Production History, published by Hip Pocket Theater, 2002.

50 Ibid.

51 Correspondence with Joseph K. Dulle, president, White Elephant Enterprises, 21 December 2001.

52 Interview with Jerry Russell, founder of Stage West Theater, 4 May 2004, Fort Worth, Texas.

53 Ibid. Stage West souvenir program for grand opening of TCU Theater location, 19–20 October 1994, n. p.

54 Ibid.

55 Ibid.

56 Ibid. Stage West annual report, 1987–1988 in Stage West clip files, FWPL-GLH.

57 Ibid.

[58] Ibid., Russell.

[59] Interview with Rose Pearson, co-founder of Circle Theater, 9 April 2004, Fort Worth, Texas.

[60] Ibid. *Dallas Morning News,* 10 October 1999, 7C.

[61] Ibid.

[62] Ibid.

[63] *Star Telegram,* 30 September 1983, 1; 11 August 2001, 1F; *Dallas Morning News,* 15 October 1995, n. p., found in clip files, FWPL-GLH, Caravan of Dreams.

CHAPTER FOURTEEN

[1] *Dallas Morning News,* 17 May 1913, 1.

[2] Ibid.

[3] FWP-FWTC, 18424, 20471; King, "Texas Theatrical Impresario," 134–135; *Record,* 4 April 1917, 5; *Press,* 4 January 1933, 5.

[4] Davis, *The American Opera Singer,* 327–329; *Press,* 23 July 1937; 31 July 1937, n. p. (found in 1937 Casa Mañana Women's Division Scrapbook, FWPL-GLH).

[5] *Star-Telegram,* 12 April 1931, sec. 2, 9; *Fort Worth Mind,* 16 December 1933, 1, Fort Worth Public Library, Tarrant County Black Historical and Genealogical Association Collection, (hereafter cited as FWPL-TCBHGA).

[6] *Gazette,* 25 December 1885, 8; *Dallas Morning News,* 8 May 1898, 7; 29 May 1898, 20; 13 May 1899, 7; 19 April 1901, 7, 21 April 1901, 8, 2 December 1901, 3; *Register,* 1 May 1901, 2; *Happy Town Girls' Big Minstrel Jubilee* program, season 1901-1902, FWPL-TCBHGA.

[7] *Telegram,* 4 March 1906, 6; *Dallas Morning News,* 5 March 1906, 7.

[8] Fort Worth Colored History and Directory, c. 1907, 84, 86–89, Series III, Box 1, FWPL-TCBHGA; Lillian B. Horace private journal, "School-Handley," 28, Box 1, Lillian B. (Jones) Horace papers, FWPL-TCBHGA; "Women of Achievement: Lillian B. Horace, Educator and Author," Box 2, Lillian B. (Jones) Horace papers, FWPL-TCBHGA; I. M. Terrell High School yearbook, 1923, 38, Box 3, FWPL-TCBHGA. A biographical sketch of Lillian B. Jones Horace, written as part of a program celebrating "Women of Achievement" notes that Horace taught in Tarrant County schools for six years before coming to teach English in Fort Worth public schools in 1911. The *Queen Esther Cantata* is described in a passage written during her tenure at a school in Handley, Texas.

[9] Ibid., Box 3, I. M. Terrell High School yearbook, 1929, n. p.; telephone interview with Mrs. Hazel Harvey Peace; Box 3, *Terrellife,* I. M. Terrell High School newspaper, 17 March 1936, 1; unknown date, May 1947, 1; Box 2, I. M. Terrell High School, One-Act play tournament program, 22–28 February 1944, FWPL-TCBHGA; *Press,* 4 November 1952, 9. The Junior League began taking plays to city schools around 1932.

[10] *Directory of Negro Business Enterprises and Professions* (c. 1921), FWPL-TCBHGA, Series III, Box 1; FWP-FWTC, 20475–20576.

[11] *Fort Worth Mind,* 5 August 1933, 1.

[12] Fort Worth Colored History and Directory, c. 1907, 84, 86–89, FWPL-TCBHGA; program for Grand Concert and Style Show, Masonic Lodge, 6 April 1922, FWPL-TCBHGA; *Star-Telegram,* 27 July 1985, 1A.

[13] *Fort Worth Mind,* 11 May 1951, 2; 16 January 1953, 4.

[14] *Press,* 30 November 1936, 3; 1 December 1936, 12; *Fort Worth Mind,* 23 October 1933, 3; 4 November 1933, 3; 8 June 1951, 3; 19 December 1952, 1; FWP-FWTC, 18424.

[15] *Fort Worth Mind,* 11 March 1933, 3; 25 September 1933, 3; 23 October, 1933, 3; 4 November 1933, 3; 18 November 1933, 3; 17 February 1934, 3; 21 July 1934, 2; 3 November 1934, 3; 22 December, 1934, 3.

[16] *Fort Worth Mind,* 14 April 1960, 8; historical sketch of Soul People Repertory Company, Manuscript and Visual Collections Department, collection no. BV3422, Indiana Historical Society, William Henry Smith Memorial Library, Indianapolis.

[17] Fort Worth Little Theater program, *Porgy,* 24–29 March 1935; Fort Worth Little Theater programs, Box 1, FWPL-GLH; Fort Worth city directory, 1932–1936.

[18] White newspapers of the time did not routinely follow black civic events, and issues of the *Fort Worth Mind,* the city's most prominent black newspaper, did not survive. As a result, the Little Theater program is the only known reference to the Fort Worth Black Little Theater.

[19] *Star-Telegram,* 13 April 1971 (eve.), 14A; 27 August 1972, 1G.

[20] *Star-Telegram,* 13 April 1971 (eve.), 14A.

[21] Interview with Rudy Eastman, co-founder, Sojourner Truth Players; founder, Jubilee Theatre, 24 February 2004, Fort Worth, Texas; *Star-Telegram,* 21 May 1979, B1; Minority Progress Committee report, City of Fort Worth, 1975, n. p.; *Star-Telegram,* 13 April 1971 (eve.) 14A.

[22] Ibid., Eastman; Minority Progress Committee report.

[23] Ibid., Eastman. *Star-Telegram,* 14 January 1978, 10D; invitation to opening of Sojourner Truth Cultural Arts Center, 14 June 1980, Sojourner Truth clip file; FWPL-LHG.

[24] Ibid., Eastman.

[25] Ibid. *Star-Telegram,* 19 January 1992, 1, 8.

[26] Ibid. *Star-Telegram,* 25 August 2002, 1G.

[27] Ibid.

[28] Ibid.

[29] Ibid.

[30] Ibid.

[31] Fort Worth City Directory, 1886–1887; 1894–1895; *Democrat,* 4 September 1879, 4; *Daily Gazette,* 15 January 1884, 6; partial season list of the Majestic Theater, compiled by the author. Zamora appeared at the Majestic the week of 9 March 1908.

[32] Ibid., partial season list of Majestic Theater. *Daily Gazette,* 1 June 1889, 4; 6 June 1889, 1; 14 June 1889, 2. Carrillo's Majestic appearance occurred the week of 8 March 1909.

[33] North Fort Worth Marine Commercial Historic District, National Register of Historic Places application, sec. 7, 15; sec. 8, 29; Carlos E. Cuéllar, *Stories From the Barrio: A History of Mexican Fort Worth,* Fort Worth: TCU Press, 2003, 129, 132. The theater operated under four names between 1920 and the end of the 20th century: the Rose, the Roseland, the Marine, and the Rose Marine.

[34] Ibid., National Register application. Telephone interview with Cathy Hernandez, Rose Marine Theater Executive Director; *Star-Telegram,* 4 February 1998, 1B.

[35] Telephone interview with George Rodriguez (hereafter cited as GR), Fort Worth actor and brother of Lynda Rodriguez, 13 April 2005.

[36] Ibid., Telephone interview with Lynda Rodriguez (hereafter cited as LR), Fort Worth actor/director/producer, Farmington, New Mexico, 14 April 2005; *LaEstrella/Star-Telegram,* 5 January 1996, n. p., found in clip files of FWPL-LHG; *Star-Telegram,* 24 January 1999, 19A.

[37] Ibid. LR. *Star-Telegram,* 23 April 1999, *Star Time,* section 23.

[38] Ibid., LR; interview with GR; program, Hispanic Playwrights' Festival, 2003; *Star-Telegram,* 27 January 1998, 1B; 23 April 1999, *Star Time,* section 23; Greater Fort Worth phone book, 1999–2000.

[39] Interview with Hernandez; *Star-Telegram,* 27 January 1998, 1; 4 February 1998, 1.

[40] Ibid.

CHAPTER FIFTEEN

[1] The JFK Theater was demolished in April 2002 to make way for expansion of the Fort Worth Convention Center (*Star-Telegram,* 14 April 2002, 25A).

[2] Steve Roth, Stacy Schnellenbach Bogle, Nancy O' Malley, et. al., *Let The Angels Play: the Commemorative Journal for the Nancy Lee and Perry R. Bass Performance Hall,* Fort Worth:

Magnolia Media Group, 1998, 34; *Star-Telegram,* 11 July 1990, 1; *Dallas Morning News,* 11 July 1990, 21A.

3 Ibid., Roth, 36.

4 Ibid. *Dallas Morning News,* 3 May 1998, 10R.

5 Ibid., Roth, 46, 128. *Star-Telegram,* 9 May 1998, 18A.

6 Ibid., Roth, 82. Dimensions of the facade provided by Don Fearing, Director of Operations, Nancy Lee and Perry R. Bass Performance Hall.

7 Ibid., 18, 57, 68, 74–76; *Dallas Morning News,* 3 May 1998, 5R.

8 Ibid., 73. *Star-Telegram,* 9 May 1998, 18A; *Dallas Morning News,* 3 May 1998, 5R; William Weathersby, "Texas Tradition," *Theatre Crafts International,* August-September 1998, 50.

9 Ibid., 54, 68, 73.

10 Ibid., 88. Audience chamber dimensions, Fearing.

11 Ibid., 68. 72–73.

12 Interview with Terry Simons, chief engineer, Nancy Lee and Perry R. Bass Performance Hall, Fort Worth, Texas, 7 September 2004; *Star-Telegram,* 3 April 1998, 1.

13 Ibid., Roth, 38, 40; interview with Simons.

14 Ibid., Roth, 98. Grand opening festivities continued from 1 May to 14 June 1998.

15 *Star-Telegram,* 11 May 1998, 3D; *Dallas Morning News,* 9 May 1998, 1.

BIBLIOGRAPHY

BOOKS

Alft, E. C. *Elgin: Days Gone By.* Carpentersville, Illinois: Crossroads Communications, 1992.

Anderson, John Murray and Hugh Abercrombie Anderson. *Out Without My Rubbers.* New York: Library, 1954.

Ben-Hur: Souvenir Album and Scenes of the Play. Buffalo: Courier Company, 1900.

The Book of Fort Worth. Fort Worth: Fort Worth Record, 1913.

Bogard, Travis. *Contour In Time: The Plays of Eugene O'Neill.* New York: Oxford University Press, 1972

Bordman, Gerald. *American Theatre: A Chronicle of Comedy and Drama, 1869–1914.* New York: Oxford University Press, 1994.

—————. *The Oxford Companion To American Theatre*, 2nd ed. New York: Oxford University Press, 1992.

Brock, Alan St. H. *A History of Fireworks.* London: George G. Harrap, 1949.

Brockett, Oscar G. *History of the Theatre*, 6th edition. Boston: Allyn and Bacon, 1991.

Buenger, Victoria and Walter L. *Texas Merchant: Marvin Leonard and Fort Worth.* College Station: Texas A&M Press, 1998.

Cohen, Judith Singer. *Cowtown Moderne: Art Deco Architecture of Fort Worth, Texas.* College Station: Texas A&M Press, 1988.

Conrad, Earl. *Billy Rose: Manhattan Primitive.* New York: World, 1968.

Cuéllar, Carlos E. *Stories From the Barrio: A History of Mexican Fort Worth.* Fort Worth: Texas Christian University Press, 2003.

Dauphin, Sue. *Houston By Stages: A History of Theatre In Houston.* Burnet, Texas: Eakin Press, 1981.

Davidson, Nelson M. *Pencil Trails: The Texas Centennial Exhibition in Dallas and Texas.* Dallas: Dealey and Lowe, 1936.

Davis, Peter G. *The American Opera Singer.* New York: Doubleday, 1997.

Dempsey, David and Raymond P. Baldwin. *The Triumphs and Trials of Lotta Crabtree.* New York: William Morrow, 1968.

Durham, Weldon B., ed. *American Theatre Companies, 1888–1930.* New York: Greenwood Press, 1987.

Ewen, David. *Encyclopedia of the Opera.* New York: Hill and Wang, 1971.

Faith, William Robert. *Bob Hope: A Life in Comedy*. New York: G. P. Putnam's Sons, 1982.

Farr, Finis. *Margaret Mitchell of Atlanta.* New York: William Morrow, 1965.

Flemmons, Jerry. *Amon: The Life of Amon Carter, Sr., of Texas.* Austin: Jenkins Publishing, 1978.

Frohman, Daniel. *Daniel Frohman Presents.* New York: Lee Furman, 1935.

Gallegly, Joseph. *Footlights On the Border: The Galveston and Houston Stage Before 1900.* The Hague, Netherlands: Mouton, 1962.

Gilbert, Douglas. *American Vaudeville: Its Life and Times.* New York: Whittlesey House, 1940.

Givner, Joan. *Katherine Anne Porter: A Life.* revised edition. Athens: University of Georgia Press, Brown Thrasher Book, 1991.

Green, Stanley and Kay Green. *Broadway Musicals Show By Show,* 5th ed. Milwaukee: Hal Leonard Corp., 1996.

Hall, Colby D. *History of Texas Christian University: A College of the Cattle Frontier.* Fort Worth: TCU Press, 1947.

Hall, Roger A. *Performing the American Frontier, 1870–1906.* New York: Cambridge University Press, 2001.

Harwell, Richard, ed. *Margaret Mitchell's Gone With the Wind Letters, 1936–1949.* New York: Macmillan, 1976.

Henderson, Mary C. *Theatre In America.* New York: Harry N. Abrams, 1986.

Hinga, Don. *Forty Years of Community Service: The Story of Karl Hoblitzelle and the Development of Interstate Theatres.* Dallas: Stellmacher and Son, 1946.

Hirsch, Foster. *The Boys From Syracuse: The Shuberts' Theatrical Empire.* New York: Cooper Square Press, 2000.

Hope, Bob, and Pete Martin. *Have Tux, Will Travel.* New York: Simon and Schuster, 1954.

The Israelites of Louisiana: Their Religious, Civic, Charitable and Patriotic Life. New Orleans: W. E. Myers, n. d.

Kendall, John S. *The Golden Age of the New Orleans Theater.* Baton Rouge: Louisiana State University Press, 1952

Laurie, Joe, Jr. *Vaudeville: From the Honky-Tonks to the Palace.* New York: Holt, Rinehart, Winston, 1953. Reissued by Kennikat Press, Port Washington, N.Y., 1972.

Leavitt, M. B. *Fifty Years in Theatrical Management.* New York: Broadway, 1912.

Lloyd, Herbert. *Vaudeville Trails Thru the West: Orpheum-Pantages-Interstate and Ackerman and Harris Circuits,* 1919.

Katz, Ephraim. *The Film Encyclopedia.* New York: Thomas Y. Crowell, 1979.

MacGowan, Kenneth. *Footlights Across America: Towards a National Theater.* New York: Harcourt, Brace, 1929.

MacGowan, Kenneth and William Melnitz. *The Living Stage: A History of the World Theater,* New York: Prentice Hall, 1955.

Makers of Fort Worth. Fort Worth Newspaper Artists Association, 1914.

Marsberger, Robert E. and Kathrine M. *Lew Wallace: Militant Romantic.* New York: McGraw-Hill, 1980.

Martin, Mary. *My Heart Belongs.* New York: William Morrow, 1976.

Marx, Groucho. *Groucho and Me.* New York: Dell, 1959.

Maxfield, Bernice B. and William E. Jary, Jr. *Camp Bowie Fort Worth, 1917–1918: An Illustrated History of the 36th Division in the First World War.* Fort Worth: B. B. Maxfield Foundation, 1975.

McLean, Albert F. Jr. *American Vaudeville as Ritual.* University of Kentucky Press, 1965.

Mitchell, Wilma Jo, ed. *Beyond Regionalism: The Fort Worth School (1945–1955).* Albany, Texas: The Old Jail Art Center, 1986.

Moore, Jerome A. *Texas Christian University: A Hundred Years of History.* Texas Christian University Press, 1974.

Morley, Sheridan. *The Great Stage Stars.* New York: Facts On File, 1986.

Mullins, Marion Day. *A History of the The Woman's Club of Fort Worth, 1923–1973.* Fort Worth: The Woman's Club of Fort Worth, 1973.

Naylor, David, and Joan Dillon. *American Theaters: Performance Halls of the Nineteenth Century.* New York: John Wiley and Sons, 1997.

Nelson, Stephen. *Only a Paper Moon: The Theater of Billy Rose.* Ann Arbor, Michigan: UMI Press, 1987.

Norris, J. Frank. *Inside History of First Baptist Church, Fort Worth, and Temple Baptist Church, Detroit.* n.p.: n.d.

Orrey, Leslie, ed. *The Encyclopedia of Opera.* New York: Charles Scribner's Sons, 1976.

Paddock, Buckley B. *Early Days in Fort Worth: Much of Which I Saw and Part of Which I Was.* Fort Worth: Texas Printing Co., n. d.

———. ed. *History of Texas: Fort Worth and the Texas Northwest Edition,* 4 vols. New York: Lewis Publishing Co., 1922.

Pate, J'Nell. *North of the River: A Brief History of North Fort Worth.* Fort Worth: TCU Press, 1994.

Payne, Darwin. Big D: *Triumphs and Troubles of an American Supercity in the 20th Century.* Dallas: Three Forks Press, 1994.

Quinn, Arthur Hobson. *A History of American Drama From the Civil War to the Present Day.* New York: Appleton-Century-Crofts, 1936.

Ragsdale, Kenneth B. *The Year America Discovered Texas: Centennial '36.* Texas A&M Press, 1987.

Rogers, Ginger. *Ginger: My Story.* New York: Harper-Collins, 1991.

Rose, Billy. *Wine, Women and Words.* New York: Simon and Schuster, 1948.

Roth, Steve, Stacy Schnellenbach Bogle, Nancy O'Malley, et. al. *Let The Angels Play: The Commemorative Journal for the Nancy Lee and Perry R. Bass Performance Hall.* Fort Worth: Magnolia Media Group, 1998.

Russell, Don. *The Lives and Legends of Buffalo Bill.* Norman: University of Oklahoma Press, 1960.

Selcer, Richard, David Bowser, Nancy Hamilton, Chuck Parsons. *Legendary Watering Holes: The Saloons That Made Texas Famous.* College Station: Texas A&M Press, 2004.

Silverman, Kenneth. *Houdini!!! The Career of Ehrich Weiss.* New York: Harper-Collins, 1996.

Skinner, Cornelia Otis. *Madame Sarah.* Boston: Houghton-Mifflin, 1967.

Slide, Anthony. *The Encyclopedia of Vaudeville.* Westport, Connecticut: Greenwood Press, 1994.

Sobel, Bernard. *A Pictorial History of Vaudeville.* New York: Bonanza Press, 1961.

Stein, Charles W., ed. *American Vaudeville As Seen By Its Contemporaries.* New York: Alfred A. Knopf, 1984.

Tarrant County Historical Resources Survey: Fort Worth Near North Side, West Side and Westover Hills. Historic Preservation Council For Tarrant County, 1988.

Texans and Their State. Fort Worth: Texas Biographical Association, 1918.

Weiner, Hollace Ava. *Beth-El Congregation Centennial, Fort Worth, Texas, 1902–2002.* Fort Worth: Beth-El Temple, 2002.

Williams, Mack. *In Old Fort Worth.* Fort Worth: Mack Williams, 1986.

Winter, William. *The American Stage of To-Day.* New York: E. F. Collier & Sons, 1910.

PERIODICALS

Allison, Gordon. "Music Circus." *Theatre Arts* 35 (June 1951): 87–89.

Bakshy, Alexander. "Vaudeville's Prestige." *Nation* 129 (24 September 1929): 258.

"Casa New Home of Worth Wurlitzer." *Fort Worth Magazine* 48 (August 1972): 12–13.

"Civic Music Brings Symphony and Concert Stars at Bargain Prices." *Fort Worth Magazine* (November 1947): 29.

Condon, Frank C. "A Lady Tells Her Age," *Colliers* (26 January 1935): 19-20.

"Dallas Theatrical History." *Bohemian* 3, No. 2 (Christmas 1901–1902): 69–71.

"DeBeque vs. Ligon," *South Western Reporter* 286 (29 September-17 November 1926): 750-754.

"Elbert Gruver." (obituary) *Dartmouth College Alumni Magazine* (January 1963): n. p.

Dachs, David. "Ten Years of the Music Tents." *Saturday Review* 41 (31 May 1958): 37–39.

Ferguson, Otis. "Daughters and Others." *New Republic* 97 (18 January 1939): 315.

"Fort Worth Theatrical History." *Bohemian* 3, No. 2 (Christmas 1901–1902): 67–69.

Heymont, George. "A Painful Process." *Opera News* (November 1987): 13–14.

"Neighbor McKee." *Newsweek* 21 (7 June 1943): 92–93.

Hull, Marcelle. "A Retrospective of the Reeder School of Theater and Design." *Compass Rose* (fall 1993): 4–6.

Johnston, Alva. "Colonel Carter of Cartersville." *Saturday Evening Post* (26 November 1938): 8.

"A Man of Parts," *UTA Magazine* 2 (September 1979): 16.

"Realistic 10-Year Growth Plan Next Stop for College," *Fort Worth Magazine* 37 (March 1961): 10-11.

Record, Pat. "Mr. Casa Mañana, Alias Melvin Dacus." *Fort Worth Magazine* 40 (May 1964): 17–19.

Seabury, Deborah. "A Lot From A Little." *Opera News* 44 (15 March 1980): 32–35.

Smith, Benjamin E. "The 'Ben Hur' Chariot Race." *St. Nicholas* (November 1900): 45–49.

"Stage Struck Texas." *Life* 45 (22 December 1958): 122.

"The Theater Smorgasbord: Hip Pocket Theater." *Fort Worth Magazine* 54 (June 1978): 41–42.

"Through Texas." *Harper's New Monthly Magazine* 59 (October 1879) 703–717.

Vacha, John E. "Biggest Bash: Cleveland's Great Lakes Exposition. *Timeline* (March/April 1996): 2–23.

Vollmer, Bob. "Flashback to Fame: The Biggest Summer Texas Ever Had." source and pages unknown (1946).

Weathersby, William. "Texas Tradition." *Theatre Crafts International* (August-September 1998): 49–51.

NEWSPAPERS

Billboard. Various issues,1936.

Camp Bowie Texahoma Bugler. Various issues, 1917.

Dallas Daily Herald. 5 October 1886.

Dallas Daily Times-Herald. 6 February 1892.

Dallas Morning News. Various issues, 1885.

Dallas Weekly Herald. Various issues, 1883.

Elgin (Illinois) *Daily Courier.* 1 February 1917.

Elgin (Illinois) *Daily Courier-News.* 27 July 1974.

Fort Griffin Echo. 17 May 1879.

Fort Worth Business Press. Various issues, 1990.

Fort Worth Democrat. Various issues, 1873–1883.

Fort Worth Daily Gazette. Various issues, 1883–1890.

Fort Worth Daily Mail, Various issues, 1885–1886.

Fort Worth Evening Mail. 17 December 1889

Fort Worth Mind, Various issues, 1933–1934, 1951–1960.

Fort Worth News-Tribune, Various issues 1982–1985.

Fort Worth Standard. Various issues, 1876–1877.

Fort Worth Press. Various issues 1926–1980.

Fort Worth Record. Various issues 1899–1919.

Fort Worth Register. Various issues, 1896-

Fort Worth Star-Telegram. Various issues, 1909–2004.

Fort Worth Telegram. Various issues, 1906–1908.

Galveston Daily News. Various issues, 1882–1888.

Jewish Monitor. Various issues, 1928.

La Estrella/Fort Worth Star-Telegram. Various issues, 1996.

New York Times. Various issues, 1889-1890.

San Diego Union Tribune. 16 November 2003, B7.

San Francisco Morning Call, 14 March 1885.

Temple Daily Telegram. 22 April 1979.

Terrellife, I. M. Terrell High School. 17 March 1936.

Texas Christian University Skiff, Various issues, 1936–1957.

Variety. Various issues, 1905–1936.

COLLECTIONS

Amon Giles Carter Papers, Texas Christian University Library, Fort Worth, Texas.

Casa Mañana Scrapbooks, 1958–1997, Fort Worth Public Library, Fort Worth, Texas.

Fort Worth Opera Records, Scrapbooks, 1946–1949, Fort Worth Public Library, Fort Worth, Texas.

Hill (William E.) Collection. Dallas Public Library. Theatre ephemera, photographs and cartoons of early 20th century performers.

Halbower-Umbenhour Theatre Collection. Tarrant County Historical Commission, Tarrant County Courthouse, Fort Worth, Texas.

Hoblitzelle Interstate Theatre Collection. Ransom Center for Humanities Research. University of Texas. Austin, Texas.

Interstate Theatre Collection MS-5. Special collections. Dallas Public Library, Dallas, Texas.

Max Kaye Collection. Congregation Ahavath Shalom. Fort Worth, Texas.

Samuel Losh Papers, Fort Worth Public Library, Fort Worth, Texas.

I. E. McWhirter Papers. First Methodist Church, Fort Worth, Texas.

Flora and Dickson Reeder Collection. Special Collections, University of Texas at Arlington Library.

Soul People Repertory Company Collection, Manuscript and Visual Collections Department, Indiana Historical Society, William Henry Smith Memorial Library, Indianapolis.

Tarrant County Black Historical and Genealogical Society Papers, Fort Worth Public Library, Local History and Genealogy.

Temple Beth-El Congregation Archives. Fort Worth, Texas.

E. Clyde Whitlock Papers, Fort Worth Public Library, Fort Worth, Texas.

CORRESPONDENCE

Alft, E. C.; Elgin, Illinois, historian and author of *Elgin: Days Gone By.* Correspondence with author.

Boren, Marie, secretary, office of Bob Hope, correspondence with author, 27 July 1993.

Buckman, Nancy, great-niece of William Fife; Sommerville, a director of the Texas Spring Palace and manager of the Matador Land and Cattle Company. Correspondence with author.

Deeker, John Deeker; chairman of Pain's Fireworks, England. Correspondence with author.

Dulle, Joseph K.; president, White Elephant Enterprises, Fort Worth, Texas. Letter to author.

Fearing, Don; Director of Operations, Nancy Lee and Perry R. Bass Performance Hall. E-mail correspondence with author. October 2004.

Fuller, James C. Letter to members of Casa Mañana board of directors, 15 September 1964.

Monnig, William. Letter to Arthur L. Kramer, n. d., Amon Giles Carter Papers, Texas Christian University.

Thelin, C. M.; acting director of public works, City of Fort Worth to J. D. Prince, manager of Will Rogers Memorial Auditorium. Department memoranda. 16 and 18 December 1946.

BUSINESS AND PUBLIC RECORDS

Business and Financial Records, Casa Mañana Musicals, Inc., 1980.

Chicago Fire Marshall, Annual Report, 1903, Chicago (Illinois) Public Library.

Federal Writers' Project, Fort Worth And Tarrant County.

Fort Worth City Directories, 1877–1970.

Fort Worth Opera Association, Income and Expense Summary, 1990–1991 season.

Minutes of the Board, Beth-El Reform Jewish Congregation, Fort Worth, Texas, 4 December 1933.

Minutes, Casa Mañana Musicals Board of Directors, 1959, 1965, 1974.

Minutes, Executive Committee, Casa Mañana Musicals Board of Directors, 1959.

Minutes, Fort Worth City Council, 1876–1960

Minutes, Fort Worth Opera Association, 1990.

Tarrant County Criminal Docket Ledgers, 1878–1890.

Texas Department of Criminal Justice, Convict Record Ledgers, Huntsville State Prison (1879–1882), Rusk State Prison (1870–1891), Texas State Archives, Austin, Texas.

FILM

Benge, Claudia. *Setting the Stage: The Fort Worth Theater Story.* City of Fort Worth Cable Office: City Video 45, 1990.

"Texas." *March of Time* Newsreel, c. 19 June 1936.

PAMPHLETS AND MISCELLANY

Allen, E. D. *Descriptive Story of the Texas Spring Palace.* Fort Worth: Texas Printing and Lithographic Co., 1889.

Add-Ran Christian University, commencement program, 1895.

Beautiful Arlington Heights. Fort Worth: Arlington Heights Realty Company, c. 1905.

Bulletin of Texas Wesleyan University, 1935.

Bulletin of Texas Woman's University, 1916, 1918.

Camp Bowie cantonment map, c. 1918.

Casa Mañana '58. Fort Worth Opera Association, 1958.

Casa Mañana programs, 1936-1939.

Celebrating Fifty Years of Excellence (50th anniversary commemorative program). Fort Worth Opera Association, 1995.

Directory of Negro Business Enterprises and Professions, c. 1921.

Dixon, Norwood P. *The Story of the Fort Worth Opera Association.* Fort Worth Opera Association, 1979

Faculty Bulletins. Texas Christian University. 3 March and 24 March 1965.

Fort Worth City Map. C. H. Rogers, 1919.

Fort Worth Colored History and Directory, c. 1907.

Fort Worth Little Theater and Community Playhouse magazines. Various issues, 1931, 1933.

Fort Worth Grand Opera Association programs, 1916, 1917, 1919.

Fort Worth Opera Association. Various programs, 1946-2004.

Hispanic Playwrights' Festival program, 2994.

Horace, Lillian B. Private Journal, 1905-c.1916.

The Last Days of Pompeii program, c. 1890.

Minority Progress Committee Report. City of Fort Worth, 1975.

Sanborn Fire Maps, Fort Worth, Texas, 1885, 1911.

Seating/Floor plans of North Side Coliseum for Chicago Grand Opera, 1916.

Smith, Edward J. *The Capitalist or The City of Fort Worth: A Parody of The Mikado.* Fort Worth: Texas Spring Palace, 1888.

_____. *Texas' Spring Palace City, Fort Worth: A Parody of H. M. S. Pinafore.* Fort Worth: The Texas Spring Palace, 1889.

Tarrant County Convention Center Fort Worth Texas. (informational brochure) Fort Worth: Tarrant County Convention Center, 1968.

This Month In Fort Worth. (informational brochure). March 1940.

Texas Wesleyan University: A Centennial Album. Fort Worth: Texas Wesleyan University, 1990.

The Story of Casa Mañana Musicals (informational brochure). Casa Mañana Musicals: n.d.

The TXWOCO yearbooks. Texas Woman's College, 1920-1922.

United States Department of the Interior/National Park Service National Register of Historic Places registration form. Marine Commercial Historic District, Fort Worth, Texas, n. d.

Wild and Whoopee brochure. Fort Worth Frontier Centennial, 1936.

"Women of Achievement: Lillian B. Horace, Educator and Author."

Women's Division Texas Frontier Centennial and Casa Mañana Scrapbook, 1936.

Women's Division Fort Worth Frontier Fiesta and Casa Mañana Scrapbook, 1937.

Yearbooks. I. M. Terrell High School. Fort Worth, Texas, 1923, 1929.

INTERVIEWS

Benge, Sharon, former director of Casa Mañana Playhouse and Shakespeare In the Park. Interview by author, 18 June 2001.

Cady, Cathey, former student of Mason Johnson and Johnson's assistant director, 1968–1985. Interview by author, 21 September 2004.

Clardy, Beth Lea, former Casa Mañana showgirl. Interview by author, October 1985.

Chadwick, Mrs. Ahdel, longtime board member, Fort Worth Opera. Interview by author, 12 February 2004.

Dacus, Brent and Debbie, son and daughter-in-law of Melvin and Katy Dacus. Interview by author, 31 January 2004.

Dacus, Melvin O., general manager-producer of Casa Mañana Musicals 1958–1974. Interview by author, 23 September 1980.

Eastman, Rudy, founder and producing director of Jubilee Theatre. Interview by author, 24 February 2004.

Eddleman, Olan Clyde "Tex," professional costumer, dancer, and entertainer. Interview by author, 9 July 2004.

Eureka, Leonard, arts reporter, *Fort Worth Star-Telegram, Fort Worth Weekly.* Interview by author, 9 September 2003.

Forestner, Dr. John, president of the Fort Worth Opera, 1996–1998. Interview by author, 25 May 2004.

Fuller, James C., former president of Casa Mañana Musicals, Inc. Interview by author, 7 August 1980.

Garber, William H., retired director of Fort Worth Community Theater and William Edrington Scott Theater. Interview by author, 12 March 2001.

Goodman, Wilby Lingo, former Casa Mañana dancer. Interview by author, October, 1985.

Hernandez, Cathy, executive director, Rose Marine Theater. Interview by author, 15 August 2004, 22 April 2005.

Holmes, Janice Nicolson, former Casa Mañana dancer. Interview by author, October, 1985.

Jary, William E., retired advertising executive and Fort Worth historian. Interview by author, October 1980.

Johnson, Rob, son of Robert Emerson "Rip" Johnson, former sports and Ice Capades promoter and Casa Mañana board member. Interview by author, 12 April 2005.

Kies, Gloria Petta, dancer, instructor, and former performer at the Worth Theater and other Fort Worth venues. Interview by author, 29 March 2002.

Klein, Betty Spain, co-founder of the Fort Worth Civic Opera Association. Interview by author, 29 February 2004.

Kruger, Ruth, wife of Rudolf Kruger, managing director of the Fort Worth, Opera, 1955–1983. Interview by author, 23 March 2004.

Massad, William, former assistant director and public relations manager of the Fort Worth Opera. Interview by author, 4 February 2004.

Peace, Mrs. Hazel Harvey. Interview by author, 16 September 2004.

Pearson, Rose, founder and managing director of Circle Theater. Interview by author, 9 April 2004.

Pollock, Michael, producer-stage director of Casa Mañana Musicals 1958–1965. Interview by author, 14 July 1980.

Reynolds, Kim Dacus, daughter of Melvin and Katy Dacus. Interview by author, October 2003.

Reeder, Flora Dickson. Interview by Gerald Saxon, Executive Director of Libraries, University of Texas-Arlington. Special Collections, UT-A Library.

Rodriguez, George X., local actor and program director of Hispanic Playwrights Festival. Interview by author, 13 April 2005.

Rodriguez, Lynda, founder of Fort Worth Theater's Hispanic Series and Hispanic Playwrights Festival. Interview by author, 14 April 2005.

Russell, Jerry, founder and managing director of Stage West. Interview by author, 4 May 2004.

Simons, Terry, chief engineer, Nancy Lee and Perry R. Bass Performance Hall. Interview by author, 7 September 2004.

Spiegel, Joy, actress with B'Nai B'rith Little Theater and Fort Worth Community Theater, and widow of Seymour Spiegel. Interview by author, 5 February 2004.

Volbach, Fritz, nephew of Dr. Walther Volbach. Interview by author, 9 September 2004.

Walker, William, retired managing director of the Fort Worth Opera. Interview by author, 23 March 2004.

Wayman, Mary Wynn, retired *Star-Telegram* reporter. Interview by author, July 1996.

Winesanker, Esther, widow of Dr. Michael Winesanker, music professor, Texas Christian University. Interview by author, 23 January 2002.

UNPUBLISHED MANUSCRIPTS

Barton, Henry W. *A History of the Dallas Opera House.* M.A. Thesis, Hardin College, Southern Methodist University, 1935.

Beach, Claudia Anne. *Henry Greenwall: Theatre Manager.* Ph.D. dissertation, Texas Tech University, 1986.

Blackwelder, Harold Gene. *The Fort Worth Civic Opera Association, 1946–1953.* M.F.A. Thesis, Texas Christian University, 1965.

Blackwood, David Byrne. *The Theatres of J. B. McElfatrick and Sons, Architects, 1855-1922.* Ph.D. dissertation, University of Kansas, 1966.

Dixon, Norwood P. *The Story of the Fort Worth Opera Association.* Fort Worth Opera Association, 1979.

Jones, Dora Davenport. *Additions and Corrections to the History of the Robert E. Lee Camp 158, United Confederate Veterans, Fort Worth, Texas, 1890–1938, including the Seven-Year Split-Off of the Albert Sidney Johnston Camp 1820, UCV; The Two-Year Life of the Belle Boyd Chapter United Daughters of the Confederacy, 1922–1923; and An Update on the Julia Jackson Chapter 141, UDC, Fort Worth, Texas Through 1981,* Fort Worth, Texas, 1981. Tarrant County Historical Commission, Tarrant County Courthouse.

Zolotow, Maurice. *Billy Rose of Broadway.* Billy Rose Theater Collection, New York Public Library.

INDEX